Local Knowledge, Global Stage

Histories of Anthropology Annual

EDITORS
Regna Darnell
Frederic W. Gleach

Local Knowledge, Global Stage

Histories of Anthropology Annual, Volume 10

EDITED BY REGNA DARNELL AND
FREDERIC W. GLEACH

University of Nebraska Press | *Lincoln and London*

Library of Congress Control Number: 2015960670

Set in Arno Pro by Rachel Gould.

CONTENTS

List of Illustrations   vii

Editors' Introduction   ix

1. Anthropologists and the Bible:
   The Marett Lecture, April 2012   1
   ADAM KUPER

2. Dead and Living Authorities in *The Legend*
   of Perseus: Animism and Christianity in the
   Evolutionist Archive   31
   FREDERICO D. ROSA

3. Anthropology in Portugal: The Case of the
   Portuguese Society of Anthropology and
   Ethnology (SPAE), 1918   53
   PATRÍCIA FERRAZ DE MATOS

4. A View from the West: The Institute of
   Social Science and the Amazon   99
   PRISCILA FAULHABER

5. Scientific Diplomacy and the Establishment of an
   Australian Chair of Anthropology, 1914–25   121
   GEOFFREY GRAY

6. The Saga of the L. H. Morgan Archive, or
   How an American Marxist Helped Make a
   Bourgeois Anthropologist the Cornerstone of
   Soviet Ethnography   149
   SERGEI A. KAN AND DMITRY V. ARZYUTOV

7. "I Wrote All My Notes in Shorthand": A First
   Glance into the Treasure Chest of Franz
   Boas's Shorthand Field Notes   221
   RAINER HATOUM

8. Genealogies of Knowledge in the Alberni Valley:
   Reflecting on Ethnographic Practice in the
   Archive of Dr. Susan Golla   273
   DENISE NICOLE GREEN

9. The File Hills Farm Colony Legacy   303
   CHEYANNE DESNOMIE

   Contributors   335

ILLUSTRATIONS

1. SPAE's first logo   55

2. Leopoldina Paulo, 1944   62

3. Percentage of topics at the lectures
   organized by SPAE, 1918–44   71

4. SPAE's current logo   80

5. Boas's German Kurrent script   223

6. Boas's Latin script   223

7. Boas's pencil writing   224

8. First page of Boas's 1894 Fort Rupert notes   228

9. Blankets piled up in a big house   231

10. Boas and Hunt in Fort Rupert, 1894   234

11. Typical word list by Boas   239

12. Drawing of Charles Edenshaw with
    shorthand notes by Boas   245

13. Drawing of Charles Edenshaw with
    shorthand notes by Boas   248

14. Face painting with shorthand notes by Boas   250

15. Sketch with shorthand notes by Boas   257

16. Drawing of a mask (very likely by Albert Grünwedel)   258

17. Drawing of a mask (very likely by Albert Grünwedel)   259

18. Boas scratch paper 260

19. "Franz Boas" in Boas's own shorthand writing 261

20. Charlie Watts and Morris Swadesh in
    Port Alberni, late 1930s 274

21. Doris Martin at Long Beach, Vancouver
    Island, July 1979 280

22. Doris, Bubba, Martin, April, and Gerri, ca. 1976 282

23. Susan with Cate, 1979 287

24. Cate Conmy looks through family
    photographs, October 11, 2013 296

25. Peepeekisis reserve after the second subdivision in 1906 309

This volume rounds off what would have been a decade of *Histories of Anthropology Annual* if we had met the ideal in producing an annual volume. In actuality it has taken a couple of extra years to reach this point. *HoAA* began in the book division at the University of Nebraska Press, then moved to the journals portfolio, and then returned to the book division with a renewed emphasis on the stand-alone character of each volume. Each volume now has a unique title, albeit still within the mandate of *HoAA* to provide an outlet for work in the history of anthropology broadly defined and directed to an audience of anthropologists.

Volume 10 is further distinguished as a watershed in the discipline in that we have recently lost two of our founding elders: George W. Stocking Jr. and Henrika Kuklick. The legacies of both live on in the work of their students and others they influenced. We particularly remember George as the founding father of a specialization in the history of anthropology combining disciplinary subject matter with historicist standards of archival research. Although trained in history, he became an honorary member of the anthropological tribe after his move to the University of Chicago Department of Anthropology in 1969. Stocking's own thematic series, History of Anthropology, from the University of Wisconsin Press produced eight volumes under his editorship (each containing a seminal essay of his own), three more edited by Richard Handler, and a final volume that was Stocking's own (remarkably ethnographic) autobiography (Darnell 2014; Stocking 2010).

HoAA was founded in self-conscious counterdistinction to History of Anthropology and intended to supplement its thematic interventions into the history, theory, and practice of anthropology with a more diffuse and incidental bringing together of work that crossed subject matter, subdiscipline, and national tradition, perhaps presaging where both the discipline and its historiography were heading. George will remain a significant figure in having set the directions we seek to document. His legacy continues to evolve. Both editors owe much to his mentorship: he served on Regna Darnell's dissertation committee as a result of his single semester at the University of Pennsylvania; and although Fred Gleach never officially worked with George at Chicago, they met, and talked, and shared interests in where the discipline had been and where it might be going. Contributors to this volume include George's former Chicago student Sergei Kan, and several others have published in previous *HoAA* volumes.

Our title theme asserts the indivisibility of local knowledge and global context in anthropology. It is our particular preoccupation to understand the global stage in terms of the particularities of the many cultures and societies that constitute it at any given moment in time. A. Irving Hallowell noted in the inaugural issue of *Journal of the History of the Behavioral Sciences* in 1965 that historians of anthropology tend to treat the history of their discipline as an anthropological problem. That is, they/we define history itself in terms of an accustomed professional toolkit, but one that each practitioner applies in her/his specific locale with the goal of illuminating different parts of the global whole. It is precisely this stereoscopic vision that led us to title our open-ended annual forum with the plural "histories" of anthropology. We are delighted that we continue to attract a broad interdisciplinary range of historians, anthropologists, members of communities more often studied than speaking for themselves, and others interested in writing primarily for an audience of anthropologists.

Some of the issues that preoccupy anthropologists are part of the history of the post-Enlightenment West out of which the discipline emerged. Both Adam Kuper and Frederico D. Rosa apply the methods of anthropological historiography to the West's Christian and pre-Christian heritage: Adam Kuper's elegant paper explores the Bible as persistent grist for the anthropological mill, especially the Old Testament "folklore" so beloved of Victorian England. Frederico D. Rosa turns another folklore tradition amenable to anthropological reading, tracing the legend of Perseus in relation to concepts of animism and Christianity. In both cases, anthropological method unites the gaze on diverse texts and the contexts of their production and transmission to contemporary anthropology. The motifs are in motion and the anthropologists in character.

The spatial or geographic past manifests in a contemporary global world in terms of diverse national traditions and institutions, and each of our first ten volumes has included papers on such national traditions. Here, Patrícia Ferraz de Matos focuses on the periphery versus the metropole, tying the nascent national tradition of the Portuguese Society of Anthropology and Ethnology in 1918 to a larger colonial context that frames this local within a larger global. Priscila Faulhaber turns to a quite different local version of Portuguese empire in her treatment of the Institute of Social Science in the Amazon. The local case she documents implicates larger global variations on the themes of the institute through the Rockefeller Foundation and other institutions for export. Europe and the Americas meet.

Meanwhile, Geoffrey Gray continues his meticulous examination of the development of anthropological institutions in Australia and their resonances across other anthropologies, primarily British social anthropology, foregrounding both Australian anthropology's deep ties to the metropole whence it originated and the unique constraints of geography and politics ostensibly isolated from outside influences but in practice weaving in and out of familiar stories elsewhere. The institutional machinations of the first anthropology chair in Sydney, standing alone until 1950, play out in familiar local/global manifestations, as the colonial system that developed within the British Empire entailed the circulation of personnel and the intersection of growing global ethnological databases.

Sergei Kan and Dmitry Arzyutov probe another kind of transnational intersection, one in which American Marxist Bernhard Stern aspired to publish the entire archive of Lewis Henry Morgan, transforming an American bourgeoisie entrepreneur into a communist prophet foretelling the universalism touted by Marx and Engels. It is a strange story of strange bedfellows with eerily distorted blinders about each other and the foibles of mutual foreignness misunderstood, and yet it became fundamental to the direction taken by ethnology and ethnography in the former Soviet Union. The coauthors span the traditions they examine in juxtaposition.

Another recurring theme through our first ten volumes has been the importance of the fieldwork process and the relationships of anthropologists to those whom they study, or the standpoint of the observer and its ethical consequences. Rainer Hatoum links a later stage of American anthropology to the German background of Franz Boas's early ethnography, foregrounding the fieldwork process and the relationships of anthropologists to those they study as another approach that has been featured through our run to date. In deciphering Boas's idiosyncratic form of shorthand—developed in some combination of protecting his work from curious eyes and efficiency in responding to fast-moving events—Hatoum renders possible a detailed textual comparison of Boas's field notes and their published versions. The comparison yields highly motivated changes that allowed Boas to generalize from the personal position and family relationships of his collaborator George Hunt to a cultural pattern attributable to all Kwakwaka'wakw (Kwakiutl in Boas's terminology). Paradoxically, Hunt emerges as the impresario par excellence, the manager of local performance on a global anthropological stage, while the single event recorded came to stand as "the" Kwakiutl potlatch, thereby also implicitly downplaying the agency and choreography of the events by Hunt.

Denise Green situates her contemporary fieldwork with the Nuu Chah Nulth (whom Boas and Sapir called Nootka) in the Alberni Valley in British Columbia, Canada, alongside an anthropological genealogy of research with this group. From the archives of the late Susan Golla, Green reconstructs a saga of building relationships of trust that facilitate revitalization agendas arising from communities and drawing on the support of anthropologists, again framed as learners, and thereby revealing the insider-outsider permutations of Golla's long-term engagement in the valley and Green's own position within that ongoing genealogy of researchers. Generations of elders' oral traditions have produced a plurality of valid and textured histories of the Nuu Chah Nulth parallel to the multiplicities of anthropological histories of anthropology.

Finally, Cheyanne Desnomie talks about how she came to know her own Indigenous genealogy better by exploring archival documentation of a failed social experiment among the Plains Cree of Saskatchewan, Canada, and supplementing this through oral tradition from her own family and others. Her historical scholarship, comfortably framed within an anthropology curriculum, again contributes to the revitalization program produced by honing "the native point of view" based on what has been lost to contemporary communities but remains accessible to be reconstituted in new forms. The ethics of the relationship between anthropologists and those they study emerge from historicist research, as well as from contemporary practice.

A decade of *HoAA* seems a good time to take stock. We thank our readers and our contributors for confirming our own conviction that these historicist issues are good to think with. To generalize from local knowledges of particular events and contexts to larger global trends requires a methodology for the history of anthropology that is both historicist and presentist. It may further require us to redefine history itself, calling for a dynamic process transcending the customary distinction of past, present, and future and replacing the static repetition of events, dates, and feats of great men (*sic*) representing the story from the standpoint of the victors with a more nuanced collation of histories in the plural. We look forward to seeing many more years of such scholarship.

REGNA DARNELL

FREDERIC W. GLEACH

REFERENCES

Darnell, Regna. 2014. Obituary of George W. Stocking, Jr. American Anthropologist 116:712–714.
Stocking, George Ward, Jr. 2010 Glimpses into My Own Black Box: An Exercise in Self-Deconstruction. History of Anthropology 12. Madison: University of Wisconsin Press.

Local Knowledge, Global Stage

1

Anthropologists and the Bible

The Marett Lecture, April 2012

I

A young philosophy don, a Jerseyman at Oxford, Robert Ranulph
Marett was intrigued by the subject set for the 1893 Green Prize in Moral
Philosophy: "The ethics of savage races." He immersed himself in the
literature on primitive religion, won the prize, and was befriended by
the only anthropologist at Oxford University, E. B. Tylor.

Tylor was the father figure of the new anthropology that had emerged
in the 1860s. It was a baggy, ambitious discipline, and Tylor himself
wrote about race and technology and language and marriage, but especially about religion, and this became Marett's main interest too. The
first objective of the anthropology of religion was to characterize the
earliest creeds and rites. The anthropologists then explained the advance
of humanity from the long dark age of magic and superstition to the
sunny uplands of a more spiritual religion; or they showed how meta-
physical error gave way to rationality and science.

In any case, they took it for granted that religion, technology, and
the social order advanced in lockstep through a determined series of
stages. At each stage, the beliefs and customs of societies at a similar level of development were essentially the same. So contemporary
primitive societies could be treated as stand-ins for past societies at an
equivalent stage of development. The notions of the American Indians,
perhaps, or, at a higher level, the Tahitians provided living instances of
conceptions and beliefs that had once been very widespread. To know
one was to know all. Captain Cook had introduced the word *taboo* from
Tahiti. Soon taboos were being discovered all over the place. Other
exotic terms were soon taken up—*mana*, another Polynesian word,

totem from the Ojibwa, *potlatch* from the Kwakiutl of British Columbia, *voodoo* from West Africa. All were elements of a universal primal religion. So Victorian anthropologists could write about Australian totems and American Indian taboos. They could even identify totem and taboo in ancient Israel.

Such beliefs and practices may once have been universal, but they were surely irrational. How could so many people have believed so many impossible things for so long? Some missionaries saw the hand of the Devil here, but the anthropologists argued that there was something about the ways of thinking of primitive people that led them to make mistakes of perception and logic. After all, Darwin had shown that human evolution was paced by the development of the brain. It was widely assumed that the brains of the various races developed at different rates. The smaller-brained savages, and indeed the early Israelites, were simply not capable of thinking very clearly.

So how *did* they think? Tylor argued that primitive peoples relied on "analogy or reasoning by resemblance" (1881:338). For Frazer, such "reasoning by resemblance" accounted for the belief in magic. Robertson Smith agreed that for the savage mind there was "no sharp line between the metaphorical and the literal," and he blamed the "unbounded use of analogy characteristic of pre-scientific thought" for producing a "confusion between the several orders of natural and supernatural beings" (1894:274). Prescientific thinkers were particularly likely to get into a muddle when it came to causality. Robertson Smith found that primal religion was characterized by "*insouciance*, a power of casting off the past and living in the impression of the moment" that "can exist only along with a childish unconsciousness of the inexorable laws that connect the present and the future with the past" (1894:57).

Tylor supposed that the very earliest religion arose from a misapprehension. People everywhere have dreams and visions, but primitive people confuse dreams with real experiences. When they dream of the dead they imagine that the dead exist somewhere else, in another state, the state that living people experience in dreams, trances, and fevers. And so "the ancient savage philosophers probably made their first step by the obvious inference that every man has two things belonging to him, namely, a life and a phantom" (Tylor 1871, 2:12). They then generalized this conclusion to embrace the rest of the natural world. Even trees and plants, even the planets, had souls. This was what Tylor termed "animism."

Rituals soon developed, notably sacrifices. In primitive animism, offerings were made to the spirits of the dead after they had appeared in dreams. In what might be called the higher animism, sacrifices were also made to "other spiritual beings, genii, fairies, gods." These sacrifices were gifts: "As prayer is a request made to a deity as if he were a man, so sacrifice is a gift made to the deity as if he were a man" (Tylor 1871, 2:375). Sacrifices took the form of burnt offerings, because spirits demanded spiritual food, the souls of animals or plants (Tylor 1866:77). Vestiges of the primitive cult, which Tylor called "survivals," recurred in the ceremonies of the most advanced religions.

In 1899 the young Marett achieved a certain notoriety by challenging Tylor's thesis that animism was the primeval religion. Marett identified a preanimistic religion based on the Polynesian belief in *mana*, which he took to mean a sort of psychic energy and power. Mana was inseparable from taboo. "Altogether, in mana we have what is *par excellence* the primitive religious idea in its positive aspect, taboo representing its negative side, since whatever has mana is taboo, and whatever is taboo has mana" (Marett 1911). His theory made some converts in Germany and France, most notably Marcel Mauss, who made mana the dynamic force behind both the gift and the sacrifice.

Tylor was already a frail old man when Marett became his friend, and Marett took responsibility for the development of anthropology at the university. He was instrumental in instituting Oxford's diploma in anthropology in 1908, and he succeeded Tylor as university reader in social anthropology, a position he held for a quarter of a century. When the university created a chair in anthropology in 1936, he held it for a year before the appointment of Radcliffe-Brown. From 1928 Marett was rector of Exeter College. He also served for many years as treasurer of the University Golf Club. A busy man, then, but, he recalled, "All this time . . . [a]nthropology was becoming . . . a passion with me. . . . Yet I was still attending to the subject with my left hand, while the right tackled the philosophy which after all I was paid to teach. In fact, I became a scandal to my friends, so that one of them wrote: 'A man of your talents seems rather wasted on the habits of backward races.' As it was, I divided my attention impartially between the beliefs of the savage and those of the Oxford undergraduate" (Marett 1941:164).

II

Tylor's theory of animism was hardly original. It was in the direct line of Enlightenment accounts of the development of rationality. Indeed, it was remarkably similar to the theory that had been advanced by Charles de Brosses (1760) and Auguste Comte (1830–42). But Tylor was also responding to the scandal provoked by two books that challenged traditional understandings of the Bible. *The Origin of Species*, published in 1859, presented a scientific alternative to the book of Genesis. The following year *Essays and Reviews* appeared, seven essays by intellectuals in the Church of England, including Benjamin Jowett, Mark Pattison, and Frederick Temple (who was to become archbishop of Canterbury) (Parker 1860). They downplayed miracles, questioned the story of the Creation, denied the doctrine of eternal punishment, and endorsed German critical scholarship that demonstrated that the Bible was a compilation of sometimes contradictory texts dating from different periods.

The continental champions of the new biblical criticism, Julius Wellhausen and Abraham Kuenen, further insisted that the Jewish religion had pagan roots. The original religion of Israel was a family cult. In time, the family cult became a tribal and then a national religion. Only with the emergence of great empires in Mesopotamia and Persia, which subjugated Israel, had prophets begun to formulate a universal spiritual religion, foreshadowing Christianity. But pagan elements survived (Wellhausen [1883] 1885).

Perhaps the ordinary churchgoer could ignore these challenges. Owen Chadwick remarks that Victorian churches were full of "worshippers who had never heard of Tylor, were indifferent to Darwin, mildly regretted what they heard of Huxley" (1970, 2:35). But the educated public did debate these new ideas, passionately. Samuel Wilberforce, bishop of Oxford, son of William Wilberforce, provoked a famous public confrontation with Huxley over the descent of man: "Was it through his grandfather or his grandmother that he traced his descent from an ape?" (Hesketh 2009:81). The bishop also moved to have *Essays and Reviews* condemned in the Convocation of Canterbury.

However, a new science of religion was emerging, with biblical and comparative wings, that engaged with the ideas of Darwin and Wellhausen. It brought together theologians, linguists, folklorists, archaeologists, and anthropologists (Wheeler-Barclay 2010). The particular project of Tylor and the anthropologists was to discover the origins of religion, origins that could never be completely outgrown, the vestiges of ancient cults haunting even the most advanced religions.

And they had fresh evidence at their disposal, for they were able to draw on a stream of reports on primitive religions from all over the world, many of them the work of missionaries. These sources were themselves shaped by the Bible and by biblical scholarship. Protestant missionaries especially made it a priority to translate the Bible into the local language. This obliged them to identify indigenous notions that were roughly equivalent to god, spirit, sin, sacrifice, and holiness. These concepts, and their ritual representations, were taken to be the essential constituents of a religion.

There is in fact no word for "religion" in the Hebrew Bible, but it seemed obvious that ancient Judaism was the prototype of authentic religion. The Bible also gave examples of false religions, which were those of Israel's idolatrous neighbors. Similar beliefs and practices were abundantly represented in the societies to which the missionaries were called. They could now be identified as not only pagan but also primitive. The idols of false religions were totems. Their laws were barbarous taboos and had nothing to do with justice or morality. Their ceremonies, shocking exhibitions of greed and lust, featured ghastly acts of cruelty, including human sacrifice. Missionary ethnographers read the reports of their colleagues, which described surprisingly similar pagan religions in distant parts of the world, and they welcomed the guidance of Tylor and Frazer, who pointed out what they should be looking for and explained the hold of superstition.[1]

So the anthropology of religion was from the first very largely an anthropology of the Bible, with comparative notes from all over the primitive world. Precisely because it had consequences for Christianity, the anthropology of religion seemed to be very important. Tylor was raised as a Quaker, and he believed that rituals always depended on magical thinking. Frazer argued that the comparative method "proves that many religious doctrines and practices are based on primitive conceptions, which most civilized and educated men have long agreed on abandoning as mistakes. From this it is a natural and often a probable inference that doctrines so based are false, and that practices so based are foolish" (1927:282). Robertson Smith believed on the contrary that he was clearing away the debris of folklore and tribal custom so that the prophetic and historical truths in the Hebrew Bible could be properly appreciated. For their part, missionary ethnographers delighted in discovering in the most primitive communities some faint intimations of more advanced doctrines, crude versions of biblical stories, even traces in the language of the passage of one of the lost tribes of Israel. In the 1920s and 1930s this sort of thing became a specialty of the Vienna school, then a hothouse of Catholic missionary anthropology.

III

In parallel with these studies of the development of religion, another foundational research program of anthropology addressed the rise of marriage and the family. Was there some connection between religion, morality, and social organization? In 1869 J. F. McLennan provided Tylor's animism with a social context. McLennan (1865) had himself proposed a model of the earliest societies. They were marauding nomadic bands, matrilineal and exogamous, practicing marriage by capture. He now argued that these bands had an appropriate religion. Each band believed that it was descended matrilineally from a particular natural species, its totem, which was worshiped as an ancestor god and placated with rituals. Totemism was at once a religion—rather like animism, as McLennan conceded—and a social system.

Long ago, totemism had been universal. McLennan identified traces of a totemic system in Siberia, Peru, Fiji, and even classical India. The Greeks had their natural spirits. Totemism was also the point of departure of later systems of thought. It planted the seeds not only of religion but also of science. When the names of animals were given to constellations of stars, this was a legacy of totemism but also the first inklings of astronomy. Beliefs about the descent of human beings from animals gave a faint hint of what would become the theory of evolution.

McLennan suggested in passing that the serpent story in Genesis may have had a totemic significance, but his theory of totemism was first systematically applied to the Hebrew Bible by his friend William Robertson Smith, who had been appointed to the chair of Hebrew and Old Testament at the Free Church College at Aberdeen in 1870 (see Black and Chrystal 1912). Robertson Smith accepted Wellhausen's demonstration that the Bible was a compilation of sources of various dates and that it included both mythological and historical elements. Following Wellhausen again, Robertson Smith aimed to identify the religious beliefs of the most ancient Israelites and to trace their progressive enlightenment. He also adopted Wellhausen's view that rituals were often hangovers from more primitive times but given fresh justifications.

How were the primitive elements to be identified? An obvious first step was to consider the practices and beliefs of Israel's pagan neighbors. Robertson Smith wrote that some ancient Jewish laws were based on principles "still current among the Arabs of the desert" (1880:340). He himself traveled in the Arabian interior to collect firsthand materials. However, even the Bedouin had progressed beyond the totemic stage, and they had been Muslims for many centuries. The comparative method practiced by McLennan offered an alternative approach. Early Israel could be understood with reference to better-documented societies at the same level of development.

In 1880 Robertson Smith published an essay titled "Animal Worship and the Animal Tribes among the Arabs and in the Old Testament" in which he argued that ancient Semitic societies were totemic. The evidence was admittedly patchy. Robertson Smith pointed to the queen of Sheba as proof of early matriarchy. Some Arab marriage rituals might be interpreted as survivals of marriage by capture. Taken together with other hints scattered in the literature, Robertson Smith later pronounced, "These facts appear sufficient to prove that Arabia did pass through a stage in which family relations and the marriage law satisfied the conditions of the totem system" (1894:88).

Similar bits and pieces of evidence might indicate that the early Arabian religion was also totemic. Tribal groupings were often named after animals and sometimes after the moon and sun. Sun and moon were evidently worshiped as gods, so animals presumably were also once treated as gods. And crucially, it seemed that totemic beliefs survived in ancient Israel, if in an attenuated form. Robertson Smith suggested that the heathen practices against which the Hebrew prophets inveighed were totemic in origin. And the second commandment itself was apparently directed against nature worship.

This argument did not go down well with his employers. The General Assembly of the Free Church of Scotland issued a swift condemnation: "First, concerning marriage and the marriage laws in Israel, the views expressed are so gross and so fitted to pollute the moral sentiments of the community that they cannot be considered except within the closed doors of any court of this Church. Secondly, concerning animal worship in Israel, the views expressed by the Professor are not only contrary to the facts recorded and the statements made in Holy Scripture, but they are gross and sensual—fitted to pollute and debase public sentiment" (Black and Chrystal 1912:382).

Yet Robertson Smith was not cast into outer darkness. He became coeditor of the famous ninth edition of the *Encyclopaedia Britannica* (and was reputed to have read every entry). In 1883 he was appointed reader in Arabic at Cambridge, and in 1889 he became professor. And he elaborated his initial thesis on early Semitic religion and social organization, notably in *Kinship and Marriage in Early Arabia* (1885) and in his masterpiece, *Lectures on the Religion of the Semites* (1889).

Robertson Smith remained wedded to McLennan's theory of totemism. Primitive people believed that they were physically descended from founding gods. Gods and their worshipers were originally thought of as kin who "make up a single community, and . . . the place of the god in the community is interpreted on the analogy of human relationships." A more sophisticated doctrine developed in ancient Israel. The divine father was conceived of in spiritual terms. But initially gods and their worshipers were thought of as blood relatives. This was also the origin of morality, for "the indissoluble bond that united men to their god is the same bond of blood-fellowship which in early society is the one binding link between man and man, and the one sacred principle of moral obligation" (Robertson Smith 1894:53).

The totemic gods were associated with shrines or sanctuaries. At certain times, a yet more intimate contact with the gods was required. This was achieved through sacrifice, which Robertson Smith termed "the typical form of all complete acts of worship in the antique religions" (1894:214). Sacrifice had been, of course, the central rite celebrated in the temple in Jerusalem, as in the temples of ancient Greece and Rome. It remained a vexing problem for Christian theology and for critical scholarship of the Bible. The priestly code represented sacrifices as acts of atonement, but Wellhausen insisted that this interpretation was anachronistic. Textual criticism revealed that the code was a postexilic document that superimposed a late priestly theology on earlier ritual practices. Originally, sacrifices were not even performed in the temple. They were associated with what Wellhausen called a natural religion, which was situated within the life of the family. Robertson Smith speculated that sacrifice was originally a sort of family meal. "The god and his worshippers are wont to eat and drink together, and by this token their fellowship is declared and sealed." The most primitive sacrifices were therefore not gifts, as Tylor had thought, but "essentially acts of communion between the god and his worshippers" (Robertson Smith 1894:243, 271).

But what was sacrificed, what was eaten at that communion meal? Robertson Smith declared that the totemic animal itself was the original sacrificial object. Normally, a totem animal could not be killed or eaten. It was "unclean"—taboo. Taboos were primitive anticipations of the idea of the sacred. Robertson Smith pronounced the evidence "unambiguous." "When an unclean animal is sacrificed it is also a sacred animal." He concluded that among the Semites "the fundamental idea of sacrifices is not that of a sacred tribute, but of communion between the god and his worshippers by joint participation in the living flesh and blood of a sacred victim" (Robertson Smith 1894:345).

The argument was clearly leading up to a climax in which something would have to be said about the sacrifices of gods themselves in Semitic religions, perhaps in connection with a communion rite. Robertson Smith took the step in this passage:

That the God-man dies for His people and that his Death is their life, is an idea which was in some degree foreshadowed by the oldest mystical sacrifices. It was foreshadowed, indeed, in a very crude and materialistic form, and without any of those ethical ideas which the Christian doctrine of the Atonement derives from a profound sense of sin and divine justice. And yet the voluntary death of the divine victim, which we have seen to be a conception not foreign to ancient ritual, contained the germ of the deepest thought in the Christian doctrine: the thought that the Redeemer gives Himself for his people. (1889:393)

Frazer cited this passage in his obituary essay on Robertson Smith and remarked that it was dropped in the posthumously published second edition of the *Lectures on the Religion of the Semites*, which had been edited by J. S. Black (1894:800–807).

IV

Like Robertson Smith, James George Frazer was a Scot and the son of a clergyman. When Robertson Smith arrived at Cambridge to take up his new professorship, he commissioned Frazer to write entries on taboo and totemism for the *Encyclopaedia Britannica*. Frazer's essay on totemism turned out to be too long for the publishers, but Robertson Smith encouraged him to write a book on the subject. *Totemism* marked Frazer's debut as an anthropologist in his own right.

Frazer's most famous book, *The Golden Bough*, first published in 1890, followed up Robertson Smith's speculations about the sacrifice of a totemic god. He also drew on the theory of a German folklorist, Wilhelm Mannhardt (1875), who had explained German peasant cults of sacred trees as survivals of ancient fertility rituals. Combining these elements, Frazer constructed an ethnological detective story. It began with the ritual strangling of the "King of the Wood," the priest of the sanctuary of Nemi, near Rome. This sacred king was the embodiment of a tree-spirit. He not simply was murdered but was sacrificed to ensure the fertility of nature. Clues drawn from a vast range of ethnographic sources showed that primitive people identified their wellbeing with the fate of natural spirits whose priest-kings were sacrificed in fertility rituals. "The result, then, of our inquiry is to make it probable that . . . the King of the Wood lived and died as an incarnation of the Supreme Aryan god, whose life was in the mistletoe or Golden Bough" (Frazer 1900, 2:363). Might this not imply that the Gospel accounts of Christ's crucifixion were further versions of the myth of the sacred king? Frazer wrote in a letter to a friend in 1904 that "the facts of comparative religion appear to me subversive of Christian theology" (Ackerman 2005:236).

Frazer then turned his attention to the Hebrew Bible. In 1904 or 1905 the Regius Professor of Hebrew in Cambridge, Robert Hatch Kennett, was persuaded to offer a private beginner's class in Hebrew (Ackerman 1987:183–184). It attracted a very select clientele: Jane Harrison, F. M. Cornford, A. B. Cook, and Frazer. Frazer became competent enough to read the Old Testament in Hebrew, and he gradually put together an anthropological commentary on the Bible, just as he had earlier issued a six-volume commentary on Pausanias's description of Greece. He published the three volumes of his *Folk-Lore in the Old Testament* in 1918.

Frazer's method was to select a myth or custom in the Bible and to identify parallels in "primitive societies." So in volume 2, chapter 4, a three-hundred-page essay titled "Jacob's Marriage," he analyzed Jacob's marriages to his cousins, the two daughters of his mother's brother, Laban, and posed the question whether Jacob was following established customs and whether such customs were to be found in other primitive societies. He was, of course, able to show that these practices were indeed widespread. A chapter on Cain explained that all over the world murderers were marked in order to protect them from ghosts. Similar exercises showed that "primitive peoples" also prayed and sacrificed to their gods and had their myths of creation, floods, and so on. As a modern biographer of Frazer comments, "The implicit purpose of the work . . . [was] to undermine the Bible and religion by insisting on its folkloric stratum, thereby associating it with savagery" (Ackerman 1987:182–183)

Émile Durkheim was also inspired by Robertson Smith. In *The Elementary Forms of the Religious Life* (1912) he adopted Robertson Smith's thesis that religion was rooted in social arrangements and in particular that early religions developed out of family cults (this thesis had been independently proposed for ancient Rome and Greece by Durkheim's teacher Fustel de Coulanges [1864]). Among the Aboriginal peoples of Australia—apparently the most primitive surviving society—the exogamous kinship group, the clan, was associated with an emblem, the totem, which was the object of taboos and sacrifice. It was, Durkheim declared, sacred.

For Durkheim, "the sacred was the religious" (Lukes 1973:241), and he praised Robertson Smith for remarking the ambiguity at the core of the notion of the sacred, the biblical *qadosh*. The ambiguity lies in the fact that the word *qadosh* may refer to something that is holy in the Christian sense, or it may designate something that is unpropitious and taboo, like a field sown with a mixed harvest or the *q'desha*, the temple priestess who is a cult prostitute. The key is that sacred things are set apart from profane beings. "A whole group of rites has the object of realizing this state of separation which is essential. Since their function is to prevent undue mixings and to keep one of the two domains from encroaching upon the other, they are only able to impose abstentions or negative acts" (Durkheim [1912] 1971:299).

Maureen Bloom argues that Durkheim was in reality characterizing biblical Judaism and that he was drawing upon his own education in the Hebrew Bible (2007:chap. 7). After all, Durkheim was the son of the rabbi of Épinal and had been destined for the rabbinate. So once again, by another route, the Hebrew Bible shaped the anthropology of religion.

v

The influence of the great Victorians was prolonged. The second edition of Robinson and Oesterley's influential *History of Israel*, published in 1937, still relied on Wellhausen, Robertson Smith, Tylor, and Frazer. Frazer himself continued to publish on the Hebrew Bible until the 1930s. Freud—another fan of Robertson Smith—produced exercises in speculative anthropology, *Totem and Taboo* (1913), and *Moses and Monotheism* (1937), which were, at least in point of method, thoroughly Victorian.

Within anthropology a reaction set in against just-so stories of origin, but the comparative method remained in favor. Marcel Mauss (1926), who was the grandson of a rabbi, suggested that the situation of the

Hebrew patriarchs was similar to that of pastoralist elites in East Africa, who lorded it over sedentary farmers. Franz Steiner (1954) compared the patriarchal families to Nuer clans and lineages of South Sudan. Occasional attempts were made to rewrite chapters of *Folk-Lore in the Old Testament* in a functionalist idiom, anthropologists citing observations from their own fieldwork to cast light on mysterious episodes in the Bible. Isaac Schapera (1955), for example, devoted a Frazer lecture (appropriately enough) to the sin of Cain.

Starting in the 1950s, biblical scholars began to draw on more recent anthropological theories (see Rogerson 1979, 1989). Some were influenced by theories of nomadism, though not, surprisingly, by the ideas about nomads in the Islamic world of the fourteenth-century Arab historian and theorist Ibn Khaldun (Fromherz 2010). Functionalist studies of segmentary lineage systems were taken as a model of the social system of the patriarchal age. Some scholars combined the lineage model with models of state formation or with the typology of bands, tribes, and chieftaincies developed by Elman Service (1962).

Inevitably, perhaps, biblical scholars tended to place too much confidence in their chosen anthropological models. It was readily assumed, for instance, that anthropologists were quite sure what lineages are (and, indeed, that any expert can distinguish minimal from maximal lineages).[2] The only issue was to identify the ancient Hebrew terms for these social units. This turned out to be very difficult. Experts could not agree whether the biblical *bet av* or *mispahah* should be translated as a "lineage," or whether the Hebrew words *sebet* or *matteh* referred to a "tribe" or a "clan." As Niels Peter Lemche remarks, "It is clear that the traditional literature of the OT employs a very loose terminology to describe the lower levels of the society, since [Hebrew terms usually rendered as] 'house' and 'father's house' are used indiscriminately of the nuclear family, the extended family, and also of the higher kinship group, the lineage." As for the very general view that the term *mishpaha* means "clan," "no scholar has troubled to define precisely what he meant by the word 'clan'" (Lemche 1985:260; cf. Vanderhooft 2009). Yet Lemche himself was perhaps too ready to identify "lineages" in biblical times and to conclude that "clan endogamy" was widely practiced (1985:272–274).[3]

Howard Eilberg-Schwartz (1990) has proposed a return to the comparative method, and attempts continue to generalize from exotic practices in order to illuminate puzzling biblical stories.[4] Old-fashioned ideas about primitive society still cast a long shadow in essays on the Bible. The ghosts of Robertson Smith, Frazer, and Marett might find some recent exercises in the comparative method rather familiar.

But N. H. Snaith (1944) chided biblical scholars for paying more attention to primitive parallels than to textual analysis. Within anthropology there was increasing concern with the meaning of beliefs and practices for the people themselves. Marett had demanded this almost from the first: "How then are we to be content with an explanation of taboo that does not pretend to render its sense as it has sense for those who both practice it and make it a rallying point for their thought on mystic matters? . . . We ask to understand it, and we are merely bidden to despise it" (1909:97). The post–World War I generation of anthropologists, the first to spend extensive periods in the field, insisted that customs had to be studied in action. Only modern ethnographic fieldwork could deliver a properly sympathetic understanding of exotic beliefs.

This was also the message of the newly fashionable linguistic philosophy. Wittgenstein read *The Golden Bough* in 1931 and reacted with furious contempt: "Frazer is much more savage than most of his savages, for these savages will not be so far from any understanding of spiritual matters as an Englishman of the twentieth century. His explanations of the primitive observances are much cruder than the sense of the observances themselves" (1979:8). In Wittgenstein's view, meaning was a matter of context and use.

And so they came to agree, the philosophers and the anthropologists, that concepts and practices could be understood only by appreciating their use in the business of everyday life in particular communities. Context was all. Peter Winch's *Idea of a Social Science*, published in 1958, identified the doctrines of the later Wittgenstein with the analytical practice of Oxford's new professor of social anthropology, E. E. Evans-Pritchard. As Mary Douglas put it, summing up what she took to be the position of Evans-Pritchard, "Everyday language and everyday thought set into their social and situational context have to be the subject of inquiry" (1980:26).

Evans-Pritchard had read history at Exeter College as an undergraduate, and he recalled Marett as an affable fellow. When he became in his turn professor of social anthropology at Oxford and lectured on theories of primitive religion, he borrowed Marett's critical characterization of the theories of Tylor and Frazer as "intellectualist." He also questioned the value of psychological and sociological accounts of religion. The son of an Anglican clergyman, Evans-Pritchard was a recent convert to Catholicism, and he was inclined to believe that all religions contain a kernel of spiritual truth. This now seemed to him to be their most important feature, and he urged that spiritual beliefs should be treated seriously in their own right (Evans-Pritchard 1965).

Evans-Pritchard (1963) came to deprecate the comparative method, but he was prepared to reverse the procedure, claiming in the introduction to his *Nuer Religion* that the religions of the Nuer and Dinka of South Sudan "have features which bring to mind the Hebrews of the Old Testament." He quoted in support an American Presbyterian working among the Nuer who remarked that "the missionary feels as if he were living in Old Testament times, and in a way this is true." "When therefore," Evans-Pritchard concluded, "I sometimes draw comparisons between Nuer and Hebrew conceptions, it is no mere whim but is because I myself find it helpful, and I think others may do so too, in trying to understand Nuer ideas to note this likeness to something with which we are ourselves familiar without being too intimately involved in it" (1956:vii). African informants who were familiar with the Bible often made such comparisons themselves (see, e.g., Turner 1967:135). However, Evans-Pritchard clearly intended to suggest that the Nuer had a sort of preknowledge of scriptural truths. In the very last sentences of the monograph, he wrote that the meaning of Nuer rites "depends finally on an awareness of God and that men are dependent on him and must be resigned to his will. At this point the theologian takes over from the anthropologist" (Evans-Pritchard 1956:322).

VII

According to the practitioners of the comparative method, the essential ingredients of primitive religion were totem and taboo. Its defining ritual was sacrifice. In 1950–51 Franz Steiner (1956, 1999)—an émigré Jewish mystic, a German poet, a friend of Elias Canetti, a lover of Iris Murdoch, and a lecturer in the Oxford Institute of Social Anthropology—gave a course of lectures on taboo, which were edited and published after his death. His central thesis was that the constructs of the comparative method had been lifted from specific ethnographic contexts. In the process they were stripped of their particularities and lost much of their meaning. When modern ethnographers apply these constructs in their own analyses, the constructs have to be qualified if they are to be of any use at all. "They are then redefined, and by this process they become so narrow as to lose all significance outside the individual analytical study to which they were tailored." For example, he suggested, "The broad significance which 'Totemism' had as a comparative category has evaporated" (Steiner 1999:105).

Steiner tagged taboo as "a Protestant discovery," while the notion that taboos regulated social order and morality was "a Victorian invention," one that was peculiarly interesting to prudes and snobs (1999:132). But taboo was actually a Polynesian concept, and Steiner proceeded to analyze the specific meaning of *tabu* in the context of Polynesian language, thought, and religion. It turned out that tabu was not at all the same thing as the "taboo" of the anthropologists.

Steiner then reviewed Robertson Smith's thesis that the notion of the sacred originated in ideas of taboo. Steiner had an educated knowledge of Hebrew, and he argued (along the same lines as Durkheim) that the Hebrew idea of qadosh could not be translated simply as "taboo," certainly not in the sense in which the Polynesians used the term *tabu*. He concluded that neither the Polynesian tabu nor the Hebrew qadosh was a useful cross-cultural category. The only universal was that all societies define certain acts, words, and situations as pregnant with danger.

So much, then, for taboo, and perhaps even for the category of the sacred. Evans-Pritchard gave the Henry Myers lecture in 1954, which he titled "The Meaning of Sacrifice among the Nuer." He remarked that "in Nuer sacrifice there are different shades of meaning. The pattern varies. There are shifts of emphasis." It was difficult, if not impossible, "to present a general interpretation, to put forward a simple formula, to cover all Nuer sacrifices" (Evans-Pritchard 1954:30). Many Nuer sacrifices regulated social relations and might be amenable to a sociological analysis. But Evans-Pritchard noted that Father Crazzolara, a Catholic missionary among the Nuer, had distinguished a category of piacular sacrifices that were not connected to social events but, much more interesting, were concerned with a universal quest, "the regulation of the individual's relation with God" (capitalized here, so no mere tribal deity) (Evans-Pritchard 1954:30).

So taboo was a Victorian invention. Sacrifice was a broad term for a range of ritual practices with unpredictable meanings that were resistant to sociological analysis and to comparison. That left totemism. Claude Lévi-Strauss's short book *Le totémisme aujourd'hui*, published in 1962, deconstructed the concept, concluding that totemism also was not a useful cross-cultural category. Anthropologists should instead investigate the truly universal process by which all societies classify and relate social groups and natural phenomena. In a more extended study published a few months later, *La pensée sauvage*, Lévi-Strauss demonstrated that arbitrary features of natural objects were given significance by their position in a series of binary oppositions. Natural species were classified with reference to these oppositions. So too were the parts of the society. They were, then, related to one another.

VIII

These exemplary critiques disposed of the classical components of comparative religion, totem, taboo, and sacrifice. Yet the change of paradigm was incomplete. A close reader of Steiner and Lévi-Strauss might still be inclined to study the place of taboo and totemic marriage rules in biblical religion, even if these elements were now understood rather differently. According to Lévi-Strauss, all societies establish parallel classifications of social and natural phenomena by making a series of binary contrasts. That was totemism, properly understood. And Steiner indicated that every society marks off certain social and natural categories as dangerous. Properly understood, then, taboo was a property of a system of classification. Edmund Leach and Mary Douglas now proposed structural accounts of biblical taboos on food and marriage.

Their projects might have been similar, but Leach and Douglas—like Robertson Smith and Frazer before them—began from very different points of view. Leach was a crusading atheist. His mother had hoped that he would be a missionary. Instead he became the president of the Humanist Society. Douglas was a conservative Catholic. Reviewing her *Natural Symbols* in the *New York Review of Books* in 1971, Leach wrote: "All her recent work gives the impression that she is no longer much concerned with the attainment of empirical truth; the object of the exercise is to adapt her anthropological learning to the service of Roman Catholic propaganda." Reviewing Leach and J. Alan Aycock's *Structuralist Interpretations of Biblical Myths*, also in the *New York Review of Books*, Douglas (1984) claimed that Leach imposed his own meanings on the myths, just like Frazer, and she concluded that the "ingenious argument is extremely interesting and, to readers who are unfamiliar with Old Testament scholarship, quite plausible."

And yet the two anthropologists had much in common, including a tendency to read back into the biblical world their own ideas about European Jews, whom they were inclined to think were too picky about food and unreasonably prejudiced against intermarriage. To be sure, the projection of a particular understanding of the present into the past, even the very distant past, is hardly unusual. But Leach and Douglas also shared more specialized ideas. Priority is difficult to establish— copies of papers circulated in draft before publication—but clearly they were already working on very similar lines in the early 1960s, drawing heavily from Lévi-Strauss.

In 1961 Leach published an essay, "Lévi-Strauss in the Garden of Eden" (reprinted in Leach 1969), which flagged his conversion to structuralism and introduced Lévi-Strauss as a better guide to the Bible than Frazer. Biblical scholars since Wellhausen and Robertson Smith had recognized mythical elements in the Hebrew Bible, the deposits of very ancient traditions, but they struggled to distinguish myths from historical texts. Leach insisted that it was all myth. And although the elements of the texts were no doubt of diverse origin, the editors of the Hebrew Bible had imposed a coherence upon this body of myth. The analyst should accordingly act "on a presumption that the whole of the text as we now have it *regardless of the varying historical origins of its component parts* may properly be treated as a unity" (Leach and Aycock 1983:89–112; similar pronouncements prefaced a number of Leach's biblical essays).

In his 1961 essay "Lévi-Strauss in the Garden of Eden," Leach analyzed the construction of the world and its creatures in the opening
chapters of Genesis by way of a series of binary contrasts. In Leviticus
11, "creatures which do not fit this exact ordering of the world—for
instance water creatures with no fins, animals and birds which eat meat
or fish, etc.—are classed as 'abominations'" (Leach 1969:13). Here and
in a paper titled "Animal Categories and Verbal Abuse," published in
1964, he argued that classifications constructed by a series of binary contrasts will always throw up elements that breach boundaries. These are
tabooed (Leach 1964). And taboos on anomalies reinforce boundaries.

Douglas's *Purity and Danger*, published in 1966, was directly inspired
by Steiner's lectures. It became famous for her first attempt at an anthropology of the Bible, a chapter on the abominations of Leviticus. Her
analysis was very similar to that of Leach, the argument being that classificatory anomalies were tabooed. She did not at this stage identify
the social context of these taboos, but she soon began to identify various possible functions. "We should see taboos as the performative acts
which stop the careless speaker from getting the categories confused....
The performance protects boundaries around classifications.... On this
distinctly Durkheimian approach, impurity and taboo supply back-up
for the current system of control" (Douglas 2004:159–162).

The most important taboos concern sex and food: "bed and board,"
as Douglas put it (Fardon 1999:186). Leach was more interested in
the bed side of things, and he treated the biblical stories of Adam and
Eve, Cain and Abel, Noah and Ham, Lot and his daughters, and Abraham and Sarah as a set of structural transformations on the theme of
incest and endogamy. Arguing that all societies struggle with similar
concerns, he compared these stories to the myth of Oedipus, which
Lévi-Strauss had selected for exemplary analysis in the first presentation of his structural method for the analysis of myth (Leach 1969;
Lévi-Strauss 1963:chap. 11).

According to Lévi-Strauss, myths grapple with existential issues, generating temporary resolutions of intractable problems. In "The Legitimacy of Solomon," Leach set out "to demonstrate that the Biblical
story of the succession of Solomon to the throne of Israel is a myth
which 'mediates' a major contradiction" (1969:31). The contradiction

is between the assertion that God gave the land of Israel to the Jewish people and that they should be endogamous, and the reality that the land accommodated a number of different populations, with whom Jews—even kings—intermarried, and for good political reasons. Leach argued that central myths in the Hebrew Bible offered resolutions of this structural contradiction.

Douglas came to agree that the ancient Hebrews were obsessed by endogamy. Rereading Leach's essay, "The Legitimacy of Solomon," "brought home . . . with a resounding thud something which Old Testament scholarship had been agreed upon for a very long time . . . that the Pentateuch was full of concern for the evils that flowed from marriage with foreigners" (Douglas 1975:208). Commenting on this passage, Richard Fardon remarks, "Tracing a general analogy between animal classification, food rules and sexual mating required, as she put it, something of a 'conversion' to alliance theory in the analysis of kinship" (1999:186).

Dating the redaction of the Tanach is still a controversial matter, but Leach (and Douglas after him) adopted the view, held by some experts, that it had been put together in its final form shortly after the return from Babylon in the sixth century BCE and the construction of the second temple. Leach and Douglas assumed that the editors imposed a unity on the various texts incorporated into the Hebrew Bible. The editors' motives were political. Leach accepted the thesis that the editors were following the party line of Ezra and Nehemiah, who led the return from exile and ruled Palestine for their Persian overlords. The texts were edited to support the policies of these satraps: their land grabbing, their xenophobic nationalism, and their insistence on Jewish endogamy. Yet if there was a party line, it was not always consistent. Leach thought that myths were bound to put alternatives into play and that myth makers were never completely in control of their material: "What the myth then 'says' is not what the editors consciously intended to say but rather something which lies deeply embedded in Jewish traditional culture as a whole" (1969:53).

Douglas took the view that different factions had edited particular sections of the Bible. She agreed with Leach that the Persian satraps Ezra and Nehemiah, who had led the exiles back from Babylon, were concerned with imposing endogamy, which enforced social and political boundaries.[5] But a priestly party, responsible for what biblical scholars identify as the P sources in the Bible, were prepared to tolerate exogamy. Their power base was in the temple, and their special privilege was the performance of sacrifices. In consequence, the priests were obsessed with the Levitical taboos, the rules of purity and holiness. And so distinct and conflicting political interests could be discerned behind the purity rules, on the one hand, and the rules on intermarriage, on the other.

The ark, the tabernacle, and the temple were the most sacred sites of Judaism. Leach (1976:84–93) sketched the outlines of structuralist geography of these sacred places. Douglas argued that the rules regulating behavior in sacred sites provided models for everyday activities. The concern for purity that regulated temple sacrifices also informed the food taboos. This was because the body was itself a temple. "To conclude," she wrote in her final collection of essays, *Jacob's Tears*, "the levitical food prohibitions have plenty to do with the tabernacle. They frame the analogy between tabernacle and body: what goes for one, goes for the other" (Douglas 2004:172). It was not enough to analyze systems of classification. One had to connect: food taboos and marriage rules; the laws of *kashrut* and the laws of sacrifice; the body and the temple; the temple and Mount Sinai and the sanctuary. In *Leviticus as Literature*, published in 1999, she introduced a further structural parallel, that between the form of the book itself—a "ring structure"—and the layout of the temple.

Some French literary structuralists also wrote essays on the Bible.[6] Yet although he had provided the inspiration, Lévi-Strauss (a grandson of the rabbi of Strasbourg) disapproved of these studies. A year after the publication of *La pensée sauvage*, the journal *Esprit* arranged a discussion between Lévi-Strauss and a group of philosophers led by the Christian existentialist Paul Ricoeur (see Lévi-Strauss 2004). Ricoeur had just made his famous linguistic turn, and he now believed that only a hermeneutic interpretation of signs, symbols, and texts could yield an understanding of the human condition. Lévi-Strauss was, of course, all in favor of a linguistic turn, but his linguistics were very different. Ricoeur charged Lévi-Strauss with privileging syntactics over semantics, structure over meaning. He conceded that this might be appropriate in analyzing the ideas of simple societies, which really had very little to say for themselves. It was not helpful when it came to more complex intellectual systems. Similarly, the play of transformations in the myths of "cold" societies was very different from the historical, logically sequential myths of "hot" societies like ancient Greece and Israel. They had produced great narratives that were vehicles of profound reflections about human existence. Could Lévi-Strauss's method be applied to such myths?

Lévi-Strauss responded that myths did not make sense in the way that Ricoeur imagined. They did not send messages; rather, they commented on one another. Symbols had only a positional significance. But Lévi-Strauss rejected the notion that there was a difference in kind between the mythologies of cold and hot societies. After all, persuasive structuralist studies of Greek myths were being published. However, the Bible was different. The problem with the Bible was, first, that while it incorporated mythical sources, these had been edited and, Lévi-Strauss said, distorted. Moreover, to understand myths one had to have some basic ethnographic information about the society in which they were current, but the ethnographic information to be gleaned from the Bible had very probably itself been mythologized (cf. Lévi-Strauss 1987).

IX

Biblical scholars may well share Paul Ricoeur's reservations about the structuralist approach. Another reasonable complaint is that anthropologists generally lacked the scholarly preparation that their projects required. For instance, J. A. Emerton (1976) exposed Leach's dubious etymologies and other errors. He also pointed out that Leach's approach to the Bible was very selective. Leach exaggerated any biblical concern with purity of blood and ignored that fact that intermarriage was denounced for religious rather than for racial or political reasons. The real fear was that men would follow their wives and worship foreign gods. However, Douglas has been treated with more respect than Leach, perhaps in part because she was a believer and he was a crusading atheist. Distinguished scholars of the Hebrew Bible, Jacob

Milgrom (2004:passim) and Jacob Neusner (2006:149), have made gracious comments on her work (and see Duhaime 1998; Hendel 2008).

In any case, structuralism, broadly defined, remains the prevailing method of anthropological studies of the Bible. Leach was followed by a number of scholars who delivered persuasive readings of biblical myths. For instance, David Pocock (1975) analyzed the structural opposition of North and South in the book of Genesis; Seth Daniel Kunin (1995) covers much the same ground as Leach, but with impressive scholarship; and Édouard Conte (2011a, 2011b) is engaged in the structural analysis of Koranic texts on descent and incest that present further transformations of the myths of the patriarchs and the genealogy of Israel. Other anthropologists, following on from Douglas, have brought out unexpected and suggestive connections—between systems of classification, rules governing sacrifices and food prohibitions, pollution beliefs, restrictions on marriage, the politics of legitimacy, and sacred architecture and landscape. The themes of these studies are, however, rather restricted. Strangely, neither Leach nor Douglas considered the ample evidence of a preference in biblical times for cousin marriage, which had been documented long ago by Frazer (1918, 2:chap. 4). And studies of the Israelite monarchy have been limited to rather old-fashioned exercises in the comparative method.

The Gospels have also been relatively neglected. Leach's (1966) rather old-fashioned comparative essay on virgin birth did not attract attention from biblical scholars. His hint that the Christian Mass is a transformation of the Jewish Passover (Leach 1976:93) was, however, developed by Gillian Feeley-Harnik, who analyzed the Last Supper as a structural transformation of the Passover seder, where "every critical element in the Passover is reversed" (1981:19). The Talmud and the Koran are still little studied by anthropologists, though Maureen Bloom (2007) has produced a sophisticated anthropological analysis of mysticism and magic in the Talmud, relating Talmudic conceptions to biblical and to Babylonian sources.

Biblical scholars may be reassured that these authors do usually know Hebrew and Aramaic, even if they seldom have a mastery of the tools of Bible criticism. For their part, biblical scholars are usually uncritical in their application of anthropological examples and rely too often on dated and discredited anthropological models. There are exceptions—R. R. Wilson's superb study of biblical genealogies comes to mind. Yet more interdisciplinary collaboration would obviously be a good idea. "While a number of scholars make more or less overt reference to advice or counsel given by anthropology colleagues in the course of their work," James Martin remarked in 1989, "no publication has appeared over the joint names of an anthropologist and an Old Testament scholar" (1989:103). I believe that the same statement could be repeated now, after a quarter of a century.

But perhaps the deeper problems are conceptual rather than methodological. It could very well be argued that anthropologists have constructed exotic "religions" in the image of their own. "From one point of view," Clifford Geertz wrote, "the whole history of the comparative study of religion from the time Robertson Smith undertook his investigations into the rites of the ancient Semites . . . can be looked at as but a circuitous, even devious, approach to a rational analysis of our own situation, an evaluation of our own religious traditions while seeming to evaluate only those of exotic others" (1971:22).

Although the Hebrew Bible had no word for religion, it bequeathed enduring paradigms of both genuine and false religions, setting the parameters for the classification of exotic beliefs and rituals. The "high religions" of the East were distressingly polytheist, even inclined to idolatry, but they might be accepted as genuine because they had sacred texts, temples, hymns, and prayers. Pagan cults, however, were equated with the false religion of the Philistines. They had idols instead of deities, magicians in the place of priests, orgies rather than solemn rituals. A romantic like Andrew Lang (see, e.g., Lang 1887) might prefer pagan sensuality, fairy tales, and nature worship to the Puritan church. But his was a challenge to the orthodox believer, not to the idea of religion itself. In the twentieth century, relativist anthropologists were inclined to treat all religions as equal, but the notion of religion itself was seldom put in question.

And so a distinctive realm of study was constituted: the anthropology of religion. It was a sacred space occupied by myths, taboos, idols, and sacrifice. Even the most secular and skeptical anthropologists accepted the parameters. They might argue about whether the distinctive feature of religion was belief or ritual and what, if anything, distinguished religion from magic, but despite a succession of paradigm changes, the field—and its subject matter—remained remarkably stable for 150 years. Yet surely its analytical core, the very notion of religion, is ripe for deconstruction.

NOTES

I am grateful to Mark Geller, Richard Fardon, Maureen Bloom, and Richard Kuper for their comments on earlier drafts.

1. Some missionary scholars were also aware of the new biblical criticism. The first Anglican bishop of Zululand, John Colenso, produced sympathetic account of Zulu beliefs and practices, even endorsing polygamy, which, he noted and as the Zulu remarked, had been practiced by the biblical patriarchs. Colenso also published contributions to the new biblical criticism and was duly tried for heresy in Cape Town (Guy 1883).
2. For a critique, see Kuper (2005:chap. 8).
3. For some sophisticated attempts to apply the segmentary lineage model to ancient Israel, see Bendor ([1986] 1996); Frick (1985); Wilson (1977). For a review, see Goldberg (1996).
4. For instance, Pitt-Rivers (1977) suggested that enduring themes of Mediterranean culture explained some puzzling biblical episodes. Gilbert Lewis (1987) compared the treatment of lepers in New Guinea and ancient Israel. Meyer Fortes (1959) identified the biblical figure of Job as the prototype of some West African beliefs. Notwithstanding his clearly stated reservations, Lévi-Strauss (1988) himself published a playful comparison of origin myths of circumcision among the ancient Israelites and the penis-sheath among the Amazonian Bororo.
5. In her treatment of these Persian satraps, Douglas seems to have projected back from an understanding of contemporary Middle Eastern politics. Richard Fardon remarks: "Parallels with the range of political positions occupied in contemporary Israel may be implicit in Douglas's account, but they are certainly not lost on her" (1999:203).
6. French scholars from various disciplines contributed structuralist analyses of biblical texts. See, for example, Barthes et al. (1971); and Soler (1979).

Ackerman, Robert. 1987. J. G. Frazer: His Life and Work. Cambridge: Cambridge University Press.

———, ed. 2005. Selected Letters of Sir James George Frazer. Oxford: Oxford University Press.

Barthes, R., F. Bovon, F.-J. Leenhardt, R. Martin-Achard, and J. Starobinski. 1971. Analyse structural et exégèse biblique. Neuchâtel: Delachaux et Niestlé.

Bendor, S. (1986) 1996. The Social Structure of Ancient Israel. Jerusalem: Eisenbrauns.

Black, John, and George Chrystal. 1912. The Life of William Robertson Smith. London: A. and C. Black.

Bloom, Maureen. 2007. Jewish Mysticism and Magic: An Anthropological Perspective. London: Routledge.

Brosses, Charles de. 1760. Du culte des dieux fétiches ou parallès de l'ancienne religion de l'Egypte avec la religion actuelle de Nigritie. Paris.

Chadwick, Owen. 1970. The Victorian Church. 2 vols. Oxford: Oxford University Press.

Comte, Auguste. 1830–42. Cours de philosophie positive. 6 vols. Paris.

Conte, Édouard. 2011a. Adam et consorts: Germanité et filiation de la Genèse au Deluge selon les traditions musulmanes. In L'argument de la filiation. Paris: Editions de las Maison des sciences de l'homme.

———. 2011b. Elles seront des soeurs pour nous: Le marriage par permutation au proche-orient. Études rurales 187:157–200.

Coulanges, Fustel de. 1864. La cité antique. Paris: Durand.

Douglas, Mary. 1966. Purity and Danger. London: Routledge.

———. 1975. Implicit Meanings. London: Routledge.

———. 1980. Edward Evans-Pritchard. London: Fontana.

———. 1984. Betwixt, Bothered and Bewildered. New York Review of Books, December 20.

———. 1999. Leviticus as Literature. Oxford: Oxford University Press.

———. 2004. Jacob's Tears: The Priestly Work of Reconciliation. Oxford: Oxford University Press.

Duhaime, Jean. 1998. Lois alimentaires et pureté corporelle dans le Lévitique: L'approche de Mary Douglas et sa réception par Jacob Milgrom. Religiologiques 17:19–35.

Durkheim, Émile. (1912) 2001. The Elementary Forms of the Religious Life. Oxford: Oxford University Press.

Eilberg-Schwartz, Howard. 1990. The Savage in Judaism: An Anthropology of Israelite Religion and Ancient Judaism. Bloomington: Indiana University Press.

Emerton, J. A. 1976. An Examination of a Recent Structuralist Interpretation of Genesis XXXVIII. Vetus Testamentum 26(1):79–98.

Evans-Pritchard, E. E. 1954. The Meaning of Sacrifice among the Nuer. Journal of the Royal Anthropological Institute 84(1/2):21–33.

———. 1956. Nuer Religion. Oxford: Oxford University Press.

———. 1963. The Comparative Method in Social Anthropology. Atlantic Highlands NJ: Athlone Press.

———. 1965. Theories of Primitive Religion. Oxford: Oxford University Press.

Fardon, Richard. 1999. Mary Douglas. London: Routledge.

Feeley-Harnik, Gillian. 1981. The Lord's Table: Eucharist and Passover in Early Christianity. Philadelphia: University of Pennsylvania Press.

Fortes, Meyer. 1959. Oedipus and Job in West African Religion. Cambridge: Cambridge University Press

Frazer, J. G. 1887. Totemism. Edinburgh: A. and C. Black.

———. 1894. William Robertson Smith. Fortnightly Review 60:800–807.

———. 1900. The Golden Bough. 2 vols. 2nd ed. London: Macmillan.

———. 1918. Folk-Lore in the Old Testament. 3 vols. London: Macmillan.

———. 1927. The Gorgon's Head. London: Macmillan.

Freud, S. (1913) 1919. Totem and Taboo: Resemblances between the Psychic Life of Savages and Neurotics. London: Routledge.

———. (1937) 1939. Moses and Monodeism. London: Hogarth Press.

Frick, Frank S. 1985. The Formation of the State in Ancient Israel. Sheffield, England: Almond.

Fromherz, Allen. 2010. Ibn Khaldun: Life and Times. Edinburgh: Edinburgh University Press.

Geertz, Clifford. 1971. Islam Observed: Religious Development in Morocco and Indonesia. Chicago: University of Chicago Press.

Goldberg, Harvey E. 1996. Cambridge in the Land of Canaan: Descent, Alliance, Circumcision and Instruction in the Bible. Janes 24:9–34.

Guy, Jeff. 1983. The Heretic: A Study of the Life of John William Colenso, 1814–1883. Durban, South Africa: University of Natal Press.

Hendel, Ron. 2008. Remembering Mary Douglas: Kashrut, Culture, and Thought-Styles. Jewish Studies 45:3–15.

Hesketh, Ian. 2009. Of Apes and Ancestors. Toronto: University of Toronto Press.

Kunin, Seth Daniel. 1995. The Logic of Incest: A Structuralist Analysis of Hebrew Mythology. Sheffield, England: Sheffield Academic Press.

Kuper, Adam. 2005. The Reinvention of Primitive Society: Transformations of a Myth. London: Routledge.

Lang, Andrew. 1887. Myth, Ritual and Religion. 2 vols. London: Longmans, Green.

Leach, E. R. 1964. Animal Categories and Verbal Abuse. *In* New Directions in the Study of Language. Eric H. Lenneberg, ed. Pp. 23–63. Cambridge MA: MIT Press.

———. 1966. Virgin Birth. Proceedings of the Royal Anthropological Institute 96:39–49.

———. 1969. Genesis as Myth and Other Essays. London: Cape.

———. 1971. Mythical Inequalities. New York Review of Books, January 28.

———. 1976. Culture and Communication. Cambridge: Cambridge University Press.

Leach, E. R., and J. Alan Aycock. 1983. Structuralist Interpretations of Biblical Myths. Cambridge: Cambridge University Press.

Lemche, Niels Peter. 1985. Early Israel: Anthropological and Historical Studies on the Israelite Society before the Monarchy. Leiden: E. J. Brill.

Lévi-Strauss, Claude. 1962a. La pensée sauvage. Paris: Plon.

———. 1962b. Le totémisme aujourd'hui.

———. 1963. The Structural Study of Myth. *In* Structural Anthropology. Pp. 206–231. New York: Basic Books.

———. 1971. Totemism. Boston: Beacon Press.

———. 1987. De la fidelité au texte. L'homme 27(101):117–140.

———. 1988. Exode sur exode. L'homme 28(106):13–23.

———. 2004. Autour de *La pensée sauvage,* réponses à quelques questions. Entretien du "groupe philosophique" d'*Esprit* avec Claude Lévi-Strauss. Esprit, November 1963:169–192.

Lewis, Gilbert. 1987. A Lesson from Leviticus: Leprosy. Man 22(4):593–612.

Lukes, Stephen. 1973. Emile Durkheim. London: Allen Lane.

Mannhardt, Wilhelm. 1875. Der Baumkultus der Germanen und ihrer Nachbarstämme. Berlin: Borntröger.

Marett, R. R. 1911. Mana. *In* Encyclopaedia Britannica. 11th ed.

———. 1936. Tylor. London: Chapman and Hall.

———. 1941. A Jerseyman at Oxford. Oxford: Oxford University Press.

Martin, James. 1989. Israel as a Tribal Society. *In* The World of Ancient Israel: Sociological, Anthropological and Political Perspectives. R. E. Clements, ed. Pp. 94–114. Cambridge: Cambridge University Press.

Mauss, Marcel. 1926. Critique interne de la "legend d'Abraham." Revue des études juives 82:35–44.

McLennan, J. M. 1865. Primitive Marriage. Edinburgh: A. and C. Black.

———. 1869–70. The Worship of Animals and Plants. Fortnightly Review 6:407–582; 7:194–216.

Milgrom, Jacob. 2004. Leviticus. Minneapolis: Fortress Press.

Neusner, Jacob. 2006. Neusner on Judaism: Religion and Theology. Aldershot, England: Ashgate.

Parker, John W., ed. 1860. Essays and Reviews. London: John W. Parker.

Pitt-Rivers, Julian. 1977. The Fate of Shechem: The Politics of Sex: Essays in the Anthropology of the Mediterranean. Cambridge: Cambridge University Press.

Pocock, David F. 1975. North and South in the Book of Genesis. In Studies in Social Anthropology. J. H. M. Beattie and R. G. Lienhardt, eds. Pp. 273–284. Oxford: Clarendon Press.

Robertson Smith, William. 1880. Animal Worship and the Animal Tribes among the Arabs and in the Old Testament. Journal of Philology 9:75–100.

———. 1885. Kinship and Marriage in Early Arabia. Cambridge: Cambridge University Press.

———. (1889) 1894. Lectures on the Religion of the Semites. Edinburgh: A. and C. Black.

———. 1894. The Old Testament in the Jewish Church. Edinburgh: A. and C. Black.

Robinson, W., and T. Oesterley. 1937. A History of Israel. 2 vols. 2nd ed. Oxford: Clarendon Press.

Rogerson, J. W. 1979. Anthropology and the Old Testament. Atlanta: John Knox Press.

———. 1989. Anthropology and the Old Testament. In The World of Ancient Israel: Sociological, Anthropological and Political Perspectives. R. E. Clements, ed. Pp. 17–38. Cambridge: Cambridge University Press.

Schapera, Isaac. 1955. The Sin of Cain. Proceedings of the Royal Anthropological Institute 85(1/2):33–43.

Service, Elman. 1962. Primitive Social Organization: An Evolutionary Perspective. New York: Random House.

Snaith, N. H. 1944. Distinctive Ideas of the Old Testament. London: Epworth Press.

Soler, J. 1979. The Dietary Prohibitions of the Hebrews. New York Review of Books, June 14.

Steiner, Franz. 1954. Enslavement and the Early Hebrew Lineage System: An Explanation of Genesis 47. Man 54:73–75.

———. 1956. Taboo. London: Cohen and West.

———. 1999. Taboo, Truth, and Religion. Jeremy Adler and Richard Fardon, eds. New York: Berghahn.

Stocking, George W. 1987. Victorian Anthropology. New York: Free Press.

Turner, Victor. 1967. The Forest of Symbols. Ithaca NY: Cornell University Press.

Tylor, E. B. 1866. The Religion of Savages. Fortnightly Review 6:71–86.

———. 1871. Primitive Culture. 2 vols. London: John Murray.

———. 1881. Anthropology. London: Macmillan.

Vanderhooft, D. 2009. The Israelite MISPAHA, the Priestly Writings, and Changing Valences in Israel's Kinship Terminology. *In* Exploring the Longue Durée: Essays in Honor of Lawrence E. Stager. J. D. Schloen, ed. Pp. 485–496. Warsaw IN: Eisenbrauns.

Wellhausen, Julius. (1883) 1885. Prolegomena to the History of Israel. Edinburgh: A. and C. Black.

Wheeler-Barclay, Marjorie. 2010. The Science of Religion in Britain, 1860–1915. Charlottesville: University of Virginia Press.

Wilson, R. R. 1977. Genealogy and History in the Biblical World. New Haven CT: Yale University Press.

Winch, Peter. 1958. The Idea of a Social Science. New York: Routledge.

Wittgenstein, Ludwig. 1979. Remarks on Frazer's *Golden Bough*. Rush Rhees, ed. Corbridge, Northumberland, England: Brynmill Press.

2

Dead and Living Authorities in *The Legend of Perseus*

Animism and Christianity in the Evolutionist Archive

Since the demise of Hartland, social anthropology and folklore studies have followed ever diverging courses, forgetful of the happy union
between the two he had promoted so successfully.

RICHARD DORSON, *The British Folklorists: A History*, 1968

Edwin Sidney Hartland (1848–1927) was a British solicitor and politician whose proficiency as a self-made folklorist and evolutionary
anthropology went far beyond dilettantism, following in the footsteps
of his principal mentor, Edward B. Tylor (1832–1917). Hartland was a
prominent figure in the Folklore Society, which he presided over at the
turn of the century. Indeed, he was one of the members of the "Great
Team" of British late Victorian folklorists, to use the expression coined
by Richard Dorson (1968:2c2). Between 1884 and 1924 Hartland's pro-
lific production included his magnum opus: a three-volume work titled
The Legend of Perseus: A Study of Tradition in Story, Custom and Belief,
which at the time enjoyed "a reputation commensurate with *The Golden
Bough.*"[1] One of the reasons for this parallel with James Frazer's anthropological best seller was the religious implications of Hartland's book.
Published in 1894, the first volume subtly heralded a challenging agenda
of universal comparativism by focusing on the myth of Perseus's first
"train of incident"—the hero's supernatural (or virgin) birth, which
obviously echoed that of Jesus Christ (Hartland 1894–96, 1:1).

No doubt, Hartland was above all a Tylorian anthropologist or folklorist (synonymous words to him) who saw in Tylor's *Primitive Culture*
(1870), like so many others did, the standard and the main intellectual
inspiration of his own endeavors. His work, like Tylor's, had therefore

this rather peculiar characteristic of combining empiricism with universalism. The idea of a long-lasting or, better still, of an everlasting legacy of prehistorical mankind and particularly of its animist stock of notions was inseparable from a cumulative perspective of ethnographical or historical data. The "promiscuity" of "civilized" and "savage" man, not only from an evolutionary point of view but also psychologically speaking, had its methodological counterpart in the quotation of a "galaxy of sources" (Dorson 1968:19) solely for their empirical content, irrespective of other scholars' analysis or theoretical reflections—or, for that matter, irrespective of their fieldwork problems, whenever the case applied.[2] This is, I think, a crucial aspect of British nineteenth-century evolutionary anthropology and particularly of the Folklore Society's intellectual networks. By the same token, the importance of objective data, as they were held to exist, created a common ground between all authorities that someone such as Sidney Hartland might invoke, whether those authorities were dead or alive. The illustration or even the recapture of this much-forgotten epistemological perspective is the challenge that I will try to defend, using the first volume of *The Legend of Perseus* as a case study. My purpose is actually twofold, since I also intend to recall that Tylorian anthropologists were obsessed with Christianity.

BEYOND ANTIQUITY: FROM OVID TO NINETEENTH-CENTURY FOLKLORISTS

Classical written versions of the myth of Perseus, in particular that of Ovid's *Metamorphoses*, were the starting point of Hartland's enterprise. And yet the urge to transfer the inquiry "from literature to tradition" (Hartland 1894–96, 1:11), that is, to oral tradition, soon manifested itself, following the suspicion or hypothesis that Roman and Greek authors ignored the oldest, rudest forms of the myth and instead conveyed more sophisticated variants, whose contents they further embellished via the literary process. This was evident in the case of Zeus/Jupiter's visit to the imprisoned Danae in the form of a shower of gold, thus causing Perseus to be conceived. Since Ovid overlooked or even rejected folk versions of this tale, the popular cult of this specific hero was lost. Only the work of the Roman writer Claudius Aelianus, *De natura animalium,* or Περὶ Ζῴων Ἰδιότητος (On the nature of animals), provided ethnographic data from the second century CE that could be taken into account. According to Aelianus, Greek-related populations of the Red Sea used the name Perseus to denominate a specific fish species and deemed it to be sacred. This was a rare but extremely faint clue. Was the primitive cult therefore beyond recovery?

The evolutionary assumption that European oral tradition had followed a deeply conservative parallel course, practically independent from literature, directly linked Hartland's quest to the folklore collectors of his time. The first comparisons in *The Legend of Perseus* were indeed historically and geographically circumscribed to Europe and the Near East. He looked in the present for a more remote Perseus, not exactly a prehistorical one, but in any case nearer to the origin than the versions of Ovid, Strabo, or Lucian. Hartland was obviously well placed to be acquainted with and follow the Folklore Society's intellectual networks, and he quoted abundantly from contemporary sources. He initially directed his attention to folktales through the works of many collectors of his time (or of recent times since the Grimm brothers), namely, from Italy, Albania, Ireland, Germany, Sweden, Russia, France, Norway, Denmark, Greece, England, Hungary, Lithuania, Holland, Bosnia, Portugal, Scotland, and Poland. I will quote just a few of those folklorists who were direct or close contemporaries with Hartland's generation: Robert Auning (1834–1914), Gunnar Hyltén-Cavallius (1818–89), Domenico Comparetti (1835–1927), Emmanuel Cosquin (1841–1919), Thomas Frederick Crane (1844–1927), Svend Grundtvig (1824–83), Adalbert Kuhn (1812–81), Wilhelm Schwarz (1821–99), Teófilo Braga (1843–1924), August Leskien (1840–1916), Adolfo Coelho (1847–1919), Christian Schneller (1831–1908), and Heinrich Von Wlislocki (1856–1907). Two specific cases nonetheless suffice for us to recall that the heuristic value of nineteenth-century folktales played a key role within Hartland's goals.

GIUSEPPE PITRÈ'S MEDUSA: "THE TENACITY OF POPULAR TRADITIONS"

In *Novelle popolari toscane* (Tuscan folktales), Giuseppe Pitrè included a folktale collected from an old illiterate lady in the village of Pratovecchio in 1876 by his friend, the lawyer Giovanni Siciliano. Titled "La maga" (The witch), it had the most striking resemblance with the classical legend of Perseus in practically all of its main incidents. Hartland composed his own English-language version instead of citing the exact words used in the version of Siciliano and Pitrè. I quote here one of the many passages that are instantly connectable to the Greek myth:

> Now, the witch in question was so terrible that all who looked at her became statues; and the king hoped that the youth would perish in the adventure. But on the way he met an old man who gave him a flying steed, and directed him to a palace wherein dwelt two women who had only one eye between them, from whom he was to obtain a mirror. And the old man warned him always to regard the witch in the mirror, and never to look at her otherwise, lest he should become a statue. (Hartland 1894–96, 1:12)

As a matter of fact, Hartland never or seldom quoted the original texts of his authorities and used them solely as data, minimizing any intellectual contribution from the original collectors, including aspects of style. In this particular case, it was irrelevant to Hartland that Pitrè was his intellectual peer and very much aware of the anthropological sensibility of British Tylorian folklorists. Hartland could have mentioned that Pitrè himself had affirmed: "Come si vede, la nostra novella è il mito di Medusa" (As we may see, our tale is the myth of Medusa) (Pitrè 1885:8). Hartland formulated a very similar idea, but independently and on his own terms, so to speak. Although I lack hard evidence, it is quite possible that the idea of writing *The Legend of Perseus* came from reading "La maga." In any case, this "petrifying" piece of oral tradition was Hartland's best demonstration of the profoundly conservative disposition of European peasantry over the centuries. He rejected, as very unlikely, the possibility that the Tuscan tale might be connected to literary influences; instead, he believed that it derived from antiquity's rural populace and its prehistorical ancestors. The fact that "La maga" is historically connected to the myth of Perseus seems to lie beyond all reasonable doubt. Let us take Hartland seriously:

> That there should be so striking a resemblance between this story

and that of the classical writers is not surprising to anyone who realizes the tenacity of popular traditions. It is not, indeed, necessary
to suppose that it has been handed down from pagan times in Tuscany: it may only date, as a popular tale, from the revived paganism
of the 15th and 16th centuries. If so, however, it would stand alone
among Italian traditions, not one of which has been traced to the
great movement known as the Revival of Learning, and a large number of which were already current while that movement was in progress. The assumption, therefore, that the Tuscan tale is a relic of two
thousand years or more does not seem unwarranted. (1894–96, 1:13)

PAUL SÉBILLOT AND AELIANUS: SALVAGING
THE KING OF THE FISHES

Pitrè's witch story nonetheless had a flaw: the hero's supernatural birth
had been lost in the storytelling chain of transmission. If Tuscany
opened the door to a broader comparison in European soil, Brittany
(France) filled the gap of conception and gave Hartland a richer and
undoubtedly older version than Ovid's retelling, from that perspective. In *Contes populaires de la Haute-Bretagne* (Folktales of Upper Brittany), published in Paris in 1880, Paul Sébillot (1843–1918) included
a tale titled "Le roi des poissons" (The king of the fishes), which he
had heard the previous year from the lips of a certain Marie Jamet of
the village of Ercé. The story had other incidents that were similar to
those of the legend of Perseus, but above all it presented the advantage of linking pregnancy to the agency of a fish:

> A poor and childless fisherman once caught in his net a fish whose
> scales shone like gold. He was going to put it into his basket, when,
> to his surprise, the fish addressed him. "I am the king of the Fishes,"
> it said; "spare me and thou shalt find many." . . . Finding its prayers
> vain, the fish directed its captor to give its head to his wife . . . , prom-
> ising that his wife should give birth to three beautiful boys with stars
> on their foreheads. (Sébillot 1880:24, translation mine)

Along with Sébillot's style—a style that the French folklorist had
tried to preserve as near as possible to the storyteller's own words—

other elements of his book were not recorded in *The Legend of Perseus*, such as the author's acute sense of salvaging tradition in changing times, the description of his own working conditions, or the revelation of his close relationship with the humble people of French-speaking Brittany. After all, Sébillot himself wrote: "I leave to others the task of searching for the source ever so difficult to find from which my storytellers have drawn. I have limited myself to the compilation of those tales, and what I here make public is nothing more than a series of studies from life, if I may use an expression borrowed from an art which is more familiar to me than literature" (1880:9).[3]

Bearing in mind Aelianus's Red Sea material, Hartland was solely interested in the fish as a more primitive cause of conception than Zeus's or Jupiter's shower of gold. The folktale comparisons, under the heading "king of the fishes," confirmed the advantage of treating separately the theme of supernatural birth. Even if he identified four main types of incidents (supernatural birth, life token, quest for the gorgon's head, and rescue of Andromeda), they weren't fully connected in any pristine version.[4] Sometimes missing, often combined with additional elements, they always appeared in different order and with different details. "Tradition, conservative as it is, is in its nature shifting and liable to endless combinations." The Perseus cycle, Hartland said, was but an "abstract ideal whole," because the process of variation had started long before mankind could write it down (1894–96, 2:440; 3:183).[5] If the story was to be understood as a prehistorical product, one had better explore the savage ideas, practically universal in their range, upon which each of its incidents was grounded.

This should be the moment to consider nineteenth-century amateur ethnographies of African, Oceanic, and American "primitive" peoples. There are some paramount authorities to explore in *The Legend of Perseus*, for example, the missionary Henry Callaway (1817–90), whose Zulu ethnography was published in bilingual editions (1870 in particular) with the contribution of the Folklore Society; or Alfred Cort Haddon (1855–1940), whose first ethnographical findings in the Torres Straits in the late 1880s were published in the journal of the (not yet Royal) Anthropological Institute (1890). Hartland was, after all, a "savage folklorist," as Richard Dorson dubbed Tylor's progeny (1968:187).

I shall leave this main road of Tylorian thought and method to concentrate on yet other kinds of European records. As I said before, the purpose of this chapter is not to identify those contemporary scholars who had personal or institutional connections to the Folklore Society, let alone to Sidney Hartland. As its title suggests, it deals with both past and present authorities. It stresses the importance of quotations from all epochs, going beyond contemporary networks. I could speak of a "timeless network" of dead and living authorities, not from the point of view of intellectual affinities in their own epoch nor genealogically speaking, but from the point of view of "pure" historical data—if such a thing exists. Hartland, in any case, believed so.

VULGAR ERRORS OR ARCANA MICROCOSMI? SAVAGERY AND LITERATURE

"Folktales, when written down, cease to be traditions. They are merely evidence of tradition preserved for us by reporters. Their value depends on the accuracy with which they have been reported. The more closely they represent the very words of the tellers of the tales—the bearers of the traditions—the more valuable, the more authentic, they are" (Hartland 1894–96, 1:90).

Hartland didn't mean by this that oral tradition vanished the moment it was recorded in print. In this particular passage, he was just pinpointing the difference between those who were the legatees of primeval mankind and those who somehow looked at that legacy from the outside. This is the very category of *authorities*, a term that I borrow from Hartland himself; and the reference I make to dead and not just living authorities is intended to emphasize the contribution of reporters from other centuries—reporters of traditions they didn't share and of creeds they didn't believe in. In his work *The British Folklorists*, Richard Dorson reminds us of the importance of seventeenth- and eighteenth-century antiquarians such as John Aubrey (1626–97). The manuscript of *Remaines of Gentilism and Judaism* was printed by the Folklore Society in 1881, with extracts from other works in an appendix, and Aubrey's *Miscellanies upon Various Subjects* was reprinted in 1890 by Reeves and Turner of London. As Dorson says, the folklorists of the golden age were thus "acknowledging a direct debt to their predecessors" (1968:10). After all, Aubrey had made "probably the earliest statement in English of the value in recording folk traditions": "Old customs and old wives fables are grosse things, but yet ought not to be buried in oblivion; there may be some trueth and usefulnesse be picked out of them, besides 'tis a pleasure to consider the errours that enveloped former ages: as also the present" (qtd. in Dorson 1968:7).

Aubrey is among the authorities listed by Hartland in the very beginning of the first volume of *The Legend of Perseus*. This was not the case with all his literary sources. There was indeed another category of authors who were not to be considered as authorities, since their writings betrayed in one way or another their active participation in the subject that they described. They were themselves a living link in the continuous chain of "animism" and "magic." Sometimes in the state of survival, partial or absolute but forcibly disguised under developed forms, "savagery" was not incompatible with literature at all.[6] Besides, I intend to demonstrate that Hartland dealt with Christian texts (as Tylor had done in *Primitive Culture*) with an eclecticism and an erudition that most anthropologists today—perhaps unfortunately—can only dream of. To begin with, let us recall Edmund Leach's accusation against the "Frazer-Hartland generation," as he coined it in his renowned 1966 article "Virgin Birth":

> It seems evident that Western European scholars are strongly predisposed to believe that *other people* should believe in versions of the myth of the Virgin Birth. If *we* believe in such things we are devout; if *others* do so they are idiots. . . . It is a striking fact that the five volumes which Hartland devoted to the discussion of Virgin Birth contain scarcely a single reference to Christianity. . . . Two pages from the end of his three volume work, *The Legend of Perseus*, Hartland remarks: "I cannot hide from myself the important bearing that some of the subjects dealt with in these pages may have upon Christian controversy"; but his heretical daring gets no further than that. (1966:39–42)

Simply put, Leach's verdict is a highly slanted history of anthropology. Apart from the many historical or ethnographical references to Christianity in *The Legend of Perseus*, Hartland's final remarks on it are much longer than the sentence quoted by Leach. The following excerpt is probably sufficient proof that Hartland's anthropology (or, for that matter, Frazer's) was *all about Christianity*:

I have written of the Legend of Perseus with no polemical object. Yet, valuing the science of folklore, as I do, chiefly for the light it throws on the mental constitution of mankind and the genesis of ideas and of institutions, I cannot hide from myself the important bearing that some of the subjects dealt with in these pages may have upon matters of Christian controversy. . . . If these legends [of the Supernatural Birth] be universal, if they must be rejected in every case but one as the product of an inevitable tendency of human imagination, then why not in that one case also? Assuredly that one case can be regarded as exceptional, only if it stands upon historical evidence totally different in kind from the others, and of inevitable cogency. But can anyone who sits down (as it is the duty at least of every educated man to do) calmly and, so far as he can, with scrupulous impartiality to weigh the evidence, say that the testimony of ecclesiastical tradition, or even of our Gospels, is different in kind from, or of greater cogency than, that which we reject, without hesitation, in the case of Sákyamuni, or of Alexander the Great? About ecclesiastical tradition I need say nothing. The records in the two Gospels which bear the names of Saint Matthew and Saint Luke are, carefully considered, irreconcilable. Both Gospels are now admitted to be secondary documents. . . .

Doubt is often a more imperative duty than belief. Nor is it the less a duty because it is painful. To the priest, everywhere and in all time, it is the gravest of sins; for the corporate interest of a priesthood adds strength to the sincere belief of the individual, a belief usually founded upon complete ignorance of all but his own side of the question. Priests, therefore, always favour the growth of beliefs of which they are the centre, so leading men deeper and deeper into the slough of superstition. . . .

But abhorrent as doubt and inquiry may be to the priest, they are the means whereby we have gradually reached a more correct and adequate view of the universe, and of human history, than was formerly imposed in the name of divine revelation. He who seeks truth by such means bears a more devoted allegiance to himself and to humanity than he who, for the sake of safety or of ease, flings himself into the lap of a priesthood. . . . He will recognize it as a duty to withhold his assent from dogmas, even though the most solemn articles of the Christian faith, until in the open court of reason his objections have been answered and his difficulties solved by sounder arguments and a deeper historical and scientific knowledge than have yet been applied by apologists to the issues. (1894–96, 3:187–190)

But let's go back to Hartland's sources. In the opening pages of *The Legend of Perseus* he presented a list of authorities that included many authors from former centuries, yet he excluded some of the dead writers whom he had consulted. Why? Because they were not authorities, they were not *avant la lettre* folklore collectors; instead, they were reproducers of the very animist categories in question. In other words, some had been observers, while the others were observed—that is, observed by Hartland himself through their writings. As a paradigm of his dichotomy between these two kinds of sources, we may refer to the seventeenth-century clash between Thomas Brown (1605–82) and Alexander Ross (ca. 1590–1654), in particular over the issue of supernatural births.

Published in 1646 and also known as *Vulgar Errors*, Brown's *Pseudodoxia Epidemica: or, Enquiries into Very Many Received Tenets and Commonly Presumed Truths* contained a passage, quoted by Hartland, where the English doctor and philosopher denounced long-lasting beliefs in miraculous pregnancies other than the Virgin Mary's (understandably left untouched). This was the case, for instance, of the intercourse between Merlin's mother and an incubus as an actual creed and not just a literary fantasy:

If as he [Aristotle] believeth, the inordinate longitude of the organ, though in its proper recipient, may be a means to improlificate the seed; surely the distance of place must prove an effectual impediment, and utterly prevent the success of a conception. . . . And therefore what is related of devils, and the contrived delusions of spirits, that they steal the seminal emissions of man, and transmit them into their votaries in coition, is much to be suspected; and altogether to be denied, that there ensue conceptions thereupon, however husbanded by art, and the wisest menagery of that most subtile impostor. And therefore also that our magnified Merlin, was thus begotten by the devil, is a groundless conception; and as vain to think from thence to give the reason of his prophetical spirit. (Brown 1672:chap. 16)

Partly as a reaction to Brown's work, in 1651 Scottish clergyman Alexander Ross published *Arcana Microcosmi: Or, the hid secrets of man's body disclosed . . . With a refutation of Doctor Browns Vulgar Errors, and the ancient opinions vindicated*. Quite exceptionally, Hartland quoted Alexander Ross's own words upholding the belief in incubi: "He [Alexander Ross] reproves Sir Thomas Browne's incredulity by saying: 'Hee that denyeth a matter of fact, must bring good witnesses to the contrary, or else shew the impossibility of the fact.' This, he declares, had not been done. Then, after arguing in favour of the 'fact', he goes on to uphold the belief in *Incubi*, 'for to deny this is to accuse the ancient Doctors of the Church and the Ecclesiastic Histories of falsehood', and 'to contradict the common consent of all Nations, and experience'" (1894–96, 1:135). No need to say that Alexander Ross didn't have a place in the list of authorities cited in *The Legend of Perseus*. But Thomas Brown did.

ANTHROPOLOGY AND THE MIDDLE AGES: TRACKING
GERVASE OF TILBURY AND HERMAN DE VALENCIENNES

Hartland's perusal of literary sources of past centuries was sometimes dependent on living authorities. His access to medieval documents, for instance, was often facilitated by other scholars' contemporary references or annotated editions. This was the case of his reading of Gervase of Tilbury's *Otia Imperialia* (Recreation for an emperor) in its profusely annotated 1856 edition by German folklorist Felix Liebrecht (1812–90). Written in the early thirteenth century by an English canon lawyer and courtier of Holy Roman Emperor Otto IV, whom the work was intended to amuse, *Otia Imperialia* was "an encyclopedic melange of cosmographical, historical, and geographical information

and a wealth of learned and original accounts of folklore and popular belief," as its 2002 translators and editors put it (Gervase of Tilbury 2002:back cover). In spite of his epoch, could Gervase of Tilbury
be an authority in Hartland's eyes? Hadn't he been a compiler of the
superstitions of his epoch? In the first volume of *The Legend of Perseus*,
Hartland never made any direct quotation from *Otia Imperialia*. After
saying that the Middle Ages "believed that Antichrist, in rivalry with
Christ, would declare himself born of a virgin," he simply relegated
the reference to a footnote (Hartland 1894–96, 1:134). But then, most
surprisingly, this specimen of "speculum" literature appears in his list
of authorities.[7]

In the passage Hartland had before his eyes, Gervase of Tilbury initially seemed to distance himself from such opinions: "Merlin *is said* to
have been fathered by one of these [incubi], for he was born, according to the *History of Britons*, of a woman but had no human father. And
they say that the Antichrist will be begotten in this way, and will claim
on this account to be the son of a virgin" (2002:97, emphasis added).
When we go back to the source, we realize nonetheless that Gervase of
Tilbury later explicitly participated in the incubi creed: "We know that
many things are seen every day relating to these phenomena. We have
actually observed that some demons love women with such passion
that they break out into unheard-of acts of lewdness, and when they
come to bed with them they bear down upon them with extraordinary
pressure, and yet are seen by no one else" (2002:97). We may conclude
that Hartland's dichotomy was relative, not absolute; after all, it had
to be so, for he knew so well—as all Tylorians did, with Frazer at their
head—that magic, religion, and science had always been intertwined
in the history of mankind (see Rosa 1997, 2003:14–29).

But there is another reason why Liebrecht's edition of *Otia Imperialia* is of interest to our case. In order to demonstrate that supernatural births could come about by other means than eating or drinking,
not just in *Märchen* (folktales) but also in sagas, Hartland mentioned
a poem written in Old French by a priest at Valenciennes about the
middle of the thirteenth century, according to which Abraham's daughter became pregnant by the scent of a blossom broken off from the
Tree of Knowledge, and she bore Phanuel. He didn't quote the poem

directly; his authority on this matter was precisely Liebrecht in the following note to *Otia Imperialia*: "Furthermore, in an Old French poem about Saint Anne's childhood we are told that Patriarch Abraham had planted in his garden the Tree of Knowledge, flung by Our Lord out of Paradise after Adam's fall (and over which wood Christ was to be crucified); and that his daughter one day became pregnant solely by the scent of a blossom broken off from it and so was born Phanuel(*)" (Gervase of Tilbury 1856:68).

This note was related to the passage of Gervase of Tilbury I have already discussed, but the note itself had a footnote (notice the asterisk) informing the reader of the existence of two nineteenth-century prints of the medieval poem, one by the German antiquary, bibliophile, and manuscript collector Joseph von Lassberg (1870–55) in *Ein schoen alt Lied von Grave Fritz von Zolre, dem Oettinger, und der Belagerung von HohenZolren, nebst noch etlichen andern Liedern* (A beautiful old song by the Earl Friedrich von Zollern to Oettinger, the Siege of Hohenzollern, and some other old songs) (1842); and the other by the French medievalist and bibliophile Antoine Le Roux de Lincy (1806–69) in *Le livre des légendes* (The book of legends) (1836): "(*) The author of this poem was Father Herman de Valenciennes in the middle of the 13th century. See Leroux de Lincy, *Livre des Légendes*, p. 24. . . . As an addition to his *Lied von Grave Fritz von Zolre etc.*, published in 1842, Lassberg printed the beginning of an Old French legend (about 550 verses) from a 15th-century manuscript belonging to him, though he couldn't do much as concerns its author, since the first folio was missing" (Gervase of Tilbury 1856:68).

Hartland didn't have the ability to follow all these threads, but they allow us to imagine a larger labyrinth of connections between contemporary and past sources. In any case, the same poem was again mentioned by him to illustrate "impregnation" of unusual parts of the body, including parts of the male's body (Hartland 1894–96, 1:94). According to Father Herman de Valenciennes, Saint Anne, the mother of Mary, had that kind of supernatural birth, namely, from the thigh of the aforementioned Phanuel.[8] Here is Joseph von Lassberg's transcription of the original piece of Christian "savage literature" (with my own tentative English translation):

Se vous voulez que je vous die	If you want me to tell you
De dieu et de sainte marie	About God and Saint Mary
Or faitez paix sy mescoutez	Listen and don't say a thing
Je vous dyrei se vous voulez	I'll tell you, if you want me to
Sy com ly roys ihesus naisqui	How Jesus our King was born
Et sa douce meire autresy	And his sweet mother as well
Sy com sainte anne fut pourtée	How Saint Anne came to life
Qui ainz ne fut de meire nee	She wasn't born from a mother
Fors par le terdre don coutel	But from the touch of a knife
En la cuisse saint fanoel	In the thigh of Phanuel
Il la pourta sy longuement	Who carried her for such a long time
Com dam dieu vint a talant	Like a maid, God came to the aid
. . . .	. . . .
Quant il vit son coutel moille	When he saw the knife was moist
De la pome quil ot taille	From the apple it had cut
A sa cuisse le ressuia	He cleaned it on his thigh
Et la seue ly engenra	And its juice was there to bear
Une mout gentil demoiselle	Such a gentle damsel
Qui mout parfut cortoise et belle	Courteous and fair
. . . .	. . . .
Et de la cuisse deliura	And from his thigh he gave birth
Iceille gentil demoiseille	To that gentle damsel
Qui tant fut cortoise et belle	So courteous and fair
Ce fut sainte anne don ie dy	It was Saint Anne, who one day
De la meire ihesu nasqui	Gave birth to Jesus's mother
	(Lassberg 1842)

This is, after all, one of the reasons why the universal comparisons of Tylorian anthropologists may still be stimulating to twenty-first-century readers. They incite us to follow our own tracks in unpredictable but often rewarding directions. I found, for example, Le Roux de Lincy's *Le livre des légendes* to be not just fascinating but much closer to Hartland's preoccupations (and yet absent from his bibliography). Here is a passage that is connected to the subject of my chapter: "There is a more modern source that we must not leave unsaid: that is the historical and literary compilations that the patient erudition of the last three centuries' scholars have left us in heritage. Today more than ever, we can appreciate just how noble and beautiful was the laborious and solitary life those men chose to live, in order to devote themselves entirely to the science whose parts they have unravelled or fully elucidated" (Le Roux de Lincy 1836:12).

ANIMISM AT THE NATIONAL GALLERY: VISUAL REMAINS OF JESUS CHRIST'S CONCEPTION

Still in the chapter concerning sagas and "impregnation" by unusual parts of the body, Hartland explored yet another surprising source—not written or oral but visual. In a visit to the National Gallery in London, with all his senses permanently alert to (what he believed to be) the crudest elements of any religion, he was struck by Fra Filippo Lippi's *Annunciation* (ca. 1449):

> The Virgin is seated in a chair with her Book of Hours in her hand, and the angel Gabriel bows before her. Above is a right hand surrounded with clouds. A dove, cast from the hand amid circling floods of glory, is making for the Virgin's navel, which it is about to enter; while she, bending forward, curiously surveys it. The picture is well worth studying, not merely for its exquisite grace, colouring and finish, as one of the masterpieces of Tuscan art in the earlier half of the fifteenth century, but also as an exposition of the ideas which were prevalent at that time under the sanction of the Church. (Hartland 1894–96, 1:131)

Needless to say, Hartland considered that this and similar depictions were apprehended in the most literal way, if not by all its fifteenth-century viewers, in any case by most of them and probably by its very creator. The Holy Spirit had assumed the shape of a dove and entered the body of Mary through her navel. Hartland mentioned other religious paintings that were indicative of different ways of understanding Mary's material conception of Jesus: "In the Church of the Magdalen at Aix, in Provence, is a picture of the Annunciation attributed to Albert Dürer, wherein waves of glory descend from God the Father, and in the midst of them a microscopic babe floats down upon the Virgin."[9] Without mentioning his authorities in this particular case, Hartland said that "during the 15th century the opinion seems to have been common that Our Lord entered already completely formed into the Virgin's womb" (1894–96, 1:131). The fact that the church pronounced the opinion heretical was after all a confirmation that the symbolical dimension of a painting such as this should not be taken for granted—quite the contrary.

But above all, Hartland considered the paintings (and even the literary sources) to be nothing more than the tip of an iceberg—the iceberg of all popular representations of Jesus Christ's supernatural birth, more often than not unrecorded, whether in the fifteenth or, for that matter, in the first century CE. In spite of the church's continual efforts to fix dogma, those representations were a tradition—and as a tradition they could be compared in their shifting nature, in their transformations, to the instability of the Perseus cycle. The Virgin Mary's pregnancy was an "abstract ideal whole" whose contradictions not even the Gospels, even the canonical ones, could reconcile.

THE VIRGIN MARY'S TRANSFORMATIONS: GEORGE SALE'S KORAN AND JONAS HANWAY'S PERSIA

I shall now consider two eighteenth-century authorities who gave Hartland additional material on the variations of Jesus Christ's supernatural birth, enlarging this saga beyond Christianity itself. The translation of the Koran by the Orientalist George Sale was originally published in 1734, with a long "Preliminary Discourse" and many "Explanatory Notes." In a five-page foreword to the reader, Sale (1697–1736) explained that, contrarily to "writers of the Romish communion," he had avoided "all reproachful language" and "endeavoured to do the original impartial justice." The notes were meant "briefly to explain" the more "difficult and obscure passages" or to enrich the reading with quotations from other sources, including Muslim authors "for whose opinions or expressions where liable to censure I am not answerable." Both in the Preliminary Discourse and the notes, he took care "constantly to quote my authorities and the writers to whom I have been beholden" (Sale [1734] 1871:v, vi, ix). Hartland probably consulted the sixth edition of 1871.

Here is Sale's translation of the Koran's most direct excerpt concerning Jesus Christ's supernatural birth through the agency of God not as his son but as his servant:

> And remember in the book of the Koran the story of Mary; when she retired from her family to a place towards the east, and took a veil to conceal herself from them; and we sent our spirit Gabriel unto her, and he appeared unto her in the shape of a perfect man. She said, I fly for refuge unto the merciful God, that he may defend me from thee: if thou fearest him, thou will not approach me. He answered, Verily I am the messenger of thy Lord, and am sent to give thee a holy son. She said, How shall I have a son, seeing a man hath not touched me, and I am no harlot? Gabriel replied, So shall it be: thy Lord saith, This is easy with me; and we will perform it, that we may ordain him for a sign unto men, and a mercy from us: for it is a thing which is decreed. Wherefore she conceived him(g), and she retired aside with him in her womb to a distant place; and the pains of childbirth came upon her near the trunk of a palm-tree. ([1734] 1871:250)

In note (g) Sale wrote: "For Gabriel blew into the bosom of her shift, which he opened with his fingers and his breath reaching her womb, caused the conception" ([1734] 1871:250). Hartland couldn't follow Sale's Arabic references (Yahia, Jalaluddin, and Al-Badawi), but it is very significant that he used the word *tradition* in his rendering of Sale's piece of information: "Mohammedan tradition ascribes the miraculous conception by the Virgin to Gabriel's having opened the bosom of her shift and breathed upon her womb" (1894–96, 1:131).

A broader picture of the shifting nature of Jesus's conception in the Muslim world was given by yet another kind of authority. English traveler, businessman, and philanthropist Jonas Hanway (1712–86) published a four-volume work in 1754 about his travels to Persia a decade before. In the city of Astrabad, alongside mercantile discussions, he befriended a few Persians who, at a certain point, asked him if he believed Jesus Christ to be the son of God: "My good friends Naseer Aga and Hahdgee made me a visit, and brought several other persons with them. Their business was to enquire if I believed Jesus Christ to be the son of God; intimating this to be the persuasion of Christians, and without waiting long for an answer, they pronounced me an idolater" (1754:172).

This was the beginning of long conversations whose contents were developed in a specific chapter, "Idolatry being imputed to the author, he attempts to defend Christianity." Hanway learned that his interlocutors didn't dispute Jesus's saintly existence but only his divinity. But Hanway also learned something else: "That his birth was miraculous, is confessed even by the Mahommedans; for they say he was conceived of a virgin by the smell of a rose. To grant there was such a person, and that he was thus conceived, is being half a Christian, with regard to the supernatural birth of Christ" (1754:179). In a footnote on Jonas Hanway, Hartland wrote: "I have not been successful in tracing his authority" (1894–96, 1:123). But wasn't authority before his very eyes? It was Jonas Hanway's authority, which was based not on other books but on the very testimony of his Persian "good friends."

My last example suggests the importance of dead authorities in the work of a major representative of the Folklore Society and of late Victorian evolutionary anthropology. Undoubtedly, much got lost through the uniformity of Hartland's way of quoting without really quoting; but the original documents are still there for us to grasp as complementary universes of the history of anthropology. At the same time, rereading a book such as *The Legend of Perseus* may remind us today that quite a few evolutionary forerunners of our discipline, contrary to some common views, did not accentuate the distance between "savage" and "civilized" humanity. Their mission was provocative, and their data were universal. In the words of Andrew Lang, which may be read as a synthesis of the Tylorian enterprise, "Man can never be certain that he has expelled the savage from his temples and from his heart" (1887, 1:338). As I said at the beginning of this chapter, the paramount idea of a long-lasting animistic heritage affected all religions, Christianity included. It therefore promoted the anthropological perusal of European historical materials from all centuries and in a way that most twentieth-century anthropologists, converted to ethnography, could not possibly follow. This is one of the reasons why, in the 1950s and 1960s, Evans-Pritchard tried to alert the (British) anthropological community to the risks of systematically ignoring ancient, medieval, and modern contexts; but more than half a century later, and in spite of the alleged historic turn in the social sciences, we keep turning our back on history in that particular sense. Considering that the contrast between Hartland's anthropology and present concerns couldn't be greater, this chapter promotes a humbler attitude toward the past of the discipline: instead of searching for our predecessors' faults, I prefer the intellectual challenge of trying to learn something with them.

NOTES

This chapter was originally a paper presented at the workshop "The Folklore Society and the Continent, 1878–1914: Intellectual Networks and the Development of the Social Sciences," held in October 2013 at the École des Hautes Études en Sciences Sociales, Paris.

1. See the bibliography for a selection of Hartland's other monographs (1891, 1899, 1921).
2. Significantly, Dorson applies this expression to the British antiquarians of the seventeenth and eighteenth centuries.
3. Sébillot was also a painter.
4. "Life token" was used by British anthropologists and folklorists to refer to an object supposed to be the safeguard vessel of an individual's life.
5. Hartland uses this expression to deny the empirical existence of such an "abstract ideal whole."
6. According to the Tylorian perspective, a survival was the permanence of an old custom or idea without a proper adaptation to its new, more civilized context. It was absolute when its prior religious meaning was simply lost and partial when it lingered. Survival contrasted with development, although some historical combinations were possible between the two.

7. A medieval encyclopedic genre from the twelfth through the sixteenth centuries.

8. Hartland's reference was in this case Jacob Grimm: "The birth from feet or legs seems to be remembered in an O.[ld] Fr.[ench] poem: Fanuel, whom his mother had conceived out of the smell of flowers, touches his thigh with a knife that had just cut an apple; the thigh conceives and bears St. Anne" (1888, 4:1449).

9. Art historians now attribute this painting to Bartholomew of Eyck (1443–45).

REFERENCES

Aubrey, John. (1696) 1890. Miscellanies upon Various Subjects. London: Reeves and Turner.

——. (seventeenth century) 1881. Remaines of Gentilism and Judaism. James Britten, ed. London: Folklore Society.

Brown, Thomas. (1646) 1672. Pseudodoxia Epidemica: or, Enquiries into Very Many Received Tenets and Commonly Presumed Truths. London: J. R. for Nath. Ekins.

Callaway, Henry. 1870. The Religious System of the Amazulu, Izinyanga Zokubula; or, Divination as existing among the Amazulu, in their own words, with a translation into English. Springvale, Natal: J. A. Blair, Folklore Society.

Dorson, Richard. 1968. The British Folklorists: A History. Chicago: University of Chicago Press.

Frazer, James George. 1890. The Golden Bough: A Study in Comparative Religion. London: Macmillan.

Gervase of Tilbury. (fourteenth century) 1856. Des Gervasius von Tilbury Otia Imperialia (The Gervase of Tilbury's Recreation for an emperor). Felix Liebrecht, ed. and notes. Hannover: Karl Rümpler.

——. (fourteenth century) 2002. Otia Imperialia: Recreation for an Emperor. S. E. Banks and J. W. Binns, trans. and eds. Oxford: Clarendon Press.

Grimm, Jacob. (1835) 1888. Teutonic Mythology. Steven Stallybrass, trans. and ed. Vol. 4. [London]: G. Bell and Sons.

Haddon, Alfred Cort. 1890. The Ethnography of the Western Tribe of Torres Straits. Journal of the Anthropological Institute of Great Britain and Ireland 19:297–440.

Hanway, Jonas. 1754. An Historical Account of the British Trade over the Caspian Sea: With the author's journal of travels from England through

Russia into Persia; and back through Russia, Germany and Holland. To which are added, the revolutions of Persia during the present century, with the particular history of the great usurper Nadir Kouli. Illustrated with maps and copper-plates. Vol. 1. London: T. Osborne.

Hartland, Edwin Sidney. 1891. The Science of Fairy Tales: An Enquiry into the Fairy Mythology. London: Walter Scott Publishing Co.

——. 1894–96. The Legend of Perseus: A Study of Tradition in Story, Custom and Belief. 3 vols. London: David Nutt.

——. 1899. Folk-Lore: What Is It and What Is the Good of It? London: David Nutt.

——. 1921. Primitive Society: The Beginnings of the Family and the Reckoning of Descent. London: Methuen and Co.

Lang, Andrew. 1887. Myth, Ritual and Religion. 2 vols. London: Longmans, Green and Co.

Lassberg, Joseph von. 1842. Ein schoen alt Lied von Grave Fritz von Zolre, dem Oettinger, und der Belagerung von HohenZolren, nebst noch etlichen andern Liedern (A beautiful old song by the Earl Friedrich von Zollern to Oettinger, the Siege of Hohenzollern, and some other old songs).

Leach, Edmund. 1966. Virgin Birth. Proceedings of the Royal Anthropological Institute of Great Britain and Ireland:39–49.

Le Roux de Lincy, Antoine. 1836. Le livre des légendes (The book of legends). Paris: Silvestre Librarie.

Pitrè, Giuseppe. 1885. Novelle popolari toscane (Tuscan folktales). Florence: G. Barbèra Editore.

Rosa, Frederico D. 1997. À Frazer ce qui est de Frazer: Vers une réinterprétation de l'intellectualisme du Golden Bough (To Frazer what is Frazer's: Toward a reinterpretation of The Golden Bough's intellectualism). European Journal of Sociology 38(2):301–310.

——. 2003. L'âge d'or du totémisme: Histoire d'un débat anthropologique (1887–1929) (The golden age of totemism: History of an anthropological debate [1887–1929]). Paris: CNRS Éditions, Éditions de la Maison des Sciences de l'Homme.

Ross, Alexander. 1651. Arcana Microcosmi: Or, the hid secrets of man's body disclosed . . . With a refutation of Doctor Browns Vulgar Errors, and the ancient opinions vindicated. London: N.p.

Sale, George, trans. and ed. (1734) 1871. The Koran: Commonly called The Alcoran of Mohammed; translated into English immediately from the original Arabic with Explanatory Notes, taken from the most approved

Commentators, to which is prefixed a Preliminary Discourse. Philadelphia: J. B. Lippincott.

Sébillot, Paul. 1880. Contes populaires de la Haute-Bretagne (Folktales of Upper Brittany). Paris: G. Charpentier Éditeur.

Tylor, Edward Burnett. 1870. Primitive Culture: Researches into the Development of Mythology, Philosophy, Religion, Art and Custom. 2 vols. London: John Murray.

3

Anthropology in Portugal

*The Case of the Portuguese Society of
Anthropology and Ethnology (SPAE), 1918*

In recent years, several works have been published on the history of anthropology in specific national contexts (e.g., Stocking 1974, 1995; Kuklick 1991; Barth et al. 2005; Ranzmaier 2011) but little on the history of anthropology in Portugal—and the exceptions have largely been written from and for the Portuguese community (e.g., Areia and Rocha 1985; Branco 1986; Pereira 1986, 1998; Pina-Cabral 1991; Leal 2000, 2006; Roque 2001; Santos 2005; Sobral 2007; Matos 2013). Even then, with the exception of some authors such as Guimarães (1995), Pereira (1998), Roque (2001), Santos (2005), and my own work (Matos 2013), it has been uncommon for Portuguese anthropologists and historians to recognize the existence of a distinct school of anthropology connected to the city of Porto, originating with the Portuguese Society of Anthropology and Ethnology (SPAE, Sociedade Portuguesa de Antropologia e Etnologia) and its legacy. This chapter intends, therefore, to contribute to a more inclusive international history of anthropology, as suggested by Richard Handler (2000), who reminded us of the need to interpret past anthropological practices in relation to specific historical and cultural moments.

The SPAE was founded in the city of Porto on December 26, 1918, with its first general meeting, when its statute was approved. The author of the initiative was António Augusto Esteves Mendes Correia (1888–1960). Mendes Correia obtained his degree in medicine at the Porto Surgery Medical School in 1911 and developed both anthropological and political interests.[1] In the process of creating SPAE, Mendes Correia counted on the support of some elder figures, such as Luís Bastos de Freitas Viegas (1869–1928),[2] Aarão Ferreira de Lacerda (1863–1921),[3] and Bento Carqueja (1860–1935).[4] The society's logo (fig. 1) illustrates the initial division between anthropology (the study of mankind in its physical and biological dimensions) and ethnology (the study of mankind in its social and cultural dimensions). SPAE held its activities at the facilities of the Anthropology Institute of the University of Porto (IAUP); organized several scientific meetings; and regularly published the *Trabalhos de Antropologia e Etnologia* (TAE), which included a bibliographical chapter aimed at informing the reader on developments in anthropology in Portugal and abroad.

The creation of SPAE was also understood as a response from Porto, a city in the north of Portugal, to the failed attempt to create an anthropological society in Coimbra around the oldest university in the country.[5] As with other such societies in Europe and the United States, SPAE gathered a small group of savants and experts who had shared interests with other members of their academic and social environments. Considering the creation dates of the anthropology societies in Europe—in Paris (1858), Berlin (1869), Vienna (1870), Italy (1871), and Sweden (1872)—SPAE (1918) was a late starter. Nevertheless, like other international societies (Ranzmaier 2011), it actually turned out to be a considerably dynamic institutional space from a scientific point of view, as well as a privileged environment for debate and the exchange of ideas. Joaquim Rodrigues dos Santos Júnior, former student and one of the main collaborators of the society's main founder, argued that SPAE was born due to the "resolute will" of Mendes Correia—a man who "was able to gather around him a company of superior men" like Aarão Ferreira de Lacerda (1863–1921), Luís Bastos de Freitas Viegas, and Bento Carqueja, who, along with him, "have built the Society's initial core" (Júnior 1969:38).

In order to obtain a better knowledge of SPAE's activities and operating methods,[6] I analyzed its statute and the minutes pertaining to its members' meetings and the events it organized. The statute approved at the first general meeting of December 26, 1918, remained in effect until the middle of the 1980s, with some minor changes introduced in 1924.[7] This statute was organized in twenty-four articles divided into six chapters: objectives, headquarters, and fiscal year; members; meetings; funding; administration; and general and provisional terms. According

Fig. 1. SPAE's first logo.

to article 1, chapter 1 of the 1918 statute, the objective of SPAE was "to promote and cultivate, in Portugal, the study of anthropological methods, zoological anthropology, ethnic anthropology, prehistoric anthropology and archaeology, experimental psychology, ethnography, and the scientific branches of its derivative or applied sciences, such as military, pedagogical, clinical, criminal, forensic anthropologies, etc." (*Estatutos da* SPAE 1918:3).

Article 1 also mentions that, in order to reach its aims, SPAE must

1. organize periodic and extraordinary scientific meetings;
2. publish original works and studies on anthropology and anthropological sciences;
3. organize and maintain a library with a reading cabinet;
4. establish contacts with counterpart societies both in Portugal and abroad;
5. intend to organize anthropological, archaeological, and ethnographic collections and to promote anthropological methods, mainly among doctors, professors, travelers, and colonial citizens;
6. publicize as much as possible the advantages of anthropological methods in schools and as a contributing element for scientific police investigation;
7. organize surveys and scientific missions with the means at its disposal, mainly in Portugal and in the colonies; and
8. sponsor the intensification and extension of the teaching of anthropology and of anthropological sciences in Portugal. (*Estatutos da* SPAE 1918:3–4)

Based on these objectives, it is clear that anthropology was intended, as a science, to generate specialized knowledge in the country and abroad, acting within the practical scope of daily life, spreading knowledge, and issuing opinions on clinical, criminal, and forensic topics. In order to enforce item 2 of article 1 of the statute, SPAE began to publish the *Trabalhos da Sociedade Portuguesa de Antropologia e Etnologia* (the title from volume 1 of 1918 to volume 10 of 1945, afterward called *Trabalhos de Antropologia e Etnologia* [TAE]), and for a long time this was the main means of presenting the society's activities. As a periodical publication, the TAE demonstrated the crucial role a journal can play in the institutionalization of a scientific discipline; it built on the former historical and natural tradition in anthropological studies, evidenced by the earlier journals *Revista de Ciências Naturais e Sociais* (1889–98) and *Portugália* (1899–1908), both published in Porto.

SPAE's headquarters were located in Porto, but the 1918 statute considered the possibility of organizing regional centers in Lisbon and Coimbra. It could include honorary, permanent, and corresponding members, the latter being "the authors of worthy anthropologic publications or individuals who in some way have provided services to anthropology and anthropological sciences" (*Estatutos da SPAE* 1918:6). Only honorary and permanent members were allowed a decision vote and to be part of managing bodies (1918:7).

When comparing this statute with the statute of the Coimbra Society of Anthropology, dated 1899, we realize that SPAE's statute is more extensive and detailed and also more ambitious. Furthermore, according to SPAE's statute, official residence in Porto was not a requirement for permanent members, unlike Coimbra's society. The 1918 statute was modified at the general meeting that took place on January 11, 1924. One noteworthy change was introduced in item 7 of article 1: the term "metropolis" replaced "country," and "overseas" replaced "colonies" (*Estatutos da SPAE* 1924:4).[8]

SPAE's objectives were vast and included multiple interests or areas of specialty. This diversity was also expressed in the variety of scientific and professional fields from which members originated. All this can be inferred from meeting minutes and annual reports. I will highlight the most relevant aspects.

THE FOUNDATION OF SPAE AND ITS FOUNDING MEMBERS

The minutes of SPAE's first meeting record that it took place in the office of the director of the Museum of Geology of FCUP, with Luís Bastos de Freitas Viegas, Aarão Ferreira de Lacerda, José da Rocha Ferreira (engineer and paleontology assistant professor in FCUP), and Mendes Correia, "summoned by the latter to an inaugural meeting of the new Society of Anthropology and Ethnology." Freitas Viegas, "appointed by all present to take on the role of Chairman, . . . gave the floor to the summoner, who explained the objectives of the meeting, subsequently presenting the project for a series of studies for the new society, which was discussed and finally approved with the wording" that would then become SPAE's statute (Livro de actas, vol. 1).

Once the statute was approved at the general meeting, Mendes Correia presented the new members of the society: José Leite de Vasconcelos (professor at FLUL and director of the Portuguese Museum of Ethnology), Vergílio Correia (curator of the National Ancient Art Museum and editor of the journal *Terra Portuguesa*), Eusébio Tamagnini (professor of anthropology at FCUC), Baltazar Osório (professor of anthropology at FCUL), Henrique de Vilhena (professor of anatomy at FMUL),[9] Manuel Valadares (director of the Lisbon Central Archive for Criminal Identification and Statistics), Cláudio Basto (director of the journal *Lusa*, from Viana do Castelo), António Aurélio da Costa Ferreira (director of Casa Pia de Lisboa),[10] Father António de Oliveira (superintendent of the Lisbon Correctional Schools), Joaquim Fontes (doctor and archaeologist from Lisbon), José Tomás Ribeiro Fortes (editor of the former journal *Portugália*), Abel de Lima Salazar (professor of histology at FMUP), Alfredo Mendonça da Costa Athayde (bachelor in natural history and science in Porto), José de Sousa Machado Fontes (bachelor in law and secretary of the Portuguese Society of Social Service of Porto), Eduardo de Sousa Soares (businessman from Porto),[11] José Álvares de Sousa Soares (doctor in Porto), Filinto Elísio Vieira da Costa (teacher of free education from Famalicão), António Ferreira Loureiro (bachelor in mathematics and philosophy and teacher at the Alexandre Herculano High School in Porto), Diogo Portocarrero (teacher at the same high school), João Grave (director of the City Museum of Porto), Joaquim Costa (bachelor in law and deputy director of that same museum), Francisco dos Santos Pereira de Vasconcelos (lawyer and former magistrate in Porto), António Correia da Costa e Almeida (lawyer in Ermesinde), Father Claudino Nazareth Brites (missionary from Lubango, Angola), António Mesquita de Figueiredo (lawyer and archaeologist in Lisbon), the viscount of Guilhomil (lawyer in Porto), and António Leite de Magalhães (captain-major in Dembos, Angola) (Livro de actas, vol. 1).

All of these individuals, along with the founders named previously, were considered permanent members from the beginning, totaling around thirty founding members. Most of these members originated from an educated bourgeoisie, although we could also find some elements from Porto's social and financial elites. This list included two priests (António de Oliveira and Claudino Nazareth Brites), who in time would be joined by others: Manuel Alves da Cunha (vicar capitulary of the episcopate of Angola), António de Miranda Magalhães (former superior of the mission in Dembos, Angola), D. Florentino Lopez Cuevilhas, José Augusto Tavares, Eugénio Jalhay, Manuel de Sousa Maia, and Avelino de Jesus Costa.

Following a proposal by Mendes Correia, José Leite de Vasconcelos was elected honorary chairman. SPAE's board in 1919 was composed of the following elements: Freitas Viegas (chairman), Bento Carqueja (vice-chairman), Mendes Correia (secretary), José da Rocha Ferreira (treasurer), and Abel de Lima Salazar (member). Alfredo Athayde was the first general secretary, and Rui Correia de Serpa Pinto was the second member with librarian responsibilities; he also organized the society's library.[12] At the first meeting, Mendes Correia also proposed the creation of the sections of prehistoric archaeology and ethnography. The governing bodies of the former section included José Fortes (chairman), Joaquim Fontes (vice-chairman), Vergílio Correia, and António Mesquita de Figueiredo (members). Those of the latter section included Vergílio Correia (chairman), Cláudio Basto (vice-chairman), Father Claudino Nazareth Brites, Captain António Leite de Magalhães, and António Costa e Almeida (members).

The main founders were all connected to the city of Porto, but from the organization's inception there were also members from the north of Portugal (Vergílio Correia and Leite de Vasconcelos), as well as from other regions of the country (e.g., Sebastião Pessanha [1892–1975], ethnographer and art critic, and Orlando Ribeiro [1911–97], geographer, both from Lisbon).[13] Based on the extensive list, we can infer SPAE's nature not as a regional organization (Porto or North) but as a national one. It was also inclusive of experts from several different areas beyond anthropology (although the latter has played a dominant role), and some were true experts in more than one domain. The founding members included at least one engineer and two priests, as well as people working in Portuguese overseas territories. Some later became prominent in national scientific congresses of the 1920s, 1930s, and 1940s; in the creation of scientific societies such as the Portuguese Society of Eugenic Studies (founded in 1937); and in the organization of the grand exhibitions in which Portugal participated or that it organized (Matos 2014). However, as mentioned by Santos Júnior, the creation of SPAE was mainly due to Mendes Correia "with a double aim: to create it '*ab initio*' and to create it by supporting it, providing the conditions required for it to prosper" (1969:41).

Even with the range of interests represented, the majority of the founding members originated from the domain of the sciences. From the natural sciences (zoology, mineralogy, paleontology, agronomy) we find Aarão Ferreira de Lacerda (education in zoology and medicine), José da Rocha Ferreira (professor of paleontology), and Bento Carqueja (education in the physical and natural sciences). From medicine, we find Freitas Viegas and Abel de Lima Salazar. And some members had oriented their careers toward areas other than their fields of education. According to the report of SPAE's first year (published in the minutes from January 22, 1920), at the inaugural general meeting thirty-two members were elected, and "during that year, the managing board approved, under the statute, a further twenty-three permanent members, totaling fifty-five members, of which only two refused the election." This was considered "a flattering number for a society that, in Portugal, was dedicated to a specialized branch of science."

SPAE'S NEW MEMBERS, BOTH NATIONAL AND FROM ABROAD

After the founding members, other permanent members were added, including renowned figures connected to science and other areas. Among these stand out Sebastião Pessanha, proposed by Vergílio Correia e Mendes Correia on January 21, 1919; Joaquim Alberto Pires de Lima (professor of medicine and ethnographer), Francisco Nunes Guimarães Coimbra (professor of medicine), and Mário de Moraes Afonso (engineering and philosophical science student, both at UP), all proposed by Mendes Correia on January 21, 1919; António Simões Pina (doctor), proposed by Rocha Ferreira on January 21, 1919; Jaime Alberto de Castro Moraes (captain-lieutenant doctor from Lisbon), Armando de Almeida Prisco (assistant professor of mineralogy at FCUP), and José Marques de Ansiães Proença (doctor in Porto, elected on April 19, 1919); Tomaz Lobo (graduate in philosophy from Leça da Palmeira), Alberto Brochado (doctor from Porto), Mário de Vasconcelos e Sá (professor at the Instituto Superior do Comércio do Porto), and Manuel B. Barbosa Soeiro (assistant professor at FMUL), elected on May 12, 1919; João Diogo (director of the Anglo-Latin School, from Porto) and Francisco de Oliveira Santos (governor of Lunda, Angola), proposed by Mendes Correia and elected on November 3, 1919; Ricardo Severo (engineer), elected in 1920;[14] Augusto de Oliveira, proposed by Mendes Correia in 1931;[15] Carlos Teixeira (geologist),[16] Maria Irene Leite da Costa (professor at both intermediate and university levels),[17] and Amílcar de Magalhães Mateus (assistant professor of zoology and anthropology at FCUP),[18] all Mendes Correia's former students at FCUP and elected in 1934; Leopoldina Ferreira Paulo (assistant professor of anthropology at FCUP), elected in 1935; and Orlando Ribeiro, elected in 1942.

I particularly sought to identify any women as permanent members during the period under consideration and found that SPAE has counted women among its members from its inception—a noteworthy fact, since they were not always present in counterpart societies. For example, at the Berliner Gesellschaft für Anthropologie, Ethnologie und Urgeschichte—where topics of debate included archaeological findings, ethnographic objects, or physiology and physical aspects—somatic characters were used as arguments to stop women from becoming members (Schouten 2001:159). The acceptance of Leopoldina Ferreira Paulo as SPAE's permanent member in 1935 is a noteworthy fact, however, not so much because she was a woman—since the society welcomed women from its beginning—but rather because she was Mendes Correia's assistant professor in the discipline of anthropology at FCUP, as well as the first woman to obtain a doctorate degree at UP in 1944 (fig. 2).[19]

It is also important to describe the external relationships that SPAE sought to maintain, widening the debate and exchanging works internationally. This effort can be seen in the invitations to foreign figures to join the society as correspondent and honorary members and by the exchange offers with foreign journals. Among the names elected as correspondent members the following stand out: Eduardo Hernandez Pacheco (University of Madrid), Telesforo d'Aranzadi (University of Barcelona),[20] Arthur Keith (Royal College of Surgeons of Great Britain and Ireland), Vincenzo Giuffrida-Ruggeri (University of Naples), Henri Breuil (Paris Institute for Human Paleontology), and Aleš Hrdlička (National Museum, Washington DC),[21] all proposed by Mendes Correia on December 26, 1918; René Verneau and Marcellin Boule (Natural History Museum in Paris), proposed by Aarão Ferreira de Lacerda on December 26, 1918; Eugenio Francours (Polish ethnographer in Madrid) on January 21, 1919; Eugenius Frankowski (assistant professor at the University of Crakow), proposed by Vergílio Correia on June 2, 1919; Yves Guyot (director of the Paris School of Anthropology), Georges Hervé (professor at this same school), Herman ten Kate (Dutch anthropologist and doctor, from Kobe),[22] and professor Manuel Antón y Ferrándiz (director of the National Anthropology Museum in Madrid), proposed by Mendes Correia on June 2, 1919; Sergio Sergi (University of Rome), proposed on November 3, 1919; Fabio Frassetto (Bologna, Italy), Francisco de las Barras de Aragon (Madrid), Hugo Obermaier (Madrid), Mario Carrara (Turin, Italy), Nello Puccioni (Florence, Italy), Quintiliano Saldaña (Madrid), proposed on June 11, 1920;[23] Alfredo Niceforo (Paris), Otto Schlaginhaufen (Zurich), elected in 1921; the count of Bégouen (French archaeologist and professor of prehistory at the University of Toulouse), elected in 1922; Rudolph Martin (anthropologist, born in Switzerland but studied and worked in Germany), J. P. Kleiweg de Zwaan (Dutch physical anthropologist), and Renato Kehl (Brazilian doctor),[24] accepted in 1923; Oliveira Viana (Brazilian lawyer and historian), elected in 1934; Hernan Lundborg (director of the Uppsala Institute for Racial Biology, Sweden), elected in 1936; Pedro Calmon (professor of law and member

Fig. 2. Leopoldina Paulo, 1944. The first woman to obtain a doctoral degree in the University of Porto. *UPorto Alumni, Revista dos Antigos Alunos da Universidade do Porto*, 2nd ser., 1 (June 2007). Used with permission of the University of Porto.

of the Brazilian Academy of Letters, over which he presided in 1945),[25] Angyone Costa (professor of archaeology at the Historical Museum of Rio de Janeiro), and Alvaro de Las Casas (Galician, author of ethnographic works), elected in 1937. Among SPAE's honorary members we could also find other names, such as Giuseppe Sergi (Italian anthropologist), Émile Cartailhac,[26] and Salomon Reinach (both archaeologists), proposed on December 8, 1919. The cooperation of foreign specialists at the TAE is another noteworthy fact. For example, Vincenzo Giuffrida-Ruggeri (Italian physical anthropologist) collaborated with the TAE on an unpublished work in 1920, and Pedro Bosch-Gimpera (Catalan archaeologist and also an SPAE member) published an article in one of the two parts of TAE published in 1928.[27]

SPAE's meetings also provided space to recognize figures who deserved tribute after their death. Among these the following stand out: Joseph Deniker (anthropologist), Ferreira Deusdado, and Felismino Ribeiro Gomes (who had devoted themselves to anthropological works in Portugal) on December 26, 1918;[28] Léon Paul Choffat (geologist) on July 7, 1919; José Fortes (archaeologist) in 1920; Aarão Ferreira de Lacerda (permanent member and SPAE's vice-chairman), Émile Cartailhac (SPAE's honorary member), and Giuffrida-Ruggeri (SPAE's correspondent member) in 1921; Freitas Viegas (SPAE's president since its foundation) in 1928; Salomon Reinach and Georges Hervé (SPAE's honorary and correspondent member, respectively) in 1932; Rui Correia de Serpa Pinto (SPAE's librarian) in 1933, to whom the society also paid tribute in 1934; Bento Carqueja in 1935; Ricardo Severo (honorary member living in São Paulo, Brazil) in 1940; and Aleš Hrdlička in 1943.

THE SPAE AND THE RECOGNITION OF
ANTHROPOLOGY AT THE UNIVERSITY LEVEL

On January 21, 1919, Mendes Correia proposed that the "suitableness of introducing the discipline of anthropology within the scope of medical preparatory studies" should be presented to the country's medical schools. According to a letter sent to SPAE, the Medical School, despite its "heavily overloaded staff," applauded the integration of anthropology in the curriculum or the creation of a special improvement course on that science aimed at doctors (minutes from May 12, 1919). On January 22, 1920, in a written document, wishes were expressed toward a rapid integration, since "it is not understandable that a doctor ignores man's natural history, in many of its aspects." According to the 1920 activities report, SPAE's managing board also proposed "a motion aiming at the development of the teaching of anthropology and prehistory at the university level."

At the same time, according to the minutes from December 27, 1920, SPAE's board also requested of the government "the separation of anthropology within the scope of the faculties of science, as a section or an autonomous group, considering its close relationships with the most diversified scientific branches, and not only with botany and zoology, to which it was associated within the same biological science group." This request also defended "the need to create institutes for anthropology, to develop the teaching of related sciences and applications, and to include general anthropology in the context of medical studies." This demand was partially satisfied by a decree dated from February 1920 that "divided the group of biological science of the faculties of sciences in three subgroups: one for botany, the other for zoology, and the third for anthropology; the latter included the discipline of general anthropology, but also allowing the creation of six-monthly or quarterly courses in criminal anthropology, ethnography, and prehistoric archaeology." Anthropology was not included in medical studies, but the effort was "valuable," according to foreign journals, in "honorably discussing the Portuguese decree"; it was considered, at least, as an official recognition of the importance and individual character of the discipline as a science. This was formalized by the Portuguese-Spanish Congress, where the natural science section was subdivided into two subsections, one for botany and zoology, the other for geology and anthropology, placing the latter on "an equal standing with other scientific branches" (minutes dated December 27, 1920). Furthermore, the congress recognized "the prominent role undertaken by geologists in the development and advancements of anthropology, mainly in the area of human palaeontology and prehistory" (minutes dated December 27, 1920).

By comparison, we may also mention the case of the Anthropological Society in Vienna (founded in 1870), where geologists played an important role in the affirmation of anthropology as a scientific discipline. However, in the Austrian case the predominance of geologists over doctors led to a greater focus on prehistory and less on physical anthropology (Ranzmaier 2011:18). In the case of SPAE, a balance between the two areas prevailed (as seen in figure 3) but, as shown in the institutionalization of anthropology at UP, with a closer relationship between science and medicine and less attention to aspects of the humanities.

As we will see, social and cultural anthropological studies were initially conducted by amateurs, missionaries, military personnel, and individuals holding offices in the colonial administrations both within Portugal and in the colonies. This might relate more to the fact that people working to define anthropology as an academic discipline were trained in the areas of science or medicine, as is the case with Mendes Correia, and less due to any possible rivalry between science and the humanities. In the case of the University of Vienna, for example, it was hard to integrate anthropology as a discipline in the Faculty of Philosophy, which was attempted around 1889, since that faculty had traditionally drawn rigid boundaries between science and the humanities. The relationship between these two domains became increasingly competitive, and physical anthropology arose mainly attached to natural science, while ethnology was attached to historical-philosophical science; in the opinion of Irene Ranzmaier, this was not beneficial to the institutionalization of either area (2011:12). In the early 1920s the ideal anthropology professor at the University of Vienna had to be able to cover both physical anthropology and ethnology (Ranzmaier 2011:15).

NATIONAL AND INTERNATIONAL
PARTNERSHIPS AND EXCHANGES

On January 21, 1919, Mendes Correia invited SPAE to cooperate in the organization of the International Institute of Anthropology, conceived by the Paris School of Anthropology, members of which had sent to the latter and to António Aurélio da Costa Ferreira a letter on the subject. SPAE joined the initiative, since it had the potential to provide interesting anthropological research in the context of the European war (1914–18). According to the minutes dated June 2, 1919, the Paris School of Anthropology thanked SPAE for joining the initiative and proposed the organization of a preparatory congress for that purpose in 1920. According to that year's report, SPAE's managing board provided for the representation and collaboration of the society in the organizing meeting of the International Institute of Anthropology, which, as proposed by the Paris School of Anthropology and by the Society for the Teaching of Anthropological Sciences, was held in Paris in September 1920. Intended SPAE representatives were Baltasar Osório, Aurélio da Costa Ferreira, and Mendes Correia, but only the latter was able to travel and bear testimony to "the praises" SPAE "received in the anthropological community and to the cordiality and opinion of unanimity that prevailed in the meeting" (Livro de actas, vol. 1).

Portugal and SPAE were represented in the board of the new International Institute of Anthropology by Eusébio Tamagnini and Barros e Cunha,[29] both connected to the University of Coimbra, Aurélio da Costa Ferreira, and Mendes Correia, constituting the first Portuguese delegation. In the Paris meeting were also present Salomon Reinach (an honorary member of SPAE) and Henri Breuil, René Verneau, and Georges Hervé (all correspondent members of SPAE). On that occasion, Mendes Correia drew Hervé's attention to the fact that Spain was not represented in the congress nor in the new institute, but Hervé answered by informing Mendes Correia that the International Institute had delegated to him the "mission of organising the Spanish Committee"; Mendes Correia then invited the Spanish comembers, Francisco de las Barras de Aragón (Madrid), Telesforo Aranzadi (University of Barcelona),[30] and Hernandez Pacheco (University of Madrid), to join the institute. Mendes Correia also represented the SPAE at the meeting to create a Portuguese section of the International Institute of Anthropology in 1922; at the time he was its vice-chairman, and he was elected secretary to that section. He also represented SPAE at the meeting of the International Institute of Anthropology in 1927, at which SPAE members Barros e Cunha and Henrique Miranda were also present.

SPAE's 1929 report mentions the International Congress of Anthropology to be held in 1930—which was to be the XV International Congress on Anthropology and Prehistoric Archaeology—and the fact that the society's chairman (Mendes Correia) and the vice-chairman (Hernâni Monteiro) had traveled to Coimbra seeking to arrange to hold the congress both there and in Porto. It was confirmed that the opening sessions and the sessions of the first four days would be held in Coimbra, with the last two days in Porto for "plenary conferences, visits, and the closing session." However, later on "an organising committee [was created], not consulting with Porto's elements," of which "only one was part of the committee"; this fact gave rise to protests in Porto "against such an ill-natured and discourteous act, as per the letter sent" to the comembers. The resolution of this situation led to two independent committees, "one for Porto and another for Coimbra, absolutely indifferent," with Alberto Rocha from Coimbra acting as intermediary in the process (Livro de actas, vol. 2). This and other episodes occurring during the time both schools existed contemporaneously point to the fact that UC's and UP's representatives did not maintain the most amicable and productive relationships for scientific work.

In 1930 several people associated with SPAE participated in the Portugal Section of the XV International Congress on Anthropology and Prehistoric Archaeology, held in France, where presentations were mainly in physical anthropology.[31] Some of the subjects debated were heredity of blood groups (Mendes Correia 1931b), craniology of Angola (Mendes Correia and Athayde 1930), anthropological study of Portuguese Guinea (Lima and Mascarenhas 1930; Mendes Correia and Athayde 1931), angles at the base of the skull in native inhabitants of Portuguese colonies (Pina 1931), and "race" differentiation through blood (Ferreira 1932). In 1934, under SPAE's initiative, the First National Congress on Colonial Anthropology was held in Porto, where "about eighty scientific communications were presented, all related to colonial matters." Perhaps because this meeting was so successful, the organizing committee of the Congresses on the Portuguese World, to which Mendes Correia belonged, and the Portuguese World Exhibition, both in Lisbon in 1940, sought from the beginning to surpass the 1934 congress and the Portuguese Colonial Exhibition, both held in Porto (Matos

2013). Several members of SPAE from Porto participated in the congress, presenting communications at the 1940 congresses: the First National Congress and the CNCP (which was integrated with the Congresses on the Portuguese World), which took place in July and September, respectively. Some of SPAE's members also presented communications at the IV Congress of the Portuguese Society for the Advancement of Science and at the XVII Congress of the Spanish Society for the Advancement of Science, held in Porto in 1942.

Another way for SPAE to disseminate the work of its members, to set themes for debate, and to get to know what other societies were doing was through the exchange of scientific periodicals. According to 1919's report (January 22, 1920), the managing board had received "friendly answers and promises for work exchange relationships" from several scientific institutions, including ACL, SGL, the Paris School of Anthropology, the Smithsonian Institution (Washington DC), the Royal Anthropological Institute of Great Britain and Ireland (London), the Società Romana di Antropologie (Rome), and the Società Italiana de Antropologia e Etnologia (Florence). SPAE also received "motivational words" from scientific journals such as the *Revue Anthropologique*, *Lusa*, and *Terra Portuguesa*. Although still in an initial phase in 1919, the library started to grow with national publications, such as the *Arquivo de Anatomia e Antropologia* (FMUL) and the journal *Contribuições para o Estudo da Antropologia Portuguesa* by IAUC.

After 1919 the *Revue Anthropologique* (by the Paris School of Anthropology and the International Institute of Anthropology), the *Rivista di Antropologia* (Roman Society for Anthropology), the journal of the Smithsonian Institution, the journal of the Società Italiana di Antropologia e Etnologia, and publications by the Bureau of American Ethnology (Washington DC) were added to the library. From 1921 onward SPAE received publications by the Société Royale de Archéologie de Bruxelles and the Institut Archéologique Liégeois (Belgium) and the journal *Ethnos* (Mexico).[32] In 1922 SPAE began to receive the journal *Man* (London) and *Mitteilungen der anthropologischen Gesellschaft* (Vienna). From 1925 SPAE also exchanged the following publications: *Société Archéologique, Historique et Géographique du Département de Constantine* (Algeria), *Bulletin de Institut des Recherches Biologiques de l'Université de Perm* (Russia), *L'Universo* (Military Geographic Institute of Florence), *Lud* (publication by the Polish Ethnological Society in Warsaw), *Investigación y Progresso* (Madrid), *Anthropos: Revue Internationale d'Ethnologie et de Linguistique* (Austria), *Journal Russe d'Anthropologie*, *La Tradizione* (Palermo, Italy), *Boletim do Museu Nacional do Rio de Janeiro* (Brazil), and *Acta Archaeologica* (Copenhagen). According to the 1920s report, several other scientific journals maintained "friendly" contacts with SPAE, such as the Italian journals *Archivio di Antropologia Criminale, Psichiatria e Medicina Legale* (Turin) and *Archivio per l'Antropologia e l'Etnologia* (Florence). Besides the journals referred to above, from 1919 onward SPAE was offered original publications from Telesforo d'Aranzadi (Barcelona), Sergio Sergi (Rome), Giuffrida-Ruggeri, Joseph de Barandiaran (specialist in prehistory and ethnologic studies in the Basque country, Spain), Enrique de Eguren (Faculty of Science of the University of Oviedo, Spain), and some permanent members (Livro de actas, vol. 1). The 1928 report mentions that, thanks to Rui de Serpa Pinto, the library was completely cataloged, missing numbers of national and foreign journals had been ordered, and new exchanges had begun. In 1929 the number of exchanges almost doubled, to 100, and in 1930 they reached 125. Members considered the library one of the most important for anthropological sciences.

PUBLICATION IN *TAE* AND SUBJECTS PRESENTED AT SPAE'S LECTURES

Some of the works presented at SPAE's lectures were later published through the journal *TAE* under the initiative of the society's managing board. These generally reflected the topics of interest and study dear to the society and were consistent with others produced at the time, both European and American (Stocking 1968, 1988). The *TAE* also published other works that had not been previously presented at SPAE's sessions and had a bibliographical review section describing new publications both national and international. The articles published by SPAE (through the *TAE*) began with posthumous notes by Artur Augusto da Fonseca Cardoso (1919), "Em terras do Moxico: Apontamentos de etnografia angolense" (In Moxico territory: Notes on an Angolan ethnography),[33] which included the "portrait of the unfortunate anthropologist" and "biographical and tribute words,"[34] as well as numerous illustration plates, some of which were offered by Henrique de Vilhena (FMUL). This article was followed by others, such as "Subsídios para o estudo etnológico de Timor" (Subsidies for the ethnological study of Timor) by Major António Leite de Magalhães (1919). On average, one to two volumes of the journal were published every year. The minutes mention several times the material difficulties of this publication series, with high costs not allowing its speedy printing. The 1926 report highlights that this journal was "unique among its kind" in the country, but (maybe because it lay "so distant from the Terreiro do Paço"),[35] it was "not considered worthy of a benevolent glance from the high ranks of government." Nevertheless, João Camoesas, minister for public education, twice offered an amount to fund the publication expenses of the TAE (in 1923 and in 1925). Furthermore, Artur Ricardo Jorge,[36] when reviewing the budget for 1926, had "doubled the provisions allowed"; as a result, during that year "2,400 escudos were available for its publications," which would allow TAE to "print an instalment every four months." SPAE's financial situation was better in 1927 thanks to the subsidy that was then allocated to it by the government, but by 1928 the 2,400 escudos subsidy and the membership fee of the members were once more insufficient, largely due to the increase in printing costs. In 1929 the National Education Board allocated a subsidy of 1,500 escudos, making it once more possible to print two installments every year. In 1935 three were published, and in the following years the publication of two per year was made possible. However, in 1940, for example, SPAE's financial situation did not allow for the publication of any installment.

SPAE organized, on average, three scientific sessions a year, and each session might include more than one lecture. For example, it organized five in 1923,[37] four in 1924,[38] three in 1925,[39] seven in 1935 (the highest number until then), and five in 1936. Mendes Correia always presented at least one lecture a year in these sessions, and the remaining lecturers varied. These presentations were "very well attended," according to SPAE's reports, by outsiders with no connection to the society and by members. Anthropology in a generic sense was the topic of several lectures. For example, on June 2, 1919, Freitas Viegas made an "inau-

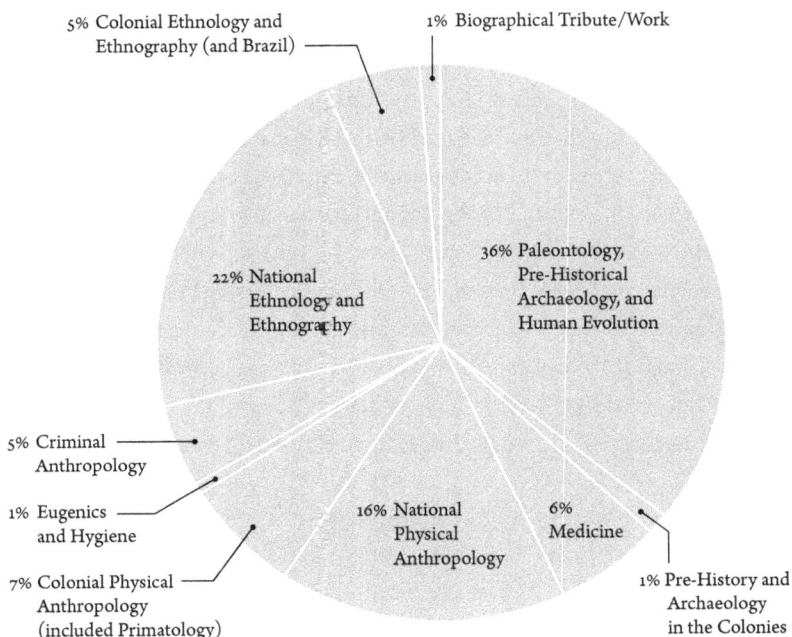

5% Colonial Ethnology and Ethnography (and Brazil)

1% Biographical Tribute/Work

22% National Ethnology and Ethnography

36% Paleontology, Pre-Historical Archaeology, and Human Evolution

5% Criminal Anthropology

1% Eugenics and Hygiene

7% Colonial Physical Anthropology (included Primatology)

16% National Physical Anthropology

6% Medicine

1% Pre-History and Archaeology in the Colonies

Fig. 3. Percentage of topics at the lectures organized by SPAE, 1918–44, classified by the author.

gural speech" on the aim and progresses in anthropology. However, other more specific topics were also presented. The diversity in topics would be related to the broad and inclusive vision of anthropology by Mendes Correia and to the way his collaborators were encouraged to address diversified research topics. Through a systematic review of the 165 lectures presented from 1918 to 1944, we can conclude that 23 percent address topics in the scope of physical anthropology and 27 percent in ethnology and ethnography (fig. 3).[40]

The most common lectures were related to paleontology, prehistoric archaeology, and human evolution. The collection of archaeological material within Portugal was easier to fund than archaeological research that involved traveling to distant places or ethnographic/ethnologic research. Furthermore, there were no researchers specifically qualified to do the latter, what today would be social or cultural anthropology. On January 22, 1920, Mendes Correia presented a lecture titled "A paleontologia e a origem do homem" (Paleontology and the origin of man), which he accompanied with light projections and the presentation of models and archaeological finds.[41] According to the minutes, "after mentioning the morphological, physiological, embryological, etc. arguments in favour of the animal origin of man," the author "described the discoveries of fossil primates" carried out until then and addressed "in particular the Maptomorphus, the Propliopithecus, the Pliopitecus, the Dryopithecus, the Sivapithecus, the Pithecanthropus, and the quaternary man." His lecture included the presentation of "genealogical trees of primates and man" by Dutch paleoanthropologist Eugène Dubois (1858–1940), German paleoanthropologist Gustav Schwalbe (1844–1916), German zoologist and paleontologist Max Schlosser (1854–1932), English geologist and paleontologist Guy Ellock Pilgrim (1875–1943), and Scottish anthropologist and anatomist Arthur Keith (1866–1955), which he assessed as "very conjectural and premature." Finally, he mentioned the "neopoligeny (in particular the pananthropoid thesis by Kloatich) and the neomonogeny (Giuffrida-Ruggeri), preferring the latter." He concluded by saying that "paleontology was not yet able to provide the human genealogical tree, but it has faith in it, first because it has provided many extinct primate species; second because it has provided some generalized forms of primates; . . . third because it has revealed the existence, in geological times, of simians that were more anthropomorphized than the current ones and of men more simian than today."

After this communication Mendes Correia presented others, including on archaeological topics. In fact, although he was the mentor of a school of anthropology, in the beginning of his career he wrote numerous texts on archaeology, and, for a long time, he wrote mainly on this topic, occasionally addressing other subjects. The themes of the lectures presented at SPAE by Mendes Correia until the 1940s illustrate this: among about twenty-seven lectures from 1919 to 1940, nineteen are related to paleontology, prehistoric archaeology, and human evolution.[42] The remaining eight are distributed between criminal anthropology,[43] physical anthropology,[44] and anthropology and history,[45] or they were intended to act as a biographical tribute,[46] some of them having been partially or fully published, although some publication titles differ slightly from the conference titles.

Another area included in SPAE's lectures was medicine, mainly with rather unknown subjects or ones that were considered aberrant. For example, the presentation "Fístula auricular congénita" (Congenital atrial fistula) by José Maria de Oliveira, on "a very curious and scarcely studied anomaly" (June 11, 1920), supported with "numerous personal observations, with photos and light projections," was published by the society in full (Oliveira 1921). Physical anthropology was also submitted to debate. For example, in the national context, Joaquim A. Pires de Lima presented a communication titled "Um caso de braquidactilia hereditária" (A case of hereditary brachydactyly) (June 13, 1922), and, from a colonial context, Hernâni Monteiro presented "Mutilações dentárias da região do Humbe" (Dental mutilations in the Humbe region) (June 13, 1922). In ethnology and ethnography in the national context, one might mention the communication by Joaquim Pires de Lima titled "O dente santo de Aboim de Nóbrega e a Lenda de S. Frutuoso Abade" (The holy tooth of Aboim de Nóbrega and the legend of Saint Frutuoso Abade) (May 6, 1921), and also the lectures presented by Armando Leça,[47] who was called a "distinguished folklorist" in the 1936 annual report, such as "O cancioneiro na vida portuguesa" (Anthology of music in Portuguese living) (1936), "Nótulas sobre o cancioneiro português" (Short notes on the anthology of Portuguese music) (1938), and "O canto e a dança no cancioneiro português" (Singing and dancing in the anthology of Portuguese music) (1939).

There was great interest in the Portuguese colonial contexts from the beginning, as illustrated by the lectures and publications in the TAE, and similar cases of examining physical or biological aspects in ethnology and ethnography can be noted among these. This focus on more physical or biological aspects was not the single prevailing tendency or inclination in the majority of the works by Mendes Correia and other figures connected to the society; it was a common one, but it cannot be seen as a general tendency. For example, Major António Leite de Magalhães presented a lecture titled "Estudo etnológico de Timor" (Ethnological study on Timor), in which he described the "results of his studies on linguistics and ethnography in the Portuguese part of the island" (June 2, 1919). Colonel Alexandre José Sarsfield devoted his lecture to the subject "African Ethnography" (January 14, 1922).

These lectures could be more or less detailed and promote debate, as is the case with the presentation by Second Lieutenant David José Gonçalves Magno (1877–1957) on the Dembos region in Angola (July 25, 1919), in which he provided a summary of the "history of Congo and its invasions, demonstrating the existing ethnic affinities between the current *dembos* and the peoples of that ancient Empire."[48] He referenced the works performed there by the colonial officials Major Leite de Magalhães and the Reverend António de Miranda Magalhães, concluding with the "*luango* or the *mubire*, the *mahungo*, the *quibaxe* and many other populations, mainly from *Caculo Cahenda*, describing their material and intellectual life, their clothing, diet, and arts, as well as their family organization, . . . birth, marriage, death, divinities, cults, sorceries, the 'oaths' ceremony, their social organization, their classes and their castes, their political organization, property, and judiciary practices" (Livro de actas, vol. 1). Following David Magno's explanation, Major Leite de Magalhães "praised the lecture" and discussed "some of its topics based on data he personally collected in the Dembos region"; there was therefore room for the exchange of experiences, which allowed enriching the knowledge on the colonies at the time. In that same session (July 25, 1919), Mendes Correia presented a lecture by missionary António de Miranda Magalhães "on the *luango* from the Dembos region, to which he added his own results on some of the skulls of the *dembado* of Zambi-Aluquem," which were sent to him by the aforementioned priest, referred to in the minutes as an "untiring researcher."[49] Therefore, to the rather ethnographical knowledge collected by the missionary on a group, Mendes Correia added his analysis of some skulls belonging to members of that same group with a modus operandi quite characteristic of a professor at FCUP for whom the study of a human group should include both its physical analysis and its sociocultural aspects.

Although the interest in the colonial field had emerged as early as 1919, as noted previously, it is mainly from the 1930s onward—and resulting from the works within the scope of the anthropological missions, promoted by Mendes Correia himself—that in SPAE's lectures more communications begin to emerge on the "anthropology of the colonies" in physical, biological, and sociocultural terms. Some of these were later published in the TAE or in other journals and are indexed in the miscellaneous collections I consulted referring to the Porto School of Anthropology.[50] In fact, SPAE's production contributed greatly to the publications by IAUP and FCUP and to the growth of a great part of the estate that today is identified with the Porto School of Anthropology.

Also relevant here is the journal *Contribuições para o Estudo da Antropologia Portuguesa* by IAUC (Anthropological Museum and Laboratory), published for the first time in 1914. Despite this journal having counted on subsidies allocated by the National Education Board and IAC, some of the works, due to the lack of funds, were published as offprints of the *Revista da Universidade de Coimbra* and of the *Revista da Faculdade de Ciências da Universidade de Coimbra*. The last example of this is the eighth installment of the sixth volume (1959). When the journal *Contribuições para o Estudo da Antropologia Portuguesa* appeared, it aimed at publishing original works in installments and to be exchanged with similar publications on a national and international level, such as the TAE. In the period from 1914 to 1981, ten volumes of the journal *Contribuições para o Estudo da Antropologia Portuguesa* were published, with a varying number of instalments each. In 1981 the journal printed a volume collecting the tables of contents for this series. The contents divided the articles into three topics: physical anthropology (seventy-nine entries), cultural anthropology (seven), and archaeology (one); that is, among the eighty-seven works published by the Coimbra School of Anthropology, physical anthropology accounted for 91 percent and cultural anthropology 8 percent of the content; archaeology (in contrast to the Porto School of Anthropology) assumed here a merely residual value (1 percent). Within the scope of the works presented at SPAE, the difference between the number of works belonging to physical anthropology was smaller than the number belonging to ethnology and ethnography.

Some of the articles in Coimbra's journal can be classified as archaeological, like the ones I classified as archaeological from the SPAE lectures, some of them published in the TAE journal. One remarkable aspect of the tables of contents of that journal is not only the smaller number of works in ethnology and ethnography compared to physical anthropology but also the fact that none of the ethnological and ethnographical works addressed the Portuguese population (such as in thirty-six works published by SPAE in the period under analysis).[51] They focus instead on populations from the Portuguese colonies, mainly Angola, like the work in archaeology (Martins 1976).[52] The lectures presented at the National Congress of Colonial Anthropology in 1934 also confirm Coimbra's interest in the colonial context.[53]

From this analysis of SPAE-related activities, we can conclude that individuals with an education in medicine, whether they practiced or not, wrote most frequently on physical anthropological subjects, while priests wrote on social and cultural anthropological subjects (terminology, vocabulary, and sociocultural practices). Research with a more social and cultural nature (linguistics, rituals, cultural practices, clothing, and diet) also was carried out mainly by people in the colonial administration or by missionaries (as I suggested previously [Matos 2013], although SPAE's materials strengthen that argument). When the titles of articles mention an "anthropological study," they often mean a study in physical anthropology; when they mention an "ethnological study," they mean topics that we would today include in social and cultural anthropology, although some are more purely ethnographic than ethnological. On the other hand, anyone who writes on prehistoric archaeology might also write on colonial physical anthropology (as is the case of the doctor, professor, and naturalist Júlio Guilherme Bettencourt Ferreira or of Santos Júnior, doctor and professor at FCUP); this means that the case of Mendes Correia, who, over time, devoted himself to several topics, is by no means unique. But some connected to SPAE, like Rui de Serpa Pinto, wrote mainly on archaeology.

FROM SPAE'S FOUNDATION TO TODAY

SPAE was the starting point of a great amount of work that would be carried out later on and served as a model for ways that ideas and individuals (Portuguese and foreign) could be joined and new structures created. It gathered together people connected to the Porto School of Anthropology and others and developed themes for discussion and means to exchange works from the impetus created by Mendes Correia. Among the people connected to SPAE we find specialists from several areas educated in medicine, science, and the humanities but also members of the military, priests, and people connected to industry. Some of the members and collaborators were amateurs in the domain of anthropology but possessed a university education in other areas and were professionally active in other domains—the humanities, science, or medicine. It was not a large organization, compared to its foreign counterparts, but that must be considered in the context of Portugal—a small country with correspondingly smaller societies. Nevertheless, if we consider the internationalization effort—namely, the inclusion of honorary and correspondent members outside the country—in that smaller context, it is a proportionate or even greater effort than, for example, societies in Great Britain and the United States.

João Leal noted that "despite a dominant preference for physical anthropology and archaeology" SPAE did not cease to promote ethnographical research (2000:35). However, I believe it achieved more than that by stimulating all areas related to anthropology, according to the comprehensive and inclusive vision with which Mendes Correia viewed the discipline, as seen in figure 3. The precedence of works in physical anthropology and archaeology may reflect the regular contributions of Mendes Correia and others educated in medicine and the natural sciences. That is to say, although the lectures presented at SPAE point to different and diversified interests, not all were published, or they were published in other places, which may have led to the lack of recognition of the society's existence and publications. The diversity of studies is also evidence of the fact that, during this period, pioneering methods and new research areas were being developed—science disciplines were more diverse and inclusive than exclusive. The conditions that led to the creation of the Porto School of Anthropology were intrinsically connected to the creation of SPAE through its statute and its activities in presenting lectures and publishing works that interested all members and in electing foreign correspondent members. The institution constituted a central core that grew in parallel to the Porto School of Anthropology.

SPAE and IAUP are institutionally distinct organs but were mixed up for a long time—perhaps because both were led by Mendes Correia. However, from the middle 1950s to 1985, this society's activity depended mainly on Santos Júnior, one of the closest collaborators of Mendes Correia who performed works in archaeology and ethnography in Trás-os-Montes e Alto-Douro (a region in the north of Portugal) and also in archaeology in Angola and Mozambique until he retired in 1971.[54] When SPAE's first chairman, Freitas Viegas, died in 1928, Mendes Correia took on the position, with Hernâni Monteiro, an anatomy professor, as vice-chairman.[55] When Mendes Correia went to Lisbon, Hernâni Monteiro took on the role of chairman and Santos Júnior, an anthropology professor, became vice-chairman. Hernâni Monteiro was later followed by Santos Júnior as chairman, and Abel Sampaio Tavares, an anatomy professor, became vice-chairman. A pattern is clear of alternating between anatomy professors and anthropology professors as chairmen of this institution due to the close relationships existing between the Department of Anthropology of FCUP and the Department of Anatomy of FMUP. When Santos Júnior resigned, a new group of candidates was elected in 1985. Vítor Oliveira Jorge became chairman of the board, an office he maintains to this day.

The SPAE's physical location, maintaining files partially gathered in dozens of boxes, has changed places on several occasions. When SPAE was created in 1918, its headquarters were in Santa Catarina's Street, no. 207, in Porto. Mendes Correia's father, António Maria Esteves Mendes Correia, offered his clinical practice in that same street, and the offer was accepted at the second meeting of the society on January 21, 1919 (Livro de actas, vol. 1). Shortly thereafter, the society began to meet in FCUP's building at Praça dos Leões (or Praça Rodrigues Teixeira), where nowadays we can find the Rectory of UP (probably as early as 1920, since SPAE's annual report for that year included an acknowledgment to FCUP for lending its facilities to hold the meetings). After the revolution on April 25, 1974, SPAE stayed at Praça dos Leões. Subsequently, its files, packed in boxes shipped by the Rectory of UP, were transferred to the former building of CICAP, but the society's headquarters were maintained in the same facilities. Once more, however, by order of UP's rector, the files were returned to Praça dos Leões. As far as I know, the last time this collection of files changed places was in May 2010, when the boxes were shipped to a storeroom assigned by the Rectory that is located in the building of the School of Journalism, in the proximity of the Faculty of Law, which I visited in June 2010. Meanwhile, it was agreed with the Rectory of UP that the publications up to 1930 would from then on be maintained in the Biblioteca do Fundo Antigo of UP in the building that houses the Rectory nowadays. There is yet no inventory of the contents of the files. However, SPAE's managing board and its current chairman, Vítor Oliveira Jorge, have made every effort to preserve these materials and to supervise all removals, and they have tried to guarantee the continuity of the society with dignity by pursuing its activities and publishing the TAE.

Regarding continuity of activities, I would highlight the fact that in 1985 SPAE began a new phase with a new managing board, reorganizing the former statute, admitting new members, and organizing scientific sessions. In 1987 it received the status of Legal Entity of Public Utility, as published in the Portuguese official journal *Diário da República*, no. 89, second series, dated April 16, 1987. The following year, it organized a conference on social anthropology and, together with the Porto Group of Archaeological Studies, organized the Colóquio de Arqueologia do Noroeste Peninsular (Conference on Archaeology of the Peninsula's Northwest). Afterward, the resulting reflections were published in the TAE. Under the same imprimatur, in volumes 30, 31, and 32 (from 1990, 1991, and 1992), articles were published that offered a posthumous tribute to the significant Portuguese ethnographer Ernesto Veiga de Oliveira. In 1992 SPAE organized a round table under the title "Existe uma cultura portuguesa?" (Is there a Portuguese culture?) and in 1993 organized the 1st Congress on Peninsular Archaeology. On the occasion of this congress, SPAE created a specific logo to promote this event and after that adopted it on some occasions as an alternative logo also used inside the TAE, although the official logo remains the original one (fig. 4). Besides promoting activities and organizing conferences, it still published the TAE journal—without interruption since 1919—with works from all areas of the social sciences (anthropology, archaeology, cognitive sciences, education sciences, information and communication sciences, law, economy, philosophy, history, linguistics, patrimony, psychology and sociology), revealing an open-minded attitude toward the publication of "essays on general issues that are of

S.P.A.E.
SOCIEDADE
PORTUGUESA·DE
ANTROPOLOGIA
E·ETNOLOGIA

Fig. 4. SPAE's current logo.

interest towards understanding the contemporaneous world."[56] It is one of the oldest journals in Portugal maintaining an exchange relationship with counterparts all over the world. SPAE's documentary record is of great value, above all due to the journal exchanges, although it also includes books. It possesses, for example, journals from the Smithsonian Institution, starting with no. 1, and is the only entity in Portugal that possesses such a set of journals. The several TAE volumes gather, therefore, many articles that offer a true goldmine of information on the history of science produced in the country.

CONCLUSION

The stories of anthropology can be told in various ways based on the narratives of individuals, institutions, ideas, and traditions. Very often, however, they are more focused on individuals rather than on ideas, and this leads to omitting significant phenomena. My aim here was to contextualize the foundation and the development of a scientific society, its objectives, and the individuals who were tied to it and who together generated the necessary conditions for intellectual production and an increase in the knowledge of and interest in a discipline that was trying to achieve academic recognition. The Porto School of Anthropology is partly a result of work developed by the SPAE and continues the tradition of the core inherited from the Carlos Ribeiro Society, to which belonged Ricardo Severo, Rocha Peixoto, José Fortes, Fonseca Cardoso, and other prominent figures.[57] This means that, in a way, Mendes Correia and his collaborators continued the work of the generation of the *Portugália* journal. This is illustrated by the fact that, for example, the first study published in the TAE was a posthumous memoir on Fonseca Cardoso. When Mendes Correia began his anthropology classes at FCUP in 1912, Rocha Peixoto and Fonseca Cardoso were already deceased, and Ricardo Severo had migrated to Brazil, but José Fortes still visited on occasion the Department of Anthropology, bringing his motivation and counsel.

The creation process of the Porto School of Anthropology, in parallel to SPAE's, is similar to that in other circles or scientific societies. These examples and others at an international level allow us to see that, from a small network of intellectuals (many of them connected to organizations such as the Geological Commission or to medium and higher education institutions) or people interested in the so-called emerging sciences, led by charismatic figures, an institutionalized debate was set in motion—of ideas, subjects, methods, and new ways to do research.[58] There are several reports mentioning each one of these schools,[59] including the choice of the topics or areas to be studied. The stories connected to the institutionalization of anthropology as a science—the introduction of the discipline in university curricula and its professionalization—were also important. Therefore, Mendes Correia is a central figure in the understanding of the strategies of the path taken by anthropology in Portugal and the way some different areas of knowledge were interconnected. The Porto School of Anthropology would be impacted by much diversified influences; its collaborators exhibited different educations and interests, and this happened at a time when anthropology was still scarcely institutionalized in Portugal. On the other hand, and because the limits of the discipline were permeable, some of the works by the collaborators of the school showed there was an interdisciplinary dialogue and the sharing of information. Sometimes the approaches may not have been the best ones, but in that context its practitioners were still learning, gathering knowledge, and defining new paths.

In Porto we encounter a kind of naturalist and physical anthropology that was dominant in France, Germany, Italy, and Spain and that also existed (and still exists) in Great Britain and the United States, combined with an anthropology that promotes sociocultural studies not only in Portugal but also in the then-Portuguese colonies. The Porto School of Anthropology has promoted exchanges with institutions originating from several European countries such as France, Italy, Belgium, the United Kingdom, Austria, Poland, Spain, and Denmark; from American countries such as the United States, Brazil, and Mexico; from Eurasian countries such as Russia; and from North African countries such as Algeria. The exchanged journals are dedicated to publishing works with a biological but also sociocultural content, including linguistics studies and studies on religion. However, a certain anachronism regarding theory and method was observed in the works produced, a reality that actually lasted throughout a large part of the twentieth century. Besides, the anthropological studies produced in Portugal were marginal on an international level, where the French, British, and North American contexts were dominant. Nevertheless, for example, German anthropology, which strongly influenced its North American counterpart and also the study of cultures inspired by Romanticism, has motivated some of the works that made their way through SPAE and the Porto school. National traditions are very distinct, even among close countries—even between Iberian neighbors Portugal and Spain.

Furthermore, when comparing the scientific societies created in Portugal in the late nineteenth and early twentieth centuries to other societies on an international level, it is imperative to consider the scale of comparison we are referring to, as well as the way that the science produced within the country at the time was somewhat peripheral to the larger world. Some authors who have written on the history of science in Portugal describe the country's situation as peripheral or, better said, as semiperipheral. According to João Arriscado Nunes and Maria Eduarda Gonçalves, "the term 'semiperiphery' is used to characterize Portugal's or Portuguese science's position in a *world* system organized in central, peripheral, and semiperipheral regions," while "the term 'periphery' is used to designate Portugal's position towards the *European* science-producing centers" (2001:14). In fact, science production depends not exclusively on the actors involved but on its conditions for production, which in Portugal, during most of the twentieth century, were associated with the restrictions connected to Catholicism, to the existence of an authoritarian political regime (1933–74), and to very low literacy levels, which did not promote innovation and technological development. Only recently, after the events on April 25, 1974, when the anthropology degree was integrated in universities, and therefore when anthropology was definitely institutionalized and professionalized, has the approach within the anthropologist community become more endogenous.

NOTES

ACL	Academia das Ciências de Lisboa / Lisbon Academy of Sciences
CICAP	Centro de Instrução de Condutores Auto do Porto / Porto Vehicle Driver Teaching Centre
CNCP	Congresso Nacional de Ciências da População / National Congress for Population Sciences
ESC	Escola Superior Colonial / Higher Colonial College
FCUC	Faculdade de Ciências da Universidade de Coimbra / Faculty of Sciences of the University of Coimbra
FCUL	Faculdade de Ciências da Universidade de Lisboa / Faculty of Sciences of the University of Lisbon
FCUP	Faculdade de Ciências da Universidade do Porto / Faculty of Sciences of the University of Porto
FLUL	Faculdade de Letras da Universidade de Lisboa / Faculty of Humanities of the University of Lisbon
FLUP	Faculdade de Letras da Universidade do Porto / Faculty of Humanities of the University of Porto
FMUL	Faculdade de Medicina da Universidade de Lisboa / Faculty of Medicine of the University of Lisbon
FMUP	Faculdade de Medicina da Universidade do Porto / Faculty of Medicine of the University of Porto
IAC	Instituto para a Alta Cultura / Institute for High Culture
IAUC	Instituto de Antropologia da Universidade de Coimbra / Anthropology Institute of the University of Coimbra
IAUP	Instituto de Antropologia da Universidade do Porto / Anthropology Institute of the University of Porto
ISEU	Instituto Superior de Estudos Ultramarinos / Higher Institute of Overseas Studies
JMGIC	Junta das Missões Geográficas e de Investigações Coloni-

	ais / Committee for Geographical Missions and Colonial Research
JMGIU	Junta das Missões Geográficas e de Investigações do Ultramar / Committee for Geographical Missions and Overseas Research
SGL	Sociedade de Geografia de Lisboa / Geographic Society of Lisbon
SPAE	Sociedade Portuguesa de Antropologia e Etnologia / Portuguese Society of Anthropology and Ethnology
TAE	*Trabalhos de Antropologia e Etnologia / Works on Anthropology and Ethnology*
UC	Universidade de Coimbra / University of Coimbra
UL	Universidade de Lisboa / University of Lisbon
UP	Universidade do Porto / University of Porto

This work was supported by FCT (SFRH/BPD 91349/2012) and by ICS-UL (UID/SOC/50012/2013).

1. Mendes Correia taught at the Faculty of Science and at the Faculty of Humanities of the University of Porto, where he gathered a group of colleagues; he was mayor of Porto (1936–42) and a member of the National Assembly (1945–57); he presided over the Council of Geographical and Colonial Investigation Missions—named Council of Geographical and Overseas Investigation Missions as of 1951 (1946–59); and he took on the presidency of the Lisbon Geographical Society (1951–60).
2. Doctor and anthropologist, director of the Anthropometric Station of Porto (Posto Antropométrico do Porto), and anatomy professor at FMUP.
3. Zoologist and doctor. He taught zoology at FCUP and was the father of Aarão Soeiro Moreira de Lacerda (1890–1947), who was a professor at FLUP.
4. After completing his studies in physical and natural sciences, Carqueja was appointed professor of agriculture and of physical and natural sciences at the Polytechnic Academy; he served as director of the newspaper *Comércio do Porto* and professor of political economy at UP and as director of *Portugália* (scientific journal existing from 1899 to 1908). He offered SPAE the estate of the Carlos Ribeiro Society (a scientific society created in Porto in 1888) and of *Portugália*, thus enabling the collections to be completed. At SPAE's general meeting on December 28, 1927, it was decided that the estate would be transferred to IAUP. The Carlos Ribeiro Society aimed at "studying natural sciences," promoting "pub-

lic lectures" and periodical and occasional publications, and organizing museums and exhibitions (Mendes Correia 1941a:9); it was divided
into four sections (geology and paleontology, zoology and botany,
anthropology, and ethnography), and from its inception it encouraged
interest in the study of natural and social facts.

5. In 1898 the Society of Anthropology was created (the first scientific
society in the area of anthropology founded in Portugal) by Bernardino
Machado (1851–1944), who also created the discipline of anthropology,
human paleontology, and prehistoric archaeology at the UC in 1885, thus
beginning the official studies of anthropology in Portugal. However, the
society soon lapsed, as Bernardino Machado, its first and only chairman,
was increasingly involved in the Republican Party in the early 1900s.

6. There is also an entry on SPAE in the well-known *Enciclopédia Luso-
Brasileira*.

7. SPAE's current statute was published in the Portuguese official bulletin
Diário da República, no. 89, second series, dated April 16, 1987.

8. This is a surprising change in terminology for the time, since the change
of the term "colonies" to "overseas" (which designated the territories
under Portuguese colonial administration) was only incorporated in
the Portuguese Constitution in 1951. The expression "overseas" was considered more appropriate by the Estado Novo dictatorial regime, since
it expressed the existence of Portuguese territories spread all over the
world, as if they were on equal terms with the metropolis, depriving
them of the colonial component, which possessed a distinguishing and
hierarchizing character.

9. However, in SPAE's meeting on March 14, 1919, Henrique de Vilhena had
a letter read on his behalf in which he thanked the society for his election as a member but declined to be part of it (Livro de actas, vol. 1).

10. Costa Ferreira (1879–1922) obtained his degrees at the Faculties of Philosophy (1899) and Medicine (1905) of the UC. Following several short
stays in Paris, he took up residence in Lisbon in 1907. He took the office
of minister for development (1912–13), and in 1914 he created the first
Medical-Pedagogical Institute, aimed at teaching the mentally disabled.

11. The Sousa Soares family owned a considerable fortune. However, in
this case, as in others, based on the analyzed materials, we cannot know
if or to what extent some of SPAE's members supported the society or
some of its research projects.

12. Rui Correia de Serpa Pinto (1907–33), with studies in engineering, was
assistant professor of geology at FCUP and one of the most promis-

ing archaeologists of his time; he was considered the "natural heir" of Mendes Correia.

13. Sebastião Pessanha was the director of the City Museum of Sintra, chairman of the board of the Sintra Institute, and delegate in the sixth section (Art and Archaeology) of the National Education Council.

14. Ricardo Severo (1869–1940) was one of the founding members of the Carlos Ribeiro Society in 1887. He completed a degree in public works engineering in 1890 and a degree in mining engineering in 1891, both at Academia Politécnica do Porto. SPAE's report dated from 1920 mentions him as the "only survivor of the editing committee of the high-quality journal *Portugália*."

15. General inspector of the child protection services of the Ministry of Justice, he was involved in the organization of the International Congress on Child Protection in Lisbon.

16. Carlos Teixeira (1910–82) was one of the most influential Portuguese geologists in the twentieth century. He was a student of Mendes Correia at FCUP in the disciplines of geology, physical geography, paleontology, and anthropology; he was primarily interested in topics of physical anthropology, archaeology, and ethnology and, later, stood out as a geologist and palaeobotanist. In 1934 he published a work in the TAE on popular medicine and superstitions in Vieira do Minho (Teixeira 1934); he also published in the area of archaeology (Teixeira 1935c, 1936b), on physical anthropology (Teixeira 1935a, 1935b, 1936c), and on factors connected to human reproduction, where he concluded that "man is subject to a period of greater reproductive activity, confirmed not only by birth statistics, but also by sexual criminology statistics, suicide statistics, etc." (Teixeira 1936a:14). In 1940 he participated in the Congress on Portuguese Pre- and Protohistory (Athayde and Teixeira 1940) and in the CNCP (Teixeira 1940), integrated in the Congresses on the Portuguese World; he made the academic praise speech for Mendes Correia at ACL (Teixeira 1964), highlighting the notability of IAUP.

17. Maria Irene Leite da Costa (1911–96) obtained a degree in natural history science and in pharmacy at UP in 1934; that same year, she was distinguished in the discipline of anthropology. She worked with Mendes Correia in the studies on the natives from Portuguese colonies who participated in the Colonial Exhibition that took place in Porto in 1934. She received education in psychology and childhood pedagogy at the University of Geneva. She taught and performed research works with psychological and pedagogical tests. In the 1950s and the 1960s she was

a member of the National Assembly, where she intervened in health and childhood support matters.

18. He was one of Mendes Correia's close collaborators and accompanied him to Guinea (1945–46) to prepare the anthropological mission there that took place under the scope of JMGIC, dependent on the Ministry of the Colonies.

19. Only with the creation of a university in 1911 did women gain access to teaching positions in higher education, but always at lower levels, such as assistant professor, and with temporary appointments, not reaching any doctoral dissertation. By comparison, note the case of the UC, which in 1911 invited Carolina Michaëlis de Vasconcelos to teach, but also the absence of women in the first FLUP. Perhaps for that reason, when Leopoldina Ferreira Paulo scheduled her doctoral exams (for November 23, 1944, with the dissertation "Alguns caracteres morfológicos da mão dos portugueses"), it made the front pages of some morning papers in Porto: "At the University of Porto, a woman is going to obtain her doctoral degree in science, something unheard-of in our city's academic life" (*Jornal de Notícias*, November 21, 1944); "For the first time in the history of the University of Porto, a woman is subjected to doctoral exams in the Faculty of Science" (*O Comércio do Porto*, November 23, 1944). More recently, the journal *UPortoAlumni, Revista dos Antigos Alunos da Universidade do Porto*, dated June 2007, published in its inside cover a photo of Leopoldina Paulo, dated November 1944, with her insignias.

20. When he suggested the filiation of brown-skinned (*morenos*) dolicoids in the Cro-Magnon, Mendes Correia (1919:128–129) quoted the work of Aranzadi (*De Antropología de España*, 1915), who considered the idea debatable.

21. Born in 1869 in Czechoslovakia (now the Czech Republic), studied medicine in the United States, worked as a physical anthropologist in Paris, was the first curator of physical anthropology at the United States' National Museum, and founded the *American Journal of Physical Anthropology* in 1918.

22. The reference to Kobe (Japan) comes from SPAE's minute book. That is where he practiced medicine for several years before returning to Amsterdam in 1919.

23. The new correspondent members elected on this date were nominated by "foreign savants."

24. On October 24, 1932, he presented a conference at SPAE about eugenic politics that was published in the TAE (Kehl 1933).

25. At the former library of the Department of Zoology and Anthropology at FCUP, I found several books presented by Calmon to the library or to Mendes Correia, with signed dedications.

26. Director of the Musée Saint-Raymond and professor at the University of Toulouse, Cartailhac invited Portuguese researchers to his museum and put himself at the disposal of SPAE's comembers who wished to visit the archaeological stations in the south of France. According to the 1921 report, he was very well acquainted with Portugal, where he had worked in preparing his work *Les âges préhistoriques de l'Espagne et du Portugal* (Paris: Reinwald, 1886).

27. Bosch-Gimpera identified four relatively homogeneous cultural areas in the Iberian Peninsula, one of which corresponded to the Portuguese megalithic culture. He directed the archaeological school in Barcelona, with German influence.

28. On this date, Mendes Correia also proposed a vote of condolences and of protest for the assassination of Sidónio Pais, president of the Portuguese Republic (Livro de actas, vol. 1).

29. The physical anthropologist João Gualberto de Barros e Cunha (1865–1950) drafted the curriculum of the Colonial Ethnography Course at the UC in 1912–13.

30. Telesforo Aranzadi refused this invitation.

31. IV Session of the International Institute of Anthropology, Portugal, September 21–30, 1930, session on Portugal, third section.

32. *Ethnos: Revista dedicada al estudio y mejoramento de la población indígena de México* (although the journal's title varied) was published from 1920 to 1925.

33. Interest in the publication was expressed by Mendes Correia on April 19, 1919. After the publication, SPAE received feedback from people who might have better knowledge of the field (1920 report). António Maria de Freitas (from Lisbon) listed corrections to the *bailundo* vocabulary, and F. de Oliveira Santos (governor of Lunda) presented corrections to *quioco* words, recognizing, however, that the differences might have resulted from the fact that the terms had been collected in different regions.

34. Fonseca Cardoso (1865–1912) was considered "unfortunate" because he suffered an untimely death caused by malaria when he was performing military functions in Timor (a territory then under Portuguese colonial administration). During the time he was there, and in parallel to his military functions, he developed anthropological observations with a physical focus among the local populations. His work was influenced by

authors such as Rudolf Virchow and Paul Topinard, both doctors and physical anthropologists. It was Mendes Correia who elevated Fonseca Cardoso to the category of founder of "Portuguese colonial anthropology" and published some of his works after his death. However, Fonseca Cardoso already was a renowned anthropologist, since in 1908 he had directed the chapter "Portuguese Anthropology" in the *Notas sobre Portugal*, 1:58–72 (Vasconcelos 1928:16). This text, which included a map on Portuguese skeletons—brachycephalus and dolichocephalus—was his last anthropological work.

35. Terreiro do Paço is the square in Lisbon where the Portuguese government's ministries are located.

36. Artur Ricardo Jorge (1886–1975) was a doctor, a naturalist, and a politician, holding the office of minister for public education in 1926. He was son to the famous hygienist Ricardo de Almeida Jorge (1858–1939), who taught medicine and introduced into Portugal new public health concepts.

37. The lecturers were as follows: Bettencourt Ferreira (doctor, professor, and naturalist); Joaquim Rodrigues Santos Júnior; Pedro Victorino (doctor, historian, archaeologist, ethnographer, military, and art critic); Amândio Joaquim Tavares (doctor and investigator in the area of physical anthropology and anatomy); Constâncio de Mascarenhas (doctor's degree at FMUP in 1924 with the dissertation "As Castas da Índia: Esboço de estudo antropo-social"); Carlos de Passos (author of works on archaeology and art); and Joaquim Fontes.

38. Lecturers: Mendes Correia; Georges-Louis Dubreuil-Chambardel (French doctor and SPAE member); Bettencourt Ferreira; Irene Cândida de Melo Pestana (went to FCUP and worked on anthropological observations in schools); Alberto de Sousa (studied arterial anomalies); Ferreira Soares (studied anatomical and medical terminology); and Alfredo Athayde.

39. In 1925 lectures were presented by Mendes Correia, Artur de Magalhães Basto (historian), and Jaime Magalhães Lima (writer).

40. The main sources for generating figure 3 were the following: Livros de Actas da SPAE (vol. 1 from 1918 to 1924 and vol. 2 from 1925 to 1944) and Mendes Correia (1941a).

41. Light projections were projected and enlarged onto a wall or other surface, a precursor to projected slides, which also preceded cinematographical projection.

42. "A paleontologia e a origem do homem" in 1920; "Einstein e a evolução orgânica" (Mendes Correia 1923) in 1922; "A idade do ferro em Portu-

gal" in 1924; "O suposto homem terciário do Vale das Lages" (Mendes
Correia 1925b, 1926c, 1928) and "Os achados de Alvão" (Mendes Cor-
reia 1926b) in 1926; "A arte pré-histórica em Trás-os-Montes" (Mendes
Correia 1929) in 1928; "Crânios da necrópole pré-romana de Alcácer do
Sal" (Mendes Correia 1926a) in 1931; "As origens da cidade do Porto"
(Mendes Correia 1932, 1935b) in 1932; "Impressões e insculturas de
pés humanos pré-históricos," "O problema de Moron em Estrabão"
(Mendes Correia 1934b), "Os Belitanos de Artemidoro," "O problema
lígure em Portugal" (Mendes Correia 1934c), and "Sepulturas pré-
históricas de Alpiarça" (Mendes Correia 1935d) in 1934; "Estela antropo-
morfa do Monte do Rebolido, Entre-os-Rios" in 1935; "Duas novas estações pré-históricas portuguesas (Gandra e Paúl de Magos)" and "Novos
elementos sobre o homem dos sambaquis do Brasil" (Mendes Correia
1946) in 1936; "A estação eneolítica de Vila Nova de S. Pedro (Cartaxo)"
in 1937; "Novas estações líticas em Muge" (Mendes Correia 1940) and
"Novas pinturas do dólmen de Baltar" (Mendes Correia 1930) in 1938.
43. "Antropologia criminal integral" (Mendes Correia 1925a) in 1925; "Fórmulas e perfis individuais em Antropologia Criminal" (Mendes Correia
1935c) in 1933; "Novas directrizes de antropologia criminal" (Mendes
Correia 1931a, 1936a, 1936b, 1937a) in 1936.
44. "A identificação no Brasil e o desmemoriado de Collegno" in 1934;
"A etnogenia brasílica" (Mendes Correia 1935a) in 1935; "Conceitos
genéticos de constituição e raça" (Mendes Correia 1941b) in 1940.
45. "Montaigne e a Antropologia" (Mendes Correia 1934a) in 1933. Michel
de Montaigne (1533–72) was a pioneer in the notion of cultural relativism, stating that each person considers as barbarian all that is not common in his or her own land.
46. "Homenagem à memória de Dr. Rui de Serpa Pinto" (Mendes
Correia et al. 1934) in 1934.
47. Armando Leça is the pseudonym of the composer, folklorist, and ethnomusicologist Armando Lopes (1883–1977). He studied at the School of
Music of the National Conservatorium and taught piano and composition.
48. In fact, the author attributed here the name of a region to a human
group, but this issue was clarified in the discussion after his presentation.
49. Description presented at SPAE's annual general meeting on January 22, 1920.
50. Miscellaneous collections are hardback volumes composed of articles
written by individuals connected to the Porto School of Anthropology
and by other people (Portuguese and foreign) with whom works were

exchanged. The set is composed of sixty-six volumes, with approximately twenty to fifty texts each.

51. The list of the tables of contents of the TAE journal can be consulted in Figueiras (1981).

52. The majority of the works about Angola, published in the 1970s, were by Manuel Laranjeira Rodrigues de Areia, retired full professor of anthropology at UC.

53. *Trabalhos do I Congresso Nacional de Antropologia Colonial*, vols. 1 and 2, 1934.

54. Mendes Correia left Porto (and SPAE) due to his more extensive connections at the time to Lisbon, where he was a member of the National Assembly (1945–57); director of ESC (1946–58, ISEU after 1954); chairman of JMGIC (1946–59, JMGIU after 1951); and chairman of SGL (1951–60). However, Mendes Correia never completely cut his bonds with Porto until his death (1960), and he would be buried there.

55. Mendes Correia abandoned the position of secretary and became vice-chairman of SPAE from January 14, 1922, with Freitas Viegas remaining as chairman and Alfredo Athayde becoming the secretary.

56. http://spae.no.sapo.pt/serve.htm, accessed July 2014. SPAE has a blog, which is regularly updated, available at http://sociedadeportuguesaantropologia.blogspot.com/, accessed July 2014.

57. For more information on the Porto School of Anthropology, see Mendes Correia (1937b), Mendes Correia (1941a), and Guimarães (1995).

58. The Geological Commission was created in 1848 by the Royal Academy of Science. Only in 1918 would the Portuguese Geological Services be created; it was integrated in 1993 into the current Geological and Mining Institute.

59. School Nina Rodrigues in Brazil was contemporaneous to the Porto school. This school allows us to understand the concerns of its members (doctors and social scientists), its theoretical guidelines, and its relationships with the Brazilian society and state (Corrêa 1982; Corrêa, Willems, and Pierson 1987).

REFERENCES

Areia, M. L. Rodrigues de, and M. A. Tavares da Rocha. 1985. O ensino da antropologia. *In* Cem anos de antropologia em Coimbra, 1885–1985. IAUC, ed. Pp. 13–60. Coimbra: IAUC.

Athayde, Alfredo, and Carlos Teixeira. 1940. A necrópole e o esqueleto de S. Paio de Antas e o problema dos vasos de largo bordo horizontal. *In* Congressos do mundo português, vol. 1: Congresso da Pré e Proto-História de Portugal. Pp. 667–683. Lisbon: Comissão Executiva dos Centenários.

Barth, Fredrick, Andre Gingrich, Robert Parkin, and Sydel Silverman, eds. 2005. One Discipline, Four Ways: British, German, French, and American Anthropology. Chicago: University of Chicago Press.

Bosch-Gimpera, Pedro. 1928. O neo-eneolítico na Europa Ocidental e o problema da sua cronologia. Alfredo Athayde, trans. TAE 3(4):277–288.

Branco, Jorge Freitas. 1986. Cultura como ciência? Da consolidação do Discurso Antropológico à Institucionalização da Disciplina. Ler História 8:75–101.

Cardoso, Artur da Fonseca. 1919. Em terras de Moxico: Apontamentos de etnografia angolense. TAE 1(1):11–35.

Cartailhac, Emile. 1886. Les âges préhistoriques de l'Espagne et du Portugal. Paris: Reinwald.

Corrêa, Mariza 1982. As ilusões da liberdade: A escola Nina Rodrigues e a antropologia no Brasil. PhD dissertation, University of São Paulo, Brazil.

Corrêa, Mariza, Emilio Willems, and Donald Pierson. 1987. História da antropologia no Brasil (1930–1960): Testemunhos. Campinas: Editora da Universidade Estadual de Campinas.

Estatutos da Sociedade de Antropologia de Coimbra. 1899. Coimbra: Imprensa da Universidade.

Estatutos da Sociedade Portuguesa de Antropologia e Etnologia. 1918. Porto: SPAE.

Estatutos da Sociedade Portuguesa de Antropologia e Etnologia. 1924. Porto: SPAE.

Ferreira, Cláudio. 1932. Diferenciação das raças pelo sangue. *In* Memória apresentada ao XV Congresso Internacional de Antropologia e de Arqueologia Pré-Histórica IV Sessão do Instituto Internacional de Antropologia. Pp. 3–12. Lisbon: Imprensa Nacional.

Figueiras, Isilda. 1981. Contribuições para o Estudo da Antropologia Portuguesa: Índices: Vols. 1–10 (1914–81). Coimbra: IAUC.

Giuffrida-Ruggeri, Vincenzo. 1920. O problema eugénico segundo a moderna genética. TAE 1(2):70–77.

Guimarães, Gonçalves. 1995. A escola de antropologia do Porto e os estudos pré-históricos em Portugal. Revista de Ciências Históricas 10:59–78.

Handler, Richard. 2000. Boundaries and Transitions. *In* Excluded Ancestors, Inventible Traditions: Essays Toward a More Inclusive History of

Anthropology. Richard Handler, ed. History of Anthropology 9. Pp. 3–10. Madison: University of Wisconsin Press.

Júnior, Santos. 1969. O Professor Mendes Correia, fundador e 2.o presidente da Sociedade Portuguesa de Antropologia e Etnologia. Offprint of TAE 21(1–4):37–45.

Kehl, Renato. 1933. Política eugénica. TAE 6(1):5–20.

Kuklick, Henrika. 1991. The Savage Within: The Social History of British Anthropology, 1885–1945. Cambridge: Cambridge University Press.

Leal, João. 2000. Etnografias portuguesas (1870–1970): Cultura popular e identidade nacional. Lisbon: Dom Quixote.

——— . 2006. Antropologia em Portugal: Mestres, percursos, transições. Lisbon: Livros Horizonte.

Lima, J. A. Pires de, and Constâncio Mascarenhas. 1930. Contribuição para o estudo antropológico da Guiné Portuguesa. Offprint of XV Congrès International d'Anthropologie et d'Archéologie Préhistorique.

Livro de Actas da Sociedade Portuguesa de Antropologia e Etnologia, vol. 1, 1918–24. Manuscript, SPAE, Porto.

Livro de Actas da Sociedade Portuguesa de Antropologia e Etnologia, vol. 2, 1925–44. Manuscript, SPAE, Porto.

Magalhães, António Leite de. 1919. Subsídios para o estudo etnológico de Timor. TAE 1:37–65.

Martins, Rui de Sousa. 1976. A estação arqueológica da antiga Banza Quibaxe, Dembos, Angola. Contribuições para o Estudo da Antropologia Portuguesa 9(4):243–306.

Matos, Patrícia Ferraz de. 2013. The Colours of the Empire: Racialized Representations during Portuguese Colonialism. New York: Berghahn Books.

——— . 2014. Power and Identity: The Exhibition of Human Beings in the Portuguese Great Exhibitions. Identities: Global Studies in Culture and Power 21(2):202–218.

Mendes Correia, António Augusto Esteves. 1919. Raça e nacionalidade. Porto: Renascença Portuguesa.

——— . 1923. A propósito duma nota do "homo." Einstein e a Evolução Orgânica. Offprint of A Águia 22(7):1–7.

——— . 1925a. Antropologia criminal integral: O normal delinquente e a crise moral. Offprint of Boletim do Instituto de Criminologia (Lisbon) 5:1–25.

——— . 1925b. A sepultura neolítica do Vale das Lages e os "eólitos" de Ota. Butlletín de L'Associació Catalana d'Antropologia, Etnologia i Prehist (Barcelona) 3(2):117–146.

————. 1926a. Explorações arqueológicas em Alcácer do Sal. TAE 3(1):56–58.

————. 1926b. Glozel e Alvão: Os portugueses e a invenção do alfabeto. Offprint of TAE 3(2):1–26.

————. 1926c. O homem terciário em Portugal. Offprint of Lusitânia: Revista de Estudos Portugueses 3(9):1–16.

————. 1928. Nouvelles recherches sur l'homme tertiaire en Portugal. *In* Congrès d'Amsterdam: IIIe Session, 20–29 Septembre 1927. Pp. 1–5. Paris: Librairie E. Nourry.

————. 1929. Art rupestre en Traz-os-Montes (Portugal). 1.o Pétroglyphes de la Valée de l'Avelames. 2.o Le sanctuaire d'Outeiro Machado. Revue Archéologique publiée sous la direction de MM. E. Pottier et S. Reinach (membres de l'Institut). Pp. 121–136. Paris: Librairie Ernest Leroux.

————. 1930. As pinturas do dólmen do padrão (Vandoma). Offprint of O Archeólogo Português 27:1–11.

————. 1931a. A nova antropologia criminal. Porto: Imprensa Portuguesa.

————. 1931b. Sur quelques schémas de l'hérédité des groupes sanguins. Offprint of XVe Congrès International d'Anthropologie & d'Archéologie Préhistorique. Pp. 1–6. Paris: Librairie E. Nourry.

————. 1932. As origens da cidade do Porto. Gaia: Pátria.

————. 1934a. Montaigne e a antropologia. Coimbra: Coimbra Editora.

————. 1934b. Moron. Offprint of TAE 6(3):1–7.

————. 1934c. O problema lígure em Portugal. Offprint of TAE 6(3):1–8.

————. 1935a. A etnogenia brasílica. Offprint of Anais da Faculdade de Ciências do Porto 19:1–22.

————. 1935b (1932). As origens da cidade do Porto (Cale, Portucale e Porto). 2nd ed. Porto: Fernando Machado and C.a Editors.

————. 1935c. Fórmulas e perfis individuais na antropologia Criminal. Offprint of Arquivos de Medicina Legal e Identificação (Rio de Janeiro) 7:1–17.

————. 1935d. "Urnenfelder" de Alpiarça. Offprint of Anuario de Prehistoria Madrileña 4–6:131–138.

————. 1936a. La nuova antropologia criminale. Tancredi Gatti, trans. Offprint of Giustizia penale. Parte 1.a: I presupposti del diritto e della procedura penale (Città Di Castello) 1:1–35.

————. 1936b. La nuova e la vecchia antropologia criminale. Offprint of Giustizia penale. Parte 1.a: I presupposti del diritto e della procedura penale (Città Di Castello) 7:1–50.

————. 1937a. A nova e a velha antropologia criminal. Offprint of Arquivos de Medicina Legal e Identificação (Rio de Janeiro) 13:1–30.

————. 1937b. Os estudos de antropologia na Academia Politécnica do Porto (1888–1911). *In* O ensino na Academia Politécnica (1.o Centenário da Academia Politécnica e da Escola Médico-Cirúrgica do Porto). Pp. 1–12. Porto: Universidade do Porto.

————. 1940. Novas estações líticas em Muge. Offprint of Congressos do Mundo Português, vol. 1: Congresso da Pré e Proto-História de Portugal. Pp. 1–17. Lisbon.

————. 1941a. A Escola Antropológica Portuense. Lisbon: Bertrand.

————. 1941b. Conceitos genéticos de raça e de constituição (Actas do I Congresso Nacional de Ciências Naturais). Boletim da Sociedade Portuguesa de Ciências Naturais (Lisbon) 13(2):27–29.

————. 1946. Crânes des "sambaquis" du Brésil. L'Anthropologie 50 (1941–46): 331–364.

Mendes Correia, António Augusto Esteves, and Alfredo Athayde. 1930. Contribution à la craniologie d'Angola. Offprint of XV Congrès International d'Anthropologie et d'Archéologie Préhistorique.

————. 1931. Contribution à l'anthropologie de la Guinée portugaise (Actas do XV Congrès International d'Anthropologie et d'Archéologie Préhistorique). Pp. 1–3. Paris: Librairie E. Nourry.

Mendes Correia, António Augusto Esteves, José Vitorino da Costa, and Óscar Saturnino. 1934. Rui de Serpa Pinto. Offprint of Anais da Faculdade de Ciências do Porto 18:1–8.

Nunes, João Arriscado, and Maria Eduarda Gonçalves. 2001. Introdução. *In* Enteados de Galileu? A semiperiferia no sistema mundial da ciência. João Arriscado Nunes and Maria Eduarda Gonçalves, eds. Pp. 13–31. Porto: Afrontamento.

Oliveira, José Maria de. 1921. Fístula auris congénita. TAE 1(3):85–122.

Pereira, Rui. 1986. Antropologia aplicada na política colonial portuguesa do Estado Novo. Revista Internacional de Estudos Africanos 4–5:191–235.

————. 1998. Introdução. *In* Os macondes de Moçambique: Aspectos históricos e económicos, vol. 1. Jorge Dias, ed. Pp. v–lii. Lisbon: Comissão Nacional para as Comemorações dos Descobrimentos Portugueses and IICT.

Pina, Luís de. 1931. Les angles de la base du crâne chez les indigènes des colonies portugaises africaines. Offprint of XVe Congrès International d'Anthropologie et d'Archéologie Préhistorique. Ve Session de l'Institut International d'Anthropologie. Pp 1–3. Paris: Librairie E. Nourry.

Pina-Cabral, João de. 1991. Os contextos da antropologia. Lisbon: Difel.

Ranzmaier, Irene. 2011. The Anthropology Society in Vienna and the Academic Establishment of Anthropology in Austria, 1870–1930. Histories of Anthropology Annual 7:1–22.

Roque, Ricardo. 2001. Antropologia e império: Fonseca Cardoso e a expedição à Índia em 1895. Lisbon: ICS.

Santos, Gonçalo Duro dos. 2005. A Escola de Antropologia de Coimbra. 1885–1950: O que significa seguir uma regra científica? Lisbon: ICS.

Schouten, Maria Johanna. 2001. Antropologia e colonialismo em Timor português. Lusotopie 8(1–2):157–171.

Sobral, José Manuel. 2007. O outro aqui tão próximo: Jorge Dias e a redescoberta de Portugal pela antropologia portuguesa (anos 70–80 do século XX). Revista de História das Ideias 28:479–526.

Stocking, George W., Jr. 1968. Race, Culture and Evolution: Essays in the History of Anthropology. Chicago: University of Chicago Press.

———, ed. 1974. The Shaping of American Anthropology, 1883–1911: A Franz Boas Reader. New York: Basic Books.

———, ed. 1988. Bones, Bodies, Behaviour: Essays on Biological Anthropology. History of Anthropology 5. Madison: University of Wisconsin Press.

———. 1995. After Tylor: British Social Anthropology 1888–1951. London: Athlone Press.

Teixeira, Carlos. 1934. Medicina e superstições populares de Vieira. Offprint of TAE 6(4):1–40.

———. 1935a. O índice da secção dos cabelos nos Portugueses. Offprint of TAE 6(2–3):1–7.

———. 1935b. Um caso de polidactilia familial. Offprint of TAE 7(4):1–8.

———. 1935c. Um peso bizantino, inédito, de Braga. Offprint of Alto Minho 3:1–4.

———. 1936a. A periodicidade das funções genésicas humanas. Offprint of TAE 8(2):1–15.

———. 1936b. Subsídios para o estudo da Arqueologia Bracarense, vol. 1: O Monte de Castro. Porto: Imprensa Portuguesa.

———. 1936c. Um caso de polidactilia hereditária. Offprint of Anais da Faculdade de Ciências do Porto 20:1–8.

———. 1940. A mulher portuguesa e o seu papel bio-sociológico. Offprint of Congressos do Mundo Português: CNCP. Pp. 1–12. Porto: Imprensa Portuguesa.

———. 1964. Elogio histórico de A. A. Mendes Correia: Memórias da Academia das Ciências de Lisboa 1. Lisbon: ACL.

Trabalhos do I Congresso Nacional de Antropologia Colonial. 1934. Vols. 1 and 2. Porto: I Exposição Colonial Portuguesa.

UPortoAlumni. 2007. Revista dos antigos alunos da Universidade do Porto 1. Second series.

Vasconcelos, José Leite de. 1928. A antropologia portuguesa como fonte de investigação etnográfica. Boletim de Etnografia 4:1–19.

4

A View from the West

The Institute of Social Science and the Amazon

In this chapter I focus on the significance of frontier in the history of social anthropology, especially fieldwork in the Amazon supported by the Institute of Social Science (ISS) of the University of California at Berkeley (UCB). I understand that subventions for scholarly research in the western part of the United States resonate in the scientific field of moving-frontier theories. ISS supported projects on "economic and cultural boundaries," relocating to the social domain the former biological metaphor of botanical germination. This institute supported projects that went beyond domestic U.S. issues, embracing social problems in other countries such as Mexico and the Brazilian Amazon.

During the interwar years, the social sciences emerged as a legitimate field of knowledge in the United States because entrepreneurs employed social engineering and applied social sciences as a way of seeking economic alternatives and gaining greater social control. Thus, new scientific hierarchies were established and new demarcations of competence were made as a means of fulfilling this goal. Curt Uckel (1882–1945), a German-born travel explorer who arrived in Brazil in 1903, specialized in Brazilian indigenous knowledge, collecting their artifacts for European museums and collaborating with representatives of Brazilian Indigenous state policy. He naturalized himself in 1921 as a Brazilian with the name Curt Nimuendajú, the name the Apopokuva-Guarani Indians gave him when they adopted him in 1906 during his sojourn among them. However, his ethnography, improved by the dialogue with his Berkeley mentor, Robert Lowie, produced boundary objects that later led to the revision of concepts such as acculturation, social change, and cultural areas. He received ISS grants that helped defray his travel expenses. In reports he was classified as Lowie's assistant without actually being affiliated with the ICB.

BOUNDARY OBJECTS

Boundary objects are objects having "different meanings in different social worlds," but their structure is "common enough to more than one world to make them recognizable means of translation" (Star and Griesemer 1989:393). Their creation and management develop and maintain coherence across intersecting social worlds. Thus, boundary objects appear together with the delimitation of different unities of observation, implying contrast or condensation between different worldviews.

This formulation led to demarcating boundaries between scientific fields, established in disputes for monopolizing professional authority and control over resources by a group of scientists who also used this control to exclude others. However, historical constraints imply that these delimitations vary according to specific contexts, thus making such boundaries ambiguous and flexible (Gieryn 1983). The scientific field demarcates what it denominates as properly scientific, separating this from the unstructured spheres that escape understanding and academic control; these spheres are thus thrown into the margins of a structured production of knowledge.

The social division of labor between armchair inquiry and fieldwork is in the core of the production of anthropological knowledge. Recognized as a field science, this discipline was eventually embedded by colonialist routes (Kuklick and Kohler 1996; Kuklick 2008). Even though interacting with their subjects of research during ethnographic encounter, traveling explorers perhaps inadvertently prepared the terrain for social control even after colonial times. I deal here with the relationship between the ISS and Nimuendajú's field research in the Amazon. While sociocultural anthropology configured itself as a field of knowledge, Lowie advised Nimuendajú's ethnographic research, helping him revise his travel writings into the academically recognized structure of publishable monographs.

Boundary objects involve antinomies between theoretical and empirical science, objective and subjective, limited and unbound (Gieryn 1983). Moreover, boundary objects of knowledge such as Amazonian peoples and their artifacts have supported the break of the idea of cultural authenticity (Clifford 1938). In their border character, they showed themselves as a strong means of discussing and reformulating concepts. Even though these objects and concepts had appeared as strange particularities produced in unstructured political and scientific fields, the goal was clearly the organization of domains of knowledge articulated within power systems.

ANTHROPOLOGY IN THE INTERWAR YEARS AND THE ISSN

After moving to the United States, Franz Boas became entangled with the museum field's constraints (Jacknis 1996). Boas had constructed his historic-cultural approach as an alternative to evolutionary schemes, and he sought autonomy in the field of scholarly research and academic training (Stocking 1976). Although he had trained as a geographer, his intellectual trajectory in German thought led him to avoid biological determinism. Looking for particular anthropological evidences, Boas emphasized historical individuality in cultural contexts using an approach that favored the historical reconstruction of human variability. He believed that methodological unity between particular disciplines could provide documentation for such reconstruction. Boas and his students, including his Berkeley disciples, sought information about indigenous cultures in an as yet incompletely analyzed cultural area. Conquest and colonization of indigenous territories had changed American indigenous cultures. This led Boas and his disciples to consider the "acculturation" problem.

George W. Stocking Jr. (1976) analyzes the transformations in U.S. anthropology that occurred after philanthropic agencies began to support academic programs. In 1923 Rockefeller Foundation Social Sciences Programs began to finance the Social Science Research Council (SSRC). In 1924 the SSRC defined interracial relationships and scientific aspects of human migration among its main fields of knowledge. Philanthropic financing acquired an "interested" character, incorporating, together with the intervention of social scientists (and anthropologists), inquiries into sociocultural differences as part of a definition of human sciences research (Stocking 1985), despite primarily supporting physical anthropology and saving archaeological sites from devastation. Formerly, U.S. cultural anthropology had focused mainly on national territories without comparing indigenous groups in other American countries.

In their formative years, the social sciences were informed by British social anthropology, together with British colonial administration. Academic institutions adapted their research methodology in such a way as to serve British imperial purposes. This doesn't mean that ethical dilemmas didn't arise, but they did not disrupt domination practices, and scholarly programs accepted the colonial system as a historical given (Asad 1973). Stocking (1985:133) reiterates the relevance of discussing how Rockefeller ideology—as capitalist entrepreneurs representative of Western colonialism—determined anthropologists' research agendas. Political agency eventually intervened in this relationship, for instance, when New York State governor Franklin Delano Roosevelt integrated the SSRC Advisory Committee on Business Research in 1928.

The University of California at Berkeley became, in the first half of the twentieth century, a recognized center of scientific research in the United States. Philanthropic agencies supported scholarly research in the western United States as a response to the moving theoretical frontier, commonly used at the time. Frederick Jackson Turner ([1921] 1963) conceived his thesis about the democratic meaning of frontier in American society by analyzing colonizing movements, implying that the conquest and appropriation of land were factors in the U.S. nation-state's "westward expansion." Turner employed the idea of the frontier as a metaphor for national expansion. He characterized it as the "place where the spirit of the American Nation germinated" (Machado 1992). Machado saw in Turner's conception a biological metaphor for the social mechanism of national expansion, even though his work emphasizes that social problems created "moving frontiers," which could then be incorporated and controlled by governmental policies.

The ISS/UCB was founded in 1932 in an attempt to transform crises into opportunities during the Great Depression. In an August 30, 1932, meeting, the UCB formalized the ISS council program after Alfred Kroeber attended the 1931 meetings of the Social Science Research Council (SSRC). His participation at the SSRR and his relationship with representatives of the Rockefeller Foundation were strategic in obtaining the foundation's support for the type of fieldwork that was vital for promoting anthropological training at the UCB. However, the ISS had to obtain better local and institutional funding. The executive committee, composed of C. B. Lipman, H. E. Bolton, I. B. Cross, A. L. Kroeber, and P. O. Ray, established the program. The main purposes of the institute were summarized in appendix 2 of the 1930 meeting minutes.

> The Institute undertakes, therefore, not to plan research, but to make it more readily possible for the individual to carry on by establishing certain functions of association and cooperation:
>
> 1—to provide a clearing-house to which every student of the social sciences is invited to bring his results and his plans for consideration.
>
> 2—its own initiative to inquire at intervals into the character and status of research activities on the campus, as bearing on the field of the social sciences (p. 1).
>
> 3—to further the development of scientific methodology in the social studies in general, by constructive criticism.
>
> 4—to initiate studies in neglected and important fields, and especially to support the appointment of scholars therein.
>
> 5—to foster division of labor, or collaboration, with the purpose of avoiding duplication of work or misdirection of energy.
>
> 6—to aid the university as an organization to achieve a more symmetric development of scholarship and instruction (consideration of teaching load, administrative duties, research assistants, library facilities, and working quarters).
>
> 7—to scrutinize, select and budget specific projects as in need of immediate support, and to solicit funds, through and for the Board of research.[1]

The planning for the next six years determined that "the duty of the Council of the Institute is to determine the rules, procedures, and policies of the Institute, and to define in general terms the activities of the Institute, subject to the approval of the President and the Regents. The Executive Committee has the duty of administering the Institute in accordance with the policies determined by the Council."[2]

The ISS included several UCB social science departments, mainly in the fields of anthropology, geography, and history. The institute supported interdepartmental projects, notably a cooperative research project involving the anthropology, geography, and history departments on cultural frontiers and the "culture hearts [sic]" of the U.S. Southwest and Mexico.[3] During the meeting of the Council of the ISS held at the Faculty Club on Tuesday, August 30, 1932, its counselors considered the proposal for the Research Program to be conducted by the ISS. According to the minutes of this meeting, these research projects included a "cooperative research project involving the Departments of Anthropology, Geography, and History on culture frontiers and culture hearts of our southwestern states and Mexico." It would "require extensive travel and much assistance" and involve "subjects most timely owing to the fact that every year makes it more difficult to get authentic and original records." The program was designed to take place in Latin America and the United States in order to integrate socioeconomic trends and contemporary problems, creating "an obligation of present to future social scientists by documenting rural social change in a period of great flux."[4] Carl Sauer and John Leightly, both from the Department of Geography, were in charge of creating the program's "Memorandum on Marginal Lands of the Post-frontier and the Cultural Atlas of California."

Sauer (1889–1975) founded the field of cultural and historical geography, which was based on the historic-cultural paradigm promoted by Kroeber and Lowie in the Department of Anthropology. All of them had learned systemic social theory from their German American background, which was based on Romantic and historicist theories (Kenzer 1985; Anderson 2011). Sauer conceived of human geography as in close relationship to cultural anthropology; his regional analysis of area studies was based on comparative study, empirical fieldwork, and archival inventory. Sauer (1941) discussed the idea of cultural area centers, although he was more interested in understanding margins (borders), frontiers (national expansion), and boundary (limits) dynamics. His economic and cultural frontiers projects were inspired by moving frontier theories, even while criticizing them. Following Vaughan Cornish, Sauer believed that the active frontier, independently from continued territorial expansion, was based on the increasing massive energy of people breaking barriers and acting as social frontiers. However, he criticized the Turnerian conception of advancement of the development of productive forces in a series of stages. Distrusting unfounded generalizations, Sauer (1941) preferred to undertake a historical examination of singular situations and processes of acquisition and loss.

Working at museums, Kroeber based his references on natural science classification practices and aesthetic thinking applied to organizing exhibitions. He envisaged the possibility opened by social sciences of integrating different disciplinary fields into scholarly association within the university. These three fields of employment of anthropological work were related to its threefold affiliation with research councils existing in the United States: the National Research Council (physical anthropology and archaeology), the Social Science Research Council (ethnography and ethnology), and the American Council of Learned Societies (linguistics, art, and history) (Steward 1961).

Lowie's work, also interdisciplinary, shows his awareness of the comingling of anthropology and other fields. He was interested in biology, human geography, and history, understanding an economy in terms of property or ecology, and political sciences mainly for social control purposes, seeking "specific linkages between institutions and between fields of inquiry" (Dubois 1960:187). He undertook "one of the first syntheses attempted by the Boasians" (Stocking 1976:19), since Boas's resistance to systematic conceptualization made it difficult for his students to extract a theoretical basis from his work.

This integration of different departments working in the field of social sciences had been articulated with area-studies programs within the United States but extrapolating its internal scope to areas of Latin America, described in the iss foundation document as "terra incognita": "As to both nature and man, California is the terra incognita from which many problems of the Southwest, of Latin America, of the Pacific Margin as a whole are best approached. Also, it is only in California that academic institutions exist where one may recruit and consult a sufficient body of experts for comprehensive studies relating to the Pacific Hemisphere."[5]

The iss redefined its frame of action during World War II, whereas U.S. scientific institutions had been involved in organizing the anthropological field together with governmental and military agencies directly involved in the war effort. The ISS council meetings were held until 1946, when the social sciences went into decline and Latin American funds were retracted. During the meeting of the ISS council in October 1932, the counselors considered the Department of Anthropology project conducted by Kroeber and Lowie, advocating "intensification of ethnological research under way; extension to border-line problems involving psychology, statistics, geography, etc."[6] In this same year, the ISS incorporated economics, political sciences, psychology, and social institutions departments.

The ISS supported academically structured projects for selected scholars among its faculty members. Its goal was to provide for the fullest possible participation, irrespective of departmental lines, by scholars of Berkeley's faculty associated with the ISS. Approximately fifty professors in the diverse areas of the social sciences were involved in the institute. The ISS provided support for their research activities, including "clerical" and "expert assistance" research support, travel expenses, and so on. The council especially recommended that "younger males be privileged." Other criteria included favoring methodologies geared toward "gathering data by field observation and archival study," depending on the nature of the project proposed.[7] Among the graduate students supported by ISS was Julien Steward, who received one of these grants to do research in 1938 under Lowie's direction. This research resulted in his 1939 PhD dissertation. The ISS also supported Nimuendajú's travels, even though his research had no formal academic ties. Robert Lowie was interested in comparing North American and South American indigenous cultures, the latter considered as being less affected by contact with "civilization." Lowie collaborated with Nimuendajú, who conducted field research in the Amazon from 1935 to 1941 that was financed by ISS. In the ISS reports, Nimuendajú acted as Robert Lowie's assistant.[8]

MOVING TRAJECTORIES AND SHIFTING PARADIGMS

Usually, the image of indigenous groups sparks curiosity and images of exoticism, instigating anthropologists to learn more about them. Baron Erland Nordeskiöld, who had taught a course at the UCB in late 1926,

introduced Nimuendajú to Lowie. Nimuendajú also maintained correspondence with Boas about his knowledge of indigenous groups, and in
a letter dated December 15, 1932, he offered to sell to Boas his collection
of Apinayé material culture for $900. Boas replied that he wouldn't be
able to offer financial support for Nimuendajú's work despite its significance.[9] Boas sent Nimuendajú a telegram on March 3, 1933, asking if he
could "take along future party without interference of scientific work
cable collect [sic]."[10] Boas expressed in this telegram his disagreement
with Nimuendajú guaranteeing his subsistence during his sojourns to
the Amazon by collecting artifacts and then selling them to European
ethnographic museums, entrenched as they were in the international
market for material culture. This market was based on international
networks of diplomatic connections, which involved entangled relationships of material and symbolic exchange (Penny 2002:54). As a
foreign collector (he was born in Germany but was a naturalized Brazilian), Nimuendajú was subjected to Brazilian patrimonial policy,[11]
which imposed severe restrictions on his collecting during World War
II. He was constantly suspected of being involved in exploitive practices.

During World War II, nationalist representatives of the Brazilian
state had dealt with Nimuendajú as merely a "foreign explorer" who
collaborated with those museums of natural history and ethnography
seen as great collector entrepreneurs. The idea of defending Brazilian
national heritage meant evoking values associated with the ideology
of the nation-state in Brazil (1930–45) and the consecration of national
integrity, thus leading to consequent suspicion of foreigners. Using legal
means (Decreto-Lei 22.698), the Brazilian state established the right of
national scientific institutions to incorporate foreign collections with
the goal of protecting indigenous heritage, including their images. But
Nimuendajú had become a Brazilian citizen, and his contributions to
anthropological knowledge about social organization and the cultures
of specific indigenous groups in the Amazon were recognized by other
local anthropologists who admired his devotion to fieldwork.[12]

K. G. Izikowitz strongly recommended Nimuendajú's work to Boas
in a letter dated September 1934 so that he could produce the Handbook of South American Indians (HSAI).[13] In 1932 Lowie wanted to edit
the HSAI, since he was the chair at the Division of Anthropology and

Psychology for the National Research Council. However, the project failed (Faulhaber 2012), and in 1934 Lowie abandoned the project and enrolled Nimuendajú in his ISS project, following Izikowitz's suggestion. In 1935 Nimuendajú received $700 for fieldwork expenses. From 1936 to 1941 he received $1,200 a year. In 1942, however, the institute gave him just $300.

ISS funds were evaluated according to a productivity system based on whether or not the applicants held a doctorate. Since this was not Nimuendajú's project, Lowie filled out the forms in his own name, adding a justification explaining that the fieldwork in the Brazilian Amazon would be conducted by Curt Nimuendajú. Lowie then annexed bibliographic references attesting the academic recognition of Nimuendajú's works by landmark anthropologists such as Alfred Métraux and Lowie himself.[14] Lowie's 1939 report underlines the anthropological accuracy of Nimuendajú's writings, recognized by authors such as E. Nordeskiöld and A. Métraux.

The ethnographic richness of Nimuendajú's publications enabled Lowie and his Berkeley companions to consider a comparative approach with Amazonian and U.S. Native peoples. Lowie had never visited the Amazon, obtaining information for his comparisons through Nimuendajú (Lowie 1959), who worked under Lowie's instructions (Freed 1960:371). Lowie publicly recognized Nimuendajú's skills in producing extensive monographs about several of the less well known indigenous peoples; Lowie also helped Nimuendajú publish as sole author at the University of California (Nimuendajú 1946, 1952). Afterward Nimuendajú's status was upgraded from a specialized gatherer in the symbolic goods market selling indigenous artifacts to museums to a consecrated author in the ethnological field, therefore achieving entry into the scientific productivity system. In his preface to *Primitive Society*, Lowie states: "Nimuendajú in the interior of Brazil has revealed unsuspected institutions among the simpler New World natives" (1947:viii).

Born in Jena, Thuringia (Germany), Curt Nimuendajú was a naturalized Brazilian citizen and lived in the Amazon (Grupioni 1998; Welper 2002; Oliveira 2006). His conception of anthropology was closer to Lowie's than Sauer's, eventually building on the same German cultural provenance of Julian Steward, who after 1940 worked with the DEA and thus became involved in the U.S. expansionist project and the fight for cultural hegemony in the field of Americanist studies. When Steward began to work for the Smithsonian in 1940, he envisaged the possibility of using the resources of the U.S. Congress for creating cooperation with South American republics as part of the "good neighbor" policy. This possibility was the basis for his proposal for the SI in collaborative projects such as the Handbook of South American Indians (Faulhaber 2012) and the Institute of Social Anthropology (Faulhaber 2011), whose ethos I see as stemming from the ISS/UCB.

Besides gathering detailed information about South American Indians, a remarkable region from a strategic point of view, Steward's scientific enterprise had theoretical implications. Articulated with the empirical evidence of "cultural contact," his cultural change paradigm, dealing with the results of other researchers' intensive fieldwork in Mexico and Brazil, built bases for Steward's later theories on "cultural ecology," which contemplated an ecological interpretation of sociopolitical development (Stocking 1976:27; Steward 1955; Kerns 2003). Steward proposed a new evolutionary paradigm. However, he based his analysis on his hypothesis of the inevitable "integration of cultures as subcultures" (Steward 1955) in "developmental programs" adequate to market integration embedded in a network of local relationships.

HOW ETHNOGRAPHIC FIELDWORK
PUZZLED ANTHROPOLOGY

Institutions such as the ISS/UCB, the Rockefeller Foundation, and the Smithsonian Institution didn't envisage receiving the indigenous artifacts gathered by Nimuendajú; instead, they were sent to national and regional museums. However, the objects participated in the cultural appropriation of locally produced knowledge with recourse to ethnography promoting its international circulation. In his "Report on Snr Curt Nimuendajú's Investigation for the Institute of Social Sciences" (labeled "Pranch 6, 1939"), Lowie stated:

> One of the general results of Nimuendaju's work is that of exploding the traditional scheme of Brazilian ethnography, which turns out to be far too simple. There are not merely two strata, a primi-

tive Gê and a more advanced Tupi' culture, with the latter passing on fragments of its inventory to the ruder stock. This is definitely refuted by Nimuendaju's observations on the pottery of the simpler groups, which is consistently different from the Tupi' type. The indications are that Eastern Brazil had a distinctive culture heart, largely associated with the cariri family, and representing an intermediate level of sophistication: its bearers planted cotton and sweet potatoes, made plain earthenware, and practiced the above-mentioned cult. It is from this focus rather than from a Tupi' or Arawak center that those Gê who have taken up agriculture and ceramics seem to have received influence. . . .

In the Handbook of Latin American Studies (Ed. Lewis Hanke), Cambridge: Harvard University Press, 1938, Métraux writes: "Only two brief résumés on N.'s extensive reports were published last year, but they mark a turning point in our conception of primitive cultures in South America." (1938)

The Handbook concisely summarizes these articles on page 44.

Lowie recognized as well the accuracy of Nimuendajú's criticism on Tukuna linguistic affiliation to the Aruak language, as previously stated by Paul Rivet. In a letter from Nimuendajú to Lowie from August 9, 1942, Nimuendajú explained that he had stated this in his monograph on the Tukuna Indians (Nimuendajú 1952). The fact that the ISS changed part of its research approach to focus on Latin America explains why Nimuendajú recovered in the 1940s his Tukuna ethnography, which he had begun in 1929 while traveling in collaboration with the SPI (Brazilian State Service for Indigenous Protection) to work among this indigenous group, which lived on the triple border between the Brazilian, Colombian, and Peruvian Amazon. His work, produced from direct interaction with indigenous groups, showed their ethnic singularity and also described how they maintained their cultural uniqueness, despite having contact with nonnative groups. His ethnography had not entirely corresponded with the way those Indians were seen by European and U.S. Americanists.[15] Although Nimuendajú lamented that such Indians had changed their previous customs, he believed that knowledge about so-called deculturated Indians had great significance for ethnology.[16]

Nimuendajú's letters show that besides trying to better understand indigenous mythology and cosmology, he had also been seeking to ethically document their thought; he claimed that his translation work depended on his empathetic relationship with the peoples whom he researched. He wrote to Carlos Estevão, his friend and director of the Goeldi (Amazonian) Museum, that his desire to work with "decently dressed" Indians like the Ticuna "came from the need to save what could yet be saved" (Nimuendajú 2000:291). Although Nimuendajú lamented that they had changed their previous customs, he believed that knowledge about deculturated Indians was also important for ethnology.[17]

Nimuendajú aimed to reconstitute the mythology and cosmology of specific peoples such as the Tukuna, even though the individuals he met affirmed that they had ceased to practice the old rituals in the ways prescribed by their elders, even though they still remembered their old myths. Nimuendajú complained that he could only find fragments of a mixed cosmology without "original characteristics." Although without producing theoretical concepts refuting acculturation theories, he showed in his writings that even though indigenous cultures and mythologies had been modified by their subordination, accommodation, or adaptation to the relationships imposed by the encompassing societies (Oliveira 2006), their cultures had not entirely disappeared, as previewed in the memorandum (Redfield, Linton, and Herskovits 1936).

The limits of the adequacy of the analysis of the Amazonian Indians to the cultural area notion conceived in the interwar years may be attributed to its baseless general approach. Direct-observation inquiries into specific indigenous peoples came to invalidate generic categories such as "marginal peoples" (Lévi-Strauss 1964). Eduardo Galvão, who knew Nimuendajú in the last days of his life, used his monographs to redefine the concept of cultural areas according to regional criteria, considering the contact between different indigenous peoples and between them and national societies (Galvão 1967; Oliveira 2001). Following Nimuendajú, the question went beyond great theories or discussing the consequences of cultural change. Ulterior approaches were founded on the definition of ethnographic areas (Melatti 2001:7) and based on temporal, linguistic, and environmental criteria. The researcher's interference in delimiting the object became crucial for its definition.

CONCLUSION

I dealt in this chapter with the significance of frontier in projects supported by the ISS/UCB. The ISS/ICB itself was a boundary object for the Social Science Research Council and the Rockefeller Foundation. During the Great Depression, support for social sciences was a way of incorporating and controlling disciplines that claimed autonomy. Founded at a university in the west of the country, this institute dealt with the social "frontiers of knowledge" in areas on the border of the nation-state.

Indirectly supported by the ISS as Lowie's assistant, Curt Nimuendajú's status was upgraded from a specialized supplier of indigenous artifacts for European museums to a researcher having academic legitimacy. Without appropriating indigenous artifacts, the ISS appropriated writings about Amazonian Indians in the context of an academically controlled research project. In this case, the ethnographic knowledge itself was a boundary object. Meanwhile, this kind of knowledge remained outside of the territory established, yet science expected to incorporate it. Moreover, it contributed to modify ways of thought on acculturation, area studies, and social change. Nimuendajú showed that records on Indians in situations of contact and on their living culture were more relevant for anthropological analysis as transforming subjects than essentializing the "lost culture."

Nimuendajú had access to anthropological publications that his colleagues from Europe and the United States sent him. He managed with skill, accuracy, and aplomb social organization analysis, which he had learned through his correspondence with Lowie. The fact that actual indigenous cultures had persisted despite the virulence of colonizers—in the terms of his observations—shows the inaccuracy of the idea that indigenous social relations were inserted in evolutionary chains and that their cultures could be absorbed as "subcultures" into national societies. Amazonian records contributed to the breakdown of the essentialist foundation of the cultural area concept. The social actors themselves were seen as able to reappropriate their destinies from the regional museums, putting into question the idea that the explanation of museum exhibitions might uncritically follow theories conceived overseas. General categories, such as the Ge tribe's characterization based on "marginal tribes," lost sense. Analyses founded on historic and geographic records seemed more convincing. The anthropological commitment, together with the dialogue with native agency, became seriously considered as boundary objects.

NOTES

A preliminary version of this chapter was presented in the panel "Histories and Legacies of Berkeley Anthropology," organized by Sergei Kan and Ira Jacknis (American Anthropological Association Meeting, 2012). I would like to thank Ira Jacknis as well for the invitation to do research at UCB in November 2010.

1. December 5, 1930, meeting document, Records of the Department of Anthropology, CU 23, University Archives, Bancroft Library, University of California, Berkeley.
2. Program established with the foundation of the ISS after the nomination of its executive board. "Appendix to the General Statement of the ISS Research Program," as formulated in October 1932. It described the ISS goals and presented a "series of representative projects in progress" (unpaginated document, CU 23, p. 1).
3. On December 5, 1930, the ISS committee approved a collaborative project titled "Culture Frontiers and 'Culture Hearts' in the Southwest of Mexico." The committee later suggested that the project's name be changed to "Culture Frontiers and Culture Hearths of the Southwest and Latin America" (ISS/ICB folder, CU 23, unnumbered typed sheet, p. 1).
4. Program established with the foundation of the ISS, with the nomination of its executive board, appendix 1, p. 2.
5. Appendix 2, "Preferential Research Program of the Institute of Social Sciences University of California," ISS foundation document, ISS folder, CU 23, p. 4. Metraux evoked this same characterization of the region as "terra incognita," lacking really intensive anthropological inquiry involving cultural translation, when he wrote to Boas about his intent to move from Polynesia back to South America (Metraux to Boas, December 9, 1936, Boas Professional Papers, Getty Museum Archive, Los Angeles, hereafter cited as BPP).

6. Appendix 2, "Preferential Research Program."
7. ISS folder, CU 23, unnumbered typed sheet.
8. Objectives: intensification of ethnological research under way; extension to border-line problems involving psychology, statistics, geography, etc.

Since 1901, the Department of Anthropology has carried on systematic field investigations, especially in ethnology, also in archaeology and linguistics. This work has centered in California and for many years has been largely restricted to this area on account of economy of prosecution. . . .

The program hear outlined bases on this accomplished work but proposes its extension and deepening as follows:

Areal extension, especially to adjacent regions, to allow the attack of problems insoluble by locally restricted area.

Fuller application of points of view other than the standard descriptive-ethnographic one. For instance, "functional" analyses of selected tribal culture, where still possible; studies of attitudes of craftsmen toward their craft; processes of growth in organized and of adaptation in unorganized native religions, etc.

Problems in border-line fields such as, on the side of psychology, normal personality differentiation in native cultures; messianic cult waves; speech learning by Indian children. Methodological: controlled test studies on the value of statistics in ethnographic definition; cyclical developments; relation of types of kinship systems to types of society. Also certain studies verging into geography, demography, and ethnobotany.

The group of investigations is conceived not as a series of adventures into new terrain but as the additional sowing of new crops in the well-tilled field of native Californian anthropology (ISS folder, CU 23).
9. "I am sorry to hear that you do not see any way of continuing your valuable ethnological work. I wish you would be good enough to let me know as soon as you can how much money will enable you to continue. I have nothing to offer at the present moment but there are certain negotiations under way that might perhaps, in the not too distant future, lead to support of work, particularly in South America" (Boas to Nimuendajú, January 8, 1933, BPP).
10. Telegram, March 3, 1933, BPP. I believe that here Boas is trying to say to Nimuendajú that he is seeking scholarly research autonomy from the colonial field of indigenous material-culture appropriation.
11. As stated by a large collection of manuscripts deposited at the archive of the Conselho de Fiscalização das Expedições Artísticas e Científicas no Brasil (Brazilian Council for Inspection of Artistic and Scientific

Expeditions in Brazil, deposited at the Mast/MCT/Brazil). Nimuendajú took many photographs of indigenous peoples (Soares 2010); they were sold together with his personal archive by his widow to the Brazilian Museu Nacional of Rio de Janeiro, where they are still stored.

12. In a letter to Boas (March 27, 1933), Nimuendajú explained that he was not merely a collector, thus exposing his unhappiness with the interference of filmmakers who documented indigenous Indian culture: he felt they were more preoccupied with the public presentation of these peoples than with actual information about their real lives and culture. Moreover, Nimuendajú saw these groups as being endangered by attacks of "neobrazilians." In another letter (December 15, 1933), Nimuendajú noted that he had been accused of being a Nazi spy. Even though his original nationality was the apparent cause of these persecutions, agents in charge of indigenous policies in Brazil felt threatened by the results of his work on Indian self-esteem. Nimuendajú sketched out his main ethnographic concerns regarding the Kamkomekra in order to obtain funding necessary to support his work. He gave detailed information about the "decay" of a number of indigenous groups, noting, for instance, that the Apinayés were reduced from 273 to just 80 members and had been suffering from diseases introduced by Europeans. The Kraó were also disappearing through their union with Afro-Brazilian groups (BPP). I would like to thank Willi Bolle for translating and commenting on the German letters.

13. Izikowitz lost his position, persecuted by Nazi forces in 1934, and wrote to Lowie that he felt that Nimuendajú would be the most qualified person to edit the Brazilian part of the HSAI. Lowie consigned a number of Nimuendajú manuscripts to archaeologist John Rowe, who kept them as private archives. His widow, Patricia Lyon, kindly allowed me to copy those documents.

14. Application for research grant from funds of the Institute of Social Sciences, University of California, sent by Robert Lowie, March 6, 1941, JRA.

15. In a letter to the director of the Museu Nacional, Heloisa Alberto Torres, Boas evaluated Nimuendajú, stating that he was "evidently an excellent student of ethnology, even though he also (compared to Charles Wagley) lacked linguistic training" (January 20, 1941, BPP).

16. In a June 1933 letter to Jules Blumensohn, introduced to Nimuendajú by Franz Boas, the German Brazilian ethnographer stated, "I myself take rather more results from my studies among the deculturated Apapokúva-Guarany, who were thought to be completely known, than

from the contacts such as being the first civilized man to deal with the Kawahiwa-Parintintin, as when I had a hand in their pacification in 1922" (BPP).

17. Nimuendajú was baffled by indigenous groups whose customs differed from what he considered to be their "original" customs. He wrote to Carlos Estevão that the Ticuna Indians were very "deculturated" (Nimuendajú 2000:143). He also stated that in 1929 he could only find "remnants" of the Mura Indians, which were of no ethnographic value (Nimuendajú 2000:94). His bafflement, I suppose, was conditioned by his being primarily a collector. However, as a representative of the Brazilian indigenous policy apparatus, Nimuendajú translated indigenous claims into national policies in favor of indigenous citizenship. This professional compromise often created conflicts with local merchants who subjugated Amazon peoples by way of indentured servitude, as happened during work among the Ticuna. His presence there incited the Ticuna to stand up to the merchants who exploited them. These merchants, afraid of losing control over "their" Indians, felt threatened by Nimuendajú's presence (for further information, see page 81 of the Portuguese manuscript sent to the Handbook of South American Indians, 82 pages, 1943, Museu Nacional Arquive, Belém).

REFERENCES

Anderson, Ryan. 2011. Franz Boas: Geographer/Anthropologist. Anthropologies: A Collaborative Online Project.

Asad, T., ed. 1973. Anthropology & the Colonial Encounter. Ithaca NY: Cornell University Press.

Clifford, James. 1988. The Predicament of Culture: Twentieth-Century Ethnography, Literature, and Art. Cambridge MA: Harvard University Press.

Du Bois, Cora, ed. 1960. Lowie's Selected Papers in Anthropology. Berkeley: University of California Press.

Faria, Luís de Castro. 1981. Curt Nimuendajú. In Mapa etno-histórico de Curt Nimuendajú. Pp. 17–22. Rio de Janeiro: IBGE.

———. 2000. Introdução. In Inventário Sumário-Conselho de Fiscalização das Expedições Artísticas e Científicas no Brasil. Pp. 7–13. Rio de Janeiro: MAST.

Faulhaber, Priscila. 2001. O Instituto de Antropologia Social (EUA, Brasil e México): Um artefato da resposta antropológica ao "esforço de guerra." Revista Mana 17(May):9–39.

Freed, R. S. 1960. Robert H. Lowie, Ethnologist: A Personal Record. Social Forces 38(4):371.

Galvão, Eduardo. 1967. Indigenous Culture Areas of Brazil (1900–1959). *In* Indians of Brazil in the Twentieth Century. Janice H. Hopper, ed. and trans. Pp. 167–205. Washington DC: Institute for Cross Cultural Research.

Gieryn, T. F. 1983. Boundary-Work and the Demarcation of Science from Non-science: Strains and Interests in Professional Ideologies of Scientists. American Sociological Review 48(6):781–795.

Grupioni, Luís Donisete. 1998. Coleções e expedições vigiadas: Os etnólogos no Conselho de Fiscalização das Expedições Artísticas e Científicas no Brasil. São Paulo: ANPOCS/HUCITEC.

Jacknis, Ira. 1996. The Ethnographic Object and the Object of Ethnology in the Early Career of Franz Boas. *In* Volksgeist as Method and Ethics: Essays on Boasian Ethnography and the German Anthropological Tradition. George W. Stocking Jr. ed. Pp. 185–214. HOA 8. Madison: University of Wisconsin Press.

Kenzer, Martin S. 1985. The Making of Carl O. Sauer and the Berkeley School of Historical Geography. Open Access dissertation and theses. Paper 1083. http://DigitalCommons@master.Ca/opensdissertation /1083.

Kerns, Virginia. 2003. Scenes from the High Desert: Julian Steward's Life and Theory. Urbana: University of Illinois Press.

Kuklick, Henrika. 2008. Introduction. *In* A New History of Anthropology. Pp. 1–18. London: Blackwell.

Kuklick, Henrika, and Robert E. Kohler, eds. 1996. Introduction. OSIRIS: Science in the Field, 2nd ser., 11:1–14.

Lévi-Strauss, Claude. 1964. Le cru et le cuit: Mythologiques. Paris: Plon.

Lowie, Robert. 1939 Report on Snr Curt Nimuendaju's investigation for the Institute of Social Sciences Berkeley. Manuscript.

———. 1947. Primitive Society. New York: Liveright.

———. 1959. Field Work in Absentia. *In* Ethnologist: A Personal Record. Berkeley: University of California Press.

Machado, Lia Osório. 1992. A fronteira agrícola na Amazônia brasileira. Revista Brasileira de Geografia 54(2):27–55.

Melatti, Júlio Cezar. 2011. Por que áreas etnográficas? *In* Áreas etnográficas da América Indígena. Júlio Cezar Melatti, ed. Pp. 1–10.

Nimuendajú, Curt. 1946. The Eastern Timbira. University of California

Publications in American Archaeology and Ethnology 41. Berkeley: University of California Press.

———. 1952. The Tukuna. University of California Publications in American Archaeology and Ethnology 45. Berkeley: University of California Press.

Oliveira, João Pacheco. 2001. Galvão e os estudos de aculturação no Brasil: Ou "santo de casa também pode fazer milagres." *In* Conhecimento e fronteira: História da ciência na Amazônia. Priscila Faulhaber and Peter Man de Toledo, eds. Belém: Museu Goeldi / Paralelo 15.

———. 2006. Curt Nimuendajú et la configuration de l'ethnologie au Bresil. *In* ESSE: Actes du colloque rapports ambivalents entre sciences sociales euro péenes et américaines. Pp. 165–197. Milan: Arcipelago Edizioni.

Penny, H. Glenn. 2002. Ethnology and Ethnographic Museums in Imperial Germany. Chapel Hill: University of North Carolina Press.

Redfield, Robert, Ralph Linton, and Melville J. Herskowitz. 1936. Memorandum for the Study of Acculturation. American Anthropologist 38:149–152.

Sauer, Carl. 1941. Foreword to Historical Geography. Annals of the Association of American Geographers 31(1):1–24.

Soares, Marilia Faco. 2010. Indios do Brasil e o olhar de Curt Nimuendajú. DVD. Rio de Janeiro: Museu Nacional.

Star, Susan L., and James R. Griesemer. 1989. Institutional Ecology, "Translations" and Boundary Objects: Amateurs and Professionals in Berkeley's Museum of Vertebrate Zoology. Social Studies of Science 19:387–420.

Steward, Julian H. 1955. Theory of Culture Change. Urbana: University of Illinois Press.

———. 1961. Alfred Louis Kroeber 1876–1960. Obituary. American Anthropologist, n.s. 63:1038–1087.

Stocking, G. W., Jr. 1976. Introduction: Thoughts toward a History of the Interwar Years. *In* American Anthropology, 1921–1945. G. W. Stocking Jr., ed. Pp. 1–74. Lincoln: University of Nebraska Press.

———. 1985. Philantropoids and Vanishing Cultures: Rockefeller Funding and the End of the Museum Era in Anglo-American Anthropology. *In* Objects and Others: Essays on Museums and Material Culture. G. W. Stocking Jr., ed. Pp. 112–145. Madison: University of Wisconsin Press.

———. 2001. Delimiting Anthropology: Occasional Inquiries and Reflections. Madison: University of Wisconsin Press.

Turner, F. J. 1963. The Frontier in American History. New York: Holt, Rinehart & Winston.

Weinstein, Barbara. 2007. Modernidade tropical: Visões norte-americanas da Amazônia nas vésperas da Guerra Fria. Revista do IEB 45:153–176.

Welper, Elena Monteiro. 2002. Curt Unkel Nimuendajú: Um capítulo alemão na tradição etnográfica brasileira. PhD dissertation, Mestrado—Museu Nacional / PPGAS / UFRJ.

5

Scientific Diplomacy and the Establishment of an Australian Chair of Anthropology, 1914–25

During the first decades of the twentieth century, Australian scientists, supported by their British counterparts, worked to convince the recently formed (1901) Commonwealth government of Australia, a federation of the states and territories,[1] of the value of anthropology. They argued that it had value as an academic discipline for two reasons: first, it sought to ascertain the laws of human sociality and origins, and second, it would be useful in training colonial field officials (Kuper 1996; Kuklick 1991; Stocking 1995). To this end they argued for the establishment of a chair of anthropology in an Australian university. It was a time of rising nationalism, pride, and a sense of Australian uniqueness, an Antipodean Briton; the crimson bonds of kinship with Britain were not severed, but there was a call to "let us be Australians: Big Australians first, and all the time" (Cole 1971; see also Anderson 2002:11–40).[2]

While anthropology in Australia was generally concerned with tracing origins and seeing the indigenous inhabitants as examples of early mankind, British anthropologists had expressed the need to institutionalize anthropology for imperial ends (Quiggin 1942:117). In Australia's sole colony, Papua, administered by Australia from 1906, J. H. P. Murray, the jurist and soon to be lieutenant-governor of Papua, was first introduced to "this very fascinating science" of anthropology at the beginning of his Papuan career through the established anthropologists of the time, particularly A. C. Haddon, C. G. Seligman, and R. R. Marett.[3] Murray accompanied Seligman on his "rounds of investigation in the Port Moresby villages" (Stocking 1995:251). Nevertheless, anthropology, he wrote to his brother Gilbert, a classical scholar at Oxford, "is purely fantastic; the alleged facts being unsupported by evidence, and the inferences forced."[4] In spite of this view, anthropology and anthropologists "became tools to be harnessed by Murray in achieving his aim of being considered a paragon of the colonial administrator" (Griffiths 1977:5).

At the 1911 meeting of the Australasian Association for the Advancement of Science (AAAS), "Aboriginal welfare [as] a matter of serious debate" was raised for the first time (Mulvaney 1988:203). The following year, Herbert Basedow (a medical doctor) and Baldwin Spencer (professor of biology at the University of Melbourne) were appointed, respectively, protectors of Aborigines in the Northern Territory to assist in the administration of Aboriginal people and help define the problems and provide solutions. Neither appointment was successful in halting depopulation and preserving the indigenous population, which were the critical issues of the day (Mulvaney 1988:205; McGregor 1997:71–86). There was even an attempt by the University of Melbourne to obtain funding from the Australian government to be used by the "departments of anthropology (the science of the structure and functions of the human body) in the various universities of Australia," which would be linked up with the Tropical Diseases Institute at Townsville.[5] At the same time Murray was casting around for a government anthropologist, an appointment he did not make until 1920 (West 1968:204–235).[6]

During this period some major ethnographic studies were published in Australia. Among them were studies by W. E. Roth, a medical practitioner; Erhard Eylmann, a German ethnographer; Carl Strehlow, a Lutheran missionary; and R. H. Mathews, a surveyor. Baldwin Spencer and Francis Gillen published *The Native Tribes of Central Australia* (1899), and it attracted considerable interest. There were major scientific expeditions, such as the Haddon-led Cambridge Anthropological expedition to the Torres Strait Islands in 1898 and the Oxford Anthropological Expedition led by A. R. Radcliffe-Brown. This spate of research and publications stimulated great interest in Europe, especially among British anthropologists and scientists.

Concerted calls for a chair of anthropology in an Australian university began with the eighty-fourth meeting of the British Association for Advancement of Science (BAAS) held in Sydney, Melbourne, and Adelaide in 1914 (MacLeod 1988).[7] This meeting signaled a more specific and direct interest in the development of anthropology as a university subject.[8] It was proposed that a committee be appointed to examine how the teaching of anthropology could be extended in the British white dominions of Australia, New Zealand, and South Africa (Hammond-Tooke 1997:20–25). It also urged that the vanishing tribes of Australia should be studied "before it was too late" (Elkin 1970:10; Mulvaney 1988:204). The meeting was interrupted by the declaration of war and the advent of World War I.

This chapter traces the events and arguments put forward that led to the establishment of a chair of anthropology at the University of Sydney and reexamines the role of the Australian National Research Council (ANRC) and that of the Rockefeller Foundation. It challenges the conclusions of previous writers such as A. P. Elkin, who claimed that the London University anatomist Elliot Grafton Smith was "the key figure" in the establishment of the chair (1970:12; see also Blunt 1988), and J. H. P. Murray, who claimed it was "largely through the persistent efforts of the Papuan Government, [that] a Chair of Anthropology has been established at the University of Sydney" (1929:9–10).[9] Others elevate the role of the Cambridge University zoologist and anthropologist A. C. Haddon: "We owe it to you," claimed David Orme Masson, president of the ANRC and Bronislaw Malinowski's father-in-law (Mulvaney 1988:220). The twenty-third Pan Pacific Science Congress was a key event at this time: "Success arose from the standing of the Pacific Science Congress . . . and the calibre of the individual scientists concerned," men concerned "almost solely with the natural sciences, and . . . a Research Council whose members were physical and biological scientists" (Elkin 1958:230–231). In short, the emphasis was on Australian-British connections and a home-grown nationalist push.

Building on earlier scholarship (Elkin 1958, 1970; Mulvaney 1988; Peterson 1990; Campbell 1998), this chapter underlines not only the importance of the ANRC but also the overlooked role of Edwin Embree, head of the Rockefeller Foundation's Division of Studies between 1923 and 1927, and his efforts in convincing the foundation, incorporated in 1913 with the purpose to promote the well-being of mankind throughout the world, to fund Australian anthropological research and a chair of anthropology at an Australian university.[10] Moreover, it was the ANRC that successfully pressed the idea of a chair of anthropology with the Australian government, obtained the necessary funding from both the Australian and state governments, and negotiated funding from the Rockefeller Foundation with the support of Embree in particular. Financial support from the Australian government was unusual, as it was not at that time involved in university education, which was a matter for the states. Moreover, the proposal to fund a chair could be explained to the public as a government "anxious to do everything possible to improve the lot of aboriginals generally."[11] On the other hand, commentators like Elkin stressed "the value of anthropology to the administration of Papua and New Guinea" as a primary factor in the decision to fund a chair (Elkin 1970:264).

I

The ANRC, formed in 1919, was Australia's link with the International Research Council, founded in 1918 in London, and other international scientific institutions. Its membership, limited to one hundred leading scientists and fifty associates representing eighteen scientific disciplines, made it an influential body with the Australian government. Of the twenty-eight men on the council's executive board, "twenty-five were university scientists, and eighteen of them professors— virtually the whole intellectual establishment of the country's five universities" (MacLeod 1988:60–61; see also Elkin 1970:11; Lewis 1979; Jonas 1989:144–161). It was inaugurated at the 1921 AAAS conference after an interim existence since 1919 (AAAS 1921). At this meeting, under the general presidency of Baldwin Spencer and Section F (Ethnology and Anthropology) under the presidency of Murray, it was resolved:

1. That there be urged on the Federal Government the need for the formation of a Federal Museum of Australia and its Territories, and the immediate necessity for securing specimens, historical and ethnological, while they are yet available.
2. That there be urged upon the Federal Government the need

for endowment of a chair in Anthropology, especially in view of its value in the Government of subject races.

3. That there be ... notice of ... the desirability of at once investigating and recording the Ethnology of the Northern part of Western Australia. (AAAS 1921:xxxiii)

The last resolution demonstrated the influence of Spencer, who concluded his presidential address by emphasizing Australia's duty "to study carefully and [as] intensively as possible" the culture of Aborigines, because, "amongst other reasons, they would be virtually extinct in a comparatively short time and any surviving remnants would have lost all knowledge of their original habits and customs" (Elkin 1970:11; also McGregor 1997). It was a common view that northwestern Australia contained the few remaining tribes that maintained a culture that was comparatively uninfluenced by contact with "civilisation" (Gray 1997). The second resolution glances toward the new international responsibilities of Australia as a trustee nation of the League of Nations in its administration of the mandate territory of New Guinea, resulting from the defeat of Germany. Significantly, the ANRC supported the need for "the endowment of systematic scientific research in the Pacific Islands under Australian Control."[12] The first resolution underlines the notion of "before it's too late," which became the driving motive for recovering and recording the cultural practices of Aboriginal people destined to fade away. It was a commonly held belief that Aboriginal men "over middle age," about fifty-five, were best placed to have information about the law, as they were fully initiated (Gray 1997).

At the urging of the ANRC, the 1923 Pan Pacific Science Congress was held in Melbourne and Sydney. Alfred Cort Haddon chaired the anthropology section. Haddon, reader in anthropology at Cambridge University, was the preeminent British anthropologist in the first two decades of the twentieth century due in part to his leadership of the Cambridge expedition to Torres Strait in 1898 (Rouse 1998). He tirelessly promoted the importance of anthropological knowledge and its application for the governance of colonized peoples, as well as the establishment of academic anthropology in the British dominions, particularly South Africa and Australia (Bolger 1977; Gray 2003). He played a key role in the first dominion chair of anthropology at Cape Town, South Africa, in 1921 (Hammond-Tooke 1997:1–38; Stocking 1995:323–339; Quiggin 1942).[13]

The Science Congress supported the endowment of a chair to train field officers and others for work in the Australian colonies (called territories by Australia) and to engage in research. Suggestions for research priorities were received from such luminaries as James Frazer, Malinowski, Seligman, and Grafton Elliot Smith; these suggestions underlined the value of enlisting the support of overseas experts (Mulvaney 1988:207). At the conference, discussions were held on a diverse range of subjects, including linguistics in Oceania, the organization of research, and the Pacific "population problem"; the latter drew papers from G. H. Pitt-Rivers and Hubert Murray.

The resolutions reiterated and expanded on those passed at the 1921 AAAS conference. Anthropology could assist in the "preservation, progress, and welfare of the native population of Oceania" through a policy "based on the investigation of native conditions, customs, laws, religion, and the like, which is a study not merely of academic interest and importance, but points the way to a sympathetic method of dealing with and governing such peoples." Research therefore was "urgently needed" in both Oceania and Australia for the following reasons:

i) The undoubted disappearance of the native population in many areas, which will not only affect the labour problem, but involves the loss of most valuable scientific material, and in the Territories held under Mandate, is itself the most serious obstacle to the duty accepted by the Mandatory Powers of promoting the material and moral well-being and social progress of the inhabitants. . . . [With regard to Aborigines who are] of great and particular interest . . . as representing one of the lowest types of culture available for study, of the rapid and inevitable diminution of their numbers, and of the loss of their primitive beliefs and customs under the influence of a higher culture . . . that steps be taken, without delay, to organise the study of those tribes that are, as yet comparatively uninfluenced by contact with civilisation.

ii) The practical importance of the ethnological study of native
    races. . . . Experience has shown the economic value of placing
    the control of labour in the hands of a man who has a sympa-
    thetic knowledge of native conditions and thought in elimi-
    nating disputes and inducing a contented frame of mind in the
    workers.[14]

Oceania was divided into four main areas. Australian Aboriginal
ethnology was of "especial concern" for Australia, which "should more
particularly investigate Papua, the Mandated Territory of New Guinea
and Melanesia, but Great Britain and France should assist in this work."
The investigation of the Maoris should be the "especial province" of
New Zealand. The rest of Polynesia was regarded as preeminently the
field for American research, with the cooperation of France and New
Zealand. The study of Micronesia was "the particular province" of Japan
and America.

The congress, to summarize, resolved that training in anthropology
would assist government officials, missionaries, and others "who will
be brought into personal contact with the natives." It stressed that "the
scientific problem of the Pacific which stands first in order of urgency is
the preservation of the health and life of the native races." It hoped that
"governments responsible for the welfare of Oceanic peoples [would]
recognise that ethnology has a practical value in administration and is
of definite economic importance," and it urged the Australian government in particular to make "provision . . . for the teaching of Anthropology in the Universities of Australia" (Gray 2006).[15]

II

On December 7, 1923, a deputation from the ANRC, headed by Masson,
met with Earle Page, acting prime minister. The minutes of the meeting
reveal that "the definite suggestion was advanced that the Commonwealth Government should found and maintain a chair of Anthropology at the University of Sydney at an approximate cost of £1700 p.a."[16]
Cabinet approved the general concept later that day. The vice-chancellor
of the University of Melbourne wrote to the prime minister, congratu-
lating him on the decision, "which will provide training for our officers

working with the natives in [the] Mandated Territory, and will inciden-
tally encourage scientific work in Anthropology." He added that "the
Council of this University has recently been in communication with
the sister Universities of Australia," and if the announcement had not
been made, "we should accordingly have been approaching you in the
matter."[17] In January 1924 Masson drafted a memorandum to both the
prime minister and the minister for home and territories on the nature
of the proposed chair at the University of Sydney.[18]

There was, however, some doubt about the training of field officers or even the need for field officers to be trained in anthropology
at a university. Colonel John Ainsworth, chief native commissioner in
the British colony of Kenya, was asked to advise the Australian government on the administration of "native" people in the Territory of
New Guinea (see Ainsworth 1924). It was the first time Australia was
responsible to an international organization, the League of Nations,
for its colonial administration of New Guinea, which it acquired as a
result of World War I (Rowley 1958; Radi 1971). The seeking of advice
from parallel colonies under British administration, such as those in
East Africa, reflects a lack of confidence by Australian authorities in
spite of their experience in Papua.

Ainsworth advised against university-trained field officers, preferring
"men of good tone, character, personality and initiative and a tolerant
patient disposition." These attributes "combined with a fairly liberal
[private] education" were of greater value than a university degree "for
the purposes of the administration of a territory with a primitive backward people."[19] Nevertheless, there was a place for university training;
Ainsworth believed cadets for the "tropical services" should undergo
"a six or nine months course of lectures and studies" at an Australian
university in "the 'geographical and climatic conditions' of the area in
which the cadet was to serve; (ii) 'the recording of temperature and
rainfall'; (iii) 'phonetic spelling'; (iv) 'medical first aid, vaccination and
hygiene'; (v) 'tropical products'; (vi) 'legal procedure' (magistrate's
court, civil and criminal procedures); (vii) 'simple accounts'; (viii) 'land
surveying'; (ix) anthropology" (Ainsworth 1924:13–14).

He suggested that there were two ways of dealing with "the subject
of anthropology." One was "the purely scientific method . . . concerned

with research work generally." The other was directed "to the acquisition of a better understanding of the natives, and the reasons for, and explanations of, their customs and traditions." He concluded that the study of anthropology "cannot be completed before appointment and after a term of service officers will be in a better position to understand and appreciate the benefits of such knowledge and also apply the preliminary teaching they have received." Thus, before an official could obtain a "native's confidence and respect" and begin "effective administration," he must acquire "some knowledge" of the people with whom he had to deal (Ainsworth 1924:13–14).

As for obtaining an ethnographic record, Ainsworth saw no need for independent anthropological investigation supported by the government. He was confident that the appointment of Ernest William Pearson Chinnery as director of anthropology (he was then government anthropologist) for New Guinea would meet the "scientific needs" of the Territory and, at the same time, be of considerable help to district officers and others who possessed a "rudimentary knowledge" of the subject (Gray 2003).[20]

Chinnery was a promoter of anthropological training for colonial field staff and supported an anthropologically informed colonial policy and practice. He was at the forefront of training cadets in anthropology and other matters associated with the governance of colonial peoples; he not only took a direct interest but also encouraged those officers who had done preliminary training with him to attend further courses in the newly created Department of Anthropology at the University of Sydney.[21] Anthropology fitted neatly with the work of the patrol officer, described by Chinnery as the exploration of "new areas, discovering and pacifying the natives living there, and guiding them through an administrative system which includes among other things, the establishment of law and order, the improvement of sanitary and health conditions, the encouragement of contact and friendly relations between tribes, the introduction of new economic ideas and the encouragement of education" (1932:163).[22]

In the year he arrived in New Guinea, Chinnery gave instruction to the district officers, who were, he told Haddon, "men without training in native work." Most of these men were ex–Australian Infantry Forces, such as G. W. L. "Kassa" Townsend (1968).[23] The patrol officer and later director of native affairs in postwar Papua New Guinea, J. K. McCarthy, remarked on this when describing his fellow passengers on the *Marsina* in 1927: "Almost every man on board was an ex-servicemen. . . . Most had gone to New Guinea in the early 1920s" (1972:9). These men were instructed with the cadets, Chinnery told Haddon, in "the ethnography of the Territory, distributions, etc and in ethnographical methods of district administration, investigation etc."[24] Chinnery was pleased that the cadets were trained "on the spot," although he preferred them to "come to me after they have completed their other courses." He outlined the course:

> My instruction will deal with Ethnography of the Territory and its relation to Administration. . . . It will embrace a brief survey in the history of our native peoples, their distribution and culture; a general outline of the problems peculiar to the Territory (complex conditions arising out of the discovery and development of backward peoples, especially those questions connected with native labour, native institutions, population etc) and instruction (practical where possible) in scientific methods of investigating native problems together with advice as to the practical application of ethnographic knowledge. . . . To better illustrate my instructions and further to impress upon the cadets the nature and importance to their future work and obligations I shall arrange a series of "talks" dealing with the experiences of a "new tribe" from the time of its discovery until it reaches a condition of definite control. By the time the cadets are ready I trust the new museum building will be available for the proper arrangement and exhibition of native collections. I shall require it for instructional purposes.[25]

While Chinnery was planning his course and undertaking the training of field officers, J. G. McLaren, secretary of the Department of Home and Territories, used Ainsworth's report to argue that anthropology and legal procedure affected only those who would become future district officers (New Guinea) or the resident magistrate (Papua) and did not justify the expense of a university course. He went on: "The proposals of the ANRC for a three years [course] . . . appear to provide an altogether too elaborate and costly means of meeting the comparatively simple needs of the situation, as laid down by Colonel Ainsworth." He also rejected Ainsworth's suggestion for a six- or nine-month university course, arguing that it was based on the assumption that the necessary training could only be acquired at a university.

McLaren, drawing on Ainsworth, suggested a solution, which was the organizing of a local system of training in the two territories concerned. He made a case that the heads of the various departments in each territory "should be better qualified than any person outside that Territory to impart the instruction required thereto by the prospective patrol Officer." With the exception of anthropology and "elementary medical principles," no formal school needed to be created. The government anthropologist could arrange for a "three month intensive course of training," and during that time the principal medical officer could "set apart an hour daily for instruction in regard to first aid, hygiene, and identification and treatment of disease of the natives." With regard to the other matters, the cadets could be attached "for brief periods to the staffs of the Departments concerned." He thought that unless each territory could absorb at "least two Patrol Officers per annum no system of training, University or otherwise, could ... be justified." He concluded: "There does not appear to be sufficient justification for the establishment of a University Chair of Anthropology at the expense of the Commonwealth." Nevertheless, a chair of anthropology could "serve a very useful public purpose in encouraging the study of anthropology amongst the community as a whole and in promoting a better general understanding of the problems with which Australia has to deal in the care and protection of the native peoples under her control."[26] Importantly, it would not involve Australian government expenditure.

Soon after McLaren advised the minister, the Senate of the University of Sydney passed a resolution at its March meeting that stated: "That the establishment of a chair of Anthropology is eminently desirable both on the score of public utility and the advancement of Science, but that in the present position of the University finances, the University cannot see its way to proceed in this matter unless the funds are provided wholly by the Federal Government."[27] This bold move—seeking federal funds—thus underpinned the notion expressed forcefully by the ANRC that it was in the interest of the Australian government to support a chair of anthropology.

The minister, Senator George Pearce, informed the ANRC: "I have lately had an opportunity of conferring with, and ascertaining the views of, Colonel John Ainsworth on the nature of the training required." The appointment of a government anthropologist in New Guinea, as well as a government anthropologist already attached to the staff of the Papuan administration, removed "the necessity of field research" conducted by a university. He concluded that in "all circumstances, and considering the question solely from the standpoint of the training of Government officials, I do not feel that I would be justified in recommending the establishment of a University Chair of Anthropology at the expense of the Tropical Territories of the Commonwealth."[28] He did, however, invite "further observations" from the ANRC.

Masson expressed disappointment,[29] but it was left to George Knibbs (acting president) and Baldwin Spencer (vice president) to reply on behalf of the ANRC.[30] They forcibly argued two propositions, namely, "the necessity of training future Government and other officials, who are called on to deal with native races," and "the necessity of training investigators competent to undertake Anthropological research." At stake was the international "reputation of the Commonwealth [of Australia]." They embellished the position in other countries by arguing that in England, France, Germany, and America, the significance of anthropology was recognized by the endowment of "Chairs and Institutions" to ensure "the training of officials and investigators, the accurate recording of all knowledge in regard to vanishing races and to afford enlightenment to those who still believe that 'the proper study of mankind is man.'"

The responsibilities undertaken by the Australian government in regard to New Guinea and Papua, "irrespective of her own Aboriginal inhabitants, [made] it necessary that adequate [university] training should be available in Australia for . . . students who wish to take positions in the tropical territories of the Commonwealth." The system of selecting and training officials proposed by Ainsworth had not been "a conspicuous success; certainly it has failed to cope both with the investigation of native customs and beliefs" and with the problem of depopulation and the disappearance of "primitive and backward races" or "becoming modified in regard to their customs, beliefs and industries." If a record "of them is to be secured and handed on to future generations it must be obtained at once by competent investigators." Hence it was unrealistic to expect the government anthropologists to undertake the "proper investigation of these natives." No two men "could possibly deal with ethnological work over such great areas, occupied by members of tribes speaking different languages, each with its own special cultures and beliefs. . . . [P]roper investigation . . . necessitates intensive study extending over a long time in a limited area." They concluded that it was "quite certain to us that Colonel Ainsworth's view would not have the support of any anthropologist in any part of the world; that it is based upon a failure to understand the question."[31]

The minister was unmoved. He advised them that the "care of the aboriginals in the various Australian States is the immediate responsibility of the State Governments, whose co-operation should, I think, be enlisted in any movement, on general grounds, for the establishment of a Chair."[32] The Australian government accepted responsibility for New Guinea, which underwrote its support for a chair. Convincing the states that responsibility for Aboriginal people could be translated into supporting a commonwealth chair at the University of Sydney became critical in the establishment of a chair of anthropology.

III

The Rockefeller Foundation pursued a global policy of promoting the efficiency and objectivity of the social sciences during the interwar years (Fisher 1980, 1986). "Institutional centres were funded to focus development, and from 1923 a fellowship programme complemented university training. . . . The Foundation . . . emphasized anthropology as one of those disciplines most emendable to scientific methodology" (Mulvaney 1988:203; see also Mills 2008:52–53). In late December 1923 the Rockefeller Foundation received a proposal from the Galton Society for the Study of the Origin and Evolution of Man for a major study on Aboriginal people in Australia, home of the "natural society" and the "lowest human race" (Peterson 1990:11; Jonas 1989:137).[33] The Galton Society members were eugenicists devoted to the study of human well-being and fitness. Jonas describes it as "one of many impressively titled organizations spawned by the American eugenics movement; like the others, its principal purpose seemed to be the promotion of solidarity in the movement by marshalling, on one letterhead, the names of scientists and nonscientists who shared a concern about the effect of 'bad' genes on the prevailing political, economic, and moral order" (1989:133). It proposed a purpose-built field hospital, staffed by five Americans and two Englishmen, that would offer treatment as a means of attracting Aboriginal people for study. There was no intention to involve Australian scientists or institutions. The Galton Society, however, lost direct input into the project due in part to Edwin Embree, who started making the project his own, but also because the foundation's policy was to work through the institutions and scholars of countries concerned (Peterson 1991:10).

Embree had salvaged a project out of the Galton Society proposal but neglected to inform its members that he had done so. This project, which he proposed to the trustees of the Rockefeller Foundation, became a study of the vanishing Aboriginal cultures of Australia. The Division of Studies, which Embree headed, was authorized to continue its survey of new fields and bring to the board's attention "from time to time specific projects to be considered on its merits" (Jonas 1989:131). Embree wanted to work through the ANRC, which he considered the only body able to handle scientific responsibilities on a national level (Jonas 1989:144). It was a project, Embree argued, that went beyond a mere scholarly commitment to "knowledge for its own sake" (1989:132). On hearing that the foundation trustees had expressed interest in his proposed project, Embree arranged for the Australian-born Grafton Elliot Smith to undertake a fact-finding trip to Australia in order "to consult with scientists there about field studies of aboriginal cultures" (Jonas 1989:137–138). Supported by the board of trustees, Elliot Smith was entrusted with the carefully worded proposal, which he put before the Australian government:

> Our position is that if the Australian Universities either individually or collectively have or wish to develop plans for studies of aboriginal peoples, and if they need financial assistance in carrying out these

plans and care to approach the Rockefeller Foundation with respect to such assistance, we are prepared to sympathetically consider such proposals. . . . As to the scope of the studies, this will depend upon the resources, the personnel and the plans of the Australian Universities. . . . The types of studies . . . might include not only such items as are regularly thought of as falling under the general subject of anthropology, but also those which would include what might be called immunology and comparative physiology on the one hand and ethnology, social customs, and organisation on the other.[34]

Elliot Smith informed the prime minister, Stanley Melbourne Bruce, that he had been "consulted by the Rockefeller Foundation as to the establishment of a department of Anthropology in the University of Sydney and to draw up a plan for a campaign of field work in connection with it" (Dawson 1938:85). It was not, however, a firm commitment, merely "one of inquiry." Smith, accompanied by Thomas Lyle, a member of the ANRC executive, stressed that the AAAS and Pan Pacific Science conferences "emphatically re-affirmed the conviction that the provision of . . . anthropological education for all officers who are to serve in Papua and the Mandated Territories is a matter of urgent practical importance."[35] They reiterated that internationally the proposals had "excited widespread interest," and it was felt that the "adoption of these resolutions would mark the commencement of a new era in dealing more sympathetically and intelligently with the native peoples entrusted to the care of European Powers."[36]

The prime minister told Smith that he could inform the Rockefeller Foundation that the government "keenly appreciated this new demonstration of the Foundation's interest in Australia and would gratefully welcome any help the Foundation might give to promote the scientific study of the native population of Australia."[37] Smith in turn informed the foundation that the Australian government and universities "would welcome the help of the Foundation in making possible the serious scientific study of the native people in Australia before it is too late to carry out such a task," whether a department of anthropology was established or not.[38] Embree could hardly contain his enthusiasm. He "looked for far-reaching results" from the enterprise that Smith's "sympathetic and tactful assistance" had initiated (Jonas 1989:141). On November 7, 1924, the board of trustees pledged US$100,000 toward the support of anthropological studies in Australia over a five-year period; this was reaffirmed on May 26, 1926 (Jonas 1989:141, 144).

The Australian government reconsidered its decision after Smith's visit. In Masson's mind the connection between the foundation and the chair of anthropology was clear. He told the University of Sydney Senate that "Elliot Smith was authorized to say that, in the event of the Professorship being founded, Foundation funds might be available for research work."[39] The federal government now asked the ANRC to seek the financial support of the states. It was decided that the states should contribute "proportionately to their respective populations, a total sum of £1500 per annum."[40] In response to the ANRC's deputations, the governments of New South Wales, Victoria, Tasmania, and Queensland promised contributions, and South Australia "is likely to join with them." Western Australia initially declined but later contributed the same amount as Tasmania.[41] New Zealand was also approached.[42]

The ANRC had "achieved its immediate object" and thus urged the Senate of the University of Sydney to "consider the appointment of a professor and the arrangements for the work of the new School."[43] The ANRC considered three matters to be especially important:

(1) The main work of the Chair, both in teaching and in research, should be in the field of Social Anthropology. . . . [T]o lay stress upon the social or cultural side accords with the emphatic wish of those interested in the project from the beginning.

(2) It hoped that the professor chosen [a "Social Anthropologist of repute"] will be one who has had actual field research experience.

(3) Though the routine work of the new Chair will, of course, be under the control of the University . . . the Council feels that great benefit would result from the establishment of a Permanent Advisory Committee, to aid the Professor (who would be its chairman) in the organisation of field research. Such a Committee should contain one or more representatives of the Com-

monwealth and of each subscribing State, appointed by the Governments in consultation with their Universities, and also a representative of the [ANRC].

The latter committee, known also as the Committee on Anthropological Research and on Fellowships in Human Biology, would be responsible for recommending to the ANRC the administration of the Rockefeller Foundation funds for anthropological research. The duties of the new professor would be to teach anthropology and ethnology and to organize and direct field and laboratory research. The teaching would, "of necessity," be in coordination with other departments of the university, such as anatomy, geography, history, economics, and psychology, its "immediate aims being: (a) The training of Government officials, missionaries and others who, in commercial undertakings, will be in contact with the natives; (b) The training of investigators in the field who may or may not be attached to some local Government."

The University of Sydney Senate moved to establish a chair of anthropology in June 1925 and appointed a committee consisting of Haddon, J. T. Wilson (an Australian-born professor of anatomy at Cambridge), and Elliot Smith.[44] The main applicants were A. R. Radcliffe-Brown, A. M. Hocart (a British anthropologist who had written on Polynesia and Melanesia), and Arthur Grimble (a British colonial official with experience in the Gilbert Islands). Malinowski "was considered in the absence of an application but it was felt certain that he would not leave the LSE." Radcliffe-Brown, who "had university teaching experience and field work in Australia[,] was the unanimous choice," although Hocart was considered the most likely appointment (Peterson 1990:11; Elkin 1970:12).

En route to Sydney from Cape Town, Radcliffe-Brown stopped in London to deliver three public lectures at the LSE titled "Study of Backward Peoples: Its Method and Practical Value" before traveling to New York for discussions with the Rockefeller Foundation. He arrived in Sydney in July 1926.[45]

IV

By the time Embree and Clark Wissler, curator of anthropology at the American Museum of Natural History, arrived in Australia in November 1925 to investigate research in both universities and museums, the decision to establish a chair of anthropology and the appointment of Radcliffe-Brown as foundation professor at the University of Sydney had been made. Embree and Wissler's tour was to last six months, and the most important stops from the point of view of the Rockefeller Foundation were New Zealand, Australia, and Hawaii. While in Australia they visited universities and museums in Brisbane, Sydney, Melbourne, and Adelaide.

In response to a question from a reporter for the *Melbourne Herald*, asking "what the Rockefeller Foundation was likely to do in practical subsidy towards research in Australian anthropology," Embree stated:

> It is true that I am here to make inquiries how far practical interest in such questions [as the study of Aborigines and the "people of the mandated territories and other Pacific islands"] has gone in this country. . . . *It is in consequence of what happened at the Science Congress that I have been sent.* I have no power to act, but only to make a report, and recommendations. It was the great practical forward step of the establishment, by the help of your Federal Government, of a Chair of Anthropology in the University of Sydney that led us to realise that you really meant business. It is only fair to say that I think it very likely that the Rockefeller Foundation will agree to give what practical assistance towards this important object that it considers adequate.[46]

In preparation for their visit, the vice-chancellor of the University of Adelaide established a special committee. Its chairman, J. B. Cleland, cast his net widely in his attempt to gain support within the university. He received replies from the physics department, as well as from the Elder Conservatorium and from anatomists such as T. D. Campbell and Frederick Wood Jones.

It is from this visit that there has sprung a belief that Adelaide was considered as the site for the chair of anthropology. This belief is a result of the reordering of the sequence of events. Philip Jones, a historian attached to the Museum of South Australia, writes that Wood Jones, Cleland, and Campbell believed that the University of Adelaide had a very good chance of securing the chair (1987:73). The impression conveyed by Jones is that the decision remained open, probably drawing on the earlier interest of the Galton Society and Embree's earlier discussions on human biology, strongly supported by the Rockefeller Foundation.

A desire to obtain funds from the Rockefeller Foundation and a belief that a chair of anthropology could be established explain the enthusiasm of Cleland and the committee to ensure that Embree and Wissler were given every opportunity to appreciate Adelaide's resources and advantages as a center for research into Aborigines. Cleland wrote that if it was decided to make Adelaide a base, "considerable kudos will necessarily attach to the University and as a result great advances will be made in the study of the aboriginal."[47] The committee prepared a whirlwind itinerary commencing immediately after Embree and Wissler arrived. The group spent nearly four days observing, photographing, and taking blood samples of Aborigines living at Wilgena: "Within twenty four hours of leaving Adelaide we were in the midst of over 70, probably nearly 90, aboriginals, who, Wissler felt sure, had merely the veneer of civilization, and who were behaving essentially as the wild natives behave."[48] This trip was later listed as the first trip of the University of Adelaide's Board for Anthropological Research, which was established in June 1926 as a permanent committee of the university.

Wissler, in his report to the foundation, noted the enthusiasm of the University of Adelaide: "No other university in Australia seems quite so intent upon research in . . . [the Aboriginal] field."[49] Adelaide was "the gateway to central and western Australia and had the easiest access to substantial populations of traditionally-oriented Aboriginal people." Cleland hoped that a result of the visit to Adelaide would be an independent base with direct funding from the Rockefeller Foundation. In spite of the enthusiasm of the Adelaide board and the location of Adelaide as an entry to the northern desert country, Wissler concluded, somewhat surprisingly, that Sydney and Melbourne were better suited to "strictly biological studies" of Aborigines rather than

Adelaide. He did, however, recommend that US$40,000 be granted annually to the University of Adelaide for research in human biology focused on Aboriginal subjects (Wissler 1926:41–45).

The Rockefeller Foundation decided to channel all funds through the ANRC, in part because the trustees "understood that [the ANRC] ... was willing to assume this responsibility." Because of the competing claims of Sydney, Melbourne, and Adelaide, it seemed "the only proper thing for such an outside organisation as the Rockefeller Foundation was to carry its contribution through a central scientific body, leaving to that ... body ... decisions as to the allocation of funds." He was confident that Adelaide would not be disadvantaged. "It may in fact result in greater resources for South Australia, particularly during those early years when personnel for research is more available at Adelaide than at any other place." Embree hoped the Adelaide people would not be disappointed with the decision.[50] This decision also satisfied the University of Sydney, removing financial responsibility concerning the distribution of funds to other universities.

Embree pointed out to Radcliffe-Brown that the research that could be carried out with foundation support "should [be] broadly conceived [and] ... include anatomy, archaeology, ethnology, pathology, physiology, psychology and sociology." The allocation of research funds would be facilitated by a special committee headed by the professor of anthropology and including representatives of the states and universities. To help overcome the shortage of Australian-trained researchers, the foundation would grant fellowships "for men studying either anthropology or subjects in the group of sciences that may be roughly defined as human biology." Such persons should have "some graduate degree" and be assured of either a definite university post or a connection with teaching, research, or scientific work in "the country from which they come."[51] It was, Masson concluded, a "very generous offer ... quite in accord" with the ANRC's expectations "since our consultations with Embree and Wissler a few months ago."[52]

An unusual feature was the ability of the ANRC to distribute the funds as it saw fit without direct influence of the foundation. Distance and time created a unique situation: "So great a time is required for correspondence between New York and Sydney it seemed wise for us to

be taking this action without consulting you specifically in advance."
In fact, no official from the Rockefeller Foundation visited Australia
between 1926 and 1938, when funding ceased (Jonas 1989:154).

V

Resolutions from the 1914 BAAS conference, the AAAS conferences, and
the Pan Pacific Science Congress of 1923 all urged the Australian government to endow a chair of anthropology as a way of meeting Australia's
new international obligations with respect to the League of Nations'
Class C mandate territory of New Guinea. Underlying this was the
imperative to record for science and posterity all that remained of the
vanishing races, especially Australian Aborigines. These twin objectives
enabled the Australian government to show it was interested in both
the development of New Guinea and the preservation of indigenous
life in both mainland Australia and New Guinea. However, translating this into support for a chair of anthropology required advocacy
by individuals, most notably Elliot Smith, Murray, and Masson. Furthermore, a confluence of several debates about the value and purpose
of anthropology enabled its institutionalization as a university-based
discipline in Australia.

Yet to consider the establishment of a chair of anthropology as the
result of the actions of one man, as did Elkin, who claimed Elliot Smith
was the key figure in the establishment of the chair, or J. H. P. Murray, who claimed that it was "largely through the persistent efforts of
the Papuan Government [Murray himself], a Chair of Anthropology
has been established at Sydney University," or to elevate the role of
Haddon as Masson did minimizes the systematic international policy
pursued by the Rockefeller Foundation in developing the social sciences in the British Empire and the particularity of Australian funding
to "study the vanishing [Aboriginal] race." Also, the advocacy of the
ANRC and its membership in negotiating a successful outcome should
not be overlooked. The persistence of the ANRC convinced the Australian government to fund a chair of anthropology at the University
of Sydney.[53] Moreover, the work of Embree in convincing the trustees of the Rockefeller Foundation to fund research, emphasizing the
need to record the "vanishing Aboriginal race," should be recognized.

In this we cannot ignore each person's contributions either. Masson was correct to highlight the important part played by Haddon. Haddon was central to the spread of anthropology in the dominions and attended not only the BAAS conference in 1914 but the 1921 AAAS and the 1923 Pan Pacific Congresses. Masson did not acknowledge his own work as president of the ANRC, which was, in my view, critical. Masson could have acknowledged Elliot Smith, who was an envoy of the foundation. He had little direct influence over the deliberations of the ANRC executive, but his report was a crucial part of a finely orchestrated "scientific" diplomacy, with the ANRC as the central broker.

The Rockefeller Foundation continued to fund anthropological research, including the journal *Oceania*, until 1938. Embree left the organization in 1927, which coincided with the diminution and eventual abandonment of "human biology," which he had so vigorously promoted. The establishment of a chair of anthropology was the beginning of modern social anthropology in Australia, although the elasticity of professional definitions remained until after World War II.

NOTES

ANRC	Australian National Research Council Papers, National Library of Australia
AWM	Australian War Memorial, Canberra
CP	Chinnery Papers, private collection
EP	Elkin Papers, University of Sydney Archives
MFP	Murray Family Papers, National Library of Australia, Canberra
ML	Mitchell Library, State Library of New South Wales, Sydney
NAA	National Archives of Australia, Melbourne and Canberra
NLA	National Library of Australia
SAMA	South Australian Museum Archives, Adelaide

1. For convenience, I refer, unless in a direct quote, to the Australian government.
2. *Gippsland Times*, May 9, 1912.
3. Murray, draft of a book on Papua, undated typescript, MSS A3138-2, Murray Papers, ML.
4. Murray to Gilbert Murray, February 1909, 565/333, MFP.

5. *Mercury*, April 4, 1912.
6. Unable to find a suitable candidate, he appointed W. M. Strong, a physician and assistant resident magistrate. In 1922 he appointed Francis Edgar Williams, an Oxford-trained anthropologist and student of R. R. Marett, as assistant government anthropologist (Murray 1929; West 1968; Griffiths 1977).
7. MacLeod writes that this meeting was part of BAAS's mandate for "social imperialism" in science. The BAAS had pursued a progression of conferences around the British empire: it held meetings in South Africa in 1905 and in Toronto and Winnipeg in 1897 and 1907, tying Canadians "to the Union Jack" (MacLeod 1988:56).
8. "Anthropological Teaching in Universities," *Man* 59 (1913):63, 67; 61 (1914):171–172.
9. Papua was an Australian territory and as such was considered to be part of Australia, albeit separate. Right of entry to Australia was closely controlled, and no Papuan "Native" could freely enter mainland Australia. For an exposition of the tangled web of Australian rule, see Gray (2007:31–32).
10. There were a number of separate funds within the Rockefeller Foundation that underwent administrative reorganization at various times. For convenience, I use the Rockefeller Foundation to cover all.
11. Memo, Department of the Interior, March 30, 1938, A431/1, 50/1661, NAA.
12. Minute book, August 17, 1922, MS 482, ANRC Papers, NLA.
13. Haddon seemingly had no impact on the development of anthropology in Canada. See Harrison and Darnell (2006).
14. Extract from Minutes of the General Meeting of the Second Pan-Pacific Congress, Sydney, September 1923, A518, N806/1/1, pt. 1, NAA.
15. Extract from Minutes of the General Meeting.
16. MS 482, December 7, 1923, ANRC Papers, NLA.
17. J. H. Macfarland to the Prime Minister, December 14, 1923, A518, N806/1/1, pt. 1, NAA.
18. Masson, Proposed Chair of Anthropology in the University of Sydney, draft memorandum, January 30, 1924. See also Suggested Chair of Anthropology—Sydney University, Proposals of Australian National Research Council, February 25, 1924, A518, P806/1/1, pt. 1, NAA.
19. Connections to Africa and the British Empire are found throughout Australian rule in Papua and New Guinea. Character features prominently in selection processes. In 1916, for example, there was an application from a South African military man, a Lieutenant Baker, look-

ing for work in the recently Australian-occupied German New Guinea. Administrator to Minister of Defence, February 10, 1916, Australian War Memorial (AWM) 33, 12/12.

20. Chinnery was appointed to the position of government anthropologist on April 24, 1924.

21. Radcliffe-Brown to Gregory, March 17, 1930; Radcliffe-Brown to Robert Lowie, June 28, 1927, 164/4/2/17, EP; Radcliffe-Brown to McLaren, June 11, 1928, A518, N806/1/1, pt. 1, NAA.

22. Chinnery to Haddon, December 12, 1924, CP.

23. Also B883, VX117176, NAA.

24. Chinnery to Haddon, April 10, 1925, CP.

25. Chinnery to Government Secretary (Rabaul), April 6, 1925, CP.

26. Memo, Secretary, Department of Home and Territories, February 25, 1924, A518, P806/1/1, pt. 1, NAA.

27. M. W. MacCallum, Vice-Chancellor, University of Sydney, to Secretary, Home and Territories Department, March 5, 1924, A518, N806/1/1, pt. 1, NAA.

28. Pearce to Masson, March 10, 1924, A518, N806/1/1, pt. 1, NAA.

29. Masson to Pearce, March 12, 1924, A518, P806/1/1, pt. 1, NAA.

30. The following, unless otherwise noted, is from Knibbs and Spencer to Pearce, April 28, 1924, A518, P806/1/1, pt. 1, NAA.

31. Knibbs and Spencer to Pearce, April 28, 1924.

32. Pearce to ANRC, September 5, 1924, A518, P806/1/1, pt. 1, NAA.

33. For a brief discussion of eugenics and philanthropic funding, see Jonas (1989:118–125).

34. Smith to Prime Minister, September 2, 1924, A518, N806/1/1, pt. 1, NAA.

35. Memo, Prime Minister, September 15, 1924, A518, N806/1/1, pt. 1, NAA.

36. Smith to Prime Minister, September 2, 1924.

37. Smith to Embree, September 30, 1924, cited in Peterson (1991:11); Memo, September 10, 1924, A518, N806/1/1, pt. 1, NAA.

38. Smith to Embree, September 30, 1924.

39. Masson, "Proposed Chair of Anthropology. Statement prepared by the Australian National Research Council for presentation to the Chancellor of the University of Sydney," April 1925.

40. It was estimated that the annual cost of the chair would include the following: salary of professor, £1,000; pension contribution, £150; salary of lecture room assistant, £350; purchase of books, traveling expenses, and so on, £200. "It was pointed out also that, as the school developed, it would be necessary to supply a Scientific Assistant, at a salary rising

to £750, so that after a few years, the annual expense would be approximately £2500" (Masson, "Proposed Chair of Anthropology").

41. The amounts for each state were: Tasmania, £56; New South Wales, £577; Victoria, £425; Western Australia, £93; Queensland, £212; South Australia, £137. See Memo, Prime Minister's Department, April 7, 1932, A518, P806/1/1, pt. 1, NAA.

42. The reasons state governments contributed to the establishment of the chair at the University of Sydney are unclear. If an argument was accepted by the states that the chair would assist in the administration of Aboriginal affairs, then there is little evidence to suggest that this resulted in sending officials to be trained. Rather, training of officials seems to have been confined to those from Papua and New Guinea. A chair of anthropology in New Zealand (Auckland University College) was established in 1950. There was, however, some teaching in anthropology and archaeology at Otago University (H. D. Skinner) and Victoria University, Wellington (Ernest Beaglehole). See Gray and Munro (2012:49–82).

43. The following text quotes are from Masson, "Proposed Chair of Anthropology," unless otherwise stated.

44. University of Sydney Senate Minutes, June 1, 1925, University of Sydney Archives. Wilson and Elliot Smith were Sydney graduates.

45. The lectures were advertised in *Man* 36 (1926):63.

46. *Melbourne Herald*, November 18, 1925, my emphasis.

47. J. B. Cleland, "Memo re Visit of Representatives of the Rockefeller Institute, in reference to the Endowment of Research in the Anthropology of the Australian Aboriginal," AA 60, ACC 243, SAMA.

48. Cleland to Wood Jones, December 1, 1925, AA 60, ACC 243, SAMA.

49. Clark Wissler, Report of a Visit to Research Institutions in New Zealand and Australia during the Year 1925, 1926, 1.1/140/4/42, Rockefeller Foundation.

50. Embree to Wood Jones, May 28, 1926, cited in Peterson (1991:12).

51. Embree to Masson, May 27, 1926; Embree to Masson, May 27, 1926, 155/4/1/1 (separate letter). EP.

52. Masson to Radcliffe-Brown, July 10, 1926, 157/4/1/24, EP.

53. Tigger Wise states, rather dismissively, that "in a record devoid of other significant triumphs, the establishment of the Chair of Anthropology ranked as one of the ANRC's most useful contributions to Australian science" (1985:97).

REFERENCES

AAAS. 1921. Summary of Resolutions Affecting Committees of the Various Sections. Section F. Report of the Fifteenth Meeting of the Australasian Association for the Advancement of Science, 15. Melbourne.

Ainsworth, John. 1924. Report on Administrative Arrangements and Matters Affecting the Interests of Natives. Melbourne: Government Printer.

Anderson, Warwick. 2002. The Cultivation of Whiteness: Science, Health and Racial Destiny. Melbourne: Melbourne University Press.

Blunt, Michael J. 1988. Smith, Sir Grafton Elliot (1871–1937). In Australian Dictionary of Biography. National Centre of Biography, Australian National University, http://adb.anu.edu.au/biography/smith-sir-grafton -elliot-8470/text14895.

Bolger, Peter. 1977. Anthropology and History in Australia: The Place of A. C. Haddon. Journal of Australian Studies 1(2):93–106.

Callahan, Michael D. 2008. Mandates and Empire: The League of Nations and Africa 1914–1931. Brighton: Sussex Academic Press.

Campbell, I. C. 1998. Anthropology and the Professionalisation of Colonial Administration in Papua and New Guinea. Journal of Pacific History 31(1):69–90.

Cole, Douglas. 1971. The Crimson Thread of Kinship: Ethnic Ideas in Australia, 1870–1914. Historical Studies 14(56):511–525.

Dawson, Warren R., ed. 1938. Sir Grafton Elliot Smith: A Biographical Record by His Colleagues. London: Jonathan Cape.

Elkin, A. P. 1958. Anthropology in Australia: One Chapter. Mankind 5(6):225–242.

———. 1970. The Journal Oceania: 1930–1970. A History. Oceania Monographs No. 16. Sydney.

Firth, Raymond. 1956. Alfred Reginald Radcliffe-Brown 1881–1955. Proceedings of the British Academy 42.

Fisher, Donald. 1980. American Philanthropy and the Social Sciences in Britain 1919–1939: The Reproduction of a Conservative Ideology. Sociological Review 28:277–315.

———. 1986. Rockefeller Philanthropy and the Rise of Social Anthropology. Anthropology Today 2(1):5–8.

Gray, Geoffrey. 1997. "Mr Neville did all in [his] power to assist me": A. P. Elkin, A. O. Neville and Anthropological Research in Northwest Western Australia, 1927–1928. Oceania 68(1):27–46.

———. 2003. "There are many difficult problems": Ernest William Pearson Chinnery—Government Anthropologist. Journal of Pacific History 38(3):313–330.

———. 2007. A Cautious Silence: The Politics of Australian Anthropology. Canberra: Aboriginal Studies Press.

———. 2010. Dividing Oceania: Transnational Anthropology, 1928–30. Histories of Anthropology Annual 6:48–65.

Gray, Geoffrey, and Doug Munro. 2012. Establishing Anthropology and Maori Language (Studies), Auckland University College: The Appointment of Ralph Piddington, 1949. Histories of Anthropology Annual 7:49–82.

Griffiths, Deidre J. F. 1977. The Career of F. E. Williams, Government Anthropologist of Papua, 1922–1943. MA thesis, ANU.

Hammond-Tooke, W. D. 1997. Imperfect Interpreters: South Africa's Anthropologists, 1920–1990. Johannesburg: Witwatersrand University Press.

Harrison, Julia, and Regna Darnell, eds. 2006. Historicizing Canadian Anthropology. Vancouver: University of British Columbia Press.

Jonas, Gerald. 1989. The Circuit Riders: Rockefeller Money and the Rise of Modern Science. New York: W. W. Norton.

Jones, P. G. 1987. South Australian Anthropological History: The Board for Anthropological Research and Its Early Expeditions. Records of the South Australian Museum 20:71–92.

Kuklick, Henrika. 1991. The Savage Within: The Social History of British Social Anthropology. Cambridge: Cambridge University Press.

Kuper, Adam. 1996. Anthropology and Anthropologists: The Modern British School. London: Routledge.

Lewis, M. J. 1979. The Royal Society of Australia: An Attempt to Establish a National Academy of Science. Records of the Australian Academy of Science 4(1):51–62.

MacLeod, Roy. 1988. From Imperial to National Science. In The Commonwealth of Science: ANZAAS and the Scientific Enterprise in Australasia 1888–1988. Roy MacLeod, ed. Pp. 40–72. Melbourne: Oxford University Press.

McCarthy, J. K. 1972. Patrol into Yesterday: My New Guinea Years. Melbourne: Chesire.

McGregor, Russell. 1997. Imagined Destinies: Aboriginal Australians and the Doomed Race Theory, 1880–1939. Melbourne: Melbourne University Press.

Mills, David. 2008. Difficult Folk? A Political History of Social Anthropology. New York: Berghahn Books.

Mulvaney, D. J. 1988. Australasian Anthropology and ANZAAS: "Strictly Scientific and Critical." In The Commonwealth of Science: ANZAAS and the Scientific Enterprise in Australasian 1888–1988. Roy MacLeod, ed. Melbourne: Oxford University Press.

Murray, J. H. P. 1929. Native Administration in Papua. Port Moresby: Government Printer.

Peterson, Nicolas. 1991. Studying Man and Man's Nature: The History of the Institutionalisation of Aboriginal Anthropology. Australian Aboriginal Studies 1:3–19.

Quiggin, A. H. 1942. Haddon the Headhunter: A Short Sketch of the Life of A. C. Haddon. Cambridge: Cambridge University Press.

Radi, Heather. 1971. New Guinea under Mandate 1921–1941. In Australia and Papua New Guinea. W. J. Hudson, ed. Sydney: Sydney University Press.

Rouse, Sandra. 1998. Expedition and Institution: A. C. Haddon and Anthropology at Cambridge. In Cambridge and the Torres Strait: Centenary Essays on the 1898 Anthropological Expedition. Anita Herle and Sandra Rouse, eds. Cambridge: Cambridge University Press.

Rowley, C. D. 1958. The Australians in German New Guinea 1914–1921. Melbourne: Melbourne University Press.

Stocking, George W., Jr. 1995. After Tylor: British Social Anthropology 1888–1951. Madison: University of Wisconsin Press.

Townsend, G. W. L. 1968. District Officer: From Untamed New Guinea to Lake Success, 1921–46. Sydney: Pacific Publications.

West, Francis. 1968. Hubert Murray: The Australian Pro-consul. Melbourne: Oxford University Press.

Wise, Tigger. 1985. The Self-Made Anthropologist: A Life of A. P. Elkin. Sydney: George Allen and Unwin.

SERGEI A. KAN AND DMITRY V. ARZYUTOV

6

The Saga of the L. H. Morgan Archive, or How an American Marxist Helped Make a Bourgeois Anthropologist the Cornerstone of Soviet Ethnography

There is no archive without a place of consignation, without a technique of repetition, and without a certain exteriority. No archive without outside.

JACQUES DERRIDA, *Archive Fever: A Freudian Impression*, 1998

THE ARCHIVE AND THE "OUTSIDE"

There are two reasons why a volume dedicated to the memory of George W. Stocking Jr. is, in our opinion, the most appropriate venue for this chapter. First, its American author studied with George at the University of Chicago and developed a strong interest in the history of anthropology under his influence.[1] It was Stocking who encouraged him to take advantage of his knowledge of Russian and explore the history of the relationship between Boas and his Russian colleagues, such as Vladimir Bogoraz and Lev Shternberg. A paper about Shternberg written in Stocking's seminar eventually grew into a monograph on Shternberg's life and scholarly contributions (Kan 2009). One important lesson many of Stocking's students learned from him is that an anthropologist's scholarly ideas develop within larger sociocultural, intellectual, political, and institutional contexts, within which he or she matures and lives, and for that reason a historian of anthropology should explore them rather than focus exclusively on anthropological theories.

Likewise, Stocking's writings became inspirational for the Russian coauthor of this chapter. Thanks to the impact of Stocking's work, Arzyutov was able to find a new common language with his senior colleagues in Russia and understood better the logic of their past and present theoretical discussions about ethnos and ethnogenesis. This "participant observation" helped him explore the relational complexity between the academic laboratory and the field in greater depth.[2]

Second, as we learn from George's last book (Stocking 2010), driven by strong pacifist views, he joined the Communist Party in 1949 while an undergraduate at Harvard. After seven years of listening to dogmatic speeches, taking part in "self-criticism" sessions, and making fruitless efforts to bring Communist ideas to the working class, George quit the party in 1956 and went to graduate school. As he repeatedly states through his book, Khrushchev's revelations about Stalin's crimes played a major role in Stocking's parting with Communism. The one good thing that resulted from George's largely negative experience as a Communist was, in our opinion, the way he learned to think critically about and do historical research, that is, what he referred to as "historicism" (Stocking 2010:75).

Bernhard J. Stern, the main protagonist of our chapter, shared some characteristics with Stocking. He too was a historian of anthropology (as well as an anthropologist and a sociologist), and he authored the first book-length biography of L. H. Morgan. Stern was also a member of the Communist Party, having joined it in the mid-1930s. However, unlike Stocking, he remained a diehard Communist believer and a staunch advocate of Stalin's Soviet Union; Stern's blind allegiance to it would not be undermined by the show trials of the late 1930s or the Stalin-Hitler Pact of 1939. Moreover, his political views affected some of the scholarly work he did. Our chapter is about one specific important episode in his professional life.

By the beginning of the 1920s, a number of Soviet research institutes, the main one among them being the Marx-Engels Institute in Moscow, were involved in the process of collecting papers, letters, and diaries of the founders of Marxism. This was one of the key projects of the early "Stalinist science" legitimizing political ideology and the significance of the social sciences in the country (Krementsov 1997). A major starting point for the construction of Soviet Marxism was the two important purchases by the Soviet authorities: the archive of

Marx and Engels and the Morgan archive. All the documents of these "founding fathers" of Marxism not only played a scientific role but were a form of Bourdieuian "symbolic capital" for both the authorities and the academic bureaucracy (Bourdieu 1977:171–183).

In this chapter we outline a complicated history of the purchase of the Morgan archive: when, how, and why it happened. We explain the acquisition of this major intellectual product, especially in the context of its transfer from the capitalist West to the socialist East. We also address the political significance of this purchase and the role of Stern's enormous efforts to locate, duplicate, and transfer the entire body of Lewis Henry Morgan's unpublished papers (as well as the books and other publications by and about him) from the archive of the University of Rochester Library to the Institute of Anthropology and Ethnography (IAE) in Leningrad. Finally, we discuss the reasons for Stern's dedication to a project for which he earned very little money. Drawing on published sources and data from American and Russian archives, we explore the reasons for the Soviet anthropologists' keen interest in Morgan, their evolving relationship with Stern, and the project's ultimate fiasco. Thus, in the tradition of Stocking's history of anthropology, our chapter is about biographies, political ideologies, and anthropological theories and institutions.

Looking at this academic transaction, one can see that while the "donors" (the University of Rochester Library and Bernhard Stern himself) did value this archive, for its "recipients" (the staff of the Leningrad Institute of Anthropology and Ethnography / Museum of Anthropology and Ethnography), it was absolutely invaluable and represented a kind of fetish. Ironically, the archive of a "bourgeois" scholar (and thus a potential ideological enemy) became a major part of the foundation of the Soviet ethnography project,[3] defining its boundaries and linking it to Marxism-Leninism, thus making it ideologically correct and acceptable to the authorities.

The saga of the acquisition of these two archives resembles a mythic narrative in which the "Holy Scriptures" had to be wrestled from the enemies' hands. Thus from the very beginning of its establishment in 1921, the Marx-Engels Institute director, an erudite, well-connected, and independent-minded old Bolshevik, David B. Riazanov, sought to obtain not only copies of the works of the two founders of Marxism but also the originals. Using a substantial budget granted to his institution, Riazanov managed to make its archive one of the major depositories of primary sources by and about Marx and Engels, as well as the history of the nineteenth-century socialist movements and socialist thought (Beecher and Fomichev 2006; Rokitianskii 2008).[4] After Riazanov's replacement in 1931 with a much less independent and creative director, Vladimir Adoratskii, the archive scaled down its purchases of original documents and books abroad. Nonetheless, this activity never completely stopped and was actually revitalized in the mid-1930s with the help of French and German socialists who feared the documents' destruction at the hands of the Nazis.

The possession of such a collection obviously gave its holders a good deal of symbolic power. Hence, starting in the mid-1930s, Soviet ethnographers (with the approval of Academy of Sciences administrators and state and party officials) began seeking the Morgan archive. They viewed Morgan as a major precursor of Marxism, since Engels's *The Origin of the Family, Private Property and the State* was basically a compendium of Morgan's *Ancient Society* with a few additions. To take possession of the Morgan manuscripts and become the key (re)interpreters of his ideas was supposed to allow Soviet ethnographers to increase the importance of their discipline within the social sciences by giving their debates a much greater theoretical quality. Of course, for the Soviet ethnographers, Morgan's genius was not equal to that of Marx and Engels, but Morgan was closer to them in terms of his methodology and "professional identity." Given the political significance of ethnography at that time, this was a very timely phenomenon.[5]

Thus Morgan was "nationalized" by Soviet ethnographers and became, in a sense, part of their discipline's genealogy. A new lineage was created, starting with Morgan, followed by Marx, Engels, Lenin, and Stalin, and ending with present-day Soviet ethnographers. Of course, other scholars were added to this genealogy at that time, such as, for example, Lev Shternberg (1861–1927), an evolutionist and one of the founders of Soviet ethnography whose work on kinship had actually been favorably commented on by Engels himself (Chattopadhyaya 1934; see also Kan 2009:52).

Russian ethnographers had been familiar with Marxist theory before it became the official ideology in the USSR. Russian populists of the 1860s and 1870s, known as Narodniks and including the founders of Soviet ethnography, Shternberg and Bogoraz, knew the works of Morgan, Marx, and Engels, with Shternberg making references to Morgan in his studies of kinship systems (Kan 2006, 2009).

The starting point of the Soviet social scientists' shift toward Marxism took place during a series of meetings at the Communist Academy in the 1920s.[6] At that time, many young Marxists tried to create a new Marxist ideology from the multiple Marxisms of that era (Dmitriev 2007). By then, photocopies of many of the manuscripts of Marx and Engels had already been brought to Moscow.

The first Soviet editions of the collected works of Marx and Engels, including the *Archive of Marx and Engels*, appeared during the first *piatiletka* (state five-year plan, 1928–32). A staff of over one hundred social scientists carefully analyzed all of the Marx and Engels manuscripts and compared various published versions of their work (Deborin 1936; collection 142, inventory no. 2, archival document 138, SPF ARAN) in order to eliminate all misprints and mistakes.[7] Publishing these books was part of the planned work of the researchers at this academic institution, just as publishing Morgan's works became a major assignment for the IAE in Leningrad. This rigidly regulated planning system and the pyramid of institutions within the Academy of Sciences had been established by Nikolai Bukharin, one of the leading Bolshevik intellectuals (Graham 1975). Ironically, Marxism, with its own pyramidal models, reflected the pyramid of the Soviet Academy of Sciences.

The year 1929 was a crucial one for the Academy of Sciences (Tolz 2000). In January elections took place, resulting in the addition of a significant number of Marxists. This event is usually considered the beginning of the "Bolshevization" or even "Marxization" of research in the humanities and especially the social sciences. The election process itself was very complex and acrimonious. Initially, a number of candidates did not make it; among them were Vladimir Bogoraz and Abram M. Deborin (1881–1963), a party member. However, in the second round, Deborin succeeded. He eventually became one of the leading Soviet Marxist philosophers (the head of the Institute of Philosophy) and a major figure in the humanities as a whole.

This Bolshevization of the Academy of Sciences was taking place at a time when Western anthropology, including the American version, began to be harshly criticized by Soviet scholars. Even Franz Boas, who in the late 1920s to the early 1930s helped several American anthropologists obtain an affiliation with the Museum of Anthropology and Ethnography (MAE) and himself mentored Julia Averkieva, a Soviet graduate student, came under criticism (Kan 2006). It seemed that contacts and cooperation between Soviet and American anthropology would become increasingly difficult. Yet there remained a place for a special kind of anthropologist, like Morgan, and his archive.

It so happened that Morgan, a scholar badly needed for the construction of a "new Marxist ethnography," was a "person from the capitalist West" and without a "politically correct" biography. This made it difficult for Morgan's first Soviet biographers to canonize him. Still, they managed to find some characteristics of the man, such as the assistance he tried to provide for the Senecas, that could make him a more acceptable ancestor and ally of Soviet scholars (see Kosven 1935a).

As many Soviet ethnographers came to realize between the late 1920s and the early 1930s, without Morgan a true "Marxist ethnography" would not be possible, since he served as a key link in a triad: Marx/ Engels-Morgan-Soviet ethnography. One of the first ethnographers to proclaim that Marxism was absolutely necessary for ethnographers was Sergei A. Tokarev (1899–1985), a student of Petr Preobrazhenskii (1894–1941). Influenced by his mentor and the very first Marxist discussions in the Soviet social sciences, Tokarev had given a presentation entitled "Totemic Society: An Exercise in Applying the Marxist Method to Solving Certain Ethnological Problems," as early as 1925 (fond 8, AIAE RAN). A few years later, while Tokarev was still experimenting with applying Marxism to ethnological research, a series of meetings took place in the Communist Academy in Moscow. Led by Valerian B. Aptekar' (a party member and a highly political academic), the meetings repeatedly reiterated the notion that Marxism was the only correct theory in ethnography (1927: 377/2/110; 1928: 350/2/233;

1928–29: 377/4/29, all in ARAN). However, a truly major event was a conference (*soveshchanie*) of Moscow and Leningrad ethnographers in 1929 at which Morgan's works were discussed for the first time (Bertrand 2002; K-1/3/7, AMAE RAN).[8] It could be argued that this conference, which lasted seven days, determined the entire course of the development of Soviet ethnography. Having done a content analysis of the minutes of this conference, one of the authors of this chapter has calculated that Marx's name (along with its derivative "Marxism") was repeated there 473 times, Engels's name 28 times, Morgan's 30 times, and Lenin's 222; Stalin's name was not mentioned at all.

At the conference, both senior and junior scholars referred to Morgan. Almost at the very beginning of the conference, Petr Preobrazhenskii described both Morgan and E. B. Tylor as classical students of anthropology who "had to construct the prehistoric culture of humanity with the help of ethnographic data" (K-1/3/7:13, AMAE RAN). However, for many of the participants, Morgan was not "Marxist enough," with his method being characterized by them as "spontaneous materialism" (*stikhiinyi materialism*). Consequently, the scholars present felt that Morgan had to be somehow made "more Marxist" (K-1/3/7:39–41, AMAE RAN). The final verdict, however, was pronounced by Nikolai Matorin (1898–1936), the first director of the MAE/IAE to be chosen from the ranks of party members. As he put it, "The issue is not that one or another piece of data used by Morgan is no longer viable (this can happen with any scholar) but that in a number of cases, Morgan used materialist analysis and is being blamed for that [by his opponents], just like the other old classical ethnographers" (K-1/3/7:63–64, AMAE RAN). However, Matorin's most emotional statement was the following: "Marx and Engels admitted that Morgan worked through the history of the preclass society independently and in a purely Marxist manner and that he could be considered one of the founders of the theory of historical materialism. This was, if you wish, a marriage based on love" (K-1/3/7:168, AMAE RAN).

That conference resulted in a number of articles in official academic journals in which Marxism and, specifically, "Morgan's theory" were proclaimed to be the foundation of Soviet ethnography (e.g., Kosven 1932). Here is a quote referring to Morgan and other classic evolutionist-materialist anthropologists: "Soviet anthropology, while recognizing the existence of some concrete and significant methodological mistakes in their works, views any indiscriminate criticism and attacks on their works, which are especially common in the present-day bourgeois scholarship, as a manifestation of a general class struggle of the bourgeoisie against materialism" (Koshkin and Matorin 1929:117). And here is another one: "In total contrast to this, Soviet ethnography puts forward a slogan not of rejecting the classics but of making a transition from them to Marxism, from spontaneous materialism to a deliberate and conscientious application of dialectical materialism" (Koshkin and Matorin 1929:117).

This establishment of a single dominant methodology within the social sciences, including ethnography, made it very important to look for allies abroad. One of them was a young "neo-evolutionist" and a Socialist, Leslie White, who toured Soviet Russia in 1929 and visited the IAE (Peace 2004:69–72). That visit was a rather significant and festive event for the IAE, and, as a result, White's 1932 article, "Evolution of Culture and the American School of Historical Ethnology," was published in *Sovetskaia Etnografiia*, the main journal of Soviet ethnographers. A year earlier White had delivered a provocative politicized paper entitled "An Anthropological Appraisal of the Russian Revolution" at the annual meeting of the American Association for the Advancement of Science; in it he argued that the Bolshevik coup of 1917 was the most significant event in modern history (Peace 2004:72–79). Bernhard Stern, who shared some of White's (left-wing) political and professional views and interests (even though the two of them never liked each other) (Peace 1998), followed in his footsteps, becoming the key link between Morgan and his Soviet devotees. It is possible that the Soviet ethnographers' interaction with White encouraged the establishment of their contact with Stern two years later.

Soon thereafter, Matorin, in his capacity as the head of the IAE, published the lead article in the first issue of the journal *Sovetskaia Etnografiia* for 1931, entitled "The Current Stage and the Tasks of Soviet Ethnography." In it he wrote that "the modern-day attacks on Morgan are the attacks on the materialist understanding of history" and that "Engels's *Origin of the Family* . . . is the guide for every [Soviet] ethnographer" (Matorin 1931:16). Matorin must have been sympathetic toward the "diplomatic" efforts of two Soviet ethnographers in establishing ties with Stern as the liaison with the Morgan archive. It was in 1931 that Isaak Vinnikov (1897–1973), a member of the IAE staff, wrote to Stern, whose 1928 article on Morgan Vinnikov had read. And in that same year, correspondence between Stern and Mark Kosven (1885–1967), a Moscow ethnographer, was also established (see below). In this case, Stern was the one who had initiated it, but in his very first response to him, Kosven gave him Matorin's address as if to indicate that he was representing or had the blessing of a higher-ranking academic bureaucrat and a party member. The year 1931 was also when Evgenii Kagarov (1882–1942) published a series of articles about Engels and the importance of his theory for ethnography (Kisliakov 1963).

Gradually, Marxism was transformed from a platform for discussion into the dominant theory. In May 1932 another important gathering of Soviet ethnographers took place: the All-Union Conference of Archaeologists and Ethnographers (2/1(1932)/201–202, AIIMK RAN).[9] There Matorin redefined the main message of the 1929 conference in order to demonstrate that the Marxist ethnography project could be adjusted somewhat. His view of Marxism became broader by means of searching for and adding allies in other (non-Marxist) anthropologies. Contrary to some of the speeches given at the 1929 conference, he asserted that modern-day Soviet ethnographers could learn some things from such scholars of the old school as Shternberg and Bogoraz.[10] He even turned this idea into a slogan, which had supposedly been mentioned in the hallways during the 1929 conference: "From the Classics to Marxism" (2/1(1932)/201:8, AIIMK RAN).

Matorin also saw the establishment of ties with Marxist and evolutionist anthropologists in foreign countries as an important task. Thus he tried hard to claim White as a Soviet ally, demonstrating how close he was to Soviet ethnographers "in spirit" (White 1932; 2/1(1932)/201:76, AIIMK RAN). In his 1932 speech, Matorin argued that "in the very near future, we'll see at a congress of our Soviet scholars, representatives of Western European countries and America who would now come as people who wish to work with us" (White 1932; 2/1(1932)/201:88–89, AIIMK RAN). This statement revealed Matorin's eagerness to create an alternative/Marxist project in ethnography, which he must have imagined as being capable of erasing state borders. It should be mentioned that it was under Matorin's leadership that the IAE not only implemented efforts to cooperate with European and American colleagues (Matorin 1934:10) but also planned expeditions to the most distant corners of the globe. Thus a proposal existed to send an expedition to New Guinea; however, it remained on paper (Alymov 2013). Plans were also made to establish collaboration with Boas to organize an expedition to Siberia and North America as a kind of continuation of the famous Jesup Expedition (142/1-1928/7:8, SPF ARAN; Krupnik 1998).[11]

In this context, Matorin's wish to cooperate with American Marxists seems quite reasonable. As a politically engaged scholar he formulated his ideas about international cooperation among ethnographers as follows:

> Soviet ethnography, which will become stronger and stronger in the course of its struggle against the clumsy [*domoroshchennye*] enemies of Marxism, will be strong enough to challenge the enemies of Marxism on the international scholarly front, especially since we will not be alone in this struggle. An American researcher, [Bernhard] Stern, has raised his courageous voice against the attacks aimed at Morgan, although he lost his professor's position after that [see below]. A Dutch scholar, [J. J.] Fahrenfort, has raised objections to [Wilhelm] Schmidt.[12] A presentation by Leslie White at the Congress of American Anthropologists in Cleveland was published in Soviet newspapers. There is no doubt that the very first major presentations by Soviet ethnographers abroad will attract friends of the USSR, and even the last of the Mohicans of the classical school unwilling to make concessions to clericalism will come close to and support us. . . . The upcoming congresses of Americanists should be used by Soviet scholars for firmly and bravely proclaiming Marxist principles in ethnography. . . . Soviet ethnographers have a very serious and honorable obligation [to do this]. But they will fulfill it under the banner of Marxism-Leninism and with a proletarian persistence. And then the international cause of ethnographers would, as a nec-

essary component, join the international project of building culture, "national in form and Socialist in content." (Matorin 1931:37–38; see also Matorin 1934)

Thus Matorin's language transformed the concept of the proletarian revolution into an international Marxist ethnography/anthropology.

It was during his tenure as MAE director that a new (and the last) round of exchange of collections with foreign museums took place. From 1931 to 1936 an American by the name of Eugene Golomshtok (see Golomshtok 1933) visited Soviet Russia with the goal of establishing an exchange of collections between the University of Pennsylvania Museum of Anthropology and MAE, the State Hermitage Museum, and the Russian Museum in Leningrad, as well as the Museum of Anthropology, the State Historical Museum, and the Ethnographic Museum in Moscow.[13] Initially, Golomshtok concentrated on the North, but eventually his interest in the Soviet collections became much broader. However, this project of collection exchange materialized only partially (Kupina 2004).

For the first generation of young Soviet ethnographers, Morgan was turning out to be a convenient figure. On the one hand, he was an example of theorizing on the basis of field data (his own and that of others); on the other, his concepts were quite close to the official ideology, or, at the very least, they did not contradict it. Morgan's research, on the one hand, opened up a whole range of topics related to the study of kinship (primarily classificatory kinship systems) and, on the other, became the precursor of the popular future Soviet studies of ethnogenesis (i.e., all of Morgan's theories were utilized to reconstruct the primordial society [pervobytnoe obshchestvo]). Thus on the basis of the study of kinship systems and their implicit connection to the primordial society, the archaeologists of the 1930s were particularly actively engaged in formulating models of the primordial society, which further developed the logic of Morgan's ideas (Efimenko 1934).

While Western anthropology was becoming a science studying modern societies, the Soviet version was making a turn to the study of premodern ones; that is, it was becoming a historical discipline (i.e., part of the humanities) rather than a social science one. Simultaneously, however, the first articles appeared that examined the culture of the northern peoples from the viewpoint of "primordial communism" (*pervobytnyi communism*) (see Kagarov [1937] for a justification of such an approach). This was an expression of an amazing Soviet ethnographic imagination—a kind of "future in the past." This is how Ian P. Al'kor (Koshkin) described it: "Our Siberian peoples have preserved very many characteristics of the so-called primordial communism, which is very important for us to study and apply for the sake of helping them make a transition to our collective forms of economic life (fishing brigades, reindeer herding cooperatives, etc.)" (K-1/3/7:126, AMAE RAN).

A chance to acquire the Morgan archive arose at a very opportune time. In 1934, with the passing of the linguist and archaeologist Nikolai Marr (a powerful figure in the humanities and some of the social sciences, including ethnography, as far as his theories and his academic politics were concerned), the place of the number one theoretician became vacant (see Slezkine 1991, 1996; Shnirelman 1993). Despite a virtual cult of Marr, his works published both during his life and posthumously (1933–37) were very difficult to apply: most ethnographers turned out to be unable to incorporate his linguistics-based "Iaphetic theory" (cleverly garnished with Marxist phraseology) into their research. In contrast to Marr, Morgan, a much more accessible thinker and a direct predecessor of Engels and Marx, looked a lot more attractive and undoubtedly gave many ethnographers much more food for thought. Thus, for example, it appears that Vinnikov was actually planning to undertake a massive collection of field data on kinship using Morgan's model and program. He even published a guide for field researchers on kinship terminology (Vinnikov 1936b).[14] (For some reason, however, this project never materialized.)[15]

As we will see later, Morgan's theories gradually became "nationalized" or "Sovietized" to such an extent that they stopped being analyzed and came to play a special role by creating (to a significant extent) a parallel world far from the dominant concepts of ethnos and ethnogenesis. It is worth noting that over time Morgan's ideas were no longer commonly present in the works of those Soviet ethnographers who conducted field research in the European part of Russia, Siberia, Central Asia, and the Caucasus. Morgan's works on kinship continued to be used by Africanists, Americanists, and other specialists who rarely (or never) went to the "field" but who, unlike the field ethnographers, knew at least one or even several foreign languages.[16] Thus Morgan fitted perfectly into the space of scholastic constructions (see Gellner 1988). This, however, is a topic for another paper dealing with the post–World War II era. Let us now return to the main protagonist of our chapter.

BERNHARD STERN'S EARLY BIOGRAPHY

Born in 1896 in Chicago to a German Jewish émigré family, Bernhard J. Stern grew up strongly committed to both his Jewish roots and his identity as an American, viewing the latter tradition as being based on the ideas of social justice and democratic freedom (Bloom 1990:19).[17]

Stern studied for a BA and an MA at the University of Cincinnati from 1913 to 1917 and simultaneously enrolled at the Hebrew Theological Seminary, graduating as a Reform rabbi. However, after serving as a rabbi for only one year, he decided to switch careers and become a physician. However, being Jewish, he could not gain admission to a single medical school. Finally, in 1923 he was accepted by a prestigious medical school in Austria but had to give up on his plans due to poor health (Bloom 1990:19). In 1923 Stern traveled to Europe, where he studied at the University of Berlin. His biographer, Samuel Bloom, believed that witnessing German life in the midst of a major economic crisis had a major influence on Stern's "ideological development" (1990:19). In 1924 he also spent six months studying at the London School of Economics.

Returning to the United States that same year, Stern entered Columbia University to study sociology under a prominent progressive scholar, William F. Ogburn. While sociology remained his main discipline and his doctoral thesis was in it, in 1925 he also undertook an intensive study of anthropology with Franz Boas. Stern's degree was actually in both sociology and anthropology. He retained an interest in anthropology for the rest of his life, teaching courses in it, attending anthropological meetings, writing a few important articles on anthropological subjects, and coauthoring a textbook in general anthropology. Stern's PhD dissertation, "Social Factors in Medical Progress," completed in 1926 and published as a book in 1927, earned him a reputation as a serious medical sociologist and historian of sociology. In fact, he is considered one of the earliest American historians of science (see Bloom 2002).

While Stern's early academic works revealed his critical attitude toward the Western and particularly American economic system, as well as the way in which its science and medicine were organized, his left-wing views, including pro-Soviet sympathies, were even more clearly revealed in his conduct as a young college instructor. After teaching in the Sociology Department of City College for a year in 1925–26 as a tutor (substituting for a professor on leave) while finishing his dissertation, he was recommended by his colleagues for a tenure-track position. However, the president of the college turned Stern down because of his sponsorship of a controversial campus talk by a Yale economist, Robert W. Dunn, on the economic and social advances made by the USSR (Bloom 1990:21).[18] According to Stern's widow, this experience, as well as the fact that, despite his fine credentials, his job applications had been turned down by several colleges and universities (including Dartmouth) because he was Jewish, hurt him deeply and undermined his trust in America's democratic principles of freedom of speech and institutions. Nonetheless, in the late 1920s he was not yet a member of any leftist political organization (Charlotte Stern cited in Bloom 1990:21). Charlotte Todes, however, whom he married in 1923, had been a labor movement activist since the early 1920s. She joined the Communist Party USA in 1926 and encouraged her husband to become a member as well.[19]

Finally, in 1927 Bernhard secured a three-year renewable tenure-track assistant professor position in the Sociology Department at the University of Washington. According to his widow, his experience at that school was similar to the one at City College: he was a popular instructor and productive researcher, but his politics made him suspect in the eyes of the administration. According to Bernhard Stern's papers from the Miklejohn Civil Liberties Institute, at the end of his second year he was put on probation by the department chair because "local religious groups, angered by Stern's classroom advocacy of a scientific approach to the problems of life, had been pressuring the University to dismiss him. In addition, the business community was disturbed by Stern's criticism of capitalist institutions and his sympathetic discussion of the achievements of the Soviet Union" (cited in Bloom 1990:22). Stern's anticlerical views seem to have been the main reason why, after three years of teaching at UW, he was offered only one additional and final year. As the documents from the same archive indicate, a group of local ministers played a big role in his dismissal. They were critical of a speech he gave to a local auto mechanics union, in which he claimed—in good Boasian fashion—that environment was a greater force than heredity. They were especially upset "with his comparison of the Easter sunrise service and the pagan rites of Indian idol worshippers" (cited in Bloom 1990:22).

During his sojourn in Seattle, Stern strengthened his position as a left-leaning liberal who was becoming gradually more sympathetic to Communist ideas but was not yet willing to join the party. In 1927 he became very interested in the famous Sacco and Vanzetti case and wrote letters in their defense. As a result of that activity, he became interested in the rights of working people in general and minorities. He often spoke to labor organizations and to student and minority groups about labor rights and related topics (Bloom 1990:22).

STERN AS A BOASIAN ANTHROPOLOGIST

While teaching at the University of Washington, Stern undertook his only ethnographic research. Its subject was the culture of the Lummi, a Coast Salish people residing in the northern part of the Puget Sound area. In a manner typical for most ethnographers working among Native Americans at the time, he spent a few months interviewing several Lummi elders deemed to be "traditional" and then composed a one-hundred-page ethnographic text that focused mainly on the life-cycle and its rituals, other aspects of Lummi religion, and folklore (Stern 1934).[20] The book, while containing some valuable pieces of data, was a standard Boasian ethnography and not a very detailed one at that. In his review, Leslie White characterized it as "a descriptive account of a culture of one of the Salish speaking peoples of the Northwest Coast of North America . . . written in a clear and orderly manner" (1935:387–388). Ronald Olson, a specialist in the region's ethnography, was more critical, characterizing the work as being a brief and "sketchy account" and "decidedly inadequate, judged by modern standards of ethnographic research" (1935:500). He also compared it unfavorably with Verne Ray's more fundamental ethnographies of the neighboring Sanpoil and Nespelem (Olson 1935:500).

Since Stern was a Boasian, as far as his anthropological views were concerned, his book did not discuss the postcontact history of the Lummi or their present-day social and economic life. Thus his "memory ethnography" style of presenting their culture contrasted sharply with his sociological writing, which addressed issues of social change head-on.[21] It should be pointed out that for the rest of his life Stern retained an adherence to some fundamental tenets of Boasian anthropology, as well as admiration and respect for Boas himself. Thus Stern appreciated Boas's antiracist stand, his cultural relativism, and his rejection of the view of "primitives" as being inferior to Westerners. He also agreed with his mentor's critique of diffusionism, his attention to the collective and even individual meaning of cultural elements, and his belief in the importance of psychological factors in culture. As Stern wrote in his review of *Primitive Art*, Boas's "discerning discussion of the psychological factors determining the stability of cultural forms, in spite of its brevity, is superior to any previous discussion of this problem in sociological literature"; he also argued that sociologists had a lot to learn from Boas as far as theoretical formulations were concerned (Stern 1929b:163).[22] The influence of Boas and his school on Stern's anthropological views also colored the way he evaluated Lewis Henry Morgan's contribution to the development of anthropology.

THE MORGAN RESEARCH

While still at the University of Washington, Stern developed an interest in the history of the social sciences and then applied and received funding for archival research on the papers of Lester F. Ward and Lewis H. Morgan, the fathers of American sociology and anthropology, respectively.[23] Using previously unpublished writings, journals, and correspondence from the Morgan archive preserved at the University of Rochester Library, as well as his published works, Stern tried, in his words, "to cast new light on the development of Morgan's theories and to evaluate them in light of contemporary knowledge" (1931:vi). This research resulted in a 1928 article, "Lewis Henry Morgan: American Ethnologist," which summarized Stern's findings and conclusions; a 1931 monograph, *Lewis Henry Morgan: Social Evolutionist*; and several publications of valuable primary sources from the Morgan archive (Stern 1930, 1933).

In his outline of Morgan's biography, Stern pointed out a peculiar paradox: a man he viewed as a middle-class liberal who "never for a moment doubted that capitalism was the best system, the United States the best democracy, and Christianity the only true religion in this better-than-all-previous worlds" produced *Ancient Society*, a work that had become a "socialist classic" (1928:347). Thus, while sympathetic to Morgan, especially as far as his pro-Indian position was concerned, Stern criticized Morgan's political views from the Left and in no way idealized him, as many socialist admirers of the American ethnologist did.

As for Morgan's theorizing, Stern gave him high marks for his Iroquois ethnography and also gave him credit for an interpretation of the evolution and development of the state from a kinship-based organization (*societas*) to a society based on territory and property (*civitas*) presented in *Ancient Society*. At the same time, Stern found many errors and flaws in Morgan's evolutionist argument spelled out in that book and elsewhere. Like Boas and most of his students, Stern viewed Morgan's unilineal evolutionist model as untenable. As Stern put it, "The cultural and social history of a people can be explained only in the light of its historical relations and cultural contacts, and not by any general universal scheme of evolution. The evolutionary concept put forth by Morgan and others . . . must therefore be revised" (1931:136). Using the arguments made by Kroeber, Lowie, Goldenweiser, and Malinowski, Stern also took Morgan to task for his attempts to reconstruct extinct forms of marriage and family by using kin terms. Finally, he took issue with Engels's argument that Morgan's critique of private property and modern capitalist civilization was close to that of the pre-Marxist (utopian) socialists. In Stern's own view, a few comments by the Rochester lawyer that might have suggested such a view could be explained by the financial losses he suffered during the panic of 1873. Generally speaking, throughout his 1928 article and his book on Morgan, Stern took "contemporary socialist students" to task for being reluctant to accept any criticism of Morgan's theories, even while being aware of his mistakes, because of the high praise heaped upon him by Marx and Engels. At the same time, the 1931 book already reflected Stern's own commitment to Marxism, at least a critical and creative use of Marxist theory. In his discussion of Morgan's inadequate reconstruction of the development of the state, Stern stated, "In view of Morgan's popularity in socialist circles, it is important to note that he never grasped the significance of the modern state as a class institution. Not only did he fail to approximate the Marxian formulation of the state as an organ of class domination, refined by Lenin, but he also did not sense the importance of caste as a precursor of the state" (1931:154). Stern's overall conclusion was that while Morgan's evolutionist method had to be discarded, he remained a pioneer, and his *Ancient Society* was "the most significant achievement as the anthropology of its period" (1931:199).

Stern's book on Morgan was received positively but without great enthusiasm. For example, sociologist Guy Johnson characterized it as "a very readable and competent account of the life and work of an American who stands out as one of the founders of anthropology" (1932:151). Surprisingly, only a couple of reviews appeared in anthropological journals.[24] The most perceptive comment on Stern's book was actually made by another biographer of Morgan, Leslie White. Being an evolutionist and an anti-Boasian who had been doing his own research on Morgan since the 1930s, White had a very different view of Morgan's contribution to anthropological theory. Nonetheless, in his review of Carl Resek's 1961 biography of Morgan, White made the following astute observation about Stern's work. While describing the latter as "useful," he pointed out a "conflict of ideologies, which made him [Stern] take a self-contradictory view of Morgan. On the one hand he was benevolently inclined toward him because *Ancient Society* has become a Marxian classic. On the other hand, as a student of Franz Boas, he was obliged to ridicule and reject Morgan as an evolutionist and an armchair philosopher" (White 1961:72). Although White's language was unnecessarily harsh, he did identify a major contradiction in Stern's thinking about Morgan and his scholarship in general. This contradiction between an honest social scientist for whom facts mattered and a committed (Communist) ideologue willing to twist them or overlook their distortion by his ideological comrades sharpened over the years and revealed itself particularly clearly in his dealings with the Soviet anthropologists discussed here.

STERN'S CAREER IN NEW YORK CITY
AND THE COMMUNIST PARTY USA

Despite the setback in Seattle, Stern did not break stride and managed to get a job as an associate editor of *The Encyclopedia of the Social Sciences*, whose senior editor, sociologist Alvin Johnson, had a reputation as an independent liberal thinker. Stern worked with Johnson for four years, until the entire project was completed. This important undertaking allowed him to increase his network of academic ties and author a number of entries on major sociological and anthropological topics. Close collegiate relations with Johnson also helped Stern obtain a part-time teaching appointment in 1934 as a lecturer in anthropology at the New School for Social Research, known for its outstanding progressive faculty. Since Stern taught on a single-course basis, his pay was not high, and he had to supplement it with public lectures and essays on anthropological and sociological topics published under a different name (CS audio interviews 1–3). That same year he also began teaching as a lecturer in the sociology department at Columbia, initially on a single-course basis as well. Two years later, after significant pressure from his senior colleagues in the department, Columbia finally appointed him lecturer in the School of General Studies but without rank; that was the position he occupied until the end of his life in 1956 (CS audio interviews 1–3). Despite his low academic rank and leftist views, Stern was highly regarded by his students and colleagues alike. He even spent time teaching at Yale as a visiting professor and was hired by several foundations, including rather conservative ones, to conduct research and write reports and papers (Bloom 1990:23). Thanks to the respect Stern enjoyed among his Columbia colleagues, he was not fired from the university during the McCarthy era, when the House Un-American Activities Committee investigated him for his Communist activities (Bloom 1990:24–32; Price 2004:136–153).

Stern's journey toward becoming a Communist began with his joining the John Reed Club in 1932 or possibly even earlier. By 1933 he had already become a member of the club's executive committee. Founded in 1929 by the staff members of a pro-Communist magazine titled *New Masses* to support Marxist writers and artists, that organization was originally politically independent but in late 1930 became officially affiliated with Moscow and the Communist Party USA. In 1932 Stern also joined a group of active Communists and representatives of several Communist front organizations to form an American antiwar committee (Lyons 1970:148). Delegates representing similar organizations from various countries met in Amsterdam in August 1932 to form the World Congress against Imperialist War. The organization's main goal was to "support the peace policies of the Soviet Union" and sabotage (through peaceful means) the war preparations in their own countries.[25]

By the mid-1930s Stern had definitely joined the Communist Party USA. This was the time of the Popular Front, when the party, having proclaimed a new policy of cooperation with all the progressive anti-Fascist groups and organizations in the country, increased its membership significantly and enjoyed greater sympathy in the wider American society. It appears that Stern was a member of one of the New York branches of the party that was composed mainly of writers and other intellectuals. This was the unit into which in 1935 he recruited a well-known Columbia University professor and literary critic named Granville Hicks (Levenson and Natterstad 1993:85). In 1936 Stern became one of the founders and editors of a Marxist social science journal titled *Science and Society*. In addition, he contributed articles on evolution and other anthropological subjects to *New Masses* under a pseudonym, Bennett Stevens, and taught occasional courses at the Workers' School affiliated with the Communist Party. At the same time, according to his widow, he was never involved in practical party activities, preferring intellectual conversations and debates (cs audio interviews 1–3).

STERN'S CORRESPONDENCE WITH KOSVEN
AND FIRST VISIT TO THE USSR

Given Stern's work on Morgan and the new developments in his political orientation in the first half of the 1930s, it made perfect sense for him to be eager to establish contacts with Soviet ethnographers and visit the land of socialism. As we have already mentioned, he made the initial contact himself by writing to Mark Osipovich Kosven, a Soviet anthropologist of the older generation who, prior to 1917, had received a fine university education in law and the social sciences in Paris and St. Petersburg but in the late 1920s to early 1930s decided to go with the times by undertaking a study of the *pervobytnyi* (primordial) social organization by applying Marxist theory.[26]

In the course of these studies, Kosven soon realized that Morgan was a key figure whose life and scholarly contributions had to be documented and analyzed from a new (Soviet) ideological perspective. Consequently, he focused much of his 1930s research and publications on this topic, producing an article on Morgan's life in 1932, followed by a small monograph dealing with his life and work in 1933 (the second edition was published in 1935), another article in 1936, several more articles on related topics, and a book, *Matriarchate*, published after World War II (see Kosven 1933b, 1935a, 1948). As a serious researcher commanding several foreign languages, Kosven, having become aware of the Morgan archive in late 1930 or early 1931, contacted the University of Rochester Library curator, Donald Gilchrist, for information about it.

As soon as Stern heard from Gilchrist about a Soviet ethnologist interested in Morgan, he immediately wrote to Kosven on February 1, 1931, informing him that Stern had just published a study of "Morgan's anthropological theories in terms of his milieu and in the light of contemporary anthropology and have told of the use of his work by Marx and Engels" (folder 3, box 1, BJS). Stern was clearly exaggerating the degree to which his book had been written from a Marxist perspective in order to convince Kosven that Stern was his Soviet colleague's comrade-in-arms. He also claimed that his study of Morgan was written "from a historical materialist standpoint." In addition, he was eager to demonstrate to Kosven his credentials as a "fellow-traveller," if not (yet) a Communist, for whom a critical evaluation of the book by a Soviet[!] scholar was of particular importance. As Stern put it, "As a member of the John Reed Club, an organization of revolutionary artists and writers, and as a contributor to the *New Masses*, I would greatly appreciate your critical comments on the book when you read it." He even signed the letter with the words "fraternally yours," common among members of left-wing parties. Finally, the American anthropologist emphasized that his work was innovative in its reliance on a large body of unpublished materials from the Morgan archive, and to give Kosven a taste of them, he mailed him not only the book itself but also a copy of Morgan's correspondence with Lorimer Fison and Alfred William Howitt, which Stern had recently published in the *American Anthropologist* (1930).

Two months later, on March 21, 1931, Stern received a courteous response from Kosven, and thus their seven-year-long correspondence was established.[27] Once the Soviet scholar had received the Morgan book, he carefully read it and heaped a good deal of praise on it, calling it "a very significant contribution to our science." At the same time, he did offer some criticism that was typical of the way Soviet ethnographers evaluated contemporary Western works. The first main flaw he found in Stern's book was his underestimation of "the historical significance" of Morgan's contribution to the discipline in general and the development of the theory of evolution of (primitive) social organization in particular; the second one was Stern's denial of the universal existence of an evolutionary stage of matriarchate, which, following Morgan and Engels, was already becoming a dogma among Soviet ethnographers (folder 3, box 1, BJS).

Stern's response to Kosven, written on June 18, 1931, reflected the tone of his entire dialogue with his Soviet colleagues: he expressed gratitude for Kosven's Marxist criticism of his work but stood his ground as far as the main arguments made in his work were concerned. Thus, he insisted that his work did give Morgan sufficient credit for his contribution to anthropology, but Stern also sent Kosven specific references to the work of several prominent North Americanists whose data clearly undermined Morgan's argument about the universality of an evolutionary matriarchate (folder 3, box 1, BJS).

In May 1931, while Stern was just beginning his correspondence with Kosven, he received a letter from a younger Soviet ethnographer, Isaac Vinnikov, mentioned earlier. At about the same time as Kosven, Vinnikov, who previously specialized in the ethnography of the Jews, turned to the study of the Marxist theory of the evolution of primitive society and specifically to locating the major primary sources on the subject, including the Morgan archive (Kan 2009:387–389). In the process he had come across Stern's 1928 article on Morgan and saw references to his book on the same subject, the latter being unavailable in the USSR. In his first letter to the American scholar, Vinnikov wrote on May 19, 1931, that he was undertaking a major research project entitled "The Fate of Morgan's Theory" and was thus very interested in Stern's research and publications (folder USSR to Stern, box 1, SP). Stern responded on June 18, once again emphasizing that his book had been written from the point of view of historical materialism (folder Stern to USSR, box 1, SP). Three months later he received an invitation from his Leningrad correspondent to contribute a paper on Morgan's life and works (published and unpublished) to a collection of papers being prepared by the MAE and the Commission on the History of Science of the Academy of Sciences on the occasion of the fiftieth anniversary of Morgan's death. In Vinnikov's September 17, 1931, letter to Stern, he stated, "This collection will, on the one hand, consist of a series of articles that will clarify the fate of Morgan's theory, as well as its relationship with the ideas of the founders of scientific socialism, and, on the other, contain factual materials, such as data on the kinship systems of twenty-six peoples of Siberia" (folder USSR to Stern, box 1, SP). On October 27, 1931, Stern replied to Vinnikov and enclosed the book the latter had requested.[28] In addition, Stern said that he would have liked to see the anniversary volume include Marx's original marginal comments on *Ancient Society* based on Marx's copy of the book. He also added an unpublished letter written by Asher Wright to Morgan, which Engels had quoted in his *Origin of the Family*; Stern suggested that Vinnikov might wish to publish it in that same volume or in a Soviet anthropology journal. Finally, Stern suggested, "It would be very valuable also to have a critical analysis of the changes made by Engels on the first edition of his book in preparation of the fourth edition" (folder Stern to USSR, box 1, SP).

For some reason, the proposed collection was never published, and the correspondence between Vinnikov and Stern was interrupted for four years. The only clue to why this happened that is available to us is a September 22, 1935, letter the Leningrad ethnographer sent to Stern when the two of them were working together on the project of publishing Morgan's collected works (see below). In it Vinnikov apologized for not writing for such a long time and said that he would only be able to explain why this had happened if the two of them ever met (folder USSR to Stern, box 1, SP). This suggests that the reason for the hiatus in their correspondence (and possibly in Vinnikov's failure to bring out his volume of papers on Morgan) was political. It is clear from just this initial exchange of letters between Stern and his two Soviet correspondents that he had already whetted their appetite for important primary sources from the Morgan archive and positioned himself as the conduit for conveying them.

Stern's next letter to Kosven, sent in early July 1932, contained an important piece of news: he and his wife were planning to visit the USSR in August on their way to Amsterdam, where they were to take part in the peace congress mentioned earlier. This was to be largely an "exploratory visit," as Charlotte Stern called it. The couple was to arrive in Moscow on August 10 and divide their time between a longer stay in that city and a shorter one in Leningrad. They had to depart for Holland on August 27. Here is how Charlotte Stern described the goals of their trip: "We decided we must see the Soviet Union. I decided I must see it from the standpoint of what the Communists had achieved, and my husband wanted to see it from the standpoint of whether it was the ideal society" (CS audio interviews 1–4).[29] According to Bernhard Stern's letter to Kosven, written July 4, 1932, "The primary purpose of our visit is learning what the Soviet is [*sic*] doing in the field of anthropology and related subjects." Of course, he was eager to meet Kosven himself "to learn of his recent work on the Udmurt people and other Soviet minorities and discuss recent developments in anthropological theory" (folder 3, box 1, BJS).[30]

The Communist Party USA did not provide Charlotte with the names of any contact persons in Russia, but because of her interests in organized labor, she and her husband asked for and were able to visit several factories. While admitting that this visit had been "entirely a surface experience" and that the only people they had been able to speak to were English speakers, Charlotte asserted that both of them were very impressed with the "great spirit of achievement, and effort, and love of the society itself among all of the people that we met." As far as the political situation was concerned, she stated that they had been completely uninformed about it and did not notice anything dramatic, even though this was the time of a major internal struggle within the Communist Party, as well as the expulsion of Trotsky from the USSR. We might add that this was also the time of the major trials of the old intelligentsia and other forms of persecution of those intellectuals who did not follow the party line. Charlotte's evidence of the general contentment among the academics they met shows how naive she and her husband were. As she put it, "The intellectuals who met my husband were very happy and jolly and felt they had a home. There was no criticism of the Communist movement. We never met anyone who actually criticized the system, or the government, or any of the individual leaders" (CS audio interview 4).

What made Bernhard even more enthusiastic about the USSR were the impressions he got from interacting with Soviet anthropologists and other social scientists. As his widow reminisced,

> In Moscow my husband was very warmly welcomed as a young scientist—social scientist—by the anthropologists and the people in the social science field. They were very kind to him, and since he was interested in anthropology, they spent many hours telling him of their plans for the native peoples who had no written language and whose knowledge of the world outside their own little communities was absolutely primitive. The plans they had and the efforts that they made so impressed him that he became quite convinced that this was a world he could support. Furthermore, he was tremendously impressed with the developments there. (CS audio interview 4)

One specific experience that made an enormous impression upon Bernhard was a plenum of the Committee of the Peoples of the North he attended in Moscow as a guest of Bogoraz. Without any knowledge of Russia or understanding of the true nature of the policies involving non-Russian nationalities of the early Stalinist era, Stern took everything that was said from the podium at face value.[31] As he wrote a decade later in an article in which he praised Soviet policies toward ethnic minorities, "I was then struck by the eager exchange of data between the native leaders and the Soviet leaders on both economic and cultural problems of these pre-literate peoples" (Stern 1944:234; cf. Stern to Kosven, October 24, 1932, folder 1, box 3, BJS). To him, the active participation of these ethnic minorities in the decisions and policies affecting their own lives contrasted sharply with the discriminatory and paternalistic policies of the federal and state governments in the United States toward African Americans and Native Americans. As an anthropologist, Stern was also impressed with the work of the Soviet linguists and anthropologists who engaged northern minorities, especially minority students from the Institute of the Peoples of the North, in a lively discussion of the new single northern alphabet based on Latin script to avoid the appearance of Russification.

The two and a half weeks spent in the USSR not only turned Stern into a diehard supporter of the Soviet regime but also broadened and strengthened his relationship with Soviet anthropologists. From then on he not only looked at the Soviet Union as a model of progressive and just society but also became a champion of its anthropology, the leader of Marxist anthropology, in his view, despite some serious disagreements with it on specific issues. This relationship became so important for the Columbia lecturer that, following his 1932 visit to Russia and especially after the second one made in 1937, he would frequently mention it in his public presentations and published works and use it to legitimize his status as an expert on Soviet ethnic groups and state policies toward them (see below).

The American scholar's eagerness to have his work on Morgan reach his Soviet counterparts, to have it translated into Russian and reviewed by them, is easy to understand. First, his Morgan book had not received much publicity, and its reviews had not been as laudatory as he would have liked. Second and more important, he very much wished to be recognized and appreciated in the only socialist country on earth by scholars firmly adhering to Marxism.[32] Thus, in one of his early letters to Kosven, written on April 13, 1931, Stern wrote, "I am anxious to know what Marxian scholars think of the work and will appreciate your sending me copies of any reviews that appear" (folder 3, box 1, BJS). The strength of Stern's desire to be accepted by Soviet academics as a fellow Marxist and a comrade-in-arms is especially clear in his letter to Kosven written on June 16, 1933, after he read Kosven's review of his Morgan book. On the whole, the American scholar was satisfied with the review, yet he was rather disappointed that, as he put it, "it does not give, to the extent that I should desire it, the impression that my approach [to Morgan] is a sympathetic one. Your difference of opinion with me on how Marx and Engels accepted Morgan's work is, I believe, mostly verbal" (folder 3, box 1, BJS). This comment shows how hard he was trying to minimize his differences of opinion with Kosven, which in fact were rather significant. After all, in his book on Morgan, Mark Osipovich characterized *Ancient Society* as being the "revolutionary work of a genius" that "spontaneously" came close to Marx and Engels's dialectical materialism (Kosven 1933b:46).[33] Stern also expressed his regret that Kosven did not mention his membership in the John Reed Club, for, as he put it, "this would have indicated that my interest in Morgan was more than academic" (June 16, 1933, folder 3, box 1, BJS).

While Stern needed Soviet anthropologists, they in turn needed him. As we have already argued, the young Marxist discipline was in search of "progressive" Western allies, and Stern made a perfect candidate. Furthermore, in the Soviet scholars' view, others like Stern could help make American anthropology more progressive. For example, in a letter dated November 9, 1932, to Stern, Kosven characterized the present-day *American Anthropologist* as a very backward scholarly periodical "both in its content and its general direction" and asked whether Stern and his friends would consider starting a "more lively and progressive ethnographic journal" (folder 4, box 1, BJS). In the meantime, progressive anthropologists could be used as sources of critical information about Western anthropology and capitalist society as a whole. Mark Plissetskii, a physical anthropologist Stern had met in Moscow in 1932 and the editor of the *Anthropological Journal*, sent him the following letter in the fall of that year: "In our conversation at Moscow I invited you to take part in *The Anthropological Journal*. Remembering this [agreement], I beg you to write a special report about the Antimilitary Congress in Amsterdam.... This correspondence must reflect the anti-imperialistic controversy in connection with the *colonial* and *racial question* [emphasis by Plissetskii]. I hope to receive from you ... other essays and correspondences about the negro [*sic*] and racial question in America and similar works, that can be interesting for the Journal" (September 29, 1932, folder 4, box 1, BJS). Stern was happy to oblige and six weeks later sent Plissetskii a note on the World Congress against the Imperialist War he had recently attended; he also mailed him a "pamphlet on the American Negro and one on Lynching" and promised to send "anything that appears in the field" (November 12, 1932, folder 4, box 1, BJS). He also sent a letter to Bogoraz promising to prepare a brochure for the Institute of the Peoples of the North on the "treatment of minorities in America" (October 11, 1932, folder 4, box 1, BJS; fond 250, folder 4, p. 307, SPF ARAN).[34]

A more pragmatic reason for individual Soviet anthropologists to court friendly Western colleagues like Stern was the simple fact that few Western publications in their field reached the USSR at that time. Hence, someone like Stern could serve as a valuable source of academic journals and especially books, which helped his Soviet colleagues keep up with the new developments in anthropology abroad. At the same time, he could also help review and otherwise publicize their own publications outside the Soviet Union.[35]

The irony of Stern's enthusiasm about Soviet cultural anthropology or what his Soviet colleagues referred to as "ethnography" is that despite his unquestioning loyalty to the USSR, being a serious scholar, he expected Kosven and his colleagues to apply Morgan's, Engels's, and Marx's theory of social evolution creatively and without dogmatism. In fact, in one of his letters to Kosven, dated December 19, 1933, he complained about the U.S. Socialist Labor Party intellectuals who "regard everything which Morgan has said as absolutely final" and contrasted that with a fresh new approach he was anticipating to come from Moscow (folder 5, box 1, BJS). In reality, it was precisely the Soviet research on the evolution of "primitive" society that had already become quite dogmatic and was becoming increasingly even more so. Stern, who kept a close watch on that research, had to be aware of this trend but chose to downplay and excuse it, attributing the dogmatism to the growing pains of a new and young Marxist social science. Thus, for example, when a Russian émigré scholar alerted him to Matorin's misrepresentation of the reason for Stern's dismissal from the University of Washington and asked him whether he intended to do something about it, Stern replied, "I see no purpose in pursuing this correction further. Undoubtedly few people have even noticed it. I am certainly not in sympathy with any attempt to discredit Soviet scientific endeavor which, though in this field still crude, is making, I believe, valiant efforts and has vast potentialities which should not be gainsaid because of crudities manifested in the formative period. I therefore prefer omission" (Stern to Fedotov-White, January 29, 1937, folder 9, box 1, BJS).

A MOST WELCOME INVITATION

As a true friend of the Soviet Union, Stern was eager to offer it some concrete assistance. Such an opportunity presented itself in late 1933, when he learned from Kosven that the latter was in the process of editing the Russian translations of Morgan's *Ancient Society* and *Houses and House-Life of the American Aborigines* and would be grateful for any materials by or about Morgan that could be published along with these two books (Kosven to Stern, November 18, 1933, folder 5, box 1, BJS). Stern characterized Kosven's project as "an extremely important task, which will determine to a very large extent the future of Marxist anthropology," adding that the extent to which his Soviet colleague would "bring the knowledge accumulated in anthropology since the publication of Engel's [sic] *Origin of the Family* will decide to a large measure the foundation for future research in the field" (Stern to Kosven, December 19, 1933, folder 5, box 1, BJS). Not surprisingly, this American Marxist was anxious to be a part of such an important project.

Kosven was clearly delighted to receive this offer of assistance, and so his response contained the following proposition. While he told Stern he did not really need much help with the new edition of *Ancient Society*, which was being published without any additional materials except for Morgan's introduction to the book by Fison and Howitt (1880),[36] Kosven conveyed to Stern the Soviet anthropologists' interest in publishing as a separate book—with Stern's participation and under his editorship—all of Morgan's journals and letters. He added that he and his colleagues were particularly interested in having Stern locate Fison's replies to Morgan's letters, as well as Morgan's correspondence with Bandelier, Powell, and several others.[37] In late February Kosven received a letter from his American colleague in which the latter expressed his happy consent to undertake the preparation of Morgan's journals and letters for publication in the USSR despite his very busy schedule of teaching and working on *The Encyclopedia of the Social Sciences* (February 26, 1934, folder 6, box 1, BJS).

Kosven's plan was to have this new work published by the Scientific Research Association of the Institute of the Peoples of the North, which he was affiliated with at the time. Kosven's choice of that institution made good sense. Ian P. Al'kor (Koshkin) (1900–1938), the head of the institute and of its Scientific Research Association who during this time also had an appointment at the Institute of Anthropology and Ethnography (IAE), was a dedicated party member and a Marxist ideologue, as well as a serious ethnographer-linguist trained by Shternberg and Bogoraz. He also had access to some funds for publishing such significant and timely works as those by Morgan and at the same time could compose ideologically correct introductions to them. This, in fact, was the role he played in the first and second editions of *Ancient Society*, published in 1934 and 1935, respectively, as well as *Houses and House-Life of the American Aborigines*, published in 1934.[38]

As soon as Stern had expressed his eager acceptance of Kosven's offer, he began the actual work. In fact, he labored so hard that in late April 1934, he was already reporting to his Soviet colleague that he was making "rapid progress" and that the manuscript should be on its way to Russia "within a month or so." Kosven must have been very pleased, yet the issue of compensating Stern troubled him. As he informed his American correspondent, Al'kor could only pay him Soviet currency. Stern's response to this information reveals how deeply committed he was to the project and to helping his Soviet colleague: "I am motivated entirely by my desire to be of some service to Soviet ethnology. It therefore makes no difference to me that you will find it impossible to pay anything in foreign currency. When the manuscript arrives in Moscow and you see its size, you may decide what you wish to pay in Russian rubles and deposit these in a Russian bank to my account" (Stern to Kosven, April 30, 1934, folder 6, box 1, BJS).

It is important to mention that, in regard to the editorial decisions about the materials to be included or left out of the book, Kosven left almost all of them up to Stern. Of course, with Morgan having already acquired the status of a sacred ancestor of Marxist anthropology, Kosven's preference was undoubtedly to have all of his journals, letters, and field notes transcribed, translated, and published. However, when Stern pointed out that he was not planning to include in the book any of Morgan's field notes that were difficult to decipher or not very informative, Kosven did not insist on having all of them published.[39] The only thing he insisted on was that, as far as the correspondence was concerned, at least Morgan's own letters had to be published without deletions, contrary to what Stern had done in his *American Anthropologist* publication of Morgan's correspondence with Fison and Howitt (Kosven to Stern, May 20, 1934, folder 6, box 1, BJS; Stern 1930).[40]

This granting the American Marxist wide editorial freedom, however, did not mean that Kosven and his colleagues did not make any attempt to fit Morgan's biography and his writings into the particular ideological framework that currently dominated the Soviet social sciences. On the contrary, Kosven's letters to Stern indicate that he was eager to have Stern uncover certain "ideologically correct" ideas and themes in Morgan. For example, taking his cue from a brief comment made by Engels about Morgan's alleged harsh criticism of capitalist society, Stern's Soviet correspondent let him know that he and his "comrades were very interested to find out whether Morgan had been influenced by utopian socialism," that is, by Henri de Saint Simon, Robert Owen, and Charles Fourier, and Kosven encouraged Stern to carefully explore Morgan's library to see if any of their works appeared in it (May 20, 1934, folder 6, box 1, BJS).[41]

Similarly, while Kosven called Stern's Lummi book "exemplary" and praised it as a "brilliant ethnographic monograph," he took him to task for not having found any evidence of the existence of the "gens" (his term for "clan") among the Lummi. Kosven could not imagine a society, "more or less advanced, that had not passed through the gens-based stage [*rodovoi stroi*] in the course of its evolution," and certain characteristics of Lummi society convinced him that the gens still existed among them in the form of a survival. He urged his American colleague to revisit this aspect of Lummi social organization and explore it as carefully as he had studied other aspects of their culture. By doing this, wrote Kosven, "you could provide very strong material for *our* (*Morganian*) [emphasis added] theory of the development of primitive society and specifically the question of the gens" (Kosven to Stern, July 4, 1934, folder 6, box 1, BJS). Kosven strongly encouraged Stern to continue his "excellent" ethnographic research among the Lummi and other Native American peoples. In other words, realizing how difficult it would be for Soviet ethnographers to undertake research in North America, he was pushing an American Marxist colleague to continue it, but with a specific goal in mind: collecting the data that would illustrate and support the evolutionary theory developed by Morgan, Engels, and Marx.[42]

In late August 1934 Kosven received a letter from Stern informing him that the work on the Morgan materials for the Soviet publication had been completed. The manuscript Stern had just mailed to Russia consisted of the following: his own brief introduction, the entire correspondence between Morgan and Fison and Howitt, a section of Morgan's travel journal (the only one Stern found to be useful to researchers), and photostats of the complete inventory of Morgan's library. While this material was somewhat smaller than the entire body he had promised to prepare, Stern told Kosven that he did not want to delay the publication any longer. Deciphering some of Morgan's journals would take a lot of time, and for that reason Stern was postponing that portion of the work (Stern to Kosven, August 27, 1934, folder 6, box 1, BJS).

Kosven was very pleased with the results of Stern's work and in his November 1934 letters assured him that the Institute of the Peoples of the North was about to publish the materials Stern had prepared. He also for the first time introduced a new plan that he and his colleagues had recently come up with: to publish Morgan's *entire* corpus or "literary legacy" (*literaturnoe nasledie*). They were eager to have Stern continue serving as the collector of the materials and the editor (or one of the editors) of these future publications (Kosven to Stern, November 24, 1934, folder 6, box 1, BJS). This decision is a clear indication of a further elevation of Morgan within the pantheon of the key classical pre-Marxist scholars whose works had to be studied as carefully as the writings of Marx, Engels, and Lenin (and eventually Stalin). Kosven also informed Stern that Soviet scholars were very interested in purchasing the original letters from Morgan's correspondence with Fison that Stern had just discovered and that, having finished editing the Russian translation of *Ancient Society* and *Houses and House-Life of the American*

Aborigines, he was now planning to produce a Russian edition of *The League of the Ho-dé-no-sau-nee or Iroquois*. In early 1935 Stern replied that he would be happy to accept Kosven's invitation to undertake this much larger Morgan project but added that, before agreeing to take it on, he had to review the entire Morgan archive; however, at present he had no spare time to do that. Little did he know that soon it would no longer be Kosven but a group of staff members of the IAE/MAE whom he would be working with on this massive project.

ENTER THE INSTITUTE OF ANTHROPOLOGY AND ETHNOGRAPHY

In the early to mid-1930s, as Morgan's writings were becoming firmly emplaced as a major part of the foundation of the Soviet Marxist theory of social evolution, their value as "symbolic capital" was gradually increasing. Hence it is not surprising that Kosven was not the only Soviet ethnologist preoccupied with publishing and analyzing Morgan's works. Despite his failure to produce a volume of essays marking the fiftieth anniversary of Morgan's death, Isaac Vinnikov was busy pursuing his own Morgan project at this time. His approach, however, was somewhat different from Kosven's: instead of concentrating on Morgan's biography and on editing Russian translations of his major monographs, the Leningrad scholar concentrated on locating what he believed were previously unknown or underappreciated materials from the Morgan corpus and publishing them with his own Marxist commentaries and analysis. The title of his 1932 article, "We Must Publish the Classics of Marxism with Care," served as the motto of his approach.

Vinnikov had to be aware of Kosven's collaboration with Stern, since the former mentioned it in his publication. For that reason, as well as because he must have been embarrassed about the fiasco with the 1931 volume, Vinnikov chose to operate on his own by contacting Donald Gilchrist of the University of Rochester Library directly with requests for materials from the Morgan archive. Simultaneously, according to a letter written by the director of IAE to a French colleague, in the early 1930s Vinnikov was engaged in his own translation of *Ancient Society* (Reshetov 1999:29; Vinnikov 1933:25). One wonders whether he was unaware of a similar project being undertaken by Kosven at the Institute of the Peoples of the North or whether he knew about it but believed that his translation would be more accurate.

The first result of this activity was an article published in late 1933 in which Vinnikov reprinted and analyzed in detail a certain table found inside the manuscript pages of *Ancient Society*. Vinnikov had recently obtained this table (as well as some other Morgan material he chose not to name), which in his view was extremely valuable as an illustration of the development of Morgan's views on the evolution of human society from the lowest to the highest forms: the left side of the table listed human inventions and discoveries, while the right side listed the evolution of social institutions. As far as the Leningrad ethnologist was concerned, this document was an important "discovery": it gave researchers a clear idea of Morgan's views on such important topics as the evolution of language, religion, and, most important, the existence of the "primitive horde," with its sexual promiscuity, as the earliest stage of human social organization (Vinnikov 1933:24–25).

This publication by his rival undoubtedly upset Kosven, who had previously enjoyed the status of the number one expert on Morgan among Soviet ethnographers. Here is what he wrote about this to Stern in the early summer of 1934:

> A certain young Leningrad ethnographer has obtained with the help of Mr. Gilchrist a six-page-long table containing a depiction of the evolution of inventions and, parallel to them, the evolution of social institutions. It appears that this table is a preliminary scheme of the chapter of *Ancient Society* entitled "Ratio of Human Progress." Unfortunately, this young ethnographer has not made this document available to researchers. Please let me know whether you are familiar with it and whether you are planning to include it in the book you are preparing. Also, if you have a copy of this document, it would be very important for us to obtain it. (Kosven to Stern, June 12, 1934, folder 6, box 1, BJS)[43]

Kosven's letter did not mention his rival by name, which suggests that he was trying to prevent his American colleague from contacting him directly. Moreover, by referring to Vinnikov as a "young" scholar, despite the fact that there was only a twelve-year age difference between them and that the IAE ethnologist was thirty-seven years old, Kosven was emphasizing that the former was a newcomer to the Morgan research and did not really know what he was talking about.

The Kosven-Vinnikov competition over the Morgan legacy (published and unpublished) and its interpretation continued for several more years and is worth mentioning as an illustration of the way in which academic points were scored and/or lost in the fight over such valuable symbolic capital during the Stalinist era. In 1934 Vinnikov published Bachofen's letters to Morgan without saying a word about Kosven's article on Bachofen, which appeared a year earlier. This was clearly a slap in the face to the Moscow ethnologist. In addition, in order to build up his own scholarly contribution, he decided to criticize Stern by arguing that the two of them pursued very different goals: his own was a truly academic publication in which the letters were published in their entirety, whereas Stern's publication contained numerous errors and deletions (Vinnikov 1934:70). Vinnikov offered the same harsh and largely unfair criticism of Stern's work in his 1935 publication of a large body of documents that had come mainly from the Morgan archive.[44] It was published by the Academy of Sciences and edited by the new director of the IEA, Ivan I. Meshchaninov.[45] Matorin had been dismissed from that position on January 1, 1934, and then arrested in early 1935.

While not as aggressive as Vinnikov, Kosven did not appreciate these swipes at his American colleague and, by extension, at himself, and so in the second edition of his Morgan biography he devoted a footnote to his rival that was full of sarcasm. Referring to Vinnikov's 1933 article as just a "little piece" (*stateika*) that conveyed the substance of Morgan's table from *Ancient Society* "sloppily and not accurately" (1935a:67), Kosven argued that it actually did not offer much new information compared to what had already been presented by Morgan in *Houses and House-Life of the American Aborigines*. He also referred to the author of the "little article" as someone who was "busy chasing discoveries" (1935a:67).

This competition between the two Soviet scholars had much less to do with their efforts to broaden the horizons of Soviet ethnography or improve the methods of field research than with their ability to correlate ethnographic "facts" with the "grid" of the official discourse, reminiscent of Foucault's ideas about the relationship between power and knowledge. Hence, as Krementsov points out, as far as these "fundamental" texts were concerned, "most critics paid no attention to the real content of the work criticized, focusing instead on their 'contributions' to the ideas of the classics of Marxism—Marx, Engels, and Lenin. The typical line in such criticism was that the author's statements on some subject or other 'runs counter to those of the Marxist classics.' 'Distortions' and 'misinterpretations' of Marxism became the main subjects of criticism" (1997:47).

A statement by a dogmatic Marxist bureaucrat and the de facto head of the IAE in the mid-1930s gives a good sense of the kind of Marxism that had developed by this time:

> Those Soviet researchers who study the past of humankind are faced with big and very noble tasks. Taking advantage of the understanding of the primordial-communist formation developed by Marx, Engels, Lenin, and Stalin, they must constantly discover new materials, thus placing their research on such a high theoretical level that it is unattainable to the researchers of the dying class; they must also advance their science at previously unseen rates. Our class enemy is fighting a vicious battle on the theoretical front. Thus all the subdisciplines studying the primordial society have been mobilized to support the fascist racist theory. The task of Soviet scholars is to increase and sharpen the theoretical weapons of the proletariat and along with the proletariat completely defeat the adversary on this front. The cause of socialist construction also places a very big obligation on the Soviet scholars. It is their noble cause to actively help the cultural and economic growth of the peoples of the USSR by studying their history, daily life, and language and thus march in the front columns of the builders of the new society. (Busygin 1934:16)

Throughout 1935 Kosven would periodically inform Stern that the work of publishing the materials he had prepared for the Institute of the Peoples of the North was moving along but more slowly than he had anticipated. Kosven blamed the delays on his own poor health, on the fact that he was based in Moscow and rarely visited Leningrad, and on other unnamed "circumstances," which most likely had to do with an increasingly charged atmosphere of purges and arrests. More importantly, by mid-1935 Kosven and Al'kor had already lost control over the larger project of publishing the entire body of the Morgan legacy. The latter was now in the hands of the IEA. In fact, the work on that project had begun even earlier. In addition to producing the publications discussed earlier, in 1935 Vinnikov contacted Arthur C. Parker, the head of the Rochester Museum of Arts and Sciences, asking him to prepare two appendices to Vinnikov's own edition of *Ancient Society* (*Rochester Times-Union*, February 20, 1935, cited in Moses 2009:284).[46]

In addition, about this time another important player, an Indian Communist by the name of Virendranath Chattopadhyaya (1880–1937) who had been working at the IAE since 1933 was given the task of playing a major role in the Morgan project. In 1934 he contacted Stern, informing him of his work on a new English translation of Engels's *Origin of the Family* (Chattopadhyaya to Stern, August 25, 1934, folder 6, box 1, BJS; Stern to Kosven, January 10, 1935, folder USSR to Stern, SP). Chattopadhyaya (or "Chatto," as friends and colleagues called him) had already had experience working with the original texts written by the classics of Marxism-Leninism. Just a few months before joining the IAE he had published a two-volume English translation of Lenin's works (Reshetov 1998). An Oxford-educated Indian Communist and an active participant in the work of the Communist International, he was seen as a "trusted comrade" and, moreover, as someone capable of translating works written in several European languages (Baruwa 2004). In 1933 Chatto gave a presentation on Engels's *Origin of the Family* in which he compared its translation into several European languages (Reshetov 1998). In 1934 he was in charge of preparing a special issue of *Sovetskaia Etnografiia* dedicated to the fiftieth anniversary of that book. In several of his letters to Stern, Kosven described Chattopadhyaya as his friend and characterized him as a "serious and active" person (see, e.g., Kosven to Stern, June 24, 1936, folder USSR to Stern, box 1, SP).[47]

Chattopadhyaya was only one of a number of foreigners working and/or doing research at the IAE/MAE in the 1930s. They included Boas's student Archibald Finney, Roy F. Barton, Wilhelmina Trisman, and several others. Some of them worked on translating Morgan and other anthropological classics into Russian. In addition to these translations, another major project of the 1930s that had been initiated by the widow of Lev Sternberg, Sarra A. Rattner-Shternberg, and involved several staff members of the IAE was the publication of his collected works. That project was only partially realized: two collections of his articles and ethnographic notes and his lectures on the evolution of religion were published (see Kan 2009:419–420). All of these archival and publication projects represented the creation of a tangible manifestation of "symbolic capital," which gave the IAE ethnographers the right to establish a new configuration of power relations within their institute vis-à-vis ethnographers in other institutions and within the Soviet humanities and social sciences in general. The purchase of and the work on the Morgan archive were very much part of that project.

In the summer of 1935 Stern received an important letter, written in English, from the director of the IAE:

Dear Professor Stern,

Appreciating the outstanding importance of the works of Lewis Henry Morgan who layed [sic] the beginning of the materialistic history of primitive communistic society, the Academy of Sciences USSR has decided to publish Morgan's complete works in the Russian language. The carrying out of this purpose has been entrusted by Presidium of the Academy to the Institute of Anthropology and Ethnography. . . . [T]he Editorial Council of the Academy . . . organized a special Editorial Committee. In connection with this we have the honor to ask you to become the member of this committee. Your participation in this work might be as follows: preparing for publication these unpublished papers, diaries and other manuscripts of Morgan, which have been discovered by you for publication; search of other unpublished manuscripts, letters, etc. of Morgan; fulfillment of that part of the work of determining texts, commenting, etc., that might be done only in your country; some consultation and so on. (Meshchaninov to Stern, July 13, 1935, folder USSR, SP)[48]

The letter also informed the American scholar that the materials he had already submitted to the Institute of the Peoples of the North would be published by that institution but that they would eventually be included in the proposed publication of Morgan's complete works being proposed by the academy. The collected works of L. H. Morgan were to consist of six volumes and include all of his articles, correspondence, manuscripts, and published monographs. Stern was to be paid in a combination of Soviet and American currency. The letter closed with a list of the members of the editorial committee: A. Deborin (chair of the committee, academy member), I. Meshchaninov (director of IAE/MAE, academy member), Ia. Al'kor (Koshkin) (editor-in-chief), A. Busygin (associate director of MAE/IAE), S. Bykovskii, V. Chattopadhyaya, E. Kagarov, M. Kosven, B. Stern, and I. Vinnikov.

This editorial board clearly represented a compromise between the erudite scholars who had done research on Morgan and knew foreign languages (Kosven, Vinnikov, Kagarov, Chattopadhyaya) and dogmatic Marxists like Busygin, Bykovskii, and Deborin, with Al'kor occupying an intermediate position between the two groups.[49] In addition, the importance of the project was underscored by the participation of two members of the academy and both the director and the associate director of the IAE. At the same time, by appointing Al'kor the editor-in-chief, the committee was not only acknowledging his previous efforts to publish Morgan in his capacity as the head of the Institute of the Peoples of the North but also responding to an important memo he had sent in the spring of 1935 to the director of the IAE in which he presented the following argument for the "necessity of publishing the collected works of L. H. Morgan and for doing so only in the USSR":

Having been critically reinterpreted and enriched by the works of Marx and Engels in the fields of history and economics, Morgan has become part and parcel of a powerful arsenal of Marxism, and today one cannot imagine a single Marxist work on the subject of prehistory that would not incorporate his data, as well as his arguments. Given the sharply negative attitude of bourgeois science and society toward Morgan, there is no doubt that his works will not be reissued [in the West].

Given all this, it is absolutely clear that (1) the collected works of L. H. Morgan need to be published and (2) this project could only be carried out in the Soviet Union; and this is the reason I am asking you, as a representative of the Academy of Sciences of the USSR, to undertake the publication of the "Collected Works of L. H. Morgan in Russian and English." (142/1-1935/38:1–3, SPF ARAN)[50]

This was a memo the IEA director and his entourage could not possibly ignore. To do so would mean to be anti-Marxist, and that was something no social scientist could afford to be in the era of "high Stalinism." Moreover, by undertaking such a fundamental and ideologically correct project, the IEA was reaffirming its ideological purity and loyalty while also demonstrating that ethnography, like all of the other social sciences, had a very solid Marxist theoretical base.

The editorial board realized that producing a six-volume edition of Morgan's collected works, especially since it involved obtaining a large number of archival materials from abroad, was a very ambitious and costly undertaking. This was confirmed by "A Preliminary Inventory of the Morgan Manuscripts," sent by Stern to Busygin in early 1936, which indicated that the kind of thorough duplication that the editorial board had requested would amount to about seventeen thousand copies (Stern to Busygin, February 11, 1936, K-3/2/7:5a, AMAE RAN). For that reason, the board requested a substantial amount of money from the Academy of Sciences.[51] In February 1936 Stern signed an agreement with the IAE to undertake the project. Aside from the cost of copying, purchasing books and magazines, and incidental expenses, he was to be paid for his labor the sum of $1,200 plus 2,400 rubles, the latter to be deposited in his name into a Soviet bank. The work was supposed to be completed by the end of 1936. If it extended beyond 1936, Stern was to be paid an additional honorarium (Busygin to Stern, February 22, 1936, folder USSR to Stern, box 1, SP).

Throughout 1936 and part of 1937 Stern spent many hours selecting the materials for photocopying and corresponding with the University of Rochester Library staff and the Eastman Kodak Company, which did the actual photocopying. He was also busy looking for and purchasing copies of books by Morgan and journals that featured articles by and about him. In addition, he continued to make efforts to locate additional manuscripts and letters pertaining to the Morgan legacy. The American Marxist scholar undoubtedly enjoyed the work: the subject matter was of significant interest to him, he was happy to help Soviet anthropology, and it made him feel important to be a member of the editorial board of this publication. At the same time, his frustration with the periodic delays with payments from the IAE, which forced him to cover expenses out of pocket, is evidenced by the voluminous correspondence preserved in the IAE/MAE and the two Stern archives. Here, for example, is an excerpt from one irritated letter Stern sent to Meshchaninov:

> Your directions for further work are along the lines on which I had planned. However, I say with regret that I shall not be able to undertake any additional work on the Morgan materials until I receive your decision and action on the [financial] question raised in my letter of January 1937. The Morgan research has interfered appreciably with the execution of other research and writing during this period and I cannot continue unless I am certain of what your answers are to the matters raised in that letter. Furthermore, as you are aware from the expense account, which I have submitted and from the supplementary statement, which I enclose in this letter, I have no further expense money at hand and you of course recognize the impossibility of my advancing further sums. (142/1-1935/38:31, SPF ARAN)

These frustrating delays were caused not only by Soviet bureaucracy but also by changes in the IAE administration brought about by the Great Terror of 1936–38. Thus, for example, in late summer 1936 Stern received a letter from Meshchaninov instructing him not to address any of his future letters to Busygin, the associate director of the IAE/MAE, but to write only to Meshchaninov or to Al'kor, because Busygin was "no longer connected with the Academy of Sciences" (Meshchaninov to Stern, August 3, 1936, folder USSR to Stern, box 1, SP). The truth of the matter was that Busygin had been arrested earlier that summer, accused of being a member of a "Trotskyite terrorist organization," and subsequently executed. A number of other staff members of the IAE/MAE were also arrested in 1936, including Bykovskii. That same year Al'kor (Koshkin) was expelled from the party "for losing his Communist vigilance" and removed from the post as the head of the Institute of the Peoples of the North. He did, however, continue working at the IAE/MAE.

While working on the project, the American Marxist continued corresponding with his old pen pal Kosven. The latter remained a recognized authority on Morgan, and his chapter entitled "Engels and Morgan" was the lead one in a monumental volume entitled *Issues in the History of the Pre-class Society* and published in 1936 on the occasion of the fiftieth anniversary of the publication of Engels's *Origin of the Family*.[52] At the same time, having left his position at the Institute of the Peoples of the North, he rarely visited Leningrad and seems to have played a secondary role in the deliberations of the Morgan Collected Works Editorial Committee.[53] As he wrote to Stern on June 24, 1936, "In the Academy of Sciences, the work on Morgan will now be carried out mainly by Comrade Chattopadhyaya" (folder USSR to Stern, box 1, SP). He was still hoping to publish excerpts from some of the Morgan manuscripts, which Stern was preparing for the IAE edition, in the *Sovetskaia Etnografiia* journal he had been involved in, but that project did not materialize (Kosven to Stern, June 24, 1936, folder USSR to Stern, box 1, SP). He did, however, try to intervene on Stern's behalf with the editorial committee whenever his friend's interests were being ignored.

On the whole the editorial committee was quite pleased with Stern's tireless efforts and on a number of occasions told him so. All signs seemed to point in the direction of the project's eventual success, especially since Morgan's stature within the Soviet social sciences continued to grow. This was evidenced by the fact that in mid-1936 the editorial committee began planning the eventual establishment of a Morgan "study" (*kabinet*). Modeled on the existing museum studies of Marx, Engels, Lenin, and other famous revolutionaries and scholars, it was supposed to showcase all of Morgan's books and articles, as well as all the works written about him. It was also supposed to feature photographs depicting the great anthropologist's life, as well as his bust, which Stern was asked to commission in the United States (Kosven to Stern, July 20, 1936, folder USSR to Stern, box 1, SP).

In the spring of 1937, having completed most of the work on the Morgan project, Stern found what seemed like a unique opportunity to have a face-to-face meeting with members of the editorial committee while visiting the socialist paradise. He signed up to lead a summer travel seminar/excursion to the USSR for schoolteachers and social workers, organized by the Compass Travel Bureau of New York City. Here is how this travel agency advertised Stern's expertise in its promotional brochure:

> Professor Stern has visited the Soviet Union previously and has studied the life and progress of Soviet national minorities. He has established friendly contacts with leading Soviet scientists, scholars, and men of letters, and is at present American editorial consultant for the Museum of Anthropology and Ethnography of the Academy of Sciences of the USSR. Membership in the Seminar guided by Professor Stern will provide a unique opportunity for an understanding of changing Soviet life. While the seminar will devote itself mainly to the study of the Soviet policy on the national minorities, there will also be an appraisal of other aspects of Soviet life. Professor Stern will be accompanied by Mrs. Stern, an authority on labor and social security. (142/1-1935/38:71–72, SPF ARAN)[54]

The Sterns and their twelve students were supposed to sail from New York on July 12 and arrive in Leningrad on July 19. After spending two days there, they were to travel to Moscow for a four-day stay. Their itinerary also included Kharkiv, Tbilisi, Erevan, Kiev, and several other cities. They were to depart from the USSR on August 19. Since this trip was billed as an educational one, Stern was anxious to have as many Soviet scholars as possible lecture to the participants, and he asked Kosven and other colleagues for help in lining up such lectures. He also asked them to arrange presentations for his group by people in the national republics who were "most likely to impress the visitors ... with the great significance of the Soviet approach to the treatment of national minorities and the superiority of the socialist method as opposed to the imperialist" (Stern to Kosven, March 3, 1937, folder

Stern to USSR, box 2, SP). Thus, this educational tour looked more like a pro-Soviet propaganda trip. In addition, this time the Communist Party USA gave the Sterns the names of some people they were to contact in the Soviet Union (either to get some assistance or to carry messages from American comrades?) (CS audio interview 4).

As for his expectations of the trip as a whole, Stern already knew he was going to be impressed. Since his previous visit, he had become an even greater fan of the USSR. In fact, in mid-1934, having finished his work on *The Encyclopedia of the Social Sciences*, he asked Kosven for assistance in arranging his long-term visit to the USSR, a trip that would enable him to teach and possibly do research there. Despite Kosven's efforts, this plan did not work out.[55] The Marxist journal *Science and Society*, coedited by Stern, made rather frequent references to the Soviet political and social system, its economy, and its high culture, all of them being laudatory. Stern's own scholarly paper, published in that journal in 1937, dealt with the obstacles to technological progress in capitalist societies and offered high praise to the new forms of that progress, as well as industrial production (e.g., the Stakhanovite movement) in the USSR. Continuing to take the propaganda generated by the Soviets at face value, he was in awe of the new (Stalin) constitution of 1936, referring to it in a November 27, 1936, letter to Meshchaninov as "very inspiring to us here" and "having a tremendous symbolic value to the world in its struggle against Fascism" (folder Stern to USSR, box 1, SP). And like all of the American Communists and quite a few of the liberals, he was convinced that the Old Bolsheviks and other prominent Soviet leaders paraded in Stalin's show trials of 1936–37 were indeed guilty of the most heinous crimes.[56]

The Sterns must not have realized that they had picked the worst time to visit the USSR. This being July, a lot of the academics they had hoped to meet in Leningrad and Moscow had gone on vacation. As his widow reminisced, "The result was that some of the academicians Bernhard wanted to see, he did not see. They were out of town, on vacation, unavailable. . . . We could not get into the Academy of Sciences [building]. That was closed. And we could not locate the microfilms he had sent them; and no one seemed to know anything about the microfilms" (CS audio interview 4). Actually, the political climate in the country had a much greater effect on these academics than the season and the weather, and the Sterns felt it. According to Charlotte, the couple was unable to see any of the people they had met on their previous trip because those people did not want to see Americans: "There was such a restrictive atmosphere in the country. The Soviet government was discouraging people from seeing foreigners. The fear of meeting foreigners was great" (CS audio interview 4). When the Sterns went to the apartments of some of the people they had met in 1932, they were told that people were out of town. Some of the people Bernhard had corresponded with refused to see him. According to Charlotte Stern, she and her husband did not know what to think, but they did not suspect that some of the people they had met before had been arrested, since nobody talked about the purges to the Sterns. It is difficult to say whether Charlotte, who remained a die-hard Communist till her dying day, was being naive or disingenuous when she claimed that she and her husband did not know about the trials and the labor camps. At least she did acknowledge that "there was fear in the air" (CS audio interview 4). Bernhard did manage to meet with Meshchaninov, who actually gave a talk to the American visitors, and with Kosven. One wonders what those two members of the editorial committee told him about the four others (out of the total of nine!) who had been arrested in the past twelve months, two of them, Al'kor and Chattopadhyaya, not long before Stern's arrival. Despite those disappointing experiences in Moscow and Leningrad, the Sterns enjoyed their trip, especially their visits to the outlying regions, where they observed the (seeming) enthusiasm of the Soviet people continuing the construction of socialism (CS audio interview 4).

Upon his return, Stern seems to have never mentioned the negative aspects of Soviet life in 1937, which he must have justified by the threat of fascism and the need to be on the alert for foreign and domestic enemies.[57] Consequently, in 1938, without any hesitation, he added his signature to a letter signed by 150 left-wing and liberal American scholars and artists expressing their support for the trial of Bukharin and other enemies of the USSR (Lyons 1970:246–250). And unlike a large number of American Communists who left the party after Soviet Russia signed the infamous pact with Nazi Germany in August 1939,

Stern, despite being a passionate antifascist, remained steadfast in his pro-Soviet views, following the party line as far as justifying and even praising Stalin's sudden about-face.

Here is what Stern wrote about his Russian trip a few months later in a letter dated September 5, 1937, to Meshchaninov: "My trip to the Soviet Union was extremely illuminating and significant to me. My first-hand impressions were most favorable as were those of my group; we shall inform others here of the extraordinary progress which we have observed" (folder Stern to USSR, box 2, BS). Four years later, when the USSR was fighting Hitler, Stern summed up his impression of the 1937 visit in an unpublished paper, "The Soviet Fight against the Nazi Invasion":

> Everywhere we saw the courageous effort of workers and farmers to build a society without the exploitation of man by man. We saw the prodigious advances in education and science, the remarkable strides in the standard of living, not merely in a small segment of the population, but in the masses of people. The efforts that were being made to enlarge the range and extent of the depth of human happiness were apparent to us. . . . Beyond that we saw a nurturing of the creative forces among the people, a fostering of their senses of beauty and their love for knowledge and truth. . . . [Yet] the people and the government were wisely alert to the danger of attack from abroad. They were ever vigilant and ready to sacrifice. (folder 6, box 5, BJS)

THE END OF THE MORGAN PROJECT

While Stern returned from Soviet Russia full of enthusiasm (or at least he claimed to feel that way), 1937 was actually not a good year as far as the Morgan project was concerned. To begin with, even prior to his trip Stern had learned from Kosven in a letter dated April 7, 1937, that the publication of the materials Stern had prepared for the Institute of the Peoples of the North was being delayed due to "administrative reorganization, including Al'kor's departure from it" (folder USSR to Stern, box 2, SP). Since two years later the institute had still done nothing about this publication, Stern must have realized by then that the project was dead in the water. In the same 1937 letter, Kosven also indicated that not much progress had been made on the Morgan project at the IAE, except for the work of translating *The League of the Ho-dé-no-sau-nee or Iroquois* and *The American Beaver and His Works* into Russian (folder USSR to Stern, box 2, SP).

It is not difficult to imagine that in the midst of the massive arrests in Leningrad and specifically at the IAE, the remaining members of the editorial committee had more important issues to deal with than Morgan's collected works. In late 1937, after the wave of arrests had somewhat subsided, the leadership of the IAE, like that of all the other academic institutes, had to follow the latest pronouncement of Comrade Stalin and, together with their entire staff, denounce their former colleagues ("unmasked" by the secret police) as "Trotskyite-Bukharinite" bandits whose goal had been to destroy Soviet ethnography (S.A. 1938:230–232). Given this atmosphere in the country and specifically the IAE, it is not surprising that, after Stern's visit to the USSR, none of his Soviet colleagues, including his friend Kosven, continued corresponding with him. From then on, the only letters he received were the official ones from IAE directors and other bureaucrats. Unfortunately for Stern, he seemed not to appreciate the degree of fear his former correspondents experienced at the height of the Great Terror.

Besides Kosven, the only member of the editorial committee who remained enthusiastic about and committed to the Morgan project was Vinnikov. At a special plenary session of the entire IAE staff held in December 1937 that marked the twentieth anniversary of the "October Revolution," he delivered a presentation entitled "The Main Stages in the Development of L. H. Morgan's Views on the Periodization of Social Evolution" (S.A. 1938:231). In early 1938 he sent a letter to the head of IAE suggesting that, now that most of the Morgan materials had arrived, it was necessary to begin the work on the Morgan archive right away but also organize a special Morgan study by February 1, 1938, and transfer all the materials sent by Stern plus all the books related to the project there. In addition, Vinnikov mentioned the need to purchase equipment to be able to read the microfilms received from Stern. Vinnikov also claimed that the first volume of Morgan's collected works could be ready by the end of the first quarter of 1939 (142/1-1938/35:7–7a, SPF ARAN). Even in late 1940 Morgan's name remained important for academic bureaucrats. During a general meeting of the entire staff of the IAE, Vinnikov, who had recently been appointed its director, gave a presentation entitled "Marks, Engels, Morgan" that included a proposal to conduct regular colloquia named after the great American scholar (*Morganovskie chteniia*) (K-1/3/3, AMAE RAN). Between 1937 and 1941 he published several manuscripts from the Morgan archive, as well as Marx's two-hundred-page synopsis of *Ancient Society* (Marx 1941; Vinnikov 1938).[58]

A major blow to Stern was an interruption in payments owed to him by the Soviets. Over the period between January 1 and June 30, 1937, following his practice of advancing his own funds to cover the expenses involved in the project, Stern had incurred expenses involved in filming and photostatting in the amount of $300; in addition, the IAE already owed him $600 plus a 1,200-ruble honorarium for his work. From the limited references to this problem made in Stern's letters to Kosven and IAE officials, it appears that by the fall of 1937 the leadership of IAE wanted to either slow down the project or put a stop to it altogether. On October 25, 1937, Stern received the following radiogram from Vasilii Struve, the acting director of IAE: "Please stop acquiring and forwarding Morgan materials letter following." However, no letter ever came.

It seems that the instructions to slow down or terminate the project had come from the chair of the editorial committee, Deborin, an influential person who in turn might have been following instructions from some higher administrator in the Academy of Sciences. It is not clear what precipitated the mysterious telegram: the larger than anticipated amount of money the project was costing, the declining interest in it among the IAE leadership and some of the remaining editorial committee members, or both. In any case, this had to be a severe blow to Stern, not only financial but also psychological. After waiting for five months for the letter promised by Struve, he finally wrote a long memo, dated March 16, 1938, to Meshchaninov (who was still the IAE director), detailing the entire situation and requesting that the money owed to him be paid as soon as possible (folder Stern to USSR, box 2, SP). Following an exchange of several letters with Vasilii Struve, who became the actual director of IAE in the spring of 1938, the sum of $300 was finally paid to Stern. The business of the remaining money, however, continued to drag on. What upset Stern most was the way Deborin tried to justify not paying it. Here is how Stern described the insult to Kosven in a letter dated November 3, 1938:

> My recent relations with the Academy of Sciences have been quite unsatisfactory. I have as yet not received payment of $600 due me for my work for the six months in 1937. The consul here has informed me that Academician Deborin has stated that my work for the Academy has not been satisfactory. He has given no proof of this assertion, while on the other hand I have repeated letters of commendation from the various directors of the Academy telling me how pleased they were with the manner in which I was organizing and assembling the photostats and films. (folder Stern to USSR, box 3, SP)

In the summer of 1938 Stern sent a complaint to the Soviet consulate in New York about this situation and received a response informing him that Deborin had finally consented to pay him the $600 in question (Ovcharov to Stern, June 27, 1938, and Struve to Stern, October 21, 1938, folder USSR to Stern, box 2, SP). However, this ordeal continued to drag on until the fall of 1940 and even involved the Soviet ambassador to the United States. Finally, in September 1940 Stern received his $600; we can safely assume that by this time he had long given up on the 1,200 rubles that were supposed to have been deposited in his bank account in the USSR (Oumansky to Stern, February 6, 1940, folder USSR to Stern, box 2, and Stern to Oumansky, September 9 and 30, 1940, folder Stern to USSR, SP).

EPILOGUE

After the late 1930s, Stern returned to the subject of Lewis Henry Morgan's contribution to scholarship only twice. In 1945 he spoke at a symposium held at Union College, Morgan's alma mater, at the unveiling of Morgan's portrait as part of a celebration of his sesquicentennial. In his talk Stern mentioned an enthusiastic reception of Morgan's work in the USSR, where the American anthropologist had become "the best known and most respected of all ethnologists" (1946:173).

Stern's general evaluation of Morgan's contribution presented in this talk was more generous than the one offered in his 1931 book.

Whether it was the influence of his Soviet colleagues, the celebratory occasion of his lecture, or both, it is difficult to say. He mentioned that some of his critics had been more caustic in their attack on Morgan than they would have been had Marx, Engels, and other socialists, as well as the Soviets, not hailed him. In Stern's words, "Morgan's work has proved to be of more lasting worth to anthropology than of most of his contemporaries and many of his later adversaries" (1946:173). And even on the subject of Morgan's theory of evolution Stern gave the scholar a high mark, though with some reservations. He argued that others have oversimplified Morgan's scheme of human cultural evolution beyond recognition. As he put it, "This much can be said with certainty. The era of anti-evolutionism in social science has long passed" (1946:175).

It is pretty clear that Stern was moving closer to the Soviet view of Morgan's contribution and the Morgan-Engels scheme of social evolution. He might have also been moving more toward a proevolutionist position because of a renewed interest in the subject among a number of American and other Western anthropologists in the 1940s. It might also have been the case that, having spent so much of his time and energy (and probably some of his own money as well) on locating, copying, and sending Morgan's papers to Soviet Russia, Stern had to develop a more positive view of the Rochester lawyer's contribution to anthropology.

The second time Stern discussed Morgan was in a 1948 article titled "Engels on the Family," also published in *Science and Society*. In it he reminded readers that in *The Origin of the Family* Engels made a cautionary remark about the tentative nature of Morgan's scientific generalizations and conclusions: "Since Engels wrote these words, anthropological research has made significant strides and it can now no longer be said that anthropology sustains all of Morgan's basic generalizations on the family, although it is recognized that they compare favorably with the views of Morgan's contemporaries" (1948:47–48). In a footnote to this passage, Stern drew attention to his own book on Morgan and admitted that he wrote it "when the attack upon the weaknesses of early social evolutionism was at its height. It contains what I now recognize to be some errors of fact and interpretation. The [critical] position taken in the book on Morgan's view on the family, however, remains essentially correct" (1948:48).

In his 1945 lecture on Morgan, Stern did mention the work he had done for the Soviet Academy of Sciences of copying Morgan's material and sending over seventeen thousand prints and films to the Soviet Union, but, as he put it, "pressing problems incident to World War II have interrupted the project" (1946:175). This suggests that he was still hoping for a resumption and the ultimate fruition of the project in the form of a publication. In 1945 Stern also made an attempt to contact one Soviet ethnographer for the purpose of reestablishing contact with colleagues in the USSR. Having learned from an article in *Moscow News* that the Moscow Institute of Ethnography had recently held a meeting in memory of Franz Boas, he wrote to the author of that piece, Iulia Petrova-Averkieva, whom he had met in the early 1930s when she studied with Boas (October 17, 1945, folder 5, box 3, BJS). Stern did not receive an answer: being at the time in China with her husband, the Soviet ambassador to that country, Petrova-Averkieva could not possibly reply to a letter from the United States.

Following a brief period of improved relations between the two countries that had been war allies, the Cold War set in, and most Soviet citizens were forbidden to have contact with Americans and other foreigners from capitalist countries. These foreigners were especially taboo for Soviet Jews, who in the late 1940s were subject to the so-called anticosmopolitanism campaign, which in reality was an anti-Semitic / Russian nationalist one. This most likely explains why Kosven did not resume correspondence with Stern after the war. He did not, however, forget his old friend and in 1947 had enough courage to send him several of his reprints via official channels. Stern was delighted to learn that his pen pal was alive and wrote him a letter on May 12, 1947. Among other things he mentioned being pleased that at least some of the Morgan materials he had sent to Russia in the 1930s were being utilized and reprinted by Kosven and Vinnikov. Stern also expressed curiosity about the fate of the prints and microfilms he had sent, whether they had been utilized in any way, made available to researchers, and so on. He complained about not having heard from any of the staff members of the IAE, even though the war had been over for two years (folder

1, box 4, BJS). When he received no answer from Kosven, Stern never again wrote to any Soviet colleagues or officials; at least, this is what the archives available to us show.

Leslie White, who succeeded Stern as the main American anthropologist researching Morgan's life and scholarship, eventually resumed correspondence with Soviet ethnographers about this subject. In 1960 he sent a letter to Vinnikov informing him about the publication of Morgan's diaries that he had edited (Morgan 1960). Iu. Averkieva (1961) reviewed that publication but did not say a word about the Soviet Morgan project discussed here. By this time Vinnikov was no longer working on the Morgan topic, and Kosven was seriously ill. Neither of them took part in the Morgan session at the 1964 International Congress of Anthropologists in Moscow that White participated in.

Twenty years later, during the sunset years of the Soviet Union, the last product of the Morgan project, a Russian edition of *The League of the Ho-dé-no-sau-nee or Iroquois* (Morgan 1983), translated in the 1930s by Eugeniia E. Blomkvist (1898–1956), was published. For some unknown reason, the introduction by Iu. P. Averkieva and N. B. Ter-Akopian failed to mention either Bernhard Stern or the Morgan archive project. Thus ended the long saga of how an American Marxist scholar helped make a bourgeois anthropologist the cornerstone of Soviet ethnography or, more broadly, the "history of the primordial society."

CONCLUSION

In some ways this saga is also about its authors. On the one hand, both of us were born in the USSR and, despite our age difference, had to study the "history of the primordial society" using more or less the same Soviet textbooks. In them Morgan was allotted a place of honor as a "precursor of Marxism." On the other hand, one of us continues to work within the Russian Academy of Sciences system, which means that the portion of the article dealing with Soviet ethnographers represents not only a history of our discipline but also a kind of "participant observation," that is, an opportunity to understand the microstrategies of that community in its construction of theoretical concepts and its struggle for power. Between the late 1920s and the late 1930s, Morgan and his archive (most of it remaining unpublished) held together the developers and builders of Marxism in Soviet ethnography and archaeology. Despite their endless attacks on each other, which ended in many of them losing their lives, the protagonists of our saga were united in the work of constituting a Morganian evolutionist scheme aimed at justifying their own claims to being *the* interpreters of the (pre)history of the peoples of the world, whose primary field data came first and foremost from the ethnography of the peoples of the Soviet Union and very rarely that of other countries and continents. Having become firmly linked to such foundational work of Soviet ethnography as Engels's *Origin of the Family*, Morgan remained more or less "untouchable" (i.e., beyond serious criticism) until the fall of the Soviet Union, even though between the 1960s and 1980s the more progressive and audacious Soviet ethnographers began to question and even challenge some of his key postulates.

Despite Morgan's privileged status, his ideas eventually became confined to just the "history of the primordial society," as well as the largely ignored discussions of kinship that took place after World War II. By this time, Morgan, as a "culture hero" of Soviet ethnography, had definitely been overshadowed by Nikolai N. Miklukho-Maklai (1846–88), a Russian-born hero with a much more politically correct biography than his American rival (Stocking 1992:219–232). Miklukho-Maklai had actually been officially canonized before the war, when in 1937–38 he was proclaimed as the great (or even the greatest) Russian ethnographer-humanist and a tireless fighter for the rights of the Papuans against Western imperialism and colonialism. In the late 1930s and 1940s a major shift occurred in Soviet ethnography, from an internationally oriented one associated with Shternberg, Bogoraz, and Morgan to a new national or Russian-oriented one.[59] This shift must have been influenced by Stalin's decision to strengthen the popular support for his regime by combining Communist ideology with Russian nationalism. This new ideology, described by scholars as "national Bolshevism," was first articulated by Stalin in a series of important letters (i.e., directives) written in the 1930s that dealt with the writing and teaching of history to public school and university students. The cornerstone of this ideology was the rehabilitation of the pre-1917 Russian military heroes, scholars, and other outstanding personalities (see Brandenberger 2002).

It should be pointed out that neither Morgan nor Miklukho-Maklai became the subject of heated debates as far as their field methods or their theoretical concepts were concerned. We would like to suggest that the intellectual history of the Morgan archive and the later history of Miklukho-Maklai's canonization were somewhat akin to the Melanesian cargo cults, in spite of the current critics of the term in anthropology (see Otto 2009). Borrowing the term had a lot more to do with a desire to learn how the cults function than with a desire to incorporate the term into a whole tangle of intrigue within the ethnographic laboratory, where ideological demands were primary and theory secondary.

In other words, the Morgan archive, acquired as "foreign goods," stimulated the first wave of discussions in Soviet ethnography, which "nationalized" Morgan and turned his (Sovietized) ideas against "bourgeois" Western anthropology, American in particular. Such "purification" of ethnography and other social sciences resulted in a situation where, by the 1960s, Morgan came to be perceived as part of the Soviet ethnographic canon, while his actual ideas were rarely discussed. One could say that by "decolonizing" certain foreign scholars and their theories, Soviet ethnography tried to do away with their alien status.

This happened despite the fact that many of the protagonists of our saga were well acquainted with the latest anthropological works in a number of European languages, as witnessed by the minutes of the 1929 and 1932 conferences and by the reviews published in Soviet ethnographic journals. However, the conservative community of Soviet ethnographers operated not so much with Morgan's ideas per se but mainly with symbols, that is, his archive and translations of his works. This explains why so much of the work of Vinnikov and other participants in this project was nothing more than text analysis. This also explains how Vinnikov was able to make an overnight switch from the Morgan to the Miklukho-Maklai project.[60]

One wonders whether Bernhard Stern ever really understood why a project that for several years would consume much of his time, energy, and some of his own money never came to fruition. Our sense is that this naive and politically dogmatic American intellectual, who believed (or made himself believe) that the Stalinist regime was the paragon of justice and progress and that Soviet anthropology would eventually become the most advanced in the world, never fully grasped why in the late 1930s publishing the archive and the collected works of L. H. Morgan was no longer a priority for his Soviet colleagues. Judging by his letters, Stern was indeed disappointed with that state of affairs, though he probably did not feel that he had completely wasted his time. The fact that the copies of some of the documents he had transferred to Leningrad were eventually published and that the archive was now available to Soviet researchers must have given him some consolation. Moreover, while Stern approached the Morgan legacy much more critically and creatively than his Soviet counterparts, the Morgan project did play the role of "symbolic capital" in his career as well. In our view, the work of collecting thousands of Morgan-related documents and sending their photocopies to Soviet Russia gave Stern a strong sense of having been a participant in the building of the new Soviet anthropology and the Soviet social sciences in general. It also bolstered his sense of self-importance and professional identity as a specialist on Soviet nationalities and Soviet ethnography. The irony of his experience, of course, is the fact that, just as the regime he so passionately supported turned out to be a repressive totalitarian one, the academic community he assisted never used the Morgan archive in any creative fashion as he had hoped.

As soon as the ideological restraints were lifted from the social sciences in the late 1980s, Soviet and (after 1991) Russian ethnographers (ethnologists) cast aside the Morganian-Marxist evolutionist scheme and experimented with various new theoretical tool kits, especially constructivism. Unfortunately, in the early twenty-first century many of them returned to the use of "traditionalist values" and familiar essentialist categories of description, which receive the blessing of the Russian authorities, themselves promoting "traditional values."[61] Thus in this post-Soviet era, political ideology and a search for a politically correct language for describing culture and society remain part and parcel of the reality of academic life in Russia, resulting in the production of scholarly works that eclectically mix different and often conflicting anthropological ideas and theories, including recycling nationalist ones developed by Russian philosophers and social scientists of the pre-1917 era, as well as post-1917 émigrés.

NOTES

AIAE RAN   Archive of the Institute of Anthropology and Ethnography, Moscow
AIIMK RAN   Archive of the Institute of the History of Material Culture, St. Petersburg
AMAE RAN   Archive of the Museum of Anthropology and Ethnography, St. Petersburg,
ARAN   Archive of the Russian Academy of Sciences, Moscow
BJS   Bernhard J. Stern Papers, Special Collections and University Archives, University of Oregon Libraries, Eugene
CS audio
interviews   Interviews with Charlotte T. Stern, conducted and recorded by Rosalyn Baxandall in 1976–77, Tamiment Library, Elmer Holmes Bobst Library, New York University
SP   Bernhard J. Stern Papers, Huntington Library, San Marino, California
SPF ARAN   St. Petersburg Branch of the Archive of the Russian Academy of Sciences
UPENN
Museum
Archives   Archives of the Museum of Archaeology and Anthropology, University of Pennsylvania

The part of the article written by Dmitry Arzyutov is supported by the project "Etnos: A Life History of the Etnos Concept among the Peoples of the North" (Economic and Social Research Council, RGA1682 PI—Prof. David G. Anderson, University of Aberdeen, Scotland, UK). Archival research by Sergei Kan in the Special Collections and University Archives of the University of Oregon Libraries in Eugene was supported by a grant from the Claire Garber Goodman Fund administered by the Department of Anthropology, Dartmouth College.

1. Sergei A. Kan was born in the USSR in 1953 in a family of historians. Between 1970 and 1973 he was a student in the history department of Moscow State University, which included special divisions of ethnography (cultural anthropology) and archaeology. In his third year, Kan

began specializing in archaeology. In 1974 he immigrated to the United States, where he received a BA in anthropology from Boston University in 1976 and a doctorate in anthropology from the University of Chicago in 1982.

2. Dmitry V. Arzyutcv was born in the USSR in 1982. He studied archaeology at Kemerovo State University (1999–2004) and was later admitted to the postgraduate program (2004–7) at the Peter the Great Museum of Anthropology and Ethnography (Kunstkamera) in St. Petersburg. He defended his PhD dissertation in ethnology in 2007. In 2010–11 he was an Yggdrasil Research Fellow at the Department of Archaeology and Social Anthropology in the University of Tromsø (Norway). He has been a research fellow at the Peter the Great Museum of Anthropology and Ethnography (Kunstkamera) since 2008. In January 2014 he was granted a three-year research fellowship by the ESRC in the Department of Anthropology, University of Aberdeen, Scotland.

3. Until 1991 Soviet sociocultural anthropologists referred to their discipline as "ethnography," reserving the term "anthropology" for physical anthropology. In this article we use "ethnography" when talking about the Soviet case and "anthropology" when referring to Stern's work.

4. In 1931 the separate Lenin Institute was merged with the Marx-Engels Institute and renamed the Institute of Marx-Engels-Lenin; it was eventually renamed the Institute of Marxism-Leninism.

5. We ought to add that during this highly politicized era there was a very high demand for ethnographic literature. Here is what Yuliia Averkieva wrote to Boas in 1932: "I wrote [down] in detail the content of the book, thinking that it will be of interest to you. If I am able to get another copy of it, I could send it to you if you would like to have it. Imagine, 57,000 copies were published a week or two ago, but one can find it now only with great difficulty, because all are sold. But I will try to get it" (Averkieva–Boas 2006:130).

6. Established in 1918 as the Socialist Academy and renamed the Communist Academy in 1924, it was intended to allow Marxist scholars to research social science problems independent of (and implicit in rivalry with) the Academy of Sciences.

7. Usually, documents from Russian archives are divided into collections (*fondy*), which are further divided into inventories (*opisi*) and, subsequently, into documents (*edinitsy khranenia* or *dela*). Numbers after a colon refer to folios in a particular archival document.

8. The entire text of the minutes of that conference, found in the RAN

Archive, has been published in a series titled Kunstkamera-Arkhiv (Arzyutov et al. 2014). The text citations are references to the verbatim of the meeting of ethnographers from Moscow and Leningrad in 1929. K-1 is a collection, 3 is an inventory, 7 is the archival document.

9. In this archive, 2 is a collection, 1 (1932) is an inventory (actually this archive has yearly organized inventories), and 201 and 202 are two archival documents that are two volumes of the verbatim stenographic report of the meeting of archaeologists and ethnographers in 1932.

10. See Matorin (1934) for a similar presentation at the All-Union Congress of Geographers.

11. In this archive, 142 is a collection, 1 (1928) is an inventory, which is organized yearly, 7 is an archival document, and 8 is a folio number.

12. Due to Wilhelm Schmidt's status as a Catholic priest he was for many years the subject of particularly vitriolic criticism by Soviet anthropologists.

13. Box 1 Europe—Golomshtok, folder Russia—Golomshtok, correspondence 1930–31, pp. 1–2; 1932, 1933, 1934, 1935–36; letters of introduction, 1932; exchanges; correspondence and inventories, 1940, UPENN Museum Archives. See also 142/1-1932/24, 2, 142/1-1933/27, 6, and 142/1-1936/37, 19–21, SPF ARAN.

14. It is true, however, that a decade earlier some articles based on field data had already been published on "classificatory kinship systems," based on Morgan's theory. They must have been influenced by Shternberg, since their authors had been his students (Dyrenkova 1926; Karger 1927).

15. Arzyutov came across parts of this program in the archives of several Soviet ethnographers of Siberia; however, it appears that they did not follow it in their field research.

16. As Tamara Dragadze noticed, when she visited the USSR in the 1960s, she did not see any research on kinship, so typical for the British anthropology of that era (Dragadze 2011).

17. Samuel based his 1990 biographical sketch of B. Stern on an interview he conducted with Stern's widow, Charlotte Todes Stern (1897–1996), in 1984. In 1976–77 Ms. Stern was interviewed and tape-recorded by Rosalyn Baxandall. The originals of the tapes are located at the Tamiment Library, Elmer Holmes Bobst Library, New York University (see Charlotte Todes Stern Papers TAM.070 Series VIII: Oral History Transcripts). We accessed them online via the Virtual Oral / Aural History Archive of the Library of the California State University, Long Beach. Bloom also drew on "The Political Papers of Bernhard Joseph Stern," an

unpublished set of documents located at the Meiklejohn Civil Liberties Institute, Berkeley, California.

18. Robert W. Dunn, a Quaker and a Socialist who at some point became a Communist, participated in relief efforts in the Soviet Union in the aftermath of the horrible famine of 1921. He came back a firm believer in the Soviet social and economic experiment.

19. Because Charlotte Stern was working for the Workers' Health Bureau, she was a secret Communist Party member and did not make her membership public (CS audio interviews 1–3).

20. One of Stern's closest colleagues at the University of Washington was another Boasian, Mel Jacobs, who joined the anthropology department during the same period of time and became a major scholar of Salish ethnology. Suttles and Jonaitis (1990:78) speculate that it might have been Jacobs who encouraged Stern to pursue ethnographic research among the Lummi. The two of them also coauthored a popular anthropology textbook (Jacobs and Stern 1947). In addition to their common scholarly interests, the two men were on the same page as far as their political views were concerned (Price 2004).

21. To be fair to Stern we should mention that he was hoping to conduct additional ethnographic research among the Salish-speaking Indians, but the lack of funding and his return to the East Coast prevented him from carrying it out.

22. In an important and well-articulated early paper, published in a sociological journal, Stern drew heavily on the ideas of Boas and several leading Boasians, such as Kroeber and Lowie, to urge his fellow sociologists to make a clear distinction between the social and the cultural (Stern 1929a). See also Stern's article published on the occasion of Boas's death (1943).

23. Stern's research on the Ward archive at Brown University resulted in his 1935 publication *Young Ward's Diaries*.

24. However, Robert Lowie, whom Stern shared his book manuscript with, was favorably impressed with it and even tried to help get it published (letters from 1928–29, folder Lowie to Stern, box 2, SP).

25. Although a number of unaffiliated left-leaning Western intellectuals, including prominent ones, took part in this congress, it was definitely run by Moscow and its Western Communist allies.

26. In the late 1902s to early 1930s, Kosven, who had previously worked at the History Institute of the Russian Academy of Sciences, was employed by such flagships of the official ideology as the Institute of

History of the Communist Academy and the Institute of Marx and Engels (Gardanov 1967:157). At the latter institution, he, like the other staff members, was charged with collecting, analyzing, and publishing annotated editions of works by Marx and Engels, and this was the task he continued to pursue once he had made a transition from social history to ethnology. However, in early 1931 he witnessed a major purge at the Marx-Engels Institute when its director was arrested for his anti-Stalinist position and half of its staff was fired. Among the staff members fired at that time was the paternal grandfather of this article's American author, historian Sergei Borisovich Kan (1896–1960) (Rokitianskii 2008; Aleksandr Sergeevich Kan, personal communication, 2000s).

27. Not having a sufficient command of English, Kosven sent letters to Stern written in Russian (and a few times in French). Someone translated them into English, and Stern responded in English.

28. He also added a letter written by Asher Wright to Morgan that Engels had quoted in his *Origin of the Family*. Stern suggested that Vinnikov might wish to publish it in that same volume or in a Soviet anthropology journal.

29. It is worth pointing out that between the 1920s and the 1930s, Soviet Russia attracted like a magnet a large number of European and American engineers, scientists, philosophers, and social scientists, some of them quite prominent (Feuer 1962). Thus Walter Benjamin spent the winter of 1926–27 in Moscow, John Dewey visited the USSR in 1928, while Ludwig Wittgenstein toyed with the idea of working there and made a brief visit to Leningrad in 1935. Several of these visitors were anthropologists.

30. Being unable (or unwilling) to cancel his summer vacation in northern Caucasus, Kosven did not meet with Stern. He did, however, put him in contact with the All-Union Society for Cultural Ties with Abroad, which helped the Sterns with their travel arrangements and sightseeing (Kosven to Stern, July 29, 1932, and Stern to Kosven, October 24, 1932, folder 3, box 1, BJS). This "cultural" organization was actually under the control of the Communist Party and the secret police.

31. Even though Bogoraz, who interpreted the plenum proceedings for Stern, had a good command of English, he must have edited what was being said, since by 1932 he had become quite cautious in public as far as political topics were concerned (Kan 2006).

32. In his April 13, 1931, letter to Kosven, Stern told him that he had sent eight

copies of his Morgan books to various Soviet periodicals for review plus a separate copy to the Marx-Engels Institute (folder 3, box 1, BJS).

33. It is noteworthy that a younger Soviet ethnographer, Alexandr M. Zolotarev, who had no personal ties with Stern, commented much more critically on his Morgan book, attacking him for treating Morgan's evolutionist theory as being outdated and passé. In his review of Kosven's book on Morgan, Zolotarev referred to Stern as a "typical middle-rank American ethnologist whose bourgeois narrow-mindedness prevented him from correctly evaluating and appreciating the significance of Morgan [as a scholar]" (1934:138).

34. It appears that Stern was also trying to publish a Russian translation of his 1932 antireligious brochure *The Church and the Workers*, but as of 1934 it still had not come out (Stern to Kosven, April 11, 1934, folder 3, box 1, BJS). On this brochure itself, see Peace and Price (2005).

35. In fact, Kosven did ask Stern to review his own book on Morgan in an American anthropological journal. In addition, he asked him to contact Margaret Mead and ask her to send him her own monographs for review.

36. Kosven also asked Stern to send him a photograph of Morgan in his younger years, and in response his American colleague sent such a picture, as well as a photograph of Morgan's home in Aurora, New York.

37. It should be noted that Stern's letter, written a few days after the establishment of diplomatic relations between the United States and the USSR, expressed his happiness about that development. Kosven was equally happy and wrote on January 30, 1934, that he hoped "it would lead to a further strengthening of the ties between the progressive trends in American anthropology and the Soviet scientists" (folder 6, box 1, BJS).

38. In his introduction to *Houses and House-Life of the American Aborigines*, Al'kor states that "the bourgeois social science has established a conspiracy of silence" toward this book because it serves as a solid proof of the existence of "primitive communism" and is a fine example of a "materialist approach to archaeology" (1934:viii). The fact that the first (1934) edition of *Ancient Society* was also listed under the rubric "Ethnographic Materials, vol. I," of the Scientific Research Association of the Institute of the Peoples of the North indicates that Al'kor and Kosven must have had bigger plans for publishing additional volumes in that series, including Morgan's works.

39. It turned out later that there were no "fieldnotes," while what he initially referred to as "fieldnotes" were actually journal entries.

40. Kosven told Stern that in the USSR academic publications printed letters without deletions.

41. To Kosven's disappointment, Stern was not able to find any traces of utopian socialism in Morgan's writings nor any books by utopian socialists in his library.

42. Stern was pleased with Kosven's overall impressions of his book but was firm on the issue of the gens, stating that "there was none to be found" (Stern to Kosven, August 27, 1934, folder 6, box 1, BJS). To be fair to Kosven, we should mention that, despite the criticism of the monograph expressed in his letter to Stern, Kosven published a rather laudatory review of it in which he even said that the gens might have already disappeared among this particular people (1935b).

43. Stern's response to Kosven on August 27, 1934, indicated that his own opinion of this table was that it did give a good idea of Morgan's evolutionist views by presenting them in a schematic form but did not represent a very important document; that is, that Vinnikov overstated the significance of his so-called discovery (folder 6, box 1, BJS).

44. This 260-page publication included the notorious table mentioned earlier, thirty-four key letters from Morgan's correspondence with Vinnikov's annotation, Morgan's corrections made on the margins of *Ancient Society*, materials for Morgan's bibliography, a brief description of newly discovered manuscripts of Morgan's, and English-language reviews of *Ancient Society*.

45. Meshchaninov was a linguist by training and prior to 1934 was the right-hand man of the powerful and politically engaged Soviet Orientalist and linguist Nikolai Marr (1865–1934).

46. This edition of *Ancient Society* never saw the light of day, and neither did Parker's commentary on it.

47. There are reasons to suspect that Chatto's relationship with Vinnikov was far from cordial. In fact, their disagreement developed in the context of the work on the Morgan project after the former published a review of Vinnikov's publication "From the Morgan Archive" (1935), in which Chatto discussed the various errors of Vinnikov's approach to the original texts (Chattopadhyaya 1935).

48. It should be mentioned that before the editorial board invited Stern to join it and undertake the bulk of the work on this project, a proposal had been made Chattopadhyaya to take advantage of an offer made

by his American acquaintance (?) by the name of Mary Lewis, who was visiting Leningrad at the time. Lewis offered to purchase Morgan's books and articles, including antiquarian editions, in the United States, with the reimbursement being paid to her sister living in Leningrad. She also proposed having photocopies of the materials from the Morgan archive made by Robert W. Dunn of the Labor Research Association, an American Communist mentioned earlier. It appears that Dunn agreed to help with the project, but once he contacted the University of Rochester Library staff, Stern found out about these negotiations taking place behind his back and became quite unhappy (Kosven to Stern, July 24, 1935, folder USSR to Stern, and Stern to Kosven, August 20, 1935, folder Stern to USSR, box 1, SP). Fortunately for Stern, Kosven's opinion that only a single American scholar could be involved in this project prevailed (142/1-1935/38, 20–21, SPF ARAN).

49. Alexander A. Busygin (1899–1936) was not a serious scholar but a Party bureaucrat in charge of academic affairs. As the associate director of the IAE he ran its day-to-day affairs. Sergei N. Bykovskii (1896–1936), originally a teacher of history in a technical school, had not received a solid education in ethnology or archaeology yet published articles in both fields. However, with his clever use of Marxist terminology to defend the party line and browbeat his opponents, Bykovskii took on the role of a theoretician in archaeology and the so-called history of primordial society.

50. It appears that the editorial board did plan to publish Morgan's collected works in both languages, but the Russian-language publication was its priority.

51. The board also tried to get the University of Rochester Library to lend IAE some manuscripts from the Morgan Archives "for consultation," but that proposition was flatly rejected (Stern to Busygin, February 2, 1936, folder Stern to USSR, box 1, SP). Following the precedent set by the Marx-Engels Institute, the board also tried to acquire some original letters from the Morgan-Fison correspondence using Stern as an intermediary. However, that deal fell through.

52. It was followed by Vinnikov's chapter titled "The Fourth Edition of Engels' *Origin of the Family* (an Exercise in Textological Analysis)" (1936a).

53. Since 1936 Kosven taught ethnology at the University of Moscow and presided over the ethnology section of *The Great Soviet Encyclopedia*.

54. In another advertisement for this trip, Compass Travel Bureau boasted that Stern's wide range of interests, which included "active participa-

tion in the progressive movements in the United States, equip him particularly well to interpret Soviet life in all its phases" (142/1-1935/38,
71–72, SPF ARAN).

55. For a while Kosven was sending Stern promising signals about a possibility of his work in the USSR, but by the end of the year, it became
clear that he could not do anything to help his American colleague.
On December 1, 1934, the head of the Leningrad Communists, Sergei
Kirov, was assassinated, most likely upon Stalin's request. In the wake of
that event, a wave of arrests swept through the city and the country as
a whole, with many of the victims being academics, including ethnographers. This was definitely not the right time to bring a foreign scholar
(even a Communist) to Russia to conduct ethnographic research or
teach. Chattopadhyaya, a personal friend of Kirov, told his wife upon
hearing of Kirov's murder, "Well, now a repression of foreigners is going
to start" (15/2/7, 25, AMAE RAN). Sadly, he predicted his own fate and the
fate of his colleagues correctly. Arrested in June 1937, he was sentenced to
death and swiftly executed (Reshetov 1998; 15/2/7, AMAE RAN).

56. Not surprisingly, Stern signed the infamous "Letter to American Liberals," published in the Communist newspaper the *Daily Worker* and
reprinted in the pro-Soviet propaganda magazine *Soviet Russia Today*,
which attacked the Preliminary Commission of Inquiry organized in
1936 by the Committee in the Defense of Leo Trotsky and headed by
distinguished American philosopher and educator John Dewey. The
letter, signed by eighty-eight Communists, Communist sympathizers,
and a few liberals, warned American liberals that the Committee in the
Defense of Trotsky was a Trotskyite front and hence an ally of fascist
and reactionary enemies of the Soviet Union (Spitzer 1990).

57. According to his students' testimonies to the FBI given in the early
1950s, when Stern was being investigated throughout the 1940s, he had
made mention of his trips to Soviet Russia and "compared [the] cultural, economic, and physical advancements made there and in the
United States. These comparisons were usually in favor of Russia" (cited
in Price 2004:143).

58. Vinnikov sent his 1935 publication "From the Morgan Archive" to a
number of Western anthropologists, including Franz Boas and Leslie White. The latter reviewed it in the *American Anthropologist* (White
1937). Continuing to search for information on Morgan and his correspondents, the Leningrad scholar also corresponded with various foreign archives and museums.

59. A celebration of the life and work of Miklukho-Maklai was followed by a search for and showcasing of other pre-1917 Russian geographers, ethnographers, and folklorists, which was particularly intense in the 1940s to early 1950s.

60. In 1938 a special exhibit was organized at the MAE to mark the fiftieth anniversary of Miklukho-Maklai's death. The guide to it was prepared by Boris Piotrovskii and edited by Vinnikov. A year later the same two authors prepared the first volume of the Russian ethnographer's *Voyages* for publication, while Vinnikov wrote the introduction to it, titled "The Significance of N. N. Miklukho-Maklai's Research for Ethnographic Science" (Vinnikov 1939).

61. The return to the so-called traditionalist values is part of the official modern-day propaganda, particularly strong in the political discourse, as well as the educational system and the mass media. It emphasizes a return to an eclectic mix of statist, Russian nationalist, Russian Orthodox, and some of the (socialist) values of the Soviet era.

REFERENCES

Al'kor (Koshkin), Ian. 1934. Predislovie. *In* Doma i domashniaia zhizn' amerikanskikh tuzemtsev L H. Morgana [Introduction to Houses and House-Life of the American Aborigines by L. H. Morgan]. Leningrad: Institut Narodov Severa.

Alymov, Sergei S. 2013. Ekspeditsiia v pervobytnost': Ob odnoi nerealizovannoi mechte sovetskoi etnografii [An Expedition to Prehistory: An Essay on One Unrealized Dream of Soviet Ethnography]. Etnograficheskoe obozrenie 4:88–94.

Arzyutov, Dmitry V., Sergei S. Alymov, and David G. Anderson, eds. 2014. Ot klassikov k marksizmu: Sovechanie etnografov Moskvy i Leningrada (5–11 aprelia 1929) [From Classics to Marxism: The Meeting of Ethnographers from Moscow and Leningrad (5–11 April 1929)]. Vol. 7. Kunstkamera—Archives. St. Petersburg: MAE RAN.

Averkieva, Julia P. 1961. Etnograficheskie dnevniki L.-G. Morgana [L. H. Morgan's Ethnographic Journals]. Sovetskaia etnografiia 1:171–174.

Averkieva–Boas Correspondence. 2006. Perepiska Ju. P. Averkievoi i F. Boasa [Iulia Averkieva / Franz Boas Correspondence (1931–37)]. Bulletin: Anthropology, Minorities, Multiculturalism, new series, 1(2):117–159.

Baruwā, Niroda Kumāra. 2004. Chatto, the Life and Times of an Indian Anti-imperialist in Europe. New Delhi: Oxford University Press.

Beecher, Jonathan, and Valerii N. Fomichev. 2006. French Socialism in
    Lenin's and Stalin's Moscow: David Riazanov and the French Archive of
    the Marx-Engels Institute. Journal of Modern History 78(1):119–143.
Bertrand, Fredrik. 2002. L'anthropologie Soviétique des années 20–30:
    Configuration d'une rupture. Presses Universitaires de Bourdeaux.
Bloom, Samuel W. 1990. The Intellectual in a Time of Crisis: The Case of
    Bernhard J. Stern, 1894–1956. Journal of the History of the Behavioral
    Sciences 6(1):17–37.
——. 2000. The Word as Scalpel: A History of Medical Sociology. New
    York: Oxford University Press.
Bourdieu, Pierre. 1977. Outline of a Theory of Practice. Translated by Rich-
    ard Nice. Cambridge: Cambridge University Press.
Brandenberger, David. 2002. National Bolshevism: Stalinist Mass Culture
    and the Formation of Modern Russian National Identity. Cambridge
    MA: Harvard University Press.
Busygin, Alexandr A. 1934. 50 let «Proishozhdeniia sem'i, chastnoi sobst-
    vennosti i gosudarstva» F.Engelsa [50 Years of F. Engels's "Origin of the
    Family . . ."]. Sovetskaia Etnografiia 6:5–16.
Chattopadhyaya, Virendranath A. 1934. Engels i Shternberg. Primechanie k
    stat'e Engel'sa «Vnov' otkrytyi sluchai gruppovogo braka» [Engels and
    Shternberg: A Footnote to Engels's Article "A Newly Discovered Case of
    Group Marriage"]. Sovetskaia Etnografiia 4:178–179.
——. 1935. Review of Iz arhiva L'iuisa Genri Morgana by I. N. Vinnikov
    [Review of I. N. Vinnikov, "From the L. H. Morgan Archive"]. Sovets-
    kaia etnografiia 6:173–188.
Deborin, Abram M., ed. 1936. Voprosy istorii doklassovogo obshchestva.
    Sbornik statei k piatidesiatiletiiu knigi Fr.Engel'sa "Proishozhdenie
    sem'i, chastnoi sobstvennosti i gosudarstva" [Issues in the History of the
    Preclass Society: A Collection of Essays Marking the 50th Anniversary
    Publication of Engels's "Origin of the Family, Private Property, and the
    State"]. Trudy Instituta Antropologii, Arheologii i Etnografii AN SSSR,
    vol. 4. Moscow-Leningrad: Izd-vo AN SSSR.
Derrida, Jacques. 1998. Archive Fever: A Freudian Impression. Chicago:
    University of Chicago Press, 1998.
Dmitriev, Alexandr N. 2007. "Akademicheskii marksizm" 1920–30-h godov:
    Zapadnyi kontekst i sovetskie obstoiatel'stva ["Academic Marxism"
    in the 1920s and 1930s: Western Context and Soviet Circumstances].
    Novoe literaturnoe obozrenie 88:10–38.
Dragadze, Tamara. 2011. Soviet Ethnography: Structure and Sentiment. In

Exploring the Edge of Empire: Soviet Era Anthropology in the Caucasus and Central Asia. Florian Mühlfried and Sergey Sokolovskiy, eds. Pp. 21–34. Halle Studies in the Anthropology of Eurasia 25. LIT Verlag.

Dyrenkova, Nadezchda P. 1926. Rod, klassifikatsionnaja sistema rodstva i brachnye normy u altaitsev i teleut [Gens, Classificatory Kinship System, and Marriage Norms among the Altai and Teleut Peoples]. In Materialy po svad'be i semejno-rodovomu stroju narodov SSSR. V. G. Bogoraz and L. Ya. Shternberg, eds. 1:247–259. Leningrad: Izdanie Komissii po ustroistvu studencheskikh etnograficheskikh ekskursii.

Efimenko, Petr P. 1934. Dorodovoe obshhestvo: Ocherki po istorii pervobytno-kommunisticheskogo obshhestva [Pregens Society: Essays on the History of the Primordial-Communist Society]. Moscow-Leningrad: OGIZ.

Feuer, Lewis S. 1962. American Travelers to the Soviet Union 1917–1932: The Formation of a Component of New Deal Ideology. American Quarterly 14(2):119–149.

Gardanov, V. K. 1967. Mark Osipovich Kosven. Sovetskaia Etnografiia 6:156–160.

Gellner, Ernst. 1988. State and Society in Soviet Thought. Oxford: Basil Blackwell.

Golomshtok, Eugene. 1933. Anthropological Activities in Soviet Russia. American Anthropologist 35(2):301–327.

Graham, Loren. 1967. The Soviet Academy of Sciences and the Communist Party, 1927–1932. Princeton NJ: Princeton University Press.

———. 1975. The Formation of Soviet Research Institutes: A Combination of Revolutionary Innovation and International Borrowing. Social Studies of Science 5:303–329.

Jacobs, Melville, and Bernhard J. Stern. 1947. Outlines of Anthropology. New York: Barnes and Noble.

Johnson, Guy B. 1932. Review of Lewis Henry Morgan, Social Evolutionist by Bernhard J. Stern. Social Forces 11(1):151–152.

Kagarov, Evgenii G. 1931. Friedrich Engels i noveishaia etnografiia [Friedrich Engels and Present-Day Ethnography]. Izvestiia AN SSSR. Otdelenie obshchestvennykh nauk.

———. 1937. Perezhitki pervobytnogo kommunizma v obshhestvennom stroe drevnikh grekov i germantsev [Survivals of Primordial Communism in the Social Organization of the Ancient Greeks and Germans]. Moscow-Leningrad: Izdatel'stvo AN SSSR.

Kan, Sergei A. 2006. "My Old Friend in a Dead-End of Empiricism and

Skepticism": Bogoras, Boas, and the Politics of Soviet Anthropology of the Late 1920s–Early 1930s. *In* Histories of Anthropology Annual, Volume 2. Regna Darnell and Frederic W. Gleach, eds. Pp. 33–68. Lincoln: University of Nebraska Press.

———. 2009. Lev Shternberg: Anthropologist, Russian Socialist, Jewish Activist. Lincoln: University of Nebraska Press, 2009.

Karger, Nestor K. 1927. Klassifikatsionnaia sistema rodstva u gol'dov [Classificatory Kinship System among the Golds]. Sbornik etnograficheskikh materialov 2:26–34. Leningrad: Krasnaia Gazeta.

Kislyakov, Nikolai A. 1963. Evgenii Georgievich Kagarov. Sovetskaia Etnografiia 1:144–148.

Koshkin (Al'kor), Yan P., and Nikolai M. Matorin. 1929. Khronika sovechaniia etnographov Leningrada i Moskvy (5/IV–11/IV 1929 g.) [Chronicle of the Conference of the Leningrad and Moscow Ethnographers (April 4–11, 1929)]. Etnografiia 8(2):110–144.

Kosven, Mark O. 1932. L. G. Morgan (1818–1881): Biografiia [L. H. Morgan: Biography]. Sovetskaia Etnografiia 1:9–43.

———. 1933a. I. Ia. Bachofen. Sovetskaia Etnografiia 1:98–140.

———. 1933b. L. H. Morgan: Zhizn' i uchenie [L. H. Morgan: Life and Teaching]. Ia. P. Al'kor, ed. Leningrad: Institut Narodov Severa TsIK SSSR.

———. 1935a. L. G. Morgan: Zhizn' i uchenie [L. H. Morgan: Life and Teaching]. 2nd ed. Leningrad: Institut Narodov Severa.

———. 1935b. Review of *The Lummi Indians of Northwest Washington* by Bernhard Stern. Problemy istorii dokapitalisticheskikh obshchestv 2(9–10):248–249.

———. 1936. Engels i Morgan [Engels and Morgan]. *In* Voprosy istorii doklassovogo obshchestvo: Sbornik statei k piatidesiatiletiiu knigi F. Engelsa "Proiskhozhdenie sem'i, chastnoi sobstvennosti i gosudarstva." Trudy Instituta Antropologii, Arkheologii i Etnografii, vol. 4. A. M. Deborin, ed. Pp. 3–30. Moscow-Leningrad: Akademiia Nauk SSSR.

———. 1948. Matriarkhat—istoriia problemy [Matriarchate—a History of the Issue]. Moscow: Academiia Nauk SSSR.

Krementsov, Nikolai. 1997. Stalinist Science. Princeton NJ: Princeton University Press.

Krupnik, Igor. 1998. Jesup Genealogy: Intellectual Partnership and Russian-American Cooperation in Arctic / North Pacific Anthropology. Part 1. Arctic Anthropology 35(2):199–226.

Kupina, Iulia A. 2004. Utraty ili priobreteniia? (Istoriia kollektsionnykh obmenov MAE RAN s amerikanskimi muzeiami) [Losses or Acquisitions? (History of Collection Exchange between MAE RAN and American Museums)]. Kur'er Petrovskoi Kunstkamery 10–11:52–85.

Levenson, Jerry, and Leah Natterstad. 1993. Granville Hicks: An Intellectual in Mass Society. Philadelphia: Temple University Press.

Lyons, Eugene. 1970. The Red Decade. New York: Arlington House.

Marx, Karl. 1941. Konspekt knigi L. H. Morgana "Drevnee Obshchestvo" [Synopsis of L. H. Morgan's Book Ancient Society]. Deciphered, translated, and commented upon by I. Vinnikov. Arkhiv K. Marksa i F. Engel's, 9:1–215.

Matorin, Nikolai M. 1931. Sovremennyi etap i zadachi sovetskoi etnografii [The Present Stage and the Tasks of Soviet Ethnography]. Sovetskaia etnografiia 1–2:3–38.

———. 1934. 15 let sovetskoi etnografii i ee dal'neishie zadachi [15 Years of Soviet Ethnography and Its Next Tasks]. In Trudy Vsesoiuznogo geograficheskogo s'ezda (11–18 apreлia 1933 g.). Issue 2, pp. 98–105. Plenarnye zasedaniia. Leningrad: Izdatel'stvo gosudarstvennogo geograficheskogo obshchestva.

Morgan, L. G. 1983. Liga khodenosauni ili irokezov [League of the Ho-De-No-Sau-Nee or the Iroquois]. Yu. P. Averkievi N. B. Ter-Akopian, ed. E. Blomkvist, trans. Moscow: Nauka.

Moses, Daniel Noah. 2009. The Promise of Progress: The Life and Work of Lewis Henry Morgan. Columbia: University of Missouri Press.

Olson, Ronald. 1935. Review of Lummi Indians of Northwest Washington by Bernhard J. Stern. American Anthropologist 37(3):499–500.

Otto, Ton. 2009. What Happened to Cargo Cults? Material Religions in Melanesia and the West. Social Analysis 53(1):82–102.

Peace, William J. 1998. Bernhard Stern, Leslie A. White, and an Anthropological Appraisal of the Russian Revolution. American Anthropologist 100(1):84–93.

———. 2004. Leslie A. White: Evolution and Revolution in Anthropology. Lincoln: University of Nebraska Press.

Peace, William J., and David H. Price. 2005. Bernhard Stern, Leslie A. White on the Church and Religion. Histories of Anthropology Annual 5:114–131.

Price, David H. 2004. Threatening Anthropology. Durham NC: Duke University Press.

Reshetov, Alexandr M. 1998. V. A. Chatopadaia—indiiskii revoliutsioner i sovetskii etnograf: K 60-letiiu so dnia gibeli [V. A. Chattopadhyay—an

Indian Revolutionary and a Soviet Ethnographer: On the Occasion of the 60th Anniversary of His Tragic Death]. *In* Kiunerovskie chteniia 1995–1997 gg.: Kratkoe soderzhanie dokladov. A. M. Reshetov, ed. Pp. 148–151. Saint Petersburg.

————. 1999. Pis'mo N. Matorina k doktoru Andre Varanyaku [A Letter by N. Matorin to Dr. André Varagnac]. Published by Alexander M. Reshetov. Kur'er Petrovskoi Kunstkamery 8–9:201–213.

Rokitianskii, Iaakov G. 2008. Iz biografii akademika D. B. Riazanova: Razgrom Instituta K. Marksa i F. Engel'sa (mart 1931 g.) [From Academician D. B. Riazanov's Biography: The Purge of the Marx-Engels Institute in March 1931]. Otechestvennye arkhivy 4:10–23.

S.A. 1938. Plenum Instituta Etnografii (dekabr' 1937 g.) [The Plenary Session of the Institute of Ethnography (December 1937)]. Sovetskaia Etnografiia 1:230–232.

Shnirelman, Viktor A. 1993. Zlokliucheniia odnoi nauki: Etnogeneticheskie issledovaniia i stalinskaia natsional'naia politika [One Scientific Discipline's Troubles: Ethnogenetic Studies and Stalin's Policies on Nationalities]. Etnograficheskoe obozrenie 3:52–68.

Slezkine, Yuri. 1991. The Fall of Soviet Ethnography, 1928–38. Current Anthropology 32(4):476–484.

————. 1996. N. Ia. Marr and the National Origins of Soviet Ethnogenetics. Slavic Review 55(4):826–862.

Spitzer, Alan B. 1990. John Dewey, the "Trial" of Leon Trotsky and the Search for Historical Truth. History and Theory 29(1):16–37.

Stern, Bernhard J. 1928. Lewis Henry: American Ethnologist. American Anthropologist 6(3):344–357.

————. 1929a. Concerning the Distinction between the Social and the Cultural. Social Forces 8(2):264–271.

————. 1929b. Review of *Primitive Art* by Franz Boas. Social Forces 8(1):162.

————. 1930. Selections from the Letters of Lorimer Fison and A. W. Howitt to Lewis Henry Morgan. American Anthropologist 32 (2):257–279; 32(3):419–453.

————. 1931. Lewis Henry Morgan: Social Evolutionist. Chicago: University of Chicago Press.

————. 1933. The Letter of Asher Wright to Lewis Henry Morgan. American Anthropologist 35(1):138–145.

————. 1934. The Lummi Indians of Northwest Washington. New York: Columbia University Press.

——— . 1935. Young Ward's Diaries. New York: G. P. Putnam's Sons.

——— . 1937. The Frustration of Technology. Science and Society 2(1):3–28.

——— . 1943. Franz Boas as Scientist and Citizen. Science and Society 7(4):289–320.

——— . 1946. Lewis Henry Morgan: An Appraisal of His Scientific Contributions. Science and Society 10(2):172–176.

——— . 1948. Engels on the Family. Science and Society 12(1):42–64.

Stocking, George W., Jr. 1992. The Ethnographer's Magic and Other Essays in the History of Anthropology. Madison: University of Wisconsin Press.

——— . 2010. Glimpses into My Own Black Box: An Exercise in Self-Deconstruction. Madison: University of Wisconsin Press.

Suttles, Wayne, and Aldona Jonaitis. 1990. History of Research in Ethnology. In Handbook of North American Indians, vol. 7, Northwest Coast. Wayne Suttles, ed. Pp. 73–87. Washington DC: Smithsonian Institution Press.

Tolstoy, Paul. 1952. Morgan and Soviet Anthropological Thought. American Anthropologist 54(1):8–17.

Tolz, Vera. 2000. The Formation of the Soviet Academy of Sciences: Bolsheviks and Academicians in the 1920s and the 1930s. In Academia in Upheaval. Michael David-Fox and Gyogy Péteri, eds. Pp. 39–72. Westport CT: Bergin and Garvey.

Vinnikov, Isaak N. 1932. Tshchatel'no izdavat' klassikov marksizma [Let Us Publish the Classics of Marxism Carefully and Thoroughly]. Sovetskaia Etnografiia 4:143–147.

——— . 1933. Novyi material po teorii Morgana [New Materials on Morgan's Theory]. Vestnik Akademii Nauk SSSR 8–9:17–24.

——— . 1934. Pis'ma Bakhovena k Morganu [Bachofen's Letters to Morgan]. Sovetskaia Etnografiia 6:70–85.

——— . 1935. Iz arkhiva Liuisa Gneri Morgana [From the L. H. Morgan Archive]. Trudy Instituta Antropologii, Arkheologii i Etnografii. Moscow-Leningrad: Academy of Sciences of the USSR.

——— . 1936a. Chetvertoe izdanie knigi F. Engel'sa "Proiskhozhdenie sem'i, chastnoi sobstvennosti i gosudarstva" (Opyt tekstologicheskogo analiza) [The Fourth Edition of Engels's Book "The Origin of the Family, Private Property, and the State" (an Exercise in Textological Analysis)]. In Voprosy istorii doklassovogo obshchestvo. Pp. 31–194. Moscow-Leningrad: Academy of Sciences of the USSR.

——— . 1936b. Programma dlia sbora materiala po sistemam rodstva i svojstva [A Program for Collecting Materials on Kinship Systems]. Moscow-Leningrad: Izdatel'stvo AN SSSR.

————. 1938. Neopublikovannai rukopis' L. G. Morgana o pliaskakh severoamerikanskikh indejtsev [An Unpublished Manuscript by L. H. Morgan on the Dances of North American Indians]. Sovetskaia Etnografiia 1:167–184.

————. 1939. Znachenie issledovanii N. N. Miklukho-Maklaia dlia etnograficheskoi nauki [The Significance of N. N. Miklukho-Maklai's Research for Ethnographic Science]. *In* Puteshestviia by N. N. Miklukho-Maklai, vol. 1. Pp. 3–11. Moscow: Institut Etnogrpafii AN SSSR.

White, Leslie A. 1932. Evoliutsia kul'tury i amerikanskaia shkola istoricheskoi etnologii [The Evolution of Culture and the American School of Historical Ethnology]. Sovetskaia etnografiia 3:54–86.

————. 1935. Review of *The Lummi Indians of Northwest Washington* by Bernhard J. Stern. American Journal of Sociology 41:387–388.

————. 1937. Review of *Materials from the Archives of Lewis Henry Morgan* by I. Vinnikov (ed.). Moscow: Academy of Sciences of the USSR. American Anthropologist 39:158–159.

————. 1961. Review of *Lewis Henry Morgan: American Scholar* by Carl Resek. Science and Society 25(1):71–73.

Zolotarev, Alexandr M. 1934. Retsenziia na L. G. Morgan: Zhinz' i uchenie by Mark Kosven [Review of *L. H. Morgan: His Life and Teaching* by Mark Kosven]. Sovetskaia Etnografiia 3:138–140.

7

"I Wrote All My Notes in Shorthand"

*A First Glance into the Treasure Chest of
Franz Boas's Shorthand Field Notes*

I tell you, if I should not become really famous one day, I shall not
know what to do. It is a horrible thought to envision for myself a life
spent unknown and unnoticed by the people.

F. BOAS TO HIS SISTER TONI, September 5, 1875, translated
by the author

There is no doubt that Franz Boas, the personification of American
cultural anthropology and the concept of cultural relativism, eventually succeeded in making his urge come true, which he expressed in the
line from a letter to his sister Toni quoted above. More importantly for
this essay, though, is the fact that this urge led Boas to build for himself
a lasting and monumental legacy in writing that, to this day, influences
research by countless scholars both directly and indirectly. Among
them are those scholars who are still trying to cope with the enormous
amount of raw material left behind by this restless mind. My current
research and book project, which this essay reflects upon, belong to
this category. It deals with the only body of material of Franz Boas that
has remained virtually untouched to this day: his shorthand writings.

When I realized that, despite the great interest in the person of Franz
Boas and his immense influence, no one had worked on the subject
before, I came to wonder why. Soon some initial answers emerged.
Aside from the fact that he used a shorthand system that fell out of
practice at the end of the nineteenth century, another factor appeared
to be at least as daunting: his terrible handwriting. This is attested not
only by his school grades for penmanship (his worst ones), by countless documented complaints by recipients of his handwritten letters,

and by many scholarly readers of his writings but also by Boas himself.[1] Among the many excuses he put forward—often saying that he was writing in "haste" and had not time—the following explanation, related by the fifteen-year-old Boas to his sister Toni, who was in New York at that time, stands out: "You may wonder why my handwriting is even worse today than usually. The reason is that I have started learning how to write all over again. This, now, is a mixture of two forms of handwriting [German Kurrent script and Latin script]. Also, I have started with shorthand again" (September 27, 1873, APS).[2]

While trying to explain the reasons for his messy writing, Boas revealed not only when he came to start changing his longhand writing from German Kurrent (fig. 5) to Latin (fig. 6) script but also when he seriously started learning shorthand.[3] Even though not much can be said about Boas's shorthand improvements by examining surviving documents, one can state that the change in his longhand involved a process that took many years, ending about 1882, just about when he started exchanging letters with his future wife, Marie Krackowizer, and when he embarked upon his first major field trip to Baffin Land. As to his use of shorthand, it is from this trip that the oldest examples have survived, about ten years after he proclaimed to have started learning shorthand (fig. 7). This is surprising, as Boas must have practiced and used shorthand long before and in many contexts of daily life. The fact that Boas must have used shorthand in many different contexts is a particularity of Boas's surviving shorthand notes as a whole, as the only shorthand notes that have survived are those strictly work-related ones that he took down during his field trips. The next quote, taken from a letter written during one of his last field trips in 1923, is proof. It shows that neither his handwriting nor his shorthand ever improved and that his handwriting actually posed a challenge for Boas himself too, a realization that gives me great comfort and satisfaction, given the troubles I have had and still have with it at times: "Dear Toni, . . . my hand is all cramped from continuous writing in Bella Bella. My shorthand was really a great help. I wrote all my notes in shorthand. I hope that I will be able to read them" (December 18, 1923, in Rohner 1969:286).[4]

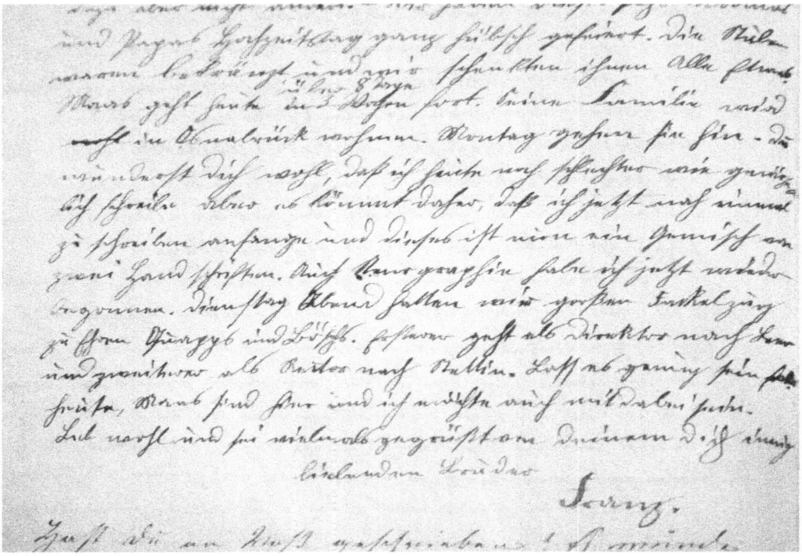

Fig. 5. Boas's early family letters (such as this example, in which he first mentions his learning of shorthand) were rendered in German Kurrent script. Sequence of letter; September 27, 1873, box 3, в в61p. Photo by the author, used with permission of the American Philosophical Society.

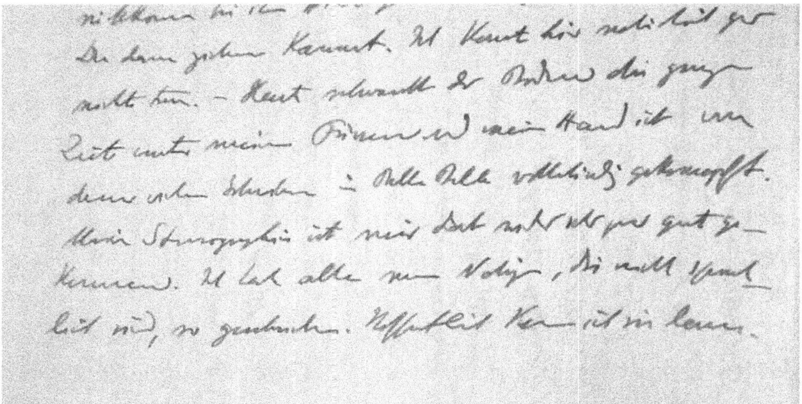

Fig. 6. Longhand filed notes and later letters by Boas (such as these lines, used in the title of this essay) were almost all written in Latin script. December 18, 1923, box 12, в в61p. Photo by the author, used with permission of the American Philosophical Society.

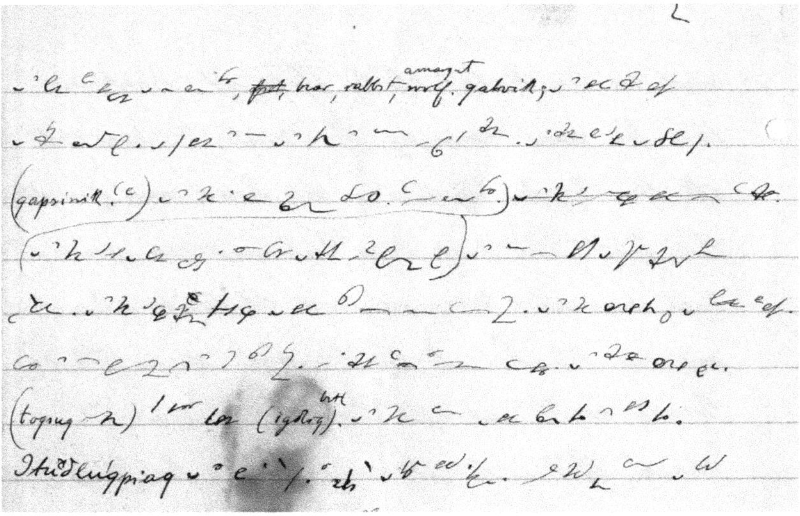

Fig. 7. Due to the peculiarities of the shorthand system employed by Boas, he almost always used a pencil when writing, making his notes usually hard to read and reproduce in images. This example is a rare exception. Sequence of manuscript page, W1a.13, 2, ACLS. Photo by the author, used with permission of the American Philosophical Society.

GETTING STARTED: A PERSONAL EXPERIENCE

Before turning to some preliminary revelations, I would like to offer a few words on how I came to work on the subject of Boas's shorthand notes, as I am confronted with this question time and again. Of course, my decision to try my luck with "decoding" Boas's shorthand did not come out of the blue. Rather, it is part of a personal story of gradually getting drawn more and more to the topic and work of Franz Boas in the course of the last eight years. It began with my involvement in two research projects: a collaborative project with the Navajo Nation on the basis of a wax cylinder collection of ceremonial songs that were collected by one of Boas's students, George Herzog; and a research project in which I came to deal intensively with Boas's first collection, compiled on the Northwest Coast, in 1886.[5] In the course of this work, a number of stimuli paved my way for a Resident Research Fellowship in 2011 at the American Philosophical Society (APS) in Philadelphia, where I first ran into Boas's shorthand materials. In this phase, Richard

Dunn, retired coexecutive officer of the APS, came to provide initial encouragement, as did the emerging "Boas 1897" project, headed by Aaron Glass at the Bard Graduate Center, and Judith Berman at the University of Victoria.[6] I eventually became part of the project, and as the team member in charge of the relevant German materials, it was among my responsibilities to secure a specialist who would be able to transcribe Boas's shorthand notes.

After several futile attempts, journalist and Boas scholar Jürgen Langenkämper, as well as a contact of his, Mrs. Beinhorn of Göttingen, put me in touch with Rosemarie Hänsel, the head of the Stenographischen Sammlungen, Sächsische Landesbibliothek Dresden. She in turn put me in contact with the head of the Stenographenverband Stolze-Schrey, Olaf Ruhe. Both turned out to be instrumental in setting me on the right path. The more I got into the process of actually deciphering some of Boas's shorthand texts, the more I became aware that the task would need to include a solid notion of Boas's larger shorthand materials beyond those immediately relevant to the "Boas 1897" project. Here, it might be important to note that in contrast, for example, to the learning of a new alphabet, that of a shorthand system usually results in highly idiosyncratic forms featuring very diverse levels of abstraction, virtuosity, and type of abbreviation.[7] Boas's shorthand is a case in point. If reading one's own shorthand is hard at times, so definitely is reading that of others. In the case of Boas's shorthand, several points added challenge to the matter: Was it really the system we eventually assumed him to be using? What language was he writing in? Did he, perhaps, switch languages from German to English in the course of his career? What was the level of competency and abstractness of his shorthand? This latter question in turn raised another one relating to the time, energy, and efforts I would have to invest to get to any level of comprehensive reading.

To render a more specific sense of the long and confusing beginning of getting to terms with what we are looking at with regard to Boas's shorthand, which simultaneously reflects on the difficulties of the topic of "shorthand" itself, I would like to present some quotes from the initial exchange of emails between Mrs. Hänsel, Mr. Ruhe, and myself. As I initially did not recognize it to be an obstacle to find someone who would be able to read Boas's shorthand, I was taken by surprise when Mrs. Hänsel remarked in one of her first emails to me, from August 29, 2012: "Unfortunately, we were not able to decipher what [the shorthand example] you sent. Nevertheless, I hope that I'll be able to ask some of the experts on the occasion of the upcoming shorthand symposium in Bayreuth [in October 2012] about it." Two months passed before the first reactions came in: "The experts in Bayreuth think that it is the shorthand system Stolze-Schrey" (November 20, 2012). In an email not long after, she added: "Let's hope that we'll now find a 'translator' . . . [as Boas's] script is (to put it politely) highly idiosyncratic and will, in any case, cause a lot of work" (November 22, 2012). A day later she added: "It is even conceivable that he [Boas] created his 'own' shorthand. Mrs. Dostojewski and Helmholtz have done that. Then it will turn into a really difficult task, as one would then have to find the 'key' first. . . . That's why it was so important for me to know whether we would have to look for German or English ('key') words. It [the pursuit of the question of what system Boas used] is, therefore, really exciting" (November 23, 2012). Initial euphoria was soon followed by disillusionment when Stolze-Schrey expert Olaf Ruhe remarked a couple of days later: "At my first reading, I haven't been able to decipher a single word as being written in Stolze-Schrey" (November 25, 2012). Only further brainstorming resulted in what turned out to be the right conclusions: "If the date [of the sent example] 1893 turns out to be correct, Stolze-Schrey has definitively to be ruled out, as Stolze-Schrey had only been introduced in 1897. The high school period [of Boas] in Minden in the 1860s and 1870s makes me think of the system Stolze, as it was widespread in northern Germany" (November 26, 2012). As they could not refer me to a specialist who might be able to read Boas's version of this shorthand system (not to mention someone having the spare time to deal with the amount of material at hand), I undertook the task myself.[8]

Of course, much more could be said about my process of coming to terms with Boas's shorthand in particular or the topic of "shorthand" in general. What is shorthand? How many systems do we know of, and what kind of rationale do they reflect? What can be said about the development of shorthand systems in Germany, and how did the basic system that Boas learned fit in? In what ways are the teachings of the numerous competing subschools that eventually developed reflected in Boas's interpretation of the system, and what are the peculiarities of his shorthand generally speaking? Quite important, too, are questions regarding the general context in which Boas—like many of his contemporaries—came to learn shorthand in the first place. While all this would be important in order to fully contextualize Boas's shorthand, these topics would overload this publication. Therefore, I would like to direct general attention to the more practical challenges in his case. They result from the fact that, even if one theoretically comes to grasp the foundation and basics of the working of Boas's shorthand script, this might not always be rewarded by a successful reading. Among these challenges, as mentioned already, his penmanship ranks quite high. In a world of signs in which accuracy and detail are key—where it really matters whether you are facing a short or a long line or a dome-shaped sign; whether this sign is placed horizontally, vertically, left, or right turned; whether such a sign is highlighted or not (and in some cases even where); and whether a sign is placed on, above, or underneath a line—in such a world it really matters if Boas presents you with "a something" that basically could be any one of these. As a result, the reader (or rather interpreter of signs) is more often than not confronted with a multitude of ways of how a given sign might possibly be "read." Resulting predicaments are in most cases only to be solved by the establishment of the context (here Boas clearly had an advantage, as he was the one who took down the notes). Therefore, one can say as a rule of thumb: the shorter a note, the harder it tends to be to render meaning from it.

In my own attempts to establish context and double-check my interpretation of what I thought I was reading, a particular body of notes took a special place: those that contained Boas's first observations of winter dances among the Kwakwaka'wakw in the winter of 1894–95 (the only known descriptions by Boas that come close to what today would be called "participant observation"). These field notes by Boas, which eventually became one of the pillars of his seminal 1897 monograph, *The Social Organization and the Secret Societies of the Kwakiutl Indians*, became my personal "Rosetta Stone," as they allowed me to

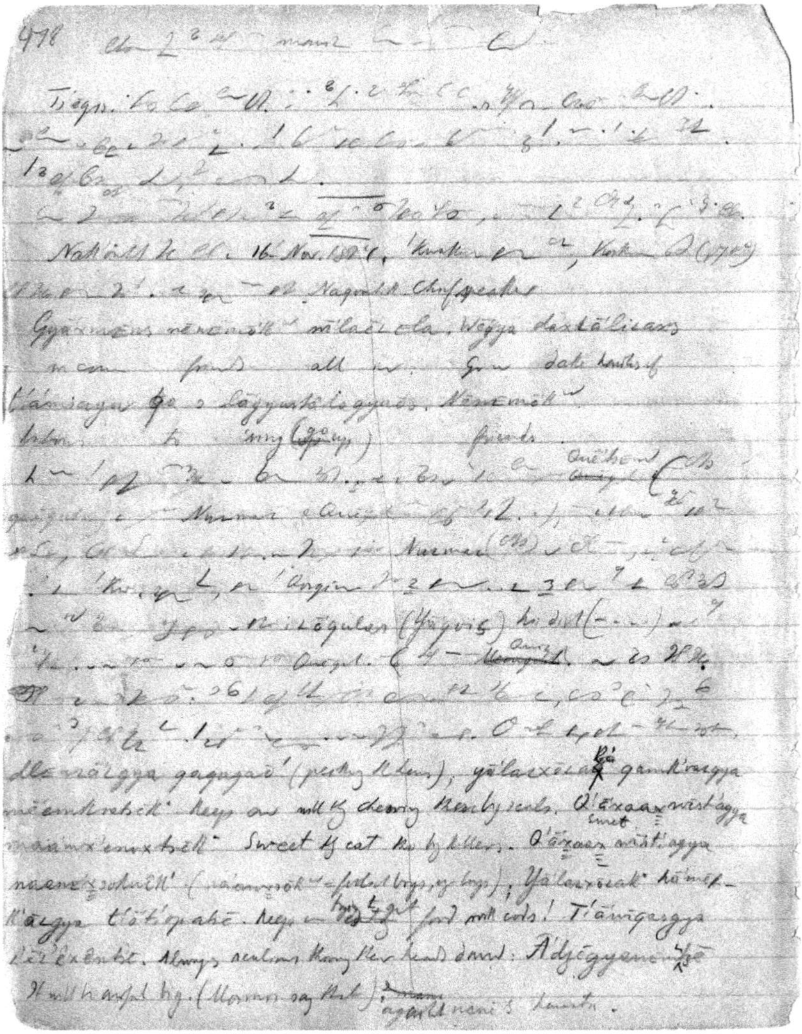

Fig. 8. First page of Boas's 1894 Fort Rupert notes on the winter ceremonials he attended. Sequence of manuscript page, W1a.10/6, 478, ACLS. Scan used with permission of the American Philosophical Society.

check the cultural content of his notes against their eventual translation into published form (fig. 8).

THE CONSTRUCTION OF "OBSERVATION"

Looking at Boas's shorthand notes, one feature is striking: he tends
to switch topics from one line to the other, quite often without any
warning or hint of doing so (e.g., by means of a title or other means
of separation). This makes it, generally speaking, extremely difficult
to browse for and identify specific topics in Boas's notes. The same
holds true for the body of field notes that is of concern here. These
notes, which ended up covering many pages, begin seamlessly, right
after some remarks on the water-monster Ts'ēqis and an interspersed
sentence reflecting on what a hunter might say at some point, as the
following quote shows:

> Ts'ēqis. *It is in part fin-back* {killer whale, or orca}.[9] *There is always
> something in the middle of the forehead like here* {there is no sketch fol-
> lowing this sentence}. *This means that it is part of the fin-back-family
> as fins or flippers are on either side below. It has a broad nose because it
> has a broad mouth. It is not cut in two. It always has a large number of
> flat round teeth, no fangs.*
>
> *When* {a} *hunter sets out he always says to the people to put up a rack,*
> {as} *he will return soon with a deer. Sometimes, they do* {it} *during feasts.*
>
> {The} Nak'oazok *gave a feast on Nov. 16th, 1894. The* KwakiuL *sat
> in the back,* Koskimo *right (north-side) The organizers of the feast did
> not sit at all. Before singing commenced* Naqoatok *chief speaker said*:
> Gyā'xmEns nēnᴣmō'kw wī'laēLela. Wēgya d'axLā'liLaxs t'ā'msayu
> qa s lā'gyustâlagyaōs. NēnEmō'kw. {interlinear translation} We come
> friends all in. Go on take handles of batons to sing (go up). Friends.
> {end of translation} *Hereupon sticks were distributed and planks laid.*
> (w1a.10/6, 478, ACLS Collection, APS)

Though the actual beginning of the related important chapter in
Boas's *Social Organization and the Secret Societies of the Kwakiutl Indians*
would open differently, all of the aforementioned elements are found
in it. The quote of the exclamation in Kwak'wala and its translation
were moved into the footnotes (Boas 1897:545), which proves beyond

a doubt that we are really dealing with the actual notes to the chapter. This is important to specify, as already a superficial comparison reveals one major discrepancy: the date on which the event is supposed to have taken place. Backed by Boas's diary entries and letters (Rohner 1969), these notes—as do numerous publications—place the described activities in the year 1894, while the published chapter, titled "The Winter Ceremonial at Fort Rupert, 1895–96," gives a different impression.

As this essay is not the occasion for a discussion of all of Boas's 1894 notes, I will select particular events described in them in order to shed light on some specific aspects that came to my attention. I would like to start with the published equivalent: "In the evening [of November 21] father of Yā'qoîs gave the promised feast, in which he was going to pay for the ecstasy of his son" (Boas 1897:555), which was part of his initiation as a *hamats'a* (cannibal dancer). As the 1897 publication is readily available, I have decided not to quote the whole text here. Instead, I would like to focus on the relevant part of the transcribed shorthand notes, which reads as follows:

> Nov. 21. *At first* xxx's[10] *mother* {i.e., Yā'qoîs's grandmother} *came in* {and called out} huhuhu. *She gave away blankets. Then, after a while* xxx {the father of Yā'qoîs} *came in singing!* HēLikya yeē'laqula (*solo-singing*) *secret song.* KyinqalaLah and *the* hamatsa *followed him*{....} *Then, he turned around and spoke to the* Nak{oatok} & Qosqimo. *He asked them to help and* heliqya *him*{, i.e., their} *great friend* {i.e., the hamats'a}. *We have tried it but haven't been able to do it. I am too small for him. Then he started singing.* (â'lakyas *sang all people*). YalaxdeEn laistai'sElayu (*see book*{,} No 3[11] {reference is elevated}) hamats'a *song. And* xxx & xxx {Yā'qoîs & his sister} *danced* [a] *dance. And they sang* 2 {songs} *for* hamats'a *and* 2 {songs} *for* kyinqalaLa: (No 7 p 50[12]). *And after that* {the} *chief of the* Qosqimo *stood up and spoke.* Yā Qōsqimox{!} *He said*{:} yā Kwā'kiuL, yā Nakoatok. *This is my* hamatsa. (*he refers to* xxx {Yā'qoîs} *as he had made him* ham***{hamats'a} *before*){....} *I* {will} *make him as heavy as I can and his father does the same.* (w1a.10/6, 498, APS)

After this quote, which should be regarded as a kind of general introduction, I will now turn to the main example and body of text that are

Fig. 9. Blankets piled up in a big house. Image #22861. Courtesy of the Division of Anthropology, American Museum of Natural History.

of primary interest here. As detail is particularly crucial with regard to comparison, both versions (i.e., the published text and the transcription of the field notes) will be quoted here in full, starting with the printed version:

> Then Yā'qoîs's father arose and [...] said: "Friends, look at me[.... .]
> Ten times I gave blankets [... and] I want you to come to my house
> ten times this year, so that I may reach to the beams of my house.
> This is not my way of doing. Chief NEqa'penk.'Em, my father,[13] and
> Â'wate taught me this way and I followed them. [...] Do you want
> to know how I obtained my ha'mats'a? [...] I received it from my
> brother-in-law, Qulî's. Therefore I am not ashamed of my ha'mats'a.
> Now I ask you one thing—do not call me Gue'tlabido. It is well when
> I live like one of you, and it is well if I act like one of the northern
> tribe, because my mother was of high blood among her tribe. I do
> not give this festival that you may call me a chief. I give it in honor
> of these two who are dancing here, that the words of their enemies

may not harm them. For this purpose I build an armor of wealth around them. (Boas 1897:556–557)

Even readers who are somewhat familiar with the ethnographic literature of the region and with an interest in the subject—just like myself before I became aware of the field notes—will probably not get too much out of this text. Although community members would understand the context, an uninitiated reader might think something like, Well, this text is about some historical, today no longer identifiable, Kwakwaka'wakw individual planning to give so many blankets as to reach to the beams of the roof of his house. This will most likely be regarded as a gross exaggeration, unless, of course, one is aware of historic photographs proving the validity of such claims (fig. 9). To read the proclamation, that he got his hamats'a from his brother-in-law, would not be too thrilling either, and even less interesting is the fact that he does not wish to be called Gue'tlabido anymore. All this changes, of course, once the field notes are taken into consideration. While these and the published text seem to be quite close at first glance, a comparison of the two proves to be quite illuminating. Boas actually wrote on November 21, 1894, the following:

Then George spoke. [*then all called out* wai yā'q'ēgysLax gyiqāmē, *speak chief and* xā'mastala gyuigamē]. *And then he said: Friends look at me, look well at me. Because I will also let* {you} *know who I am. This is my way.* {In the past} *5 years you heard, as I know*{,} *a lot about me* {and} *what I do. Then I made* hamatsa *at first* {sic; for the first time, i.e., when he received his hamats'a?}. *I gave blankets away, 10 times him* {sic; (to) them / to the} Qosqimo. *And I want you to come back to my house 10 times this year, so that I reach the two beams of my roof. It is not my way.* Neqa'p'EntyL {NEqap!EnkEm, a chief of the KwEkwakw!Em (GwitEla)}, *the chief, my father* [*he has the position* {of a} *father*] *and* Â'wate {A'wade, a chief of the Ma'Emtagila} *have taught me everything about this way and I have followed them ever since. My name is* Lāqoagyila *owing to the* {plural? singular?} *copper there* {which} *came from my grandfather. Ermine and abelon shells* {English term in shorthand} *also came from him. And therefore, my name is* Q'ōmoquē. *If you want to know how I got my* hamatsa, *I got* {my} hamatsa *from* (Q'uli's) (= OmheL) *my sister. And therefore I am not ashamed of my* hamatsa. *Don't call me* Guē'Elabidō, *don't call me* Mā'maLnatēlā. *Because when I dress myself as an Indian, then I look good, because my mother is born high in the north. And I look good when I dress like a white man because my father was known to everyone. Then he said{: "}I am not doing this so you call me a chief{!} I am doing it for these 2 here who are dancing* {his son, the hamatsa, and his daughter, the kyinqalaLala}, *so that the words of their enemies may bounce off from them. Therefore I am putting this shield of wealth around them{."}* (w1a.10/6, 498–499, APS)

Taking the whole published chapter into consideration, one realizes how thoroughly Boas has covered up the "true" identity of the organizer of the event described. Now it becomes clear that "Yā'qoîs's father" is George. In other parts of the notes, he is readily identified as George Hunt, Boas's closest Native collaborator among the Kwakwaka'wakw, with whom he ended up closely working for some forty-five years (Boas 2004; Berman 1996, 2001). The other main protagonists are Yā'qoîs the hamats'a, who is George's son David, and his sister, George's daughter, who acted as *kyinqalaLala* for her brother.[14] I am not claiming to reveal here for the first time the identity of George Hunt with regard to the described events.[15] The point is that the comparison of the field notes and the published text shows how Boas obscured Hunt's identity in his writings. It has to be added, though, as Judith Berman correctly stresses, that Boas hardly ever disclosed the identities of his informants, an action that she suggests was linked, at least in part, to the threats posed by the Indian Act (personal communication, July 6, 2014).

But it is probably also true that George Hunt, the son of a Hudson Bay trader and of Tlingit and English ancestry, did not quite match Boas's "ideal" for a protagonist in his description of an "authentic" and "prototypical" winter dance of the Kwakwaka'wakw. As is by now well known, George Hunt, though born and raised in Fort Rupert, actually came from outside of the Kwakwaka'wakw society and was only later adopted into it. Hunt was not, of course, the first outsider to marry into the Kwakwaka'wakw, but he was particularly vulnerable to charges of illegal potlatching. Only hinted at between the lines, it becomes clear

Fig. 10. Boas and Hunt during a photograph session in Fort Rupert, 1894. Photograph by Oregon C. Hastings. Image #11604. Courtesy of the Division of Anthropology, American Museum of Natural History.

that both Hunt's position in Kwakwa̲ka'wakw society and his right to that hamats'a seat did not remain uncommented upon by his village mates and neighbors. That is indicated by the "shield of wealth" that Hunt and his supporters put around that hamats'a position and around Hunt's son David to fend off challenges. It is likewise demonstrated by the names that Hunt asked his guests not to call him any longer. While the published version features only the reference to Hunt's mother and to the "father of Ya̱'qoîs" disliking one name (i.e., Gue'tlabido, which is translated as "Son of Northern Tribe" in a footnote),[16] comparison with the field notes makes clear that this is just half of the picture that Boas originally recorded. Here, reference to a second name, Ma'maLnatela, tentatively translated as "White on His Father's Side," and references to Hunt's white father are likewise included.[17] Thus, Boas not only chose to simply omit Hunt—and thus the non-Native part of his heritage— but also shifted the focus away from him to his son, who is the main protagonist in the published text. This actually follows a typical pattern in Boas's work and reflects his already well-documented and discussed understanding of anthropology, which included the ignoring of acculturative influences and the focus on the concept of precontact culture (I will not elaborate on this here, but see Glass 2011:20 ff.) (fig. 10).

I will now turn to a third example out of Boas's 1894 field notes. This example helped him prepare the first lengthy, detailed description of a Kwakwaka'wakw hamats'a dance and ceremony ever published. Boas's entries for November 23 include the following observations:

Instantly {after a previous ceremony was finished there was} *loud clapping and* {calls of} hūh *followed. Then* {there was} *whistling* {heard} *on top of the roof. After that* {a} *speaker came in with a horizontal*{ly held} *stick* {i.e., staff} *and* {a} *scalp on one end. Then came another* {speaker} *with a staff*{.} *They are clapping and attendants of the hamatsa* {appear} *with rattles* {and} *with cedar bark ring*{s} {unclear sentence in German}. *He dances squatting in* {the} *door, turns around* {, and} *then* {there is} *immediately singing in the rear.* {The hamatsa wears an} *arm ring and* {a} *broad band around the head,* {and dances} *with* {a} *blanket.* 2 *women dance in the doorway for him.* {A} *man* {in the} *rear right (*{when looking} *from the entrance*{,} *in the corner) rattles.* 2 *attendants* {are appearing} *with staffs. Then* 3 *speakers came from* {the} *rear to* {the} *front* {to stand} *in front of* {the} *fire and* {they} *followed him. One attendant had* {a} *big red and white neck ring*{.} *In the back whistles are heard*{. Now the} *attendants gather around him. The* 3 *speakers remain in some distance behind him. More women are dancing*{.} 3 {women are} *in the door now.* 1 {more is} *in* {the} *rear* {to the} *left,* {and} 4 {others in the} *rear* {to the} *right. At the end of the song*{,} *more whistles and calls* {of} *hoip* {are heard}. *Second song*{. The hamatsa} *resumes dancing again*{.} *Even more women are dancing.* {The} *hamatsa wears* {a} *thin round ring with long fringes on* 2 *places. After he made it one time around*{,} *the heily*** {hēili'qya, i.e., attendents} *closed around him again. Women are dancing with their backs to the fire*{,} *except for those in the doorway.* 3rd *dance*{, the} *hamats'a stands. First, he goes back and forth in the rear and then around* {the} *fire. He has* {a} *dance-apron and* {wears} *a blanket. Otherwise* {he is} *naked* {and wears} *no shirt* {underlined by Boas}. *In front* {of the} *fire he calls out* hāp *again and sits*{/takes a seat} *to* {the sounds of} *whistles and* {calls of} hoip. *Then* {follows another} *song and* 2 *women start dancing in the back center. All other* {women} *join in. Then the* hamatsa *begins*{,} *standing*{, to dance. The} *face of* {the} *hamatsa* {is} *all black. Then* {the} hamatsa *runs behind the curtain. After that* {the floor} *is swept for* {the next} *dance in the rear. A speaker speaks in the rear and the one who came in last leaves.* {Now the} *front is also swept.* 3 *speaker are standing in the rear. Then* 4 *men come back with blankets. After distributing the blankets* *** {the old big noses?} went around the fire. (w1a.10/6, 515, APS)

The equivalent episode in *The Social Organization and the Secret Societies of the Kwakiutl Indians* opens as follows:

Then Mā'a and G.a'loīL[18] went out, and immediately the quē'qutsa began to beat time and cried "yū!" all at the same time. When they had done so, the whistles of the hāmats'a were heard on the roof of the house. Then Mā'a returned, carrying a staff to which an imitation of a scalp was attached. He was followed by G.a'loīL. Both remained standing at the door, one on each side, and Mā'a said: "Friends did you hear that noise? If I am not mistaken, something dangerous is near us. Keep your batons in readiness." While he was speaking the door opened and the hā'mats'a Ya'xyak.alag.ilîs appeared, crying "hāp, hāp, hāp." (Boas 1897:572)

When confronted with the field notes, the reader is inclined to compare the difference between the two texts and have the same experience that a very shortsighted person would have when putting on his glasses after having had a look at a celebration without them. All of a sudden, the blurry shapes and shadows he had seen before would have turned into a startlingly clear and sharp picture. But this comparison is misleading, as it neglects one crucial aspect: the modification of the picture we are actually being presented with. Aside from the level of minor, although no less important, deviations in detail (e.g., whether people called out "hūh" [field notes] or "yūh" [Boas 1897], or whether the hamats'a wore a blanket or not), these refinements are found on other levels, too.

But instead of getting lost in details, I would prefer to lead the discussion now toward the fact that this refinement was a process, one in which both Boas and Hunt had a say. How strong the role of George Hunt actually was is reflected not only in surviving letters but also in the sheer amount of textual evidence. With regard to the particular case discussed here, surviving letters from Boas give us some revealing insights into the nature of their collaboration. In a letter Boas wrote to his wife, Marie, on November 15, 1894, for example, we learn the following: "All my free time is used for making stenographic notes, i.e., I make short notes and go over them the next day with Hunt and have him explain everything to me" (quoted in Rohner 1969:179). While this sounds like a great arrangement, Hunt was of course aware of Boas's dependence on him and obviously let him know that occasionally, as the following lines, written by a rather frantic Boas to his wife a few days later, document:

> This morning I obtained a few more items concerning last night and also wrote down a few folktales.[19] I wish I were away from here. George Hunt is so hard to get along with. He acts exactly as he did in Chicago. He is too lazy to think, and that makes it disagreeable for me. I cannot change this, though, and have to make the best of it. He left at noon with some excuse and returned only after several hours. He knows exactly how I depend on him. (November 22, 1894, quoted in Rohner 1969:183)[20]

No less interesting are the textual pieces of evidence that reflect the kind of relationship the two men had. Looking at the three examples picked out of the larger body of Boas's field notes documenting his 1894 Fort Rupert experience, one thing is striking: while in the beginning we find passages of text—some including expressions in Kwak'wala—that basically made it into the 1897 published book as they were, this level of "observational" quality is not kept throughout the notes. As Boas and Hunt's collaboration progressed, exemplified by the second example presented here, Boas stopped presenting word-for-word quotes. Still, we find Hunt breaking down for Boas the core content of some of the speeches Boas transcribed in subsequent English translations.[21] The last example is completely different again, as here we merely learn that individuals, not identified by Boas, simply spoke. When I read the notes for the first time, I wondered and bemoaned the seemingly increasing "loss in quality" in the "observations." But after I reevaluated the issue I came to see the great advantage in the ups and downs of Boas and Hunt's collaboration, as reflected in the field notes. We have reached one of those rare moments when we are able to get beyond negotiated versions of Boas's "observations," which, as we know, were usually strongly influenced by Hunt. Finally, we are able to understand that Boas, for good reasons, mistrusted his own observations the most. It is here that the value and rarity of these sections of Boas's field notes on the hamats'a ceremony lie, not because they are by any means "truer" or "less distorted," but because they are as much Boas the person as they can become, and because they resemble much more the state of confusion and ignorance we experience when we are confronted with cultural settings utterly different from our own.

WORD LISTS, MYTHS, AND MANY THINGS MORE

There are two research topics that are quite prominent in Boas's field notes: language and myth. His lifetime interest in these topics supports this impression and leaves no doubt, if there had ever been any, that Boas considered language and myth as the keys to gaining a better understanding of the cultural dimensions of humanity (see, e.g., Boas 1911, 1940; Hymes 1981 [2004]; Darnell 1998 [2000]; Berman 1996). Considering this, it is not too surprising to find most of Boas's field notes—and thus most of his shorthand material—not so much in his professional papers but rather in the Boas collection of the Committee on American Languages of the ACLS (American Council of Learned Societies). As the main instrument to commence learning a language is word lists, and as these form the basis of the survey work on Native languages, such lists came to be important elements in most of Boas's field notebooks (fig. 11). Boas's word lists typically are Native words—or, rather, whatever was considered their phonetically closest approximation at a given time—usually listed in a column on the left side, followed by their "translation" in English, German, German shorthand, or a wild mix of these languages and script forms in a column on the right side. Thus, word lists pose complex challenges in and of themselves. They are not easy to read, and they are often not what

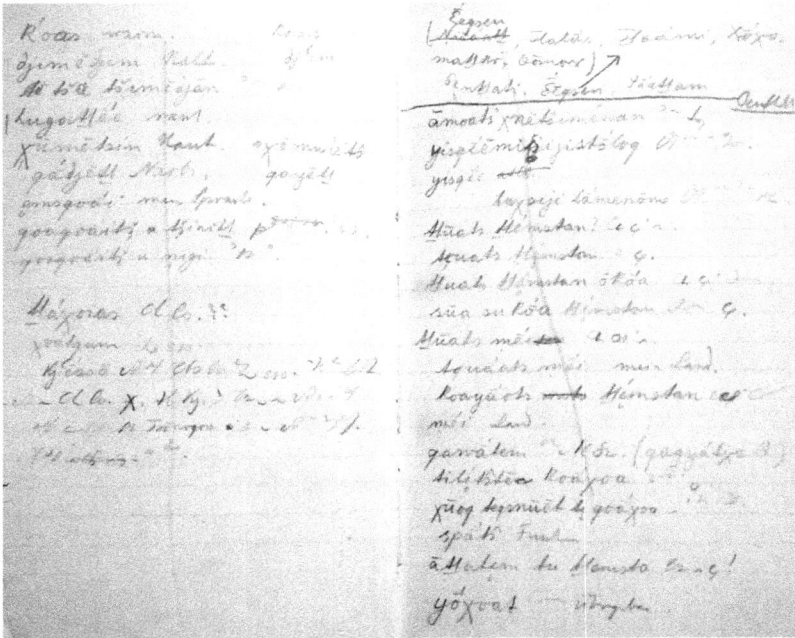

Fig. 11. A typical word list by Boas. B B61, n.p., fn 3. Photo by the author, used with permission of the American Philosophical Society.

they seem to be at first glance, that is, simple lists of words. They are the results of cross-cultural collaborations that stand, at times, for fascinating stories. Their historic value and their potential insights with regard to matters of Native language preservation make them important "cultural" (i.e., man-made) objects. An example should illustrate the point. One of the many word lists from Boas's 1886 notebooks starts like this:

Pentlatch

āmoats'xnētŝimē'wan	*I am sad.*
yisqī'ēmisijistō'loq	*I will return soon.*
tuxaiji lā'menōme	*I will see him soon.*
tlūats tle'mstan?	*Whose house is this.*
tuats tle'mstan	*My house.*
tluats tle'mstan	*Whose house is small.*

sūa su kō'a tle'mstan	*Small house.*
tlūats mē'i	*Whose land is this.*
tquā'ats mē'i	My land ... {this line is written in German longhand}

(B B61, fn 3, n.p., APS)

Admittedly, a list like this is not too exciting, especially if it goes on for pages. But our perception of it will certainly change when we gain information on how it came to be and what it stands for. This particular list, for example, takes us all the way back to Boas's first trip to the Northwest Coast, to his intensive studies of Native languages in and around the town of Comox, which he visited from November 12 to December 2, 1886. In his travel diary we read the following:

> The Comox live in the last houses of the settlement. Mr. Cliff, who has lived here for many years, introduced me so that they were very friendly. I have already written that I was under the impression that the Comox spoke two different languages. After some fruitless questioning I discovered that they have combined with the Penntatish {probably a misread version of the handwritten notes} [Pentlatch]. There is only one family of these left, the last of the tribe. I immediately made friends with them and am now learning this newly discovered language. From the few words I have obtained in one day, I know that it, too, belongs to the Salish, but it has apparently been very much influenced by the language of the Comox. Pure Penntatish [Pentlatch] seems no longer to exist. I shall spend the next week learning the language and recording the myths. (November 12, 1886, quoted in Rohner 1969:59)

Boas's notes from November 13 shed some more light on his study in the Pentlatch language and his word lists: "I have gotten another long Penntatish [Pentlatch] text and at last, with great difficulty, discovered some pronouns in it. It took me an hour to distinguish between 'I' and 'you.' They are so nearly alike that I could not hear the difference. I always have them tell me myths in the afternoons" (November 23, 1886, quoted in Rohner 1969:65).

During this—in Boas's terms—quite long stay in Comox, he attempted to document and "record" not only the languages of the Comox and Pentlatch but also those of the Lekwiltok, Sechelt, and Squamish. Managing this enormous workload with the different individual personalities of his collaborators made matters obviously worse. This becomes quite clear in his statement from November 30:

> I did not get much wiser today. I tried my luck with the Sisa'atl [Sechelt] again but was unable to get anywhere with him because he speaks too quickly and cannot understand what I want. I think I had better stop with my vocabulary instead of continuing to be annoyed and not discovering anything with certainty. I am slowly progressing with the Lequiltag [Lekwiltok] vocabulary and today got some Puntlatish [Pentlatch] texts and a few Comox stories, but nothing worthwhile. The Comox and Puntlatish [Pentlatch] vocabularies contain up to this time about 1,000 words, and I can make myself quite well understood by using the small number of these that I know. At least they can no longer speak without my knowing what they are talking about. (November 30, 1886, quoted in Rohner 1969:68–69)

When we look closer at what Boas simply termed as "texts" and "stories" in the quote cited above, it becomes apparent that we are actually dealing with a broad and complex topic. We find records of all kinds and in all forms reflecting the many ways in which Boas attempted to capture these. Boas's endeavors range from actually trying to transcribe the stories and myths in their Native language as he heard them (sometimes with, sometimes without subsequent attempts to translate them), to interlinearly rendered narratives featuring lines in Native language transcriptions followed by translations in all kinds of forms and languages (English and German) and script combinations (longhand and shorthand). His efforts also included "simple" attempts to take down myths in English and German longhand (some intermixed with parts in shorthand) or in German shorthand only.

While Boas did not comment on the recording context of most stories and myths, he did reflect on some circumstances in his correspondence with his wife, sister, or parents. These examples are particularly revealing. Among the examples that meet the criteria described and that additionally are written down in shorthand, one particular myth captured my interest. It was taken down by Boas during his 1886 trip and begins as follows:

Cowichan

A man {by the name of} Siā'latsa *came to* Xā'tsa. *He built a house. He stayed one day. Then another man descended* {from heaven, his name was} Swūtlā'q. *And a woman goes to* Qōlā'sīlwot. *And another* {man} *came down*{,} Sūqsā'qūlaq. *And another came on the next day*{,} Squē'lem. *And then again one came*{,} Swiq'ēm'ām. *And* {then} Siāiimqen. Kto'xšin, Xōāxōtšin, Hē'nqen. Xtlā'set. Xāiotsemqen{.} Xuitēxten. *And they go to* Tsuqōla. *The woman had nothing*{,} *no clothes. And she was* *** {ashamed?} *und took leaves and covered herself with them (cedar bark) and she made a fire. And the men were all painted.* (B B61, fn 1, n.p., APS)

It is worthwhile to cast a look into Boas's letter diary, as it contains a section that offers us a better understanding of the general context in which he recorded this myth. After preliminary studies in Victoria, his ensuing visit among the Kwakwa̱ka̱'wakw, and another brief stay in Victoria, Boas took some time to visit the Cowichan and other Salish peoples around the town of Duncan on Vancouver Island. He stayed there from November 4 to 10, 1886, that is, until his departure for Comox. Obviously, the visit did not at first work out as he had envisioned, as Boas complained on November 8:

I find that my notes are very scant these days owing to the slow progress I am making. I must admit that this week has been the most unpleasant one I have spent in the region. I have to run about all day—twice a day two miles to the settlement—and there is very little to be found here. At least I know that the people here have an entirely different cycle of myths from those in the north, and this strengthens my belief that the myths here [on the Northwest Coast] originate from two different sources. I was up there again yesterday and almost became impatient because of the long-drawn-out manner in which they told the stories. It really was a test of patience. (quoted in Rohner 1969:54–55)

One day later Boas's mood had changed altogether:

> It is unfortunate that I must leave tomorrow because I have just made a good beginning. An old man related so well about the first people that I shall try, if at all possible, to stop here on my way back. Perhaps I shall get the linguistic material which I need very badly in Comox; otherwise I should prefer to remain in Nanaimo. This morning I went down to the village, as arranged, only to find that my new friend [the one who told him the story about the first people], who goes under the name of [Big] Bill, was not home. (quoted in Rohner 1969:6)

It should be noted that the aforementioned myth, which had such an effect on the mood of Boas, finally ended up being published in German in a thoroughly remastered version, under the name "Siālatsa," in Boas's 1895 monograph on Northwest Coast mythology, where it is presented as the origin myth of the Cowichan (compare Bouchard and Kennedy 2002 [2008], an edited version of Boas's 1895 book translated into English; see esp. 133 ff.). Many more examples are bound to surface in the future as I continue my exploration of Boas's shorthand writings. As brilliant examples of how non-Native perception of the cultural realities on the Northwest Coast gradually and very slowly came to be shaped over time, these stories—no matter how incomplete or distorted they may be—are of particular historical value.

Boas's letter diaries record a number of remarks on this topic and on how hard he struggled. Issues of communication were particularly pressing in new contexts, for example, when George Hunt was not around. Strategies to overcome challenges of communication included the hiring of locals, such as missionaries or Natives who spoke either English or the lingua franca of the region, the pidgin trade language Chinook Jargon. It is interesting to note that Boas's first attempts to learn Chinook Jargon can be traced back to the visit of a Bella Coola group touring Germany in 1885, an event that was organized by the Jacobson brothers Adrian and Fillip, and therefore to a time before he even had made any specific arrangements to conduct research on the Northwest Coast.

A good example of the challenges of communication surfaces quite clearly, for example, in a letter he addressed to his wife in August 1897 while staying in Port Essington during the first field season of the Jessup North Pacific Expedition, which Boas organized for the American Museum of Natural History. Here we read:

> Dear Wife, […] Smith started right in to make castings, and since yesterday I have joined him. We already have sixteen—partly Haida, partly Tsimshian, and one Tlingit woman. Smith is photographing. I spent the rest of the time with a Haida painter whom I got just in time. He was ready to leave for Fort Simpson the day before yesterday when I quickly engaged him. I am showing him all the photographs which I had made in New York and Washington, as well as in Ottawa, and I am able to identify many objects with his help. I am very happy about this because our collections from now on will be much more [complete?]. (August 13, 1897, quoted in Rohner 1969:223)

And some days later: "Dear Wife, […] My Haida friend takes so long to do a painting that I lose a lot of time. I cannot do anything else while he is doing it, and I have some free time. In between I let him tell me things. Since his Chinook is rather limited however, the conversation is very difficult" (August 19, 1897, quoted in Rohner 1969:228).

One of the results of this collaboration was the following fragment of a Haida myth captured in shorthand on a drawing that is now preserved at the American Museum of Natural History in New York (fig. 12):

> Whale having devoured raven. Blanket edge with raven
> *And many people came and cut him* {the whale} *up. And raven thought, the chief's son shall find me, {and} shall cut me out. And he* {the chief's son} *cut him* {the whale} *and saw raven and he* {raven} *flew out* {of the whale's body}. *And he flew against his* {the chief's son} *breast and the son of the chief was dead. And all people ran away. And he* {raven} *flew towards the sky and came back as old man, by supporting himself on a stick{/cane}. And he asked{:} Why are you running away. When they told him he said. In the past this all happened and back then all people deserted the land and left all things back. Do it again. Don't take anything with you. Save yourself as quickly as you can. And the people ran away. And he* {raven} *took all the furs and had a lot to eat. And he ate it all up.* (folder 14, box 2, AMNH)[22]

Fig. 12. Drawing of Charles Edenshaw with shorthand notes by Boas. Z/25 K.
Courtesy of the Division of Anthropology, American Museum of Natural History.

Regarding the general nature of the design to which this story refers, we read a proud Boas reporting to his wife from aboard a ship after leaving Port Essington on August 26: "I was successful in obtaining drawings and paintings. You might remember that I planned to collect paintings done on hard-to-decorate materials in order to study the symbolism of the Indians. For this purpose I chose face paintings and paintings on edges of blankets. The results are very satisfying, because I found just what I had expected, that is, strong stylization and stressing of symbols" (August 26, 1897, quoted in Rohner 1969:231).

This quote makes the previous story about the design become even more meaningful. Though we still have not learned a name from it, this quote includes a hint that leads to the identification of the Haida artist to whom Boas refers. No news to Northwest Coast scholars, this artist's identity was revealed in Boas's essay on Haida face paintings, which was published a year later (Boas 1898) and in which we learn that his name is Ē'densâ. In cther words, Boas's previous comments to his wife referred to none other than the famous Haida artist Charles Edenshaw, whom Boas came to call "one of the most famous artists of the tribe [i.e., Haida]" (quoted in Jonaitis 1995:108).[23] Because of the general importance and fame of Edenshaw, I would like to include here, too, the legend captured on a second blanket-edge design preserved in the same collection as the previous one (fig. 13):

A man went to fish Halibutt. {The man's name was} xāusgana in his country. And raven always went there and came to his house. And x. was nice to him{.} He did not know that he {raven} was a fool {trickster}. He stayed there for a long time. And in the morning they would leave together to go fishing. And raven said {one day}, I saw an island with many woodpeckers on it. And x. believed him and he said to him{:} Let's go and have a look. And when the weather was nice one day they went *** {to the east?}. x's wife went with them {or "did not go with them," as the woman actually stays home}. But there were no woodpeckers there. He {raven} lied. And they rowed {sic; paddled} there. And raven said. Stay here, I will go into the forest to rouse them. And there were many twigs lying on {the} ground [it is actually a plait with something like berries on it] and he hit himself with it on the nose and blood leaked out. And he said. Become woodpeckers. And here {they} flew around. [sLāsk'Ema {below it} name of the wood]. And he went back to the boat and said{:} Do you see the many woodpeckers. And he {x} saw these and wanted to catch them. They tie these feathers{,} the red ones{,} onto their fish rods in order to get luck. And he went there and raven went back into the boat and thought {to himself:} I wish wind would come from the direction of the island {and} that {it} would drive the boat away. And he put {the} boat over his head {sic} and acted as if he was sleeping. And x. saw it and called him. Stop sleeping{, wake up}, you are drifting into the ocean. And x. {realized that he} was in big trouble {term in English longhand} as he was without a boat. And raven went to x's wife. Her husband was {still} on {the} island. And he came to their house. He made himself look like her husband. And he said. This one over there is raven, he is always lying {incorrect German}. And she gave him to eat. And he ate and soon he said. I am {still} hungry. Not like I used to be when I used to get full. And he kept on eating more and more. And soon he slept with his {i.e., x's} wife. And x started thinking. I wish my {sacred} rattle would come to me. And here it came. And then he *** {unified the waves, made them become one}. And then he {x} walked over the water until it turned into land {incorrect German}. And he went ashore at the place of his village. And he{,} x{,} told his wife {what happened}. And he told her{:} Raven has lied to you. Close all cracks in our house and watch the door. When all is ready close even the chimney. And I will come. And then she went back. And the woman acted as if nothing had happened. And she cooked for him {i.e., raven}. And {raven} kept on saying. I did not feel like this in the past. Now, I am hungry all the time. And when the woman finished {with all the things that her husband had asked her to do}, x entered the house and beat raven {almost?} dead. And he {raven} took his raven-fur {sic; raven skin} and flew {away, calling out} qax qax qax. But he {x} {almost?} killed him. {x} broke all his {raven's} bones. And they {x and his wife} threw him {raven} into the latrine. Into {the} water closet. And next day he was still there. And when they {x and his wife} went to have a shit {that is the expression used} there, raven spit at both of their buttocks. And x grabbed him and beat him {half?} dead again. And he took {a} big stone and beat him to powder{?}. And he {x} took {his} boat and threw him {raven} into the ocean. And he {raven} drifted about{.} And many people went out {onto the sea} to get something {i.e., they went fishing}. And they asked {raven, who was floating in the ocean:} Why does the chief {raven} go out onto the ocean? And he answered. A woman did that.*** {incorrect German; general meaning: And he thought about her and said: Come on, everyone, and eat (as he was still in powder form)}. And then came the whale and ate him. (folder 14, box 2, AMNH)[24]

These examples should have demonstrated clearly that, aside from Boas's own theoretical considerations for being interested in myths,[25] there were other reasons as well that kept his interests in them high throughout his career. To a great part this was due to his early realization that material culture, art, and countless other aspects of Native Northwest Coast cultures were deeply embedded in the world of myth and that this anchor was the key to their understanding.

Fig. 13. Drawing of Charles Edenshaw with shorthand notes by Boas. z/25 D.
Courtesy of the Division of Anthropology, American Museum of Natural History.

Boas's interest in all forms and expressions of art, including the general appreciation of Northwest Coast art and the emerging market for it in the second half of the twentieth century, has been thoroughly discussed and analyzed elsewhere (see, e.g., Boas 1927; Jonaitis 1995; Jacknis 2002). Instead, I would like to turn to Boas's work on some less tangible expressions of art. Among these, his interest in the designs and forms of face painting has already been noted. To demonstrate that his attention to this topic was by no means restricted to his study of Haida face paintings, I would like to choose the following example of a shorthand explanation from a drawing that he took down when he was with the Kwakwaka'wakw (fig. 14):

G'ä'g.ililas. *Someone who has lost his child or* {another} *close relative* (***{?; the or a} *sister). On the head* {a} *feather* {is worn} *which had been turned in red paint. When someone has died one remains lying on* {one's} *back* (yia'mxa {replaced with an arrow to "X"}) *Then all peo-*

ple gather and attempt to speak kindly with him {i.e., the one who had the loss} *so that he will forget the deceased.*{X} *This happens as soon he* {the deceased} *is buried*{.} *All enter the house* {of the mourner} *then. He lies at the back* {close to the} *wall in front of* {the} *gla**lla* {glabella?}. *And at first* KwīKw *speaks to him. And* {representatives of} *every* clan *in* {their} *order. Then he* {the mourner} *takes someone who speaks for him* (dzō'xwa) {and} *promises to give* {him} *blankets* {English term in shorthand}. *And after 4 days he gives* {the blankets to the one who is going to speak for him}. *Then the people leave* {the or his house}. *And after 4 days he has gathered his things and then he* {the mourner} *paints himself like that. And he speaks then* {i.e., he renders a speech through his speaker?}. (fig. 2, folder 4, box 1, AMNH)[26]

Another even less tangible form of art that is also linked in many ways—but not exclusively—to myths is the world of music and song. Actually, this realm constitutes one of the core topics of Boas's work, surfacing time and again from the first to the last of his field notebooks. This probably has a lot to do with the fact that music had always been an important element in Boas's life and for many of his family members as well. His sister Toni, in particular, had been a noted pianist who even took classes from Franz Liszt and Boas reportedly almost always had a piano in his living quarters throughout his life (see Boas 2004:82). A particularly interesting episode illustrating the role of music in daily life of the Boas family has been preserved by a remark of Franz Boas's wife, Marie, who dropped—ten months after their marriage—the following remark in a letter to Boas's mother, Sophie: "Franz and I had been terribly high-spirited all day long. We are singing Eskimo songs all the time" (September 6, 1887, B B61 F, APS; see also O'Neill 2010).

And so it is not too surprising to learn that Boas actually used all kinds of means to "record" Native music throughout his career. Aside from his ability to write down a song after hearing it, he discovered early on a device that caught his attention and inspired him: the phonograph. It is a stroke of luck that a letter containing Boas's initial response to his first encounter with this recording machine has survived. In a euphoric reaction, he wrote the following to his mother on December 9, 1878, about a week after he had seen his first phonograph in Bonn:

Fig. 14. Face painting with shorthand notes by Boas. z/4 B. Courtesy of the Division of Anthropology, American Museum of Natural History.

Last week a phonograph was on display here, a really interesting invention. I went there to have a look at it. It is actually weird when this device starts moving and begins to speak and sing, depending on whether you spoke or sang into it before. It really is an invention of great importance that, as I believe, will have a great future. Just imagine all the speeches at the Reichstag, recorded by means of such a machine and then having it repeat the whole hearings later on! At the same time, this device is fabulously simple. It is a real egg of Columbus.[27] This Edison must have an inventive genius that is immense. (B B61p, box 4, APS)

The phonograph did actually become part of the spectrum of Boas's attempts to "capture" and preserve culture. The first time he reportedly came to use a phonograph was at the Chicago World's Fair in 1893. On that occasion, Boas teamed up with the ethnomusicologist John C. Fillmore to realize that task.[28] At the same time, another ethnomusicologist, Benjamin Gilman, was also present. He likewise recorded songs during the fair by means of a phonograph, though his interests were broader than Boas and Fillmore's. While the latter focused on recording Kwakwa̲ka'wakw singers present at the fair, Gilman recorded all kinds of performers. Unfortunately, only a few recordings from both teams have survived to this day, leaving us with 37 (of formerly about 120) wax-cylinder recordings from Boas and Fillmore and 18 cylinders with Kwakwa̲ka'wakw songs from the Gilman collection.[29] Despite this small number of surviving cylinder recordings, we can still consider ourselves lucky, as we do have two rare examples of double recordings of the same song performances preserved in these collections, that is, songs that had been simultaneously recorded by both teams.[30] After this start, which left us with few remaining recordings, Boas came to use the phonograph to preserve Kwakwa̲ka'wakw music again some thirty-seven years later during his last research trip to Fort Rupert in 1930–31, when he was seventy-two.[31] From this effort a total of 157 wax cylinders have been preserved.[32]

While no shorthand notes have surfaced so far that can be directly linked to the 1893 recording sessions, the notes taken during Boas's second trip in 1930–31 have been preserved. These demonstrate again how broad his interest in the subject was. These notes relate by no means only to the songs that had been recorded. They also reflect on general categories of song and on the cultural importance of song as such. Three short examples demonstrate that range. An example that characterizes the kind of remarks one would find on particular songs is the following, which refers to a cylinder recording (cyl. 116/37) titled "Winter dance song, War dancer" in the records of the Archive of Traditional Music, Bloomington: "Tōx'wit: *Song of* māxwa *who was killed and caused* {through his murder} *the secession of the tribe.* {Now, the song} *belongs to* Mrs. Sam. *It belongs* {to the} Maamtag.ila{.... Now follow the words of the song in Kwak'wala and their English translation}" (Kwak field notes, p. 641, B B61p, box 22, APS).

These notes reveal Boas's constant drive to record in the greatest detail possible the relevance of music in the Native context, including the level of ownership and band attribution. Unfortunately, it is the same level that tends to be the first to be omitted when a text is prepared for publication, as it is usually deemed as too detailed for general consumption. On other issues he simply did not publish, which is not surprising, considering the amount of detailed information Boas collected. Part of my ongoing work entails making these crucial details—with all due caution—resurface wherever possible, as the notion of "preserving" culture does not make any sense to me if the levels of information most useful to the intended potential main users have been suppressed out of the fear that the general public might find this kind of information too boring.

Other notes that Boas took include—as already indicated—more general observations regarding music, among others, its use, performance, composition, and sources of inspiration. The following example demonstrates this attention to detail quite nicely:

> Love songs {are} *sung by young men of a tribe while they walk back and forth on the street. The others sing theirs* {i.e., their love songs elsewhere} *and* {wherever they?} *meet with each other*{.} *And* {they} *painted*{/ held?} *each other and the one tribe walks through the* *** {center?; the meaning of the sentence, which is probably not complete, is not quite clear}. *And they make them* {songs} *in the house*{.} *And when they have*

them {the songs, they} *sing them loud and* {then} *the others come and learn them* {the new songs} *from them.* {The} *young* {men} *make first the melodies*{.} *And* {then they} *make* {a} knot *in a string in order to keep it* {i.e., remember it. And} *then they wear the string around the neck. Young hunters* (hunters; the term is added below the shorthand term and is rendered in longhand) *make the songs* {i.e., their love songs} *on someone. And when they come to a small creek with a waterfall* {then they have the impression that} *the sound is like* {a} *song and from it they get their ideas* {for} *melodies. And waves or ancestors* {?, are also sources for songs}. hāāne˙ *say* {the} *ancestors* {?, for example} *and that gives* {the composers the} *melody and* rhythm {for a new song}. (Kwak field notes, p. 529, 3 B61p, box 22, APS)[33]

Aside from sections that clearly deal with certain songs, a category of songs or music, its performance, or its creation, the topic of music actually penetrates almost all aspects of Boas's descriptions of Native cultures, reflecting not only his interest in the subject but also the central role of music in Northwest Coast life. The following quote is a good example of how tightly the subject of music is interwoven with other topics and how references to songs slip into different forms of cultural descriptions:

Tā'ltEm {was} a L!aL!as̱quoala{. He} *spoke* Bella bella {and} *came to own coppers* {by the name} sē'gExstag'ila *and* nE'ngemala. *These were not the only* {coppers} *that came from* Bb {Bella Bella} *this way* {i.e., to the Kwakwaka'wakw}. Nä'enagwEs{?} ({had a} Kw'wākum *father*{/ ancestor?} *and* {his} *mother* {was} BB){. He} *was* {an} *old man when* G.{eorge} *was young* [*he only ate Indian food*]. {He} *claimed to be the owner of* 12 *coppers which he had brought from there and* {he} *had a long song about it.* BB: Laimag̱ūs {is} *in* BB. *his name.* = Ōdzē'stalis *of* {the} Kw'kwākūm. *And he gave the coppers away here and slaves in* BB. *His song was only bawl.* (Kwak field notes, p. 624, B B61p, box 22, APS)[34]

One of the major challenges of working with Boas's shorthand notes (as with any of his notes) is to disentangle the many different layers of meaning, for any given note is quite often meaningful in several ways. Considering Boas's enormous output, it is also not always easy to determine whether a certain piece of information found its way to the public or not. And then there is, of course, the fact that there are many ways in which a piece of information can develop a life of its own on its way to getting published. To illustrate some of the issues, two examples should be sufficient here. Both come from a set of notes dealing with Kwakwaka'wakw medicines of all sorts. The first example reads as follows:[35]

> Medizin. aā'gala. *It is chewed and spit on* {the} *swelling. It makes blisters* {go away (obviously missing).} *It is tied on* {the swollen part} *with soft*{/white?} K.ā'tsekw. *And then* {it} *makes blister* ***. (mā'sta = mustn {?}) *And then they spike the blister with broken clam* (mussle) *schell* {misspelled English term in shorthand} *in order to let out* {the} *water* {from the blister}. *And then they grease the skin with* catfish oil. *And when the skin comes off and leaves an open wound then the roots of* goose*l/b*ry t'Em*niis *are grounded in salt water and smeared on it to make it heal. It* {the wound} *is cleaned with it.* (k.ikaōkw goē's.s = wegerich {?}; plentain; written above the previous term in ink). *The leaves of it* {i.e., its leaves} *are put on the wound. And when they dry up they are changed. It pulls the bad juices* {liquids/fluids} *out. And it holds* {i.e., binds} *it.* q'ExEmē'n *grows in the south* {and} *is bought by* Lekw*lt*** {Lekwiltok?}. (W1a.28, 193, APS)

As it turned out, the basic information of the notes actually found its way into one of Boas's publications: "A plaster is made of Monseses uniflora L.S.F. Gray, (aā'gala), which is chewed and placed on swellings, where it is held by means of shredded, undyed cedar bark. It draws blisters, which are pricked with broken mussel shells. Then they are smeared with catfish oil. When the skin of the blisters comes off, so that an open wound is left, it is washed with the juice of gooseberry roots (Ribes, sp. *t!E.'ik.!aōku gwē'x.s*) and laid on to heal the wound. When dry, the leaves are removed" (Codere 1966:382).

Although at first glance the published version seemed to be quite close to the shorthand notes, I noticed modifications after I read the texts more closely. The published text uses only one Native term and adds new information, the Latin term of the main plant discussed and the source and nature of the plaster. This is one way in which notes develop on their way to publication. In other instances, though, they lose interesting aspects on their way to the public, as is the case with the second example:

George Hunt—Love charms. *A small* yew stick *6 inches* {in} *diameter and depicts a man and a woman. The people* {here} *lie on their side when they* cohabit. *And* {so} *they* {these figures} *are carved as if they were doing* wu'lxwa'ats'yu (wilxwa = love) {lying on their sides.} *The dick* {Boas uses the equivalent graphic German word here} *of the man is so depicted as if it enters the woman* {from below} *and exits her from the mouth and is then taken by the man into his own mouth. And if it* {this figure is to be} *used by a man* {he puts} *between both figures sweat from the belly of the girl and* {some of} *her spit and hair* [*they do this even for their own women* {particularly} *if they do not love their husbands*{—the term for that is} q'a'yā'nas{. It is a term used when a} *woman hates her husband* {so much}, *that she would never eat with him.* {In those cases} *his cheeks are often scratched by* {his} *wife*]. *And* {he takes} *some of her* urine *from 4 stones on which she had pissed. And he takes a kind of* L'Etā'yas *(but it is a different kind) and* Drosera *and* wī'wōmaxLawo'ye {?} *and* {the} *head of a snake*{,} sē'lEm. *And* {the} *toes of a frog*{,} wîq'a's. *(and toes* {of a,} gwā'las{, a} *lizard) and they took first these medicines and mixed them with another and then they take the underwear*{/clothes?} *of* {the} *woman and put everything together. And then they take the end-part of the snake's head and put it in there. The toes of the frogs are likewise in there. And this all is tied together with sinew* {?} *of a corpse and then put in there between the two figures. And then they take the skin of a snake and wrap it around the whole thing. If it is needed to be used on a man* {i.e., used by a woman to influence her husband} *then it* {this bundle} *is worn by the woman tied to her belt that keeps her skirt up. A man wears it under his left armpit on a string that goes over* {the} *shoulder. This means* {the} *string hangs over* {the} *right shoulder and under* {the} *left*. (w1a.28, 477, APS)

For the point I am trying to make here, it is sufficient to focus on the first part. Therefore, only that part will be quoted here as it was later published. It reads as follows: "If a man wishes to get the love of a woman, he carves a yew stick about fifteen centimeters long in the form of a cohabiting couple, the membrum virile protruding out of the woman's mouth and being held in the man's mouth. Between these two figures is placed a charm consisting of perspiration from the woman's abdomen, some of her saliva, a few of her hairs, four pebbles on which she has urinated, and also a kind of plant, *L!Eta'eyas*, Drosera, *wī'ewōmaxLāwo'wē*, and toes of the toad and lizard" (Codere 1966:153).

Even though both texts express the same kind of basic information, there are some major differences. Aside from a refined language to be expected in publications, we find the published version lacking the richness of Native terms and other relevant cultural information found in the field notes. This example demonstrates that the published version of a given body of the field notes is not necessarily the "better" and "richer" version with regard to cultural information, in detail or in Native terminology—all aspects that make Boas's notes so valuable. This means too, and this is a challenge for setting priorities, that one cannot automatically skip field notes just because one knows that Boas had published on the particular content the notes deal with. Despite the enthusiasm sparked by the possibility of now being able to compare field notes with their published versions, one should not forget that usually there have been many intermediary versions before certain texts came to be published. In some cases even these versions have survived.

While reaching the critical question of setting priorities with regard to dealing with Boas's shorthand materials, another challenge needs to be mentioned: his shorthand notes do not necessarily come in the form of a more or less closed text. Rather, they may be found in the form of short remarks on the margins of pages otherwise dominated by longhand notes, or they may be integrated with them, included as both part of the sentences or as single words inserted into a text. In short, I am talking about a category of shorthand notes for which I used the term "bits and pieces." To this category also belong brief notes like the following one, which yields some basic information about the figure in a drawing that Boas preserved in one of his sketch books (fig. 15). It says: "Ētcāa'm{,} *the first chief of the tribe.* {He} *came down from heaven.*"

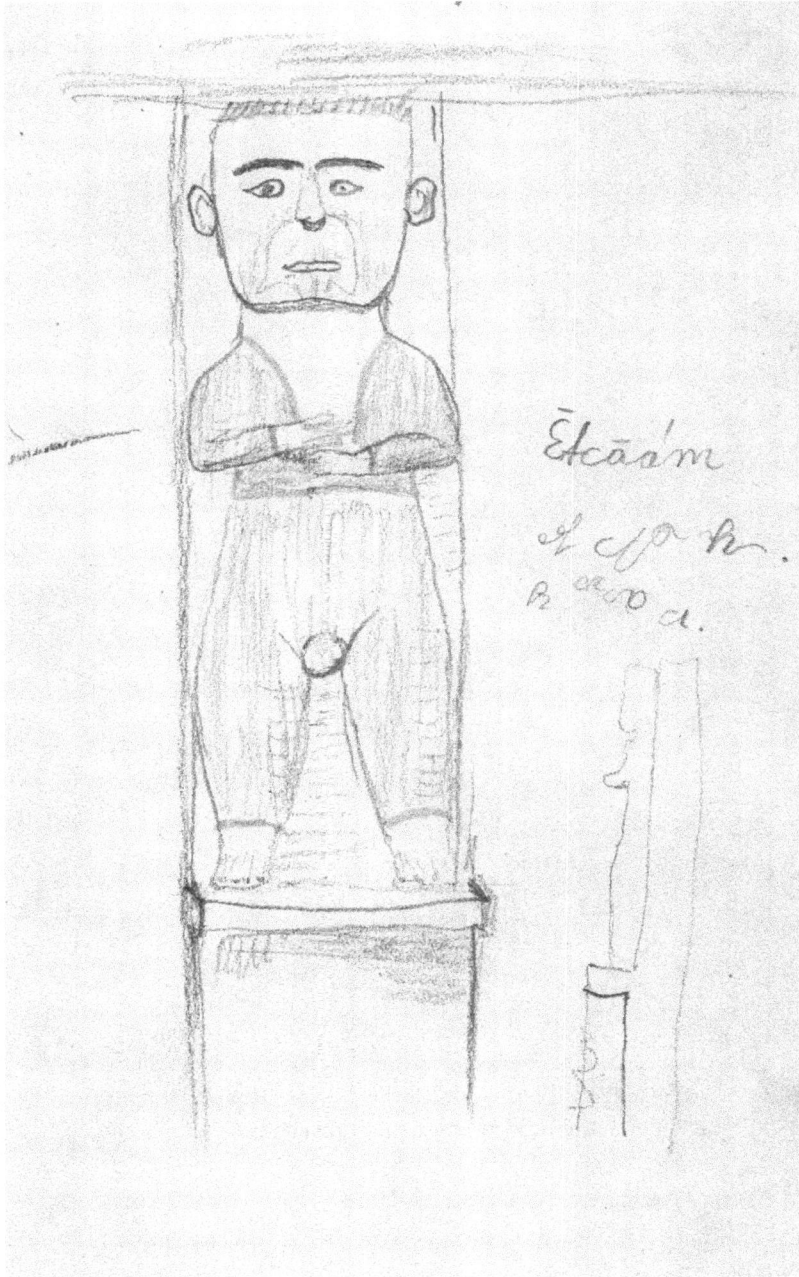

Fig. 15. Sketch with shorthand notes by Boas. z/11 z. Courtesy of the Division of Anthropology, American Museum of Natural History.

Fig. 16. Drawing of a mask (very likely by Albert Grünwedel) from the collections of the Royal Ethnological Museum of Berlin (IV A 1242). Most of the remarks are in longhand, but they also include some shorthand. z/43 1. Courtesy of the Division of Anthropology, American Museum of Natural History.

As Boas (in contrast to others) did not—to my current knowledge—use shorthand as a form of "secret script" but simply as a means to write faster and to achieve more in a given time, decoding such inserted shorthand phrases does not necessarily reveal a sensitive and tricky topic or a secret. A case in point is the example seen in figure 16, where the only

Fig. 17. Drawing of a mask (very likely by Albert Grünwedel) from collections of the Royal Ethnological Museum of Berlin (IV A 1243/1270). Most of the remarks are in longhand, but they also include some shorthand. Z/43 K. Courtesy of the Division of Anthropology, American Museum of Natural History.

shorthand remark on a whole page written in longhand simply reads: "*Forehead and cheeks as before. He wears a mustache. {It} is very thin*" (fig. 92, folder 8, box 3, AMNH). Here Boas obviously simply switched to shorthand to finish his notes faster. Yet another type of "bits and pieces" is an important addition to knowledge, which means that one cannot simply discard them as "unimportant." A case in point is the

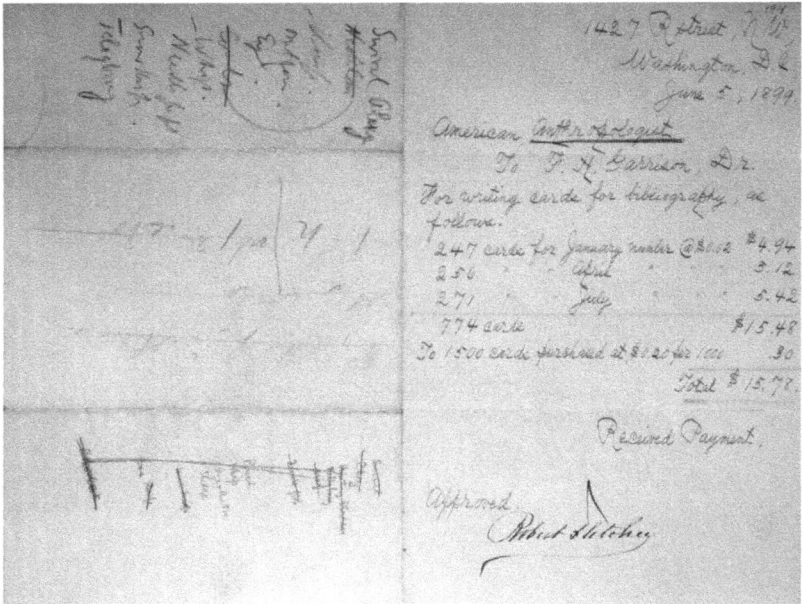

Fig. 18. An account from the *American Anthropologist* used by Boas as scratch paper. It includes checklists and some unrelated shorthand notes. Folder "American Anthropologist," box 2, B B61. Photo by the author, used with the permission of the American Philosophical Society.

few shorthand words on the drawing of a mask (fig. 17). This mask had been subject to different interpretations. The shorthand words show that there are possibly even more relevant aspects that have so far not entered the published sources. In this particular case, it was the crossed-out shorthand section that solved uncertainties about reading some of Boas's English longhand notes. Though not all of his longhand notes are readily comprehensible, the general information is clear: "probably Qōl'ōs. (*The man wears* {crossed out}) The man wears bird mask [. . .] half man half bird. . . . mouthpart is *at the same time the lower jaw* {i.e., lower beak} *of* {the} *bird*" (fig. 18, folder 8, box 3, AMNH). These notes by Boas do not by any means "solve" uncertainties with regard to the interpretation of the mask represented in the drawing; actually, they add to the confusion. This reminds us that even though we can now access his shorthand field notes, they do not necessarily bring us

Fig. 19. "Franz Boas" in Boas's own shorthand writing. Folder "Bessel," box 8, B B61.
Photo by the author, used with the permission of the American Philosophical Society.

closer to "the truth," as we can, of course, never be sure how "correct"
the information was that he recorded in the first place.

As a final remark on the subject of "bits and pieces," I would like
to point to some very rare instances of Boas's non-research-related,
personal shorthand use. Private notes are almost completely nonex-
istent in the monumental legacy of written records I reviewed, which
is very odd, as typically shorthand, if one masters it, is usually used
for all kinds of note taking. The first example includes some scribbled
notes on an account—the specific content is not important in this
context—published in the *American Anthropologist*: "*When I was still a
small boy. First Meyer*{?,} *first Boas*{,} *come in Boas*{.} *You are stupid*{!}
Do you like Brussels sprouts{?}" (folder: American Anthropologist, box
2, B B61, APS) (fig. 18). Boas obviously used these notes while explaining some shorthand basics—judging by the content—presumably to
his children. A second example is found on a different piece of scratch
paper: a letter from the Cosmos Club, also used by Boas as the basis
for a check-list. Here, a probably bored Boas left us his full name—
Franz Boas—in shorthand (folder: Bessel, box 8, B B61, APS) (fig. 19).

This introduction to my ongoing work is intended to provide a first general impression of Boas's large body of shorthand materials and of the multifold challenges faced when dealing with it. As I have indicated, we are looking at an incomplete picture of Boas's use of that form of script, because almost no notes of a private nature taken during his manifold other activities, such as meetings, have survived. Why would Boas learn and verifiably use shorthand throughout his life and then not use it for the main purpose for which it was originally developed: the taking of notes in any context? And so we are basically left to look at the only examples of Boas's use of shorthand that have survived: his ethnographic field notes, which are part of his professional legacy.

While dealing with this particular category as part of the larger body of raw data that Boas left behind, I regard my work as part of the larger current major efforts to make these primary results of early anthropological research accessible to scholars and to those Native communities among which research was conducted. This intention clearly reflects my hopes and expectations that my work on the shorthand material might prove inspiring and meaningful in several ways and for several audiences, especially the Native communities; after all, the basic body of raw material would not exist without their collaboration and knowledge in the first place (aside from Boas's own efforts).

Thus, the goals for my work, research, and book project are clearly stated: first, and as an immediate goal, to render a more substantial overview of the available shorthand material, and second, as a long-term task, to make it accessible to the interested public and to Native communities in particular. As a result, my work has already generated an ever-growing list of topics for potential studies. Many of these activities clearly call for collaborative approaches—a very exciting prospect for the future.

ACKNOWLEDGMENTS

My research has been conducted under the kind financial support offered by the American Philosophical Society (Franklin Research Grant), the Boas Documentary Edition project, and an NEH Digital

Humanities Start Up Grant for the Boas 1897 project. To all of these funding agencies I would like to express my gratitude. Beyond that, I feel greatly obliged to a number of individuals whom I would like to warmly thank for all their efforts with regard to this research endeavor. Here I would like to particularly name Regna Darnell; Richard Dunn; Aaron Glass and Judith Berman (both of whom I would also like to thank for very helpful comments on an earlier draft of this essay); Tim Powell and a number of his colleagues from the wonderful staff at the American Philosophical Society, Philadelphia: Brian Carpenter, Bayard Miller, Roy Goodman, Charles Greifenstein, Earle Spamer, and Linda Musumeci. Furthermore, I would like to thank Jürgen Langenkämper, Rosemarie Hänsel, Olaf Ruhe, and Peter Miller. I have only begun collaboration and discussion of the material with representatives of the Native communities reflected upon in the notes. For some preliminary comments, I would like to thank William Wasden Jr., whom I consider to be much more than just an extremely knowledgeable and gifted representative of his community and source of information.

NOTES

AFC	American Folklife Center, Library of Congress, Washington DC
APS	American Philosophical Society, Philadelphia, Pennsylvania
ATM	Archive of Traditional Music, Bloomington, Indiana

All translations of Boas's shorthand writings and letters are mine. See note 9 for further information.

1. A written comment left with the Baffin Land maps preserved at the National Anthropological Archives, Smithsonian Institution, in Washington DC sums up the issue quite neatly: "[The] notes on the maps include a short text in Eskimo and some notes in German and English; most of these notes are illegible, because Boas used a shorthand system of his own in writing many of them, and his handwriting is very difficult to read even when not abbreviated."
2. The following quote is from a somewhat earlier yet undated letter from Boas to his sister Toni: "You will already know that I began to learn shorthand. Still, I cannot practice it enough as I am spending too much time practicing swimming, which I likewise just started to learn. . . . I

forgot that you have started to learn English shorthand." At that time Toni was in North America, a visit that started on June 13, 1873, when she left Hamburg. This letter must have been written shortly after Boas's Uncle Abraham Jacobi married Mary Putman, an event referred to in the letter but for which I have not been able to pin down a date so far. As the later letter is dated September 27 of that year, it can only mean that Boas had started learning shorthand sometime in the early summer of 1873; at that time he was fifteen. He must have discontinued learning it during summer vacation and resumed taking courses again sometime in September. It still is not quite clear whether these courses were voluntary courses offered at school (it clearly wasn't mandatory) and/or whether Boas got his schooling in one of the many shorthand clubs that sprang up at that time. This was the beginning of the shorthand boom in Germany, which lasted until about the first half of the twentieth century.

3. Kurrent script was developed in the seventeenth and eighteenth centuries (Johnen 1924:46). Latin script first became popular among merchant families in Germany at the beginning of the nineteenth century. Called "American" or "English" script, it finally came to replace German Kurrent (its popular modern version at that time was called "Sütterlin") in the first half of the twentieth century (Johnen 1924:46). With the exception of earlier letters that included sections in the Latin language, a real breaking point seems to have been Boas's move to Heidelberg at the beginning of his university studies there in 1877. The oldest example of Boas using Latin script to write German known to me is a brief postcard he wrote on his first train ride to Heidelberg on that occasion (April 14, 1877). For a while he used Latin script when writing short postcards and German Kurrent when writing letters. His first surviving real letter in Latin script is dated January 30, 1880. But it still took him a couple more years, until about 1882, to use Latin script as his main long-hand form of writing in family letters.

4. Rohner was rather liberal in his translation here, which should be "my hand is completely cramped from the excessive writing in Bella Bella. My shorthand was there of great help again. I wrote all my nonlinguistic notes that way. I hope that I will be able to read them." However, I have held to Rohner's translation, as it does not really alter the basic meaning of the quote and fits better in the title of my essay.

5. The first project was financed by the Volkswagen Foundation (Hatoum 2009, 2010). The second project was funded by the German Federal Ministry of Education and Research (Hatoum 2014).

6. The goal of the Boas 1897 project is to produce an annotated critical edition of Boas's seminal monograph *The Social Organization and the Secret Societies of the Kwakiutl Indians*, published in 1897. See Glass and Berman (2012) and www.bgc.bard.edu/research/initiatives/the-distributed .html.

7. Reflecting these different levels of virtuosity and abstraction, today's Deutsche Einheitskurzschrift features three levels of proficiency: Verkehrsschrift (a bit faster than regular writing), Eilschrift (dictations), and Redeschrift (good enough to pick up the news or debates). Boas's level of proficiency is approximately the level of Eilschrift.

8. My latest research under the Franklin Research Grant has produced possible evidence that Boas might have adopted Gregg shorthand for writing notes in English later in his career. As evidence is too scarce and inconclusive at this point, I have chosen not to dwell upon this aspect here in any detail.

9. With regard to my transcriptions of shorthand texts, I would like to point out the following: First, I have put all of Boas's shorthand texts and terms in italics, and I have inserted my additions within curly brackets, since Boas used both parentheses and square brackets in his shorthand texts. Second, I have put all of the words or text that Boas wrote in longhand in roman type, and all my additions within the longhand quotes are in square brackets. All underlinings in the shorthand transcriptions stem from Boas's original texts.

10. I have crossed out names to establish the effect of the narrative; details will be demonstrated later in the essay.

11. This remark refers to Boas's 1893 notebook from the Chicago World's Fair (w1a.9) and shows that Boas kept on coming back to his earlier notes. This song is on page 5 with the cross-reference "M688," which points to its rendering in *The Social Organization* on that page. Two cylinder numbers are given for the song in the notebook (cyl. 13 and 14). Of interest is that the name of the composer of the song has been recorded here: "3. Hamats'a (New song) Qoayōstētsas made it" (w1a.9, p. 5).

12. Boas's Chicago notebook (w1a.9) features on page 50 a KyinqalaLala song that could be regarded as the third song on the page. The title is marked with a blue cross, while the title is underlined in red (the same applies to the previous song). It is interesting to note that altogether three cylinder numbers are given here (cyl. 24, 25, 26). This song is linked in *The Social Organization* to the same events described here in the notes (found on page 556), even though a different song (the sec-

ond) is mentioned on that particular page. The English translation and the complete text in Kwak'wala with the English translation can be found on pages 460 and 693, respectively, and they match the song given in the notebook. This is particularly interesting, as the title of the song reads in the notebook as follows: "7 KyinqalaLala. Songs belongs to 6 [i.e., the previous song], now to David's sister (м693 [page number in *The Social Organization*])." The interesting thing here is that the previous song, song number 6, is noted to be a Ha'mshamtses song. This means that it belongs to a different secret society, albeit one of the same category as the hamats'a. This song is linked by Boas (w1a.9, pp. 40–51) to one of the masks in the collections of the Berlin Ethnological Museum (iv a 1242) (fig. 16), which had originally been collected by Adrian Jacobsen (1881–83). Aside from a description of the mask, Boas also includes the name of the owner in his notebook: "Nǎ'wis Mē´emqoat *** [name?] Qalē'sEmakw = xuē´la coming & squeak in his fear [?,] Quē'qutsa name." Boas's remarks, therefore, seem to imply that the last-mentioned individual had been the former owner of the KyinqalaLala song, now sung for David Hunt's sister, and that that song had its origin in the context of a different secret society.

13. This is not his biological father. It was a sign of respect to refer to a highly respected person in the potlatch as "father" (comment by an anonymous reader).

14. Jane [Jone?] is the name I read in the notes, but Judith Berman (personal communication, July 6, 2014) suggested that it rather might be Emily Hunt, who married Charley Wilson, who is referred to here.

15. See, for example, Suttles (1991:133), and, regarding the general role of Hunt for Boas's 1897 publication, Berman (2001:195ff.).

16. The translation of this name is given in a footnote and is not particularly incriminating, as some Kwakwaka'wakw tribes were considered "northern." William Wasden Jr. offers the name Gwitaḻabidu' for the translation "Little Northerner" (personal communication, May 21, 2014).

17. Wasden added that he considers it likely that Boas might have rendered George Hunt's old nickname wrong. He suggests that it was not Mamałnataḻa (White on His Father's Side) but rather Ma'małnabidu' (Little Whiteman), which would be the older version of today's name Ma'małabidu'. Wasden explained: "The word Ma'małni 'whiteman' came from the west coast. We say Ma'mała" (personal communication, May 21, 2014).

18. These are the two speakers who also had an active role during a previously held copper purchase by George Hunt.

19. Boas's multitasking activity readily surfaces in his 1894 field notes, in which we find fragments of different myths he recorded in Kwak'wala interspersed between his observations of activities related to the winter ceremonies. For example on page 489 there is the first paragraph of a myth, rendered without title and in Kwak'wala, that was finally published in Boas's *Kwakiutl Tales* (1910:358–359) under the title "Kwô'teat (Weight-on-Floor)." Another case is found on page 492 of the field notes, where we find the last lines of a myth that would also appear in Boas's *Kwakiutl Tales* (1910:361–362) as part of "K!wadzâ'ē" (Sitting on Earth). Only the beginnings and endings of myths are found in these field notes, while the main bodies of the texts, the title, and the translation either are not recorded or are missing. Gaps in the page numbers indicate that whole bodies of Kwak'wala text had been collected but then removed at a later date (when probably their beginnings and endings were copied from the parts that remained with the original notes).

20. Berman (personal communication, July 6, 2014) points out the following: "Missing from Boas's letters (and from Rohner's book) is the point that Hunt was in the middle of his son's final Hamat'sa performance, with attendant feasts and presentations, and he obviously had a lot to do in addition to taking care of his guests."

21. That Boas was the driving force in this process is to be expected and is reinforced by quotes like "Tomorrow I will have Hunt translate the speeches for me" (November 19, 1894, quoted in Rohner 1969:182).

22. So far I have not been able to locate a printed version of this myth.

23. As one of Boas's major focuses lay on the collection of facial casts during his stay in Port Essington, it raises the question whether his collection of casts includes one of Charles Edenshaw. For more on the role of Edenshaw and his interaction with Boas, see Wright and Augaitis (2014); Jonaitis (1988:201ff.).

24. A version of this myth that differs in many details from the one given here had been published by Boas in 1895 as the last of eight episodes of Haida raven legends (see Bouchard and Kennedy 2002 [2008]:607–608). No reference to the world of art or material culture is made.

25. Among these interests was Boas's already sufficiently discussed rejection of evolutionary theories, as well as his attempts to keep his ties to Berlin anthropology (see, e.g., Stocking 1996; Cole 1999; Darnell 1998 [2000]).

26. This note, like those on the other Kwakwa̱ka'wakw face painting drawings kept at AMNH, has not been published so far, to the best of my knowledge.

27. This is a German saying that expresses the surprise regarding a strikingly simple solution for a seemingly unsolvable challenge. It is said to reflect an episode that is thought to have taken place after Columbus's return from "discovering" America. At a dinner in 1493 Columbus claimed that anyone could have discovered America. Taking a cooked egg, he asked those present to make it stand without support. All tried and failed, but Columbus cracked one end of the shell on the table, making the egg able to stand by itself.

28. After the Chicago World's Fair, Boas and Fillmore began transcribing the recorded songs, but Boas does not seem to have been very satisfied with Fillmore's work, as he wrote to his wife on November 15, 1894, while in Fort Rupert: "Today I corrected a few of the songs Fillmore wrote down in Chicago. Either the Indians sang very differently into the phonograph, or he could not hear them well. I am positive that I have written them down correctly now, and the difference between my rendering and his is immense. I have now had enough practice to write it easily" (quoted in Rohner 1969:179).

29. The number 120 is based on an estimate reflecting the songs listed in Boas's Chicago notebook (W1a.9). A number of references link songs listed in the notebook to objects in the collection of the Ethnological Museum in Berlin. From the records it is apparent that Boas sent twelve wax-cylinder recordings linked to objects in the collection to Berlin in 1895, where they received the entry number IV A 7099 (several had been reported to already have been broken upon arrival). Unfortunately, these recordings no longer exist. The Boas/Fillmore Collection (54-121-F) is housed in the Archive of Traditional Music, Bloomington. The Gilman Collection (AFS 14741) is preserved in the American Folklife Center, Library of Congress, Washington DC.

30. Boas/Fillmore cylinders 2 and 3 feature the same songs as the Gilman cylinders 85 and 86.

31. Boas also used the medium of film at that time, in some cases even actually filming the singers singing their songs into the phonograph. Katie Bunn-Marcuse of the Bill Holm Center in Seattle is currently working on connecting the content of the two forms of media.

32. These recordings are housed in the Archive of Traditional Music, Bloomington, where they are associated with two collections: 54-035-F

(81 cylinders) and 83-917-F (76 cylinders). These cylinders are copies of galvanos at the Berliner Phonogramm-Archiv in Berlin. Their "Boas-Kwakiutl" collection consists of 156 galvanos, which are copper negative copies of the original wax cylinders, which were destroyed in the process of making the galvanos. The original cylinders had been sent to Berlin for that purpose in 1931, obviously right after Boas's return from Fort Rupert. In Berlin there is another collection of Boas galvanos consisting of 44 cylinders recorded in 1897 among the Thompson-River in British Columbia. (On Boas and other cylinder recordings, see, e.g., Jacknis 2003, 2014; Ziegler 2006; Hatoum 2009, 2010.)

33. Codere includes the following remark, which echoes some ideas and remarks found in this note: "Love songs and mourning songs are designated by the same term and are often similar in character. They are sung in a way imitating crying, often falsetto and vibrato. The young man's challenging love songs used to be sung by a crowd of youths marching up and down the street of the village, with the intent of annoying and embarrassing the girls" (1966:348).

34. Coppers are important cultural objects that symbolize great value and have their own histories and names. They are important cultural items that feature prominently in potlatches, for example.

35. As many parts of the notes had been crossed out by Boas with either a blue or a red colored pencil, reading proved to be particularly difficult. This is a characteristic trait in a number of his manuscripts and obviously reflects Boas's work on the notes at some point. This habit greatly hampers the reading of such notes.

REFERENCES

Berman, Judith. 1996. The Culture as It Appears to the Indian Himself: Boas, George Hunt and the Methods of Ethnography. *In* Volksgeist as Method and Ethic: Essays on Boasian Ethnography and the German Anthropological Tradition. George W. Stocking, ed. Pp. 215–256. Madison: University of Wisconsin Press.
———. 2001. Unpublished Materials of Franz Boas and George Hunt: A Record of 45 years of Collaboration. *In* Gateways: Exploring the Legacy of the Jesup North Pacific Expedition, 1897–1902. Igor Krupnik and William W. Fitzhugh, eds. Pp. 181–213. Washington DC: Smithsonian Institution.
Boas, Franz. 1895 [1992]. Indianische Sagen von der Nord Pacifischen Küste Amerikas. Berlin: A. Asher.

——. 1897. The Social Organization and the Secret Societies of the Kwakiutl Indians. Washington DC: Government Printing Office.

——. 1889. Facial Paintings of the Indians of Northern British Columbia. American Museum of Natural History Memoirs, vol. 2, pp. 13–24.

——. 1910. Kwakiutl Tales, vol. 2. New York: Columbia University Press.

——. 1911. Introduction. *In* Handbook of American Indian Languages. BAEB 40:1–83. Washington DC: Government Printing Office.

——. 1927. Primitive Art. Reprint, 1955. New York: Dover Publications, Inc.

——. 1940. Race, Language and Culture. New York: Macmillan Company.

Boas, Norman. 2004. Franz Boas 1858–1942: An Illustrated Biography. Mystic: Seaport Authographs Press.

Bouchard, Randy, and Dorothy Kennedy. 2002 [2008]. Indian Myths & Legends from the North Pacific Coast of America. (Edited and annotated translation of Franz Boas's 1895 edition of *Indianische Sagen von der Nord-Pacifischen Küste Amerikas.*) Vancouver: Talonbooks.

Codere, Helen. 1966. Introduction. *In* Franz Boas: Kwakiutl Ethnography. Helen Codere, ed. Pp. xi–xxxii. Chicago: University of Chicago Press.

Cole, Douglas. 1999. Franz Boas: The Early Years, 1858–1906. Vancouver: Douglas & McIntyre; Seattle: University of Washington Press.

Darnell, Regna. 1998 [2000]. And Along Came Boas: Continuity and Revolution in American Anthropology. Amsterdam: John Benjamins Publishing Company.

Evans, Brad, and Aaron Glass, eds. 2014. Return to the Land of the Head Hunters: Edward S. Curtis, the Kwakwaka'wakw, and the Making of Modern Cinema. Seattle: University of Washington Press.

Glass, Aaron, ed. 2011. Objects of Exchange: Social and Material Transformation on the Late Nineteenth-Century Northwest Coast. West Haven: Yale University Press.

Glass, Aaron, and Judith Berman. 2012. The Distributed Text: An Annotated Digital Edition of Franz Boas's Pioneering Ethnography. Culture 6(1):18.

Hatoum, Rainer. 2009. In the Light of the "Scientification" of Tradition. *In* Museumsinseln / Museum Islands. Lidia Guzy, Rainer Hatoum, and Susan Kamel, eds. Pp. 23–76. Berlin: Panama Verlag.

——. 2010. Musealizing Dialogue. *In* From Imperial Museum to Communication Centre? On the New Role of Museums as Mediators between Science and Non-Western Societies. Lidia Guzy, Rainer Hatoum, and Susan Kamel, eds. Pp. 121–136. Würzburg: Königshausen & Neumann.

———. 2014. The Materialization of a Specific Knowledge Order? Reflections on the Berlin Boas Northwest Coast Collection. *In* Transforming Knowledge Orders: Museums, Collections and Exhibitions. Larissa Förster, ed. Pp. 107–134. Paderborn: Wilhelm Fink.

Hymes, Dell. 1981 [2004]. "In Vain I Tried to Tell You": Essays in Native American Ethnopoetics. Philadelphia: University of Pennsylvania Press.

Jacknis, Ira. 2002. The Storage Box of Tradition. Washington DC: Smithsonian Institution.

———. 2003. Franz Boas and the Music of the Northwest Coast Indians. *In* Constructing Cultures Then and Now: Celebrating Franz Boas and the Jesup North Pacific Expedition. Laurel Kendall and Igor Krupnik, eds. Pp. 105–122. Washington DC: Smithsonian Institution.

———. 2014. A Chamber of Echoing Songs: Edward Curtis as a Musical Ethnographer. *In* Return to the Land of the Head Hunters: Edward S. Curtis, the Kwakwaka'wakw, and the Making of Modern Cinema. Brad Evans and Aaron Glass, eds. Pp. 99–127. Seattle: University of Washington Press.

Johnen, Christian. 1924. Allgemeine Geschichte der Kurzschrift. Berlin: Verlag Ferdinand Schrey.

Jonaitis, Aldona. 1988. From the Land of the Totem Poles: The Northwest Coast Indian Art Collection at the American Museum of Natural History. New York: American Museum of Natural History; Seattle: University of Washington Press.

———, ed. 1991. Chiefly Feasts: The Enduring Kwakiutl Potlatch. New York: American Museum of Natural History; Vancouver: Douglas & McIntyre.

———. 1995. A Wealth of Thought: Franz Boas on Native American Art. Seattle: University of Washington Press.

O'Neill, Sean. 2010. No Other Art Moves Me as Deeply as Music: On the Place of Music in the Boasian "Sense" of Anthropology. Unpublished manuscript.

Rohner, Ronald, ed. 1969. The Ethnography of Franz Boas: Letters and Diaries of Franz Boas Written on the Northwest Coast from 1886 to 1931. Chicago: University of Chicago Press.

Stocking, George, ed. 1996. Volksgeist as Method and Ethic: Essays on Boasian Ethnography and the German Anthropological Tradition. Madison: University of Wisconsin Press.

Suttles, Wayne. 1991. Streams of Property, Armor of Wealth: The Traditional Kwakiutl Potlatch. *In* Chiefly Feasts: The Enduring Kwakiutl Pot-

latch. Aldona Jonaitis, ed. Pp. 71–134. New York: American Museum of
Natural History; Seattle: University of Washington Press.
Wright, Robin K., and Daina Augaitis. 2014. Charles Edenshaw. London:
Black Dog Publishing.
Ziegler, Susanne. 2006. Die Wachszylinder des Berliner Phonogramm-
Archivs. Berlin: Staatliche Museen zu Berlin—Stiftung Preußischer Kul-
turbesitz.

8

Genealogies of Knowledge in the Alberni Valley

Reflecting on Ethnographic Practice in the Archive of Dr. Susan Golla

Asking for help is important. I learned this over the five years I spent in Nuu-chah-nulth First Nations' *haahuulthii* (traditional territory) as an anthropology PhD student: I witnessed networks of relatives work together to celebrate important moments in their interwoven lives through *n'uushitl* (potlatching) and *tl'itscuu* (feasting).[1] Asking for help demonstrates an understanding that most cultural "business" is larger than the individual.[2] One must reach out to find the appropriate resource. This is how I eventually found myself, in the fall of 2013, immersed in the archive of Dr. Susan Golla. Someone asked me for help.

In May 2012 Tseshaa-aqsup Shishaa (Darleen Watts) approached me looking for information about a book her father, Charlie Watts, had contributed to in the latter years of his life.[3] Darleen explained that in the late 1980s her father began working with anthropologist Dr. Susan Golla and later linguist Dr. Suzanne Rose to translate previously unpublished texts collected by Edward Sapir during his fieldwork in Alberni in 1910 and 1913–14. "Susan worked with my Dad. He just adored her. She came by, picked him up every day," Darleen explained. "They were working on a book. She always said she would give him a copy when it was published. He asked me before he died to make sure I got a copy" (personal communication, Port Alberni, British Columbia, May 5, 2012). Five years before Charlie's death, Dr. Susan Golla herself passed away in January 1993 after a battle with cancer.

Fig. 20. Charlie Watts (*left, background*) and Morris Swadesh (*right, foreground*) in Port Alberni sometime in the late 1930s. Morris Swadesh was a student of Edward Sapir, and his notes from this time are also in the American Philosophical Society library. In the late 1980s and early 1990s Charlie Watts worked with Susan Golla to help translate stories that Edward Sapir had collected during his fieldwork in 1910 and 1913–14. Photo courtesy of Darleen Watts.

The search for Dr. Golla's notes and the book Darleen Watts spoke of began with a series of emails and phone calls. People remembered the names of Susan's family—her husband, Jim, their daughter, Cate—but could only suggest that they were "probably in New York City." Easiest to find was her ex-husband and well-known linguist, Victor Golla, who kindly put me in touch with Susan's close friend, former roommate, and PhD peer, Dr. Janet Chernela. Dr. Chernela introduced me to Cate, the daughter Jim and Susan welcomed into the world in Port Alberni. Cate connected me with her father, who was away at the time on a six-week motorcycle trip. On his return, he explained that Susan's notes had been deposited in the American Philosophical Society (APS) library nearly twenty years earlier. Susan's research was a continuation of the ethnographic fieldwork of her predecessors, Franz Boas, Edward Sapir and Morris Swadesh, whose Nuu-chah-nulth records—in their original form—were all housed in the APS.[4] Susan had spent many hours in the APS reading room, poring over Sapir's original field notebooks. She made it explicit to family and friends that it was best that her notes reside there as well.

In the fall of 2013 I found myself in the APS reading room, poring over *her* notebooks, papers, photographs, audiotapes, and manuscripts. I began connecting stories and experiences from my own fieldwork with the observations and records in Susan's notes. We lived somewhat parallel lives: both New Yorkers, conducting fieldwork in our late twenties, puttering around the Alberni Valley in unreliable old vehicles (for her, a 1960 Peugeot, and for me, a 1982 Volkswagen Rabbit), and spending much of our time with the descendants of Hamilton George (listed in Sapir's notebooks as his first Nuu-chah-nulth "informant"). Susan and I were connected through the Hupacasath and Tseshaht people who welcomed us into their homes and families and also by a history of anthropology and anthropological practice. Our stories became interwoven through ethnographic and archival fieldwork.

A few months before her untimely death, Susan wrote to her linguist collaborator, Suzanne Rose, "Much as I love stories, I don't accept the notion that we are each just the sum of our narratives" (November 9,

1992, APS). The stories of our lives create connections, networks, and genealogies that actively shape experience and memory. In this chapter I discuss stories produced and inspired by the archive of Dr. Susan Golla, an anthropologist who died far too young. Within twenty-one boxes spanning 9.5 linear feet at the APS in Philadelphia are hundreds of stories that are part of larger historical, cultural, and familial narratives.

The stories in Susan's archive link with other collections at the APS, particularly the notebooks and papers of Edward Sapir and his student Morris Swadesh. Over the years, the APS has become an archival meeting place for a lineage of anthropologists who worked with Nuu-chah-nulth people in the Alberni Valley. Papers and sundry documents reveal another level of connection across generations: Swadesh followed up with Tseshaht and Hupacasath families who worked with Sapir, and Golla did the same with another generation of descendants. My fieldwork brought me into the lives of yet another generation of grandchildren and great-grandchildren of Tom Sayach'apis, Hamilton George, and Dan Watts. These three men and their immediate relatives were the foundation for much of Sapir's work in the Alberni Valley. This project is therefore also a story of human relationships produced through ancestral ties and anthropological antecedents.

Franz Boas, Edward Sapir, Morris Swadesh, Susan Golla, myself, and many other anthropologists have spent time in the Alberni Valley, home to the Hupacasath and Tseshaht First Nations, the most interior Nuu-chah-nulth communities at the head of Barkley Sound on the west coast of Vancouver Island. Since the beginning of the twentieth century, the Alberni Valley had become a kind of "coming together place" for anthropologists and Nuu-chah-nulth people alike. The Canadian Pacific Railway arrived in 1912, and, soon after, a highway connected the area to larger cities on the island such as Nanaimo and Victoria.

Following amateur anthropologist Gilbert Malcolm Sproat (1860–80), Franz Boas arrived in August 1889 for a two-week field trip. Edward Sapir came twenty years later, in 1910, and again in 1913–14, to follow up on Boas's research as part of the Canadian Geological Survey. Over sixty-five years later, when Susan Golla arrived in 1976, people still vacillated about whether earlier generations of Tseshaht and Hupacasath people should have shared information with Sapir. Susan's description of the situation is based on an interview with two Hikuulthaht women: "They are very ambivalent about Sapir. Again, they stressed that many people wouldn't talk to him, thought it very wrong of Alec [Thomas] and Old Tom [Sayach'apis] to 'sell' their stories. . . . At the same time they are glad that what's there is there, and regretful that because of people's attitudes sometimes other (maybe more correct) versions have been lost" (November 27, 1977, APS).[5] Yet Sapir and later Swadesh were also remembered quite fondly in the valley. Chuuchka-malthnii often told me this story of his mother and grandmother first meeting Swadesh in the late 1930s:

> My mother always used to tell this story. She was at the train station with my grandmother, my father's mother, Mrs. Hamilton. They were chums, eh? This would have been sometime in the 1930s. They were approached by a man. He had kinky blonde hair, like that curly hair Jewish people have, and he was really tall and obviously white. He walked up to my mother and my grandmother and he said to each of them, "Achukthlahak?" [Who are you?]. They were just stunned by him. My grandmother turned to my mother, "Ch'ihaa" [a ghost, spirit being]. He asked them again, "Achukthlahak? Tseshaa-aksup? Huupach'esaksup? Uukthlaama Morris Swadesh. Postinat-h" [Who are you? Are you women Tseshaht? Hupacacath? My name is Morris Swadesh, I am American, from the United States]. He spoke perfectly, that's why they thought he was a ch'ihaa. See, the thing is that made that story so amazing to me is that he had never met a Kuu-as [Nuu-chah-nulth] person in his life, but he could speak our language fluently. He studied with Edward Sapir, eh? And the other thing was, it was a really racist time, and white people in Alberni didn't speak to Kuu-as in any respectful manner; they did not ask them who they were or where they came from; they were not kind toward Native women, and they certainly did not speak Quuquuatsa [the Nuu-chah-nulth language].

Swadesh and Sapir worked during times of extreme racial tension in the Alberni Valley. Sapir noted that he was often the "only white man present" at a number of potlatch ceremonies (which, keep in mind, were considered illegal, according to the 1884 revision to the Canadian Indian Act) (Sapir 1913:76; see also Sapir 1911:285). Swadesh later arrived at the height of residential schooling. Both Sapir and Swadesh expressed appreciation for and interest in Native culture at a time when most white people encountered in the valley expressed the opposite. Swadesh ensured that the appropriate Hupacasath and Tseshaht families received copies of *Nootka Texts* and *Native Accounts of Nootka Ethnography*, a consideration that did not go unnoticed. These books contained a partial collection of the legendary histories collected by Sapir. Susan Golla saw the importance of these texts to her Nuu-chah-nulth friends and later endeavored to return the remaining texts through a translation project. Each anthropologist picked up where the other had left off, continuing an ongoing history of anthropological investigation and repatriation.

Records, materials, institutions, places, people, and memories interface and connect to produce stories. Susan Golla's stories are revealed through letters, remembrances in journals, scribbles in field notebooks, photographs, and the occasional audiotape. At times, her stories create a sense of order in the archive, and in other instances they disrupt, subvert, and raise questions. Stories are a social activity, just like the archival research practice of piecing together histories from documents. As an anthropologist in the archive, I found myself regularly stealing away from the reading room to make phone calls or send emails to the living people connected to this material. I eventually traveled to Brooklyn to meet Jim, Susan's husband at the time of her death, and their daughter, Cate. Spending time in Susan's archive and later making personal connections with her friends and family made me part of the unfolding story—I was brought to the archive through stories I heard about Susan Golla while I was in the field. Once I arrived on the East Coast of the United States I found a rich collection of texts that have spurred new stories and relationships. Today, these stories are finding new life in the places and families that sparked their initial telling.

ANOTHER ANTHROPOLOGIST IN THE ALBERNI VALLEY

Dr. Susan Golla was born in 1948 and spent much of her childhood in upstate New York. She completed high school abroad in France and began university there, where she studied art history. She came to

Washington DC in the late 1960s to enroll at George Washington University (GWU), where she studied anthropology and would eventually meet her first husband, Victor Golla, a well-known linguistic anthropologist. Golla was an important mentor to Susan; it was with him that she charted her path into graduate studies. Susan completed her undergraduate degree at GWU and went on to pursue a master's degree in anthropology, but she did not conduct fieldwork for this project.

While in Washington DC Susan worked as assistant to William C. Sturtevant, curator of North American ethnology at the U.S. National Museum / Smithsonian Institution. She assisted with the research and publication of the *Handbook of North American Indians*, of which Sturtevant was general editor. After her time at the Smithsonian, she enrolled in Columbia University's anthropology PhD program in the mid-1970s. Victor joined her in New York in the 1975–76 school year as she developed her doctoral project. Her classmate Janet Chernela explained, "There is no doubt that Victor was an important influence in Susan's academic development. Her interest in the First Nations of the north Pacific evolved in relation to his. She made the choice of her field site with him, and through his introductions. He served as her informal consultant, advisor, and professional colleague in her most formative scholarly years" (personal communication, email, September 2, 2014).

Susan made her first fieldwork trip to Port Alberni in May 1976, when she was twenty-seven years old. She and Victor attended a Northwest Coast conference May 12–16 in Vancouver, where she met a number of prominent anthropologists working on the west coast of Vancouver Island: Eugene Arima (who, according to Golla's notes, said nothing more to her than "You won't have any problem because you're a very beautiful girl. I'm serious") and Barbara Efrat, who offered to bring her to the island and introduce her to some potential informants (1976 notebook, p. 3, APS).[6] Through Barbara, Susan made the acquaintance of Ben David, a young carver/painter. Ben is the son of Winifred David and grandson of Hamilton George, Edward Sapir's first informant.[7] Ben introduced Susan to his maternal aunt, Doris Martin, also daughter of Hamilton George.

Doris and Susan became fast friends throughout the summer of 1976. Susan wrote of Doris to Victor, "She's a strong, sweet old woman

Fig. 21. Doris Martin at Long Beach, Vancouver Island, July 1979.
Photo courtesy of April Thomas.

(not *so* old, 60) with a big heart and a good sense of humor" (June 8,
1976, APS). Doris took Susan under her wing, toured her around the
valley, and talked with her about certain things she knew. "There are
some things that we don't tell anybody, outside of our family," Thlotiismayak (April Thomas), Doris's daughter, explained to me. "But my
mom told Susan a lot. They were very close. My mom thought of her
like a daughter, so she was a sister to me" (personal communication,
telephone, September 23, 2013). Susan recorded only one tape of her

and Doris sitting together talking about language. A television blares in the background as Susan repeats words and phrases:

DM: Kwats'alth.
SG: Would you say that again?
DM: Kwats'alth.
SG: And "good"? How do you say that?
DM: Tl'uulth. Tl'uulth is "good," you know, and kwats'alth is "pretty."
SG: So kwats'althma is "It is pretty."
DM: Mmmm. (my transcription)

The tape runs for about an hour. "Well, this is getting better, this is getting easier," Susan declared toward the end with apparent joy. Doris also sounded happy, chuckling in reaction to Susan's delight. The APS's digitization of this tape now means Doris's children can listen to their mother speaking their language. This has become especially important to Doris's youngest daughter, Chii-ilthimakamakuu-a (Gerri Thomas). Gerri is actively involved in the Quuquuatsa Language Society, attends courses in Nuu-chah-nulth language, and has started apprenticing herself to fluent speakers in order to learn the language. "You see, we never learned from our mom," Th̲otiismayak explained. "She always spoke to us in English, 'cause that's what they spoke in school. She wanted us to do well in school, to graduate."

After Susan left Port Alberni following the summer of 1976, she kept in touch with Doris by writing letters. Susan only kept incoming letters from Doris, so it is hard to know what news she reported from New York City. Doris's letters are always signed "Love, Doris." "Susie, some days I really miss you," she wrote in one postscript (September 15, 1976, APS). Susan was the last to speak at the 1982 Thlaakt'uulthaa (End of Grief Potlatch), held one year following Doris's death. She directed her speech toward the family: "I have never spoken at a gathering like this before but tonight I felt I really had to say something. Doris was my good friend. She befriended me on the first day I came into this valley. She took me into her home, and into her family, and made me one of them. I learned a great deal from her about Indian traditions,

Fig. 22. Doris (*center*), with her youngest son, Bubba (*left*), and Doris's husband, who went by his surname, Martin (*right*). Seated in front are April (*left*) and Gerri (*right*). Ca. 1976. Photo courtesy of April Thomas.

but also just about what it means to be a good person and lead a good life" (August 28, 1982, APS).

While Susan immediately and easily developed a close relationship with Doris Martin and her family, she struggled to develop meaningful relationships with others. Eventually, she became close with Margaret and Adam Shewish, an elderly Tseshaht couple and chiefly family of the highest rank from this community. Her work with Doris (and through Doris an extended network of Hupacasath people, primarily from the Hamilton family) and the Shewishes formed the foundation for her research, but she struggled more generally with an omnipresent sentiment of distrust around anthropologists.

Developing intimacy and rapport was perhaps Susan's greatest research challenge. She conducted her fieldwork during a period of political, racial, educational, and emotional tension in the Alberni Valley. She arrived only three years after the final closure of the Alberni Indian Residential School, when groups like the Native Alliance for Red Power were gaining popularity among young Nuu-chah-nulth people.

She also began her fieldwork in the wake of a decade of what seemed to be an unending flow of white anthropologists who had appeared and just as quickly disappeared from people's lives. The entitled behavior of some of these visiting academics had left a bitter taste in the mouths of many that was not easily forgettable. In an undated note, Susan described a discussion one Sunday morning over coffee. She was told, "Anthros [are] not humble . . . ask you questions then don't let you give full answers; do all talking themselves, etc. I hope you don't do that," to which another Tseshaht woman, Kathy Robinson, added, "Not yet. She hasn't gotten her degree yet" (undated note, APS).

By the 1970s some Nuu-chah-nulth people were publicly retaliating against anthropologists. When Claude Lévi-Strauss visited Thunderbird Park, a Native carving apprenticeship program in Victoria in the early 1970s, young Hupacasath carver Ron Hamilton (now Chuuchkamalthnii) used this as an opportunity to publicly challenge him.[8] In a televised recording, Lévi-Strauss asked questions and commented about the masks Hamilton was carving. After each statement, Hamilton would quickly counter and correct him in a rather successful attempt to make Lévi-Strauss look uninformed.[9] Certainly this was the most widely broadcast example of public humiliation of anthropologists. Hamilton used the camera (and television broadcast) as an opportunity to comment on the nature of expertise and where he felt the real knowledge resides: in Native communities, with Native people. Susan experienced humiliation through everyday experiences in public spaces (not, luckily, televised). She recorded in her field notebook, for example, "Had a nasty run-in with Tat in bar in Victoria last Saturday. He was very drunk and very angry and vituperating at me for being an anthro. 'I hate you brain-pickers . . . leave the language alone . . . don't do it (ask questions?) to me,' etc. etc. etc." (December 15, 1977, APS). When Susan met Ron Hamilton, he "went out of his way to make me feel unwelcome," she remembered in a letter to Victor Golla (June 8, 1976, APS).

After her first month in the Alberni Valley, Susan reflected: "The Indians here are a lot more sophisticated in the ways of anthros than most non-anthros. They knew the difference between anthropology and archaeology, for example, and use words like 'taboo'" (July 19, 1976, APS). While the general public may seem to rarely know the difference between anthropology and archaeology, Susan was beginning fieldwork with people not only who knew this difference but whose lives were very much affected by the anthropologists and archaeologists who had frequented the valley. During her first meeting with George Clutesi, a well-respected Tseshaht painter, historian, and storyteller, she remembered: "He sat down, looked me in the eye, and, absolutely without malice said, 'I'm not going to tell you anything . . . By the time I left he was saying, 'You'll have to stay a long time before people will tell you anything.' . . . 'We've told our people not to talk to anthropologists anymore because of what they've done to us'" (July 19, 1976, APS).

Susan felt the reality of Clutesi's forecast during her first few years of fieldwork. In a report on her research to the Canadian Museum of Man (her funding agency), she lamented that people would refuse formal interviews but were more than happy to discuss genealogies, cultural beliefs, and other pertinent information "only while my hands are fully occupied in a pile of dishes following supper" (undated note, APS). Thlotiismayak told me that elder Mabel Taylor used to speak in Nuu-chah-nulth to the other old ladies: "Don't say anything when she [Susan] is around! She probably has a tape recorder in her pocket!" (personal communication, Ahahswinis, British Columbia, March 21, 2012).

Because this was Susan's first fieldwork experience, many of her letters and early diary entries are filled with disappointment in herself for not "doing enough work" or "taking enough notes." Like many anthropologists in the field, she begins by believing there is a "right" and a "wrong" way of doing fieldwork and eventually comes to a place of understanding that fieldwork methods—how one goes about collecting and recording information—depend on context. She struggled with keeping notes, explaining: "Some people are offended by the notebook and then I either have to strain my creaky memory or sneak into the bathroom to scribble. How ignoramus it would be to be caught on the throne with paper and pencil" (undated note, APS). I too in my experience was often told outright, "Put that notebook away! I am telling you something because I want you to remember it!" For a community that has relied on oral history traditions for thousands of years, memory is the place where important information should be recorded. Despite the challenges Susan faced in making records and taking notes, she explained in a letter to a friend, "I find doing fieldwork simultaneously terrifying, exhilarating, unnerving, and rewarding. Meeting people is still a big trauma, but generally once met they are amazingly generous and hospitable. There's a fair amount of suspicion of Whites and anthros, but at least people are honest about it" (June 4, 1976, APS).

After her first summer in the valley, Susan returned to New York to complete coursework and exams and advance to candidacy. She came back to Vancouver Island about a year later, in September 1977. It was a challenging time for her: her marriage to Victor Golla was, for all intents and purposes, over. She longed to have children, writing to a friend, "I have come to envy the women here, their big families" (July 5, 1976, APS). She reflected in her notebooks that she must have initially appeared quite strange to people during her first visit, having been married in her late twenties and yet without children. In a conversation Susan had with Thlotiismayak in October 1977, Thlotiismayak expressed similar feelings of alienation: "You don't know how it's like around here to be 23, not married, and no kids" (October 31, 1977, APS). Of course, Susan did have some understanding, and she wanted to have children while in the field. In Nuu-chah-nulth homes she witnessed expressions of extreme love and affection for small children, and she hoped to welcome a child into this world.[10] She fell in love with long-time friend Jim Conmy, and the two maintained a relationship long distance during her fieldwork in 1977–78; he eventually joined her in 1979. Together, they moved onto the Tseshaht Reserve and into a little home that Adam and Margaret Shewish fixed up for them. Here, they welcomed their first child, Cate (Hakumiik), born on February 18, 1979. During her pregnancy, Susan remembered:

> Following MS [Margaret Shewish] own teaching about women traditionally never announcing the fact of pregnancy (it was "too sacred" to them) I never formally told her. (Though I told DM [Doris Martin], a great gossip, in mid-Aug and I'm sure word got thru). Around 4 ½ months when I returned from Seattle MS et. al. began to comment, very favourably, and with increasing frequency, on my increasing girth. One day circa 5 months I walked into kitchen—MS eyes my belly and said "you're looking better every day." I replied, "We are."

She nodded and laughed and said, "That's good. That's really good." (undated note, ca. October—November 1978, APS)

Margaret Shewish would later give Cate her name, Hakumiik (Little Princess), in the baptism/naming ceremony hosted by Susan and Jim in Port Alberni. Other close Nuu-chah-nulth friends came forward to play a role in looking after Cate. Hilda Nookemis, for example, was a stand-in godmother, a "proxy," as she explained to me. She went on, "I treasured my time with Susan as well as Jim when he came to join her. She was a special friend to me." Hilda was a confidante and voice of reason for Susan, especially when she went through personal struggles and the general challenges associated with ethnographic fieldwork.

Each of the women involved in Susan's fieldwork played a slightly different role in Susan's life and research. Margaret Shewish was an incredible source of information, and over time, the two became close. "I was devoted to MS [Margaret Shewish], and I believe she really did like me" (1990 field notebook, p. 10, APS). Her relationship with Doris Martin was more informal. "Susan liked my mom, she loved my mom," Doris's daughter explained. "My mom took her in, and my mom teased the hell out of her, and she [Susan] hated it, and she never got it that if we love you, we tease you. If we don't love you, we don't tease you" (personal communication with Thlotiismayak, Ahahswinis, British Columbia, November 10, 2013). Susan was like a daughter to Doris. "Doris has virtually adopted me," Susan explained in an early letter to a friend. "She tells me things, she teaches me the language, she feeds me. She doesn't want money (the subject clearly embarrassed her), so I have become her personal chauffeur. I take her to the doctor; I do her shopping" (June 4, 1976, APS). Doris had witnessed many anthropologists, such as Philip Drucker and Morris Swadesh, pass through her father's door. Doris knew a lot of Hupacasath history, genealogy, and general knowledge about natural resources, and she shared this knowledge with Susan over the years. Just next door to Doris were Hilda and Cyril Charles. Susan enjoyed the rancorous debate that went on in their home. Cyril would especially provoke his Aunty Ruby. Susan wrote of one evening in 1978, "CC [Cyril Charles] and RP [Ruby Peterson] got into a rousing argument about almost everything, Indian politics, Indian

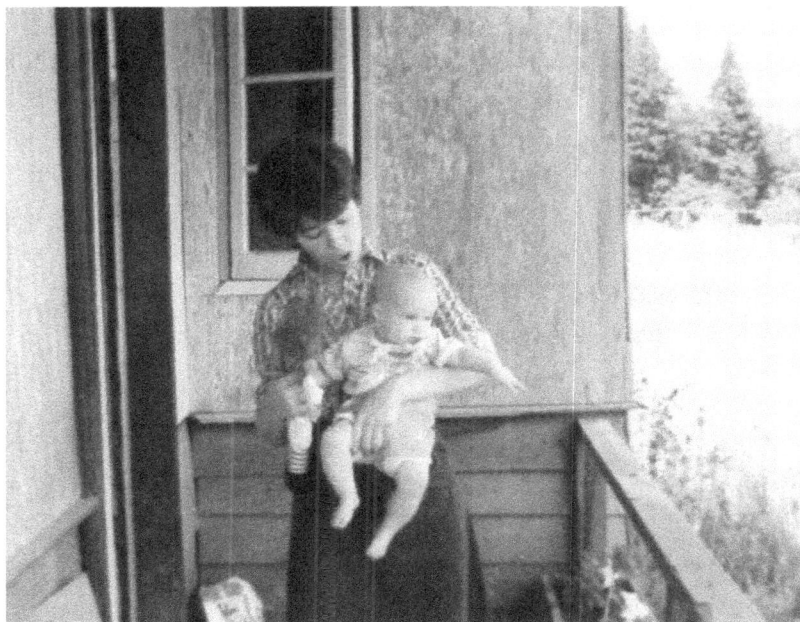

Fig. 23. Susan with Cate at their home on the Tseshaht Reserve in the summer of 1979. Photo courtesy of Jim Conmy.

identity, Canadian identity, how to tell who's Indian, Indian medicine, racism, use of Indian language at potlatches" (March 21, 1978, APS). In these moments of debate and discussion, Susan learned about the challenges facing Nuu-chah-nulth people, points of contention, and hope for the future. As the years went by, Susan and her growing family wove their lives into the lives of Nuu-chah-nulth people in the valley.

Information does not come handed down in neat packages: "You have to work for it. It's hard work," Chuuchkamalthnii has explained to me. In Nuu-chah-nulth oral history traditions, information, histories, and genealogies are repeated and repeated until a basis of knowledge is established, thus allowing future conversations to quickly reference a person, place, or story and situate the knowledge within a network of human and nonhuman actors (Latour 2005). Hence, being elbow deep in dishes following dinner, as Susan had bemoaned, is the perfect time to educate an anthropologist—he or she cannot take notes and must commit information to memory. A notebook or tape recorder is simply a crutch; instead, the information must be burned into memory so it can be called upon instantly when needed. This is not unlike what Julie Cruikshank (1998) found in her first fieldwork. She too was not getting her questions answered in the way she had anticipated. Instead, she was told stories. These stories—which at the time she felt were only peripherally related to the autobiographies she was hoping to collect—were actually cultural scaffolding. Women would later reference the stories when they told their biographies. This is the manner by which storytelling becomes part of "communicative process": one learns "what the story *says*. Then you learn what the story can *do* when it is engaged as a strategy of communication" (Cruikshank 1998:41).

Throughout her fieldwork, Susan was told stories in different contexts—while out harvesting cedar bark, picking berries, walking in the woods, cutting fish, playing Scrabble, cleaning up after meals—but rarely in formal situations where she was allowed to make an audio recording or written transcription in her notebook. She had, by some point, accepted this state of affairs. If people would not record stories, alternatively, she would bring to her research participants' stories already recorded.

TRANSLATION OF SAPIR'S NOOTKA TEXTS

Despite their abhorrence of recent anthropologists and ambivalence about the information recorded by earlier ones, Hupacasath and Tseshaht people expressed fond memories of early anthropologists Edward Sapir and Morris Swadesh to Susan Golla. Sapir recorded a number of stories, and Swadesh later played an important role in publishing a small fraction of this research. Sapir found the Nuu-chah-nulth immensely interesting and wrote to Alfred Kroeber in December 1910, "[I] hope I shall be able to spend several years on them" (Golla 1984:55; see also Darnell 1990:75). This would not turn out to be the case.[11] Nearly thirty years would elapse before Swadesh posthumously published only a portion of this material. These two publications, *Nootka Texts* and *Native Accounts of Nootka Ethnography*, were on bookshelves in the homes of many of Susan's research participants. Hugh Watts (grandson of Tom Sayach'apis) told her he read from *Nootka Texts* every night, while Adam Shewish said, "Those books make me proud to be Indian" (July 7, 1979, APS).

Nearly four years after beginning her fieldwork, Sapir's recorded stories enabled Susan to foster deeper relationships with Hupacasath and Tseshaht people. Susan traveled to the APS archives and found a series of not yet translated texts collected by Edward Sapir in 1910 and 1913–14. These texts were specifically about the Alberni Valley and included origin stories about the Hupacasath, the Tseshaht, and other groups such as the Hikuulthaht. Most of these texts were collected at the tail end of Sapir's fieldwork, when he was far less meticulous about translation. While some parts of the texts were translated, most were left in the Nuu-chah-nulth language, written in his orthography. Susan made copies and returned to the Alberni Valley. She began with one translation, "A Legendary History of the Tseshaht," and worked primarily with Mabel Taylor. Susan audio-recorded many hours of their translation work. A few years later, she employed the help of linguist Suzanne Rose to work with other fluent speakers to translate more of the unpublished Sapir texts, among them "A Hopachasaht Account of Culture Origins," "Two Swan Women Make Place Names for the Hopachasaht Country," "The Origin of the Tseshaht," and "The Story of Tlatlakokwap and Taposhinis." This translation project would ensure repatriation of these stories to origin communities.

The lapse of time between Sapir's and Golla's fieldwork (1910 to 1980) was a period of dramatic cultural upheaval. Hupacasath and Tseshaht children in the valley were forcibly removed from their homes and required to attend residential school, where they were not allowed to speak their language. Susan was acutely aware of this fact and recorded in her field notebook a conversation she had with a group of Tseshaht women in their twenties and early thirties: "She [one of the women] said that she used to speak Indian exclusively before she went to school. Then it was beaten out of her. I expressed surprise that that had happened so recently and everyone at the table was at pains to assure me that it happened, essentially, until that school was closed [in 1973]. All told stories of beatings for speaking Indian" (November 29, 1977, APS). In addition to causing physical and psychological traumas, removing children from homes also disrupted traditional forms of intergenerational knowledge transfer and oral history record records. As a result, many of the stories that Sapir collected were no longer part of the collective memories of the Hupacasath and Tsehshat living at the time of Susan's fieldwork. However, a group of elderly, fluent speakers remained and were interested in translating these texts so that they could be known to future English-speaking generations.[12]

Suzanne Rose, a linguist who had spent a decade immersed in the Nuu-chah-nulth language, helped Susan by reading Sapir's transcriptions out loud to fluent speakers. The speakers would then repeat the most accurate pronunciation back to Suzanne, who meticulously transcribed the texts, using a particular orthography. Ultimately, Susan and Suzanne created a four-line interlinear text: first, the Nuu-chah-nulth, a second line of morphemes, a third line of direct translation of the Nuu-chah-nulth morphemes into English, and finally, a fourth line of running English translation. At the time, these translations—if published—would have doubled the amount of Nuu-chah-nulth material published by Sapir and Swadesh. Perhaps more importantly, these were primordial texts that revealed who people were, where they came from, and what their purpose was for being in the valley. Some of these origin stories are about place-names, others are about the genesis of technologies related to weaving, carving, fishing, and so on, and others are about spiritual beliefs.

Bringing these stories back to the valley brought Susan closer to the community where she had previously struggled to find intimacy with research participants. I have been told at length by the descendants of her informants that this process of translation was fulfilling for their parents and grandparents. "My dad used to get so happy every day when Susan would come to pick him up," Darleen Watts told me. "They had a very close, special relationship. He was distraught when he heard of her death." In the midst of completing this translation work, Susan discovered she had cancer. She continued to work tirelessly on the project until her death in early 1993. In November 1992 she wrote to her collaborator, Suzanne, "I'm on another trial of chemotherapy, not too bad so far, but also zero results. Somehow seeing this volume into print, or at least into proofs, gives me new goals, so I'm willing to try more treatments than before." Her devotion was not without a sense of remorse. "I feel guilty that these things are so important to me," she began. "Why not just another few months with my kids? But they [the Nootka texts] are the product of so many years of work. It's hard to think of it all languishing unused." She was devoted to her family and to her work, two things that for an anthropologist are, more often than not, intertwined. Having seen proofs, she believed at the time of her death that the texts would be published, though they never were. This was the book Darleen Watts had asked me to help her find.

RETURNING SUSAN'S WORK

Just as Susan endeavored to repatriate information to Nuu-chah-nulth families, I too am working to return important documents, including Susan's translated texts. I am currently working with the new Center for Native American and Indigenous Research (CNAIR) at the APS to arrange for the digitization of documents in preparation for their return to the community. CNAIR is directed by Dr. Timothy B. Powell, with Brian Carpenter serving as the senior archivist, and is dedicated to a new initiative called Digital Knowledge Sharing. CNAIR works in partnership with indigenous communities to select and digitize archival documents that can play a significant role in language preservation and cultural revitalization. The APS received grants of $1 million from the Andrew W. Mellon Foundation to pilot Digital Knowledge Sharing partnerships with the Eastern Band of Cherokee Indians, the Penobscot Nation, the Tuscarora Nation, and Ojibwe bands in the United States and Canada. As a consulting scholar for CNAIR, I am working with the APS and Nuu-chah-nulth families to create new partnerships that will result in gifting digital copies of the Sapir and Golla collections to the communities of origin. This process will also provide an opportunity for Nuu-chah-nulth people to share their stories and protocols with the APS in order to enhance catalog descriptions and to protect culturally sensitive materials in the collection.

The translated and annotated Sapir texts Susan was working on at the time of her death were supposed to be volume 11 of the now defunct series the Collected Works of Edward Sapir, published by Mouton de Gruyter. Susan Golla and Suzanne Rose were both editors for volume 11, which would include their four-line interlinear translations alongside Golla's ethnological annotations. I located a manuscript in Susan's papers at the APS, though only the English translations with annotations. I later located the four-line interlinear text, although it is unreadable: it is a dot-matrix printout written in a computer code intended for the publisher's software program (which likely no longer exists).

The APS digitized the English translations, which I returned to Darleen Watts shortly after my return to Port Alberni in October 2013. She was thrilled to finally see her father's translation work but disappointed that it had not been formally published. She hopes to see this happen eventually. She explained, "This is something that our father did. It's a legacy that he left behind that was incomplete, and it has got to get completed sometime." We are currently working with the APS Press to find a way to publish Susan's annotations and the English translations alongside Sapir's Nuu-chah-nulth transcriptions. With a proper publication in hand, the hope is to one day host a *tl'itscuu* (feast) in Port Alberni and return the texts to the descendants of the people who helped Susan Golla with translation, as well as the descendants of Tyee Bob, Tom Sayach'apis, and William, the three men who initially told these stories to Sapir.

In Nuu-chah-nulth country, stories, which belong exclusively to certain families, are part of a proprietary, kin-based oral record. The ownership of specific histories was an ethnological distinction that fascinated Edward Sapir. He reiterated this to Kroeber after his last field trip in January 1914: "The Nootka are intensely interesting, both ethnologically and linguistically. Perhaps the most interesting thing about them in the former respect is the extremely large number of distinct kinds of things that are handed down as family privileges" (January 14, 1914, Ottawa, Ontario). In other words, as Golla argued, people are not simply a "sum of [their] narratives" but are in fact an accumulative, genealogical network of many stories and histories that produce ties to places, histories, rights, and beliefs.

Susan insisted upon ethnographic treatment of archival documents, arguing that "special potential" and "special problems" surface in Native-authored, ethnographically collected texts (Golla 1988:107). She wanted to bring "ethnographic sophistication" to archival analysis by breathing life into source material through contextualization. These nuanced source materials, she contended, were curtailed by translation and decontextualization. At the time, she was writing about Sapir's materials—but she could have been writing about her own in a kind of foreshadowing of what was to come. My role as facilitator, researcher, and ethnographer brought me to the archive, into the lives of Susan Golla's family and dear friends, and of course back to the valley and the families with whom I have developed close relationships in the context of my research. Anthropologists were, and continue to be, embroiled within genealogies—and genealogies influence what kinds of stories are known and if they will be told.

Susan's anthropological pedigree was known in the valley. At a feast Susan hosted to acknowledge the generosity and helpfulness of research participants, Tseshaht head chief Adam Shewish explained to the witnesses present: "What you see here is not a new thing. Long ago, there was a man came here. His name was Sapir. Then there was another one, his name was Swadesh. Now Susan's doing the same thing. What she's doing is not for this generation. Years from now our children will be able to read what went on on the reserve" (July 7, 1979, APS). In other words, people expected Susan to arrive knowing the stories and histories associated with her anthropological genealogy. When she eventually did bring the stories collected by Sapir, people were not only receptive but excited to work with her. She was bringing their stories home, but through an appropriate genealogical network—an anthropological one. Likewise, I have been added to this genealogy; hence, people asked me to find Susan's stories and bring them home for interpretation. While the APS has digitized these documents, we hope to formally publish these annotated, translated texts, as Susan Golla and her Nuu-chah-nulth collaborators had initially intended.

CONCLUSION

My first exposure to Dr. Susan Golla was not through published materials in a library but through the stories I listened to while conducting ethnographic fieldwork on Vancouver Island (2009–). Hilda Nookemis was the first to approach me. "You should really look at Susan Golla's work. She was my friend, a real smart lady. And gee, her hair sure was beautiful! It was a shock when we lost her, eh? Too young."

Others would mention her as well, especially Doris's children, who fondly remembered Susan's devotion to their mother. They enjoyed her company, late nights playing cards and drinking tea. Thlotiismayak would frequently remind me that Susan provided her with a pair of ruby earrings to wear at her wedding: "It was my 'something borrowed.' She was my sister, eh?" Her adversary, or "boyfriend," as Cyril Charles used to tease, Chuuchkamalthnii (Ron Hamilton), not surprisingly, had few kind words to speak of Susan. He complained of her attending his November 1983 *emtnakshitl* (naming potlatch) without invitation, and when she took photographs without permission, "Tuffy [Hupacasath hereditary chief] ripped the film out of her camera, right in front of everyone!" he relished. With few exceptions, most remembered Susan as thoughtful, helpful, and clever. "I really, really liked her," Rudy Watts explained to me when I brought him a recording Susan had made of his father, Hugh Watts, speaking in Nuu-chah-nulth. "My parents really enjoyed having her around. She knew a lot. She listened" (personal communication, Tseshaht Reserve, November 14, 2013).

In this project, I also endeavored to return copies of Susan's notes to the appropriate descendants (usually the children of her informants). When I asked Thlotiismayak about the notes I provided to her, she replied, "I read them and read them. I read them about three times. It made me miss her [Susan]." The notes also revealed dimensions of Thlotiismayak's mother that she had not known. "I'm almost sixty years old, and my mom passed away when I was twenty-six," she began. "In those twenty-six years of my life my mother never told me she was proud of me for anything. And then I get the notes, and Susan Golla's written down that 'Doris is very proud of Ape [April/Thlotiismayak] for all that Indian stuff she is learning.' That meant so much to me."

While Susan devoted herself to the preservation of Nuu-chah-nulth stories, she was not as meticulous about recording her own personal stories. Susan's daughter, Cate, described this tragic irony:

Towards the end of her life my mom couldn't speak at all. Instead, she carried a notebook, which would get filled up with giant exclamation points or emphatic underlines as she tried to communicate points of urgency or emotion to my brothers and me. For a while, she had one of those kids' toys that you could scribble on with a red plastic stylus and then clear in one magic swoop by lifting the magnetic writing surface from its cardboard back. She literally erased her stories as she was telling them. And despite everything, we didn't have the foresight to think how much we'd want to have those scribbled words forever. Somehow, we seem only to have saved one of her notebooks. Filled with one-sided conversations with my dad, and friends at home, and me and my brothers, it's a dear possession. And now you've shared the news of many more notebooks. And, just as much, you've launched a kind of collective memory mining and remembering that we just haven't had much of before. (personal communication, email, February 15, 2014)

And so when I arrived at Jim Conmy's home in Brooklyn in October 2013, I was welcomed with open arms and a delicious meal of pesto pasta. We looked through photographs and talked about memories of Port Alberni and the friendships developed there. "I'm so delighted you have landed in my mother's files, and in our lives, and the lives of others who knew her," Cate told me later. "I am sure she would also be delighted, both as an anthropologist and as a storykeeper whose own story has gotten a little lost" (personal communication, email, February 15, 2014).

Susan's life is as much part of this story as her research: the two are entangled. Her request to deposit her materials at the APS shows foresight—she knew that her death would mean that she could not keep promises to provide completed copies of research material (in published book form) to the Nuu-chah-nulth people who helped her along the way. Without a doubt, Susan did her best to keep these promises and certainly believed the annotated, interlinear translations of the unpublished Sapir texts were going to be in print. As a backup, she asked that her papers be archived at the APS. She was covering all of her bases in the worst-case scenario that volume 11 of the Collected Works of Edward Sapir would not make it into print.

In a letter Susan wrote to George Clutesi early in her fieldwork, she explained: "I would hope also that the record I would make of your traditions and your culture would be of interest and use to your chil-

Fig. 24. Susan's daughter, Cate Conmy, looks through family photographs at her father's home in Brooklyn, New York, October 11, 2013. Photo by Denise Green.

dren and grandchildren someday" (July 19, 1976, APS). Her hopes have been fulfilled, and today many of the children and grandchildren of her informants are benefiting from the information she recorded. It is my hope that I have upheld Susan's wish to treat archival documents with "ethnographic sophistication" by including source communities and direct descendants of her and Edward Sapir's informants in the research process, as well as her family, colleagues, collaborators, and close friends. I look forward to the moment when the translation work of Darleen's father, Charlie Watts, and the recording of all those that came before him are brought to life through formal publication of the Sapir texts.

ACKNOWLEDGMENTS

I would like to express my sincerest thanks to an immense network of people who connect through the life and work of Dr. Susan Golla and who have helped me with this research: Jim Conmy, Cate Conmy, April Thomas, Darleen Watts, Hilda Nookemis, Gerri Thomas, Joyce White, Rudy Watts, Janet Chernela, Sheila Dauer, Ron Hamilton, Victor Golla, and Suzanne Rose. The François André Michaux Fund Fellowship from the American Philosophical Society enabled me to spend a month of intensive investigation into Dr. Golla's notes at the APS. I would like to thank Brian Carpenter, senior archivist at the APS, who initially helped me to locate Susan's papers and later digitized all the tapes. Thank you to Tim Powell, director of the Center for Native American and Indigenous Research at the APS, for his guidance and encouragement. Charles Menzies, Gastón Gordillo, and Charlotte Townsend-Gault were all part of my PhD committee at the University of British Columbia and provided thoughtful critique and encouragement throughout my research. A Vanier Canada Graduate Scholarship from the Social Sciences and Humanities Research Council also provided financial support during the time of this research.

NOTES

1. Throughout this chapter, I use an "easy-read" orthography for Nuu-chah-nulth words, modified from an orthography created by Chuuch-kamalthnii (Ron Hamilton) that does not require special characters. Generally speaking, Nuu-chah-nulth traditional territories span the west coast of Vancouver Island, British Columbia, "from Brooks Peninsula in the north to Point-no-Point in the south, and as far inland as the Alberni Valley, at the head of Barkley Sound" (Nuu-chah-nulth Tribal Council 2014).

2. Nuu-chah-nulth people typically use the term "business" to refer to the main purpose of a potlatch (e.g., naming, seating, end of grief, etc.).

3. Tseshaa-aqsup is the female version of Tseshaht and directly translates as Woman from Tseshaa. The suffix *aht* means "people from."

4. Boas spent only two weeks in Alberni in August 1889 but was responsible for recommending Edward Sapir for the position as director of the anthropological division of the Geological Survey of Canada. His original notes are in the American Philosophical Society collection but are in shorthand, as discussed by Rainer Hatoum in this volume. Sapir's field notebooks, wax cylinder recordings, photographs, and artifacts collected in Alberni (now Port Alberni), British Columbia, in 1910 and 1913–14 were originally deposited in the Canadian Museum of Civilization (now the Canadian Museum of History). Sapir's 1914–22 correspondence with informant Alex Thomas, the audiovisual materials, and artifacts remain at the Canadian Museum of History today; however, Sapir removed the original field notebooks and some associated materials (e.g., drawing books produced by Douglas Thomas and William). After his death, these records were donated to the American Philosophical Society Library.

5. The Hiikuulthaht are a tribe of people who came from Hiikuulth, farther down Barkley Sound (closer to the west coast). The Hiikuulthaht eventually moved into the Alberni Valley sometime in the late eighteenth to early nineteenth century and remained an autonomous group, sharing the valley with the newly amalgamated (and recently arrived) Tseshaht, as well as the valley's original inhabitants, the Hupacasath. Sometime at the end of the nineteenth century, the Hiikuulthaht officially amalgamated with the Tseshaht. According to census records, this occurred before 1881; however, Boas (1891:31) identified the Hiikuulthaht ("Eku'lath = bushes on hill people") as independent. One of Sapir's main informants, William, had Hiikulthaht ancestry. The most frequently cited example of an incorrect story collected by Sapir was "A Girl Obtains Power from the Fish" (Sapir and Swadesh 1939:120–127). During Susan's fieldwork, at least three different women pointed out serious inaccuracies. All three of these women had direct genealogical connections to Asmanahey, the Hiikuulthaht woman featured in the story. During my fieldwork, I was told similar information by Chuuchkamalthnii, who learned of the inaccuracies from his aunty, Elizabeth "Lizzy" Gallic (née Lauder), granddaughter of Asmanahey. The story was dictated by William, also Hikuulthaht, but with no direct genea-

logical connection to Asmanahey or her daughter, Punii-ii (Polly). In other words, this story did not belong to William because it was not from his family; therefore, the erroneous nature of the recoding is not surprising. Many argue that he had no right to share it, since it was not from his family.

6. Today, anthropologists and source communities consider the term "informant" offensive; however, at the time of Golla's fieldwork, and Sapir before her, this was the designation used.

7. Hamilton George later changed his name to George Hamilton sometime in the 1920s.

8. In Nuu-chah-nulth cultural practice, an individual's name changes over the course of his or her life. Today, most people have English names, which are often given at birth and used in legal documents. In the early 1970s, Ron Hamilton went by the name Hupkwatchuu (Hair All Over), which was not a "big" name but a nickname used by his relatives from the time he was a baby. Over the course of his life, he has been formally named over forty times at potlatch ceremonies. In the late 1970s he used the name Kwayaatsapaalth and in 1983 was given the Hiikuulthaht name Ki-ke-in by his maternal aunt Elizabeth Gallic. He used the name Ki-ke-in until May 2009, when he became head of Takiishtakamlthlat (Earthquake House), the first-ranked house of the Tl'ikuulthat-h, one of the four septs of the Hupacasath First Nation. He now uses the name Chuuchkamalthnii.

9. Lévi-Strauss was touring British Columbia to promote his most recent book, *The Way of the Masks*, making Hamilton's antics even more compelling.

10. In many of Susan's interviews with older Nuu-chah-nulth people, they would describe the struggles of previous generations (those living in the late nineteenth and early twentieth centuries) to raise children into adulthood. During this period, children rarely survived into adulthood. For example, Dan Watts, one of Sapir's informants, had twenty-four children, and only three survived into adulthood (March 9, 1981, APS). In another example, Lizzy Gallic described "Old Hupacasath Chief John": "He and his wife got babies all the time but they couldn't grow up, couldn't survive. They gave up" (November 27, 1978, APS). Even when children did survive into young adulthood, they were forcibly removed from their homes and sent to residential school; therefore, it is not surprising that Susan witnessed such immense love and appreciation for children in the homes of Nuu-chah-nulth people.

11. Sapir spent four months during the fall of 1910, returned toward the end of 1913, and stayed until March 1914. He continued his Nootka research via correspondence with Alex Thomas (grandson of Tom Sayach'apis), whom he trained to read and write using his Nootka orthography. In total, Sapir spent approximately nine very productive months in Alberni.

12. During my fieldwork, 2009–14, only two fluent speakers remained in the Hupacasath community, and both are in their eighties. In other words, translating these texts was timely.

REFERENCES

Boas, Franz. 1891. Second General Report on the Indians of British Columbia. British Association for the Advancement of Science, 60th meeting. Pp. 582–715. London.

Cruikshank, Julie. 1990. Life Lived Like a Story: Life Stories of Three Yukon Native Elders. Lincoln: University of Nebraska Press.

———. 2005. Do Glaciers Listen? Local Knowledge, Colonial Encounters, and Social Imagination. Vancouver: University of British Columbia Press.

Darnell, Regna. 1990. Edward Sapir: Linguist, Anthropologist, Humanist. Berkeley: University of California Press.

Dunae, Patrick A. n.d. viHistory (Vancouver Island Census). http://vi history.ca/index.php. Accessed February 19, 2013.

Golla, Susan. n.d. Susan Golla Papers, Manuscript Collection #89 (not yet cataloged). American Philosophical Society Archives, Philadelphia PA.

———. 1987. He Has a Name: History and Social Structure among the Indians of Western Vancouver Island. PhD dissertation, Columbia University, New York.

———. 1988. A Tale of Two Chiefs: Nootkan Narrative and the Ideology of Chieftainship. Journal de la Société des Américanistes 74:107–123.

Golla, Victor, ed. 1984. The Sapir-Kroeber Correspondence. Survey of California and Other Indian Languages, University of California, Berkeley.

Latour, Bruno. 2005. Reassembling the Social: An Introduction to Actor-Network-Theory. New York: Oxford University Press.

Nuu-chah-nulth Tribal Council. 2014. http://www.nuuchahnulth.org /tribal-council/welcome.html. Accessed August 30, 2014.

Sapir, Edward. n.d. Unpublished field notes. American Council of Learned Societies Committee on Native American Languages. Manuscript Collection, Mss.497.3.B63.c. American Philosophical Society Archives, Philadelphia PA.

———. 1911. Summary Report of the Geological Survey, Department of Mines, for the Calendar Year 1910. Anthropological Division: Report of Field Work, Ottawa. Pp. 284–287.

———. 1913. A Girl's Puberty Potlatch among the Nootka Indians. Royal Society of Canada, Transactions, 3rd series, 7:67–80.

Sapir, Edward, and Morris Swadesh. 1955. Native Accounts of Nootka Ethnography. Research Center in Anthropology, Folklore, and Linguistics, Indiana University, Bloomington.

Sapir, Edward, Morris Swadesh, and Linguistic Society of America. 1939. Nootka Texts: Tales and Ethnological Narratives, with Grammatical Notes and Lexical Materials. Linguistic Society of America, University of Pennsylvania, Philadelphia.

9

The File Hills Farm Colony Legacy

First Nations people in Canada have experienced and continue to experience a multitude of hardships at the hand of the government through various colonial and assimilation policies. The aim of this chapter is to provide a unique perspective about a little-known facet of Canadian history, the File Hills Farm Colony, and to engage in an accurate ethnographic representation of contemporary indigenous peoples that avoids the hazards of stereotyping, idealizing, and freezing in time and space.

A social experiment grounded in British colonial expansionist ideology, the File Hills Farm Colony was created by the Canadian government in southern Saskatchewan in 1897. During the late 1800s and early 1900s, graduates from Indian residential and industrial schools were chosen to transfer to the Peepeekisis Cree Nation reserve. Land was set aside by the federal government for use in a project proposed by the Indian agent, William Morris Graham, with the intent to create an agrarian, utopian community of First Nations participants. It was hoped that the implementation of the colony would create a self-sufficient population and act as a solution to the "Indian problem" (Bednasek 2009a:88) in Canada. This chapter examines the contemporary issues that have arisen as a result of the colony's existence.

North American scholarly publications on indigenous cultures have often focused on the historical events and tragedies experienced by aboriginal peoples. The first section of this chapter presents this type of information on the File Hills community. Utilizing archival documents and previously published information, I reconstruct a brief history of the File Hills Farm Colony from the time of the 1874 signing of Treaty 4 in Saskatchewan, to the creation of the Peepeekisis band, and finally to the implementation and disintegration of the File Hills Farm Colony on the Peepeekisis reserve.

Based on this historical overview of the colony, I address the problems that have often surrounded the study of indigenous topics and the use of indigenous knowledges in academic writing.[1] I attempt to rectify these past issues in indigenous scholarly writing by adopting a methodology that involves the use of oratory and the acknowledgment of social memory as a valid method of passing on knowledge. In doing so, the use of vernacular, or "everyday," language to express information is maintained throughout the chapter. I also explore previous representations of indigenous peoples in anthropological study through a discussion of the historical use of salvage anthropology and the ethnographic present.

In order to produce an appropriate representation of the current situation that the Peepeekisis community now finds itself in, I intend this chapter to be viewed as an autoethnography. Not only have I engaged in personal communication with Peepeekisis members and visits to the reserve, but the topic I address here is directly related to my own status as a First Nations woman and registered member of Peepeekisis Cree Nation. Previous research conducted by other scholars on the colony has often been primarily focused on the transfers of ex-residential and industrial school graduates to Peepeekisis. With few exceptions, very little information has been presented about the current situation that the descendants of the "original" band members of the Peepeekisis community have experienced. It is my desire not only to share the collective history of my band but also to provide a voice for those who may not have previously had the opportunity to tell their stories.

PEEPEEKISIS AND THE FILE HILLS FARM COLONY: A HISTORICAL PERSPECTIVE

There is no denying that the relationship between the aboriginal population of Canada and the country's governing body is a historically complicated one. Evidence of this can be seen every day in the media and in news reports about various First Nation communities. For Peepeekisis Cree Nation, a reserve located in the Treaty 4 territory of southern Saskatchewan, it is no different. Unlike other reserves in Canada, Peepeekisis served as the location of a radical experiment in aboriginal assimilation and colonial policies. This scheme would be known as the File Hills Farm Colony.[2] An attempt at creating an agrarian First Nation utopia by the Canadian government, this social experiment is little known to the Canadian general public. However, at the time of its implementation and operation, the colony was heralded both in Canada and internationally as an innovative success in the management of Indigenous peoples. Despite this level of recognition, it becomes apparent under a close examination that the project was rife with eugenic implications, land displacement, and a general disregard for the original members of the Peepeekisis band.

Although the reserve is named after his son Peepeekisis, it was Chief Canahachapew (Ready Bow) who was present at the signing of Treaty 4. Described as a "much needed step" toward "bringing the Indians of the Fertile Belt into closer relations with the Government of Canada" (Morris 1991 [1880]:77), Treaty 4 was signed on September 15, 1874, after several days of negotiations. Arthur J. Ray, Jim Miller, and Frank J. Tough explain that the language of each of the numbered treaties indicates the objectives of the treaty-making process, objectives that included the "opening [of] areas for settlement in exchange for the Crown's bounty and benevolence, thereby ensuring peace and goodwill" (2000:59). Earlier Treaties 1 and 2 discussed the locations of reserve lands in regard to specific bands and chiefs; however, subsequent treaties did not specify which lands were to be set aside for reserve use. Instead, reserves were to be located "where it shall be deemed most convenient and advantageous" (2000:60) for Indian bands after consultation with government officers.

After the death of Canahachapew in 1880, Peepeekisis (Little Hawk or Sparrow Hawk) was recognized and elected by the people to succeed as chief (Indian Claims Commission 2004c:11). During the same year, the land that would become the band's reserve was surveyed in accordance with the regulations specified in the Treaty 4 text. A rectangular plot, the reserve was the southernmost of four side-by-side reserves (the other three being Little Black Bear, Star Blanket, and Okanese, north to south, respectively) in the File Hills region, an area located about twenty miles northeast of Fort Qu'Appelle (2004c:11). After completion of the land survey, this group of four reserves would become known as File Hills and would be associated with the File Hills Colony, an experimental project proposed by Indian Agent William Morris Graham to the Department of Indian Affairs.

Prior to the creation of the colony, Peepeekisis band members were already involved with agriculture and were successfully farming on the reserve. The terms laid out in Treaty 4 had specified the receiving of "Agricultural implements, Cattle, grain, Carpenter's tools, etc., proportioned to the number of families in the Band actually engaged in farming" (Canada 1874). To assist in this transition to agriculture, the bands of File Hills were aided by farming instructors, and it was the members of the Peepeekisis band who were said to "surpass any other in this section before very long" (Indian Claims Commission 2004c:13). However, by the mid-1890s the population of the File Hills bands had decreased, and Peepeekisis's namesake chief had passed away, along with his three serving headmen. The Department of Indian Affairs refused to recognize Chichiquio (Shave Tail), Peepeekisis's son, as the next hereditary chief, leaving the band leaderless for the next forty-five years. It would be during this time that Graham rose to a position of authority as a government agent in File Hills.

An ambitious man, William Morris Graham rose through the ranks of bureaucracy in the Department of Indian Affairs. Starting as a clerk in 1885, Graham not only was appointed an Indian agent but would eventually earn the title of commissioner for the reserves in the areas that eventually became the provinces of Manitoba, Saskatchewan, and Alberta in June 1895 (Titley 1983:26). At the time, Indian policy was regulated and influenced by "nineteenth century evangelical religion, cultural imperialism, and laissez-faire economics" (1983:25). Through these governing policies, it was hoped that Canada's indigenous population would become "civilized" by abandoning their own traditions in favor of adopting European culture. Successfully achieving this required not only the conversion to Christianity but also the continued practice of agriculture in hopes of creating a self-sufficient population. According to E. Brian Titley, "The triumph of Bible and plough would be followed by 'amalgamation' with the rest of the population and the eventual disappearance of the Indians as a separate people" (1983:25). A true agent of the government, Graham upheld these beliefs and was a strong supporter of Indian policy. This would become evident during the next three decades.

Using land on the Peepeekisis reserve, the purpose of the File Hills

Farm Colony was to create an agricultural community well removed from any reserve influences in order to prevent regression to the traditional way of life. Titley explains that there "was to be no contact between the colonists and the older Indians who adhered to traditional culture. And social interaction among the colonists themselves was closely monitored to prevent any lapse into tribal ways" (1983:27). In 1901, after approval from the Department of Indian Affairs, Graham began selecting graduates from residential schools based on their "progressive" attitudes in hopes of developing "a colony of Indians who readily accepted Whiteman's [sic] lifestyle, religion and culture" (Graham 1991:vii). In addition to shaping attitudes and lifestyles of the aboriginal graduates, implications of eugenics and euthenics policies also came into play, as, according to C. Drew Bednasek, "Graham's experiment selected students for their intelligence . . . favouring those of mixed white and Aboriginal blood" (2009a:445). Bednasek further explains that selected participants were "'superior' ex-pupils from neighbouring reserves" (2009a:452) and were subject to arranged marriages. Eleanor Brass, one of the first children to be born at the File Hills Colony, described her reputation as a colony resident as a student attending residential school: "One of the matrons said that [girls from the colony] were always getting into things that the other children wouldn't think of doing. I came to the conclusion that it was because of our European background. We must have inherited some aggressive characteristics which contributed to our curiosity and animation" (1987:26).

Brass's father, Fred Dieter, "was half white and reported by Graham to be the colony's first settler" (Bednasek 2009a:453). In addition, those selected as colony placements were granted membership to the Peepeekisis band and provided with farming equipment and surveyed tracts of land set aside specifically for the cultivation of crops. During this time, there was no elected chief on the reserve, so membership was granted based on the votes of already registered band members, including both colony placements and nonplacements.

Eleanor Brass wrote extensively about her experiences growing up as a colony resident. She "saw it in its various stages, through depression to approaching prosperity" (1987:11). According to Brass, "So keen was the desire for the success of the scheme that Mr. Graham made his own plans which were felt to be quite strict at times" (1987:11). Graham's role was not restricted to the selection of graduates to participate in the scheme, as various texts and accounts describe him as micromanaging every aspect of the project. "In the early days of the colony, fiddle dances, powwows and tribal ceremonies were forbidden. Mr. Graham considered them a hindrance to progress" (1987:13). Gilbert McLeod, a descendent of colony member Henry McLeod, recalled that Graham "was absolute in everything. He could not be questioned, and what he said had to go or if it didn't, if they didn't respond to the things he said, he would just ignore it. He was absolute in everything" (Indian Claims Commission 2002:55). Florence Desnomie also echoed this sentiment in her discussion with the Indian Claims Commission: "He was like Hitler. He bossed everybody around on the reserve, and we had—they had to do just what he did, what he wanted" (2002:72–73).[3]

The implementation of the colony addressed the need felt by government officials "to have a 'showpiece' reserve which could advertise Canada's sound administration" (Carter 1991:159). Visiting dignitaries in the 1920s, such as Governor General Earl Grey and his successor, the Duke of Connaught, were given tours of the colony as an example of "the best illustration of the Canadian system" (1991:158) in regard to policies dealing with the indigenous population. It was also during this time that the colony was praised in American newspapers. To outsiders, the File Hills Farm Colony appeared innovative and provided a solution to Canada's "Indian problem" (1991:157). However, the manner in which the farming experiment was conducted was not revealed to the general public. In addition to the initial tracts of land assigned to colony placements in 1901, the reserve was further subdivided in 1902 and 1906 to accommodate the influx of new colony transfers (Bednasek 2009c:59). This resulted in further displacement of the original Peepeekisis band members, who were left to occupy less than 8,000 acres of the 26,624-acre reserve (Indian Claims Commission 2004c:35).

The colony peaked between 1910 and 1920, with over thirty-six farmers and their families working and cultivating over 3,000 acres of land. During this time, the Department of Indian Affairs also recognized a new chief of the Peepeekisis band–forty-five years after the death of Peepeekisis (Indian Claims Commission 2004a:3). Along with the multi-

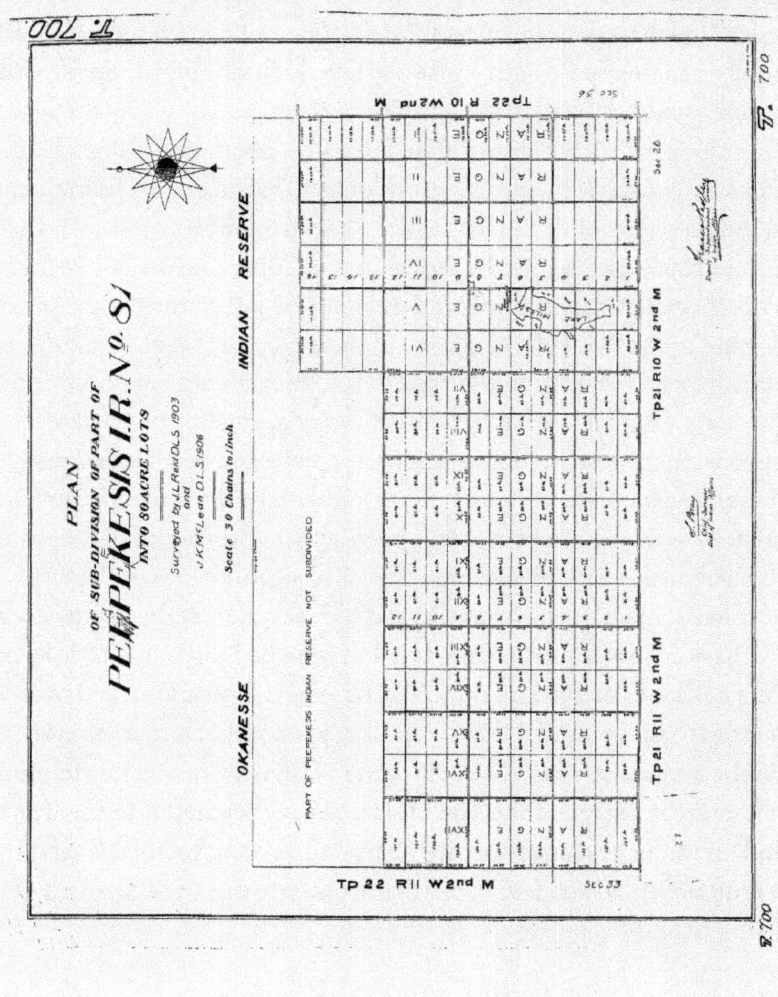

Fig. 25. Peepeekisis reserve after the second subdivision in 1906. Colony placements resided and farmed in the subdivided area, while original band members
were relegated to inhabiting and utilizing the northwest portion on the reserve
(Indian Claims Commission 2004b:7D).

ple subdivisions of land, which displaced original band members, questions regarding the validity of membership transfers to Peepeekisis were raised. Graham's conduct at membership meetings was criticized due to his "touchiness and penchant for finding insult and reproach where none was intended" (Titley 1986:186), in addition to his poor record-keeping abilities (Indian Claims Commission 2004a:3). By the 1950s, the colony had all but disintegrated due to economic hardship and the increasing suspicions and questions of band membership. In the same decade, a court ruling found that the original members of the band had a valid cause for complaint. However, a second court ruling reached a decision that declared that it would not be fair to revoke the membership of the File Hills colonists, as the majority of their families had already been residing on the reserve for an extended amount of time (2004a:3). Rather than remove the colony placements, alternative solutions were suggested, such as monetary compensation. Unfortunately, these suggestions have never been acted upon by the Canadian government. Several inquiries have since been launched on behalf of Peepeekisis band members who have requested investigations into the legitimacy of colonist membership transfers and the inception of the colony itself.

There are no physical remains left of the File Hills Farm Colony on Peepeekisis Cree Nation. Buildings have been either knocked over or burned to the ground. Despite this, the presence of Graham's agricultural scheme is still felt. Rather than manifested in architecture or monuments, the legacy of the File Hills Colony is etched into the hearts and identities of many band members, both young and old. Currently, it is an unsettled shadow that still lingers between the Canadian government and Peepeekisis Cree Nation.

CRISES OF INDIGENOUS REPRESENTATION

Indigenous Knowledges versus Academic Imperialism

There have been many academic studies of First Nations people and culture. However, previous research and studies have had a tendency to focus solely on historical occurrences, with little attention paid to the contemporary issues that continue to plague First Nations and indigenous peoples. With this thought in mind, I agree with scholars such as James Clifford and George Marcus (1986) who argue that there is a crisis of representation when it comes to indigenous people both in North America and around the globe. This is evident in academic research and publishing, as well as in the opinions of the general public. Traditional academia is saturated in ideology, hegemony, and dense language. This critique addresses the utilization of indigenous knowledges in academic study and the application of theoretical language to present such information. Those who are unversed in theoretical research and study often find it a challenge to digest the manner in which knowledge is presented. Through the act of colonization and the expansion of imperialist powers, indigenous teachings and ways of learning have often been devalued or appropriated by other dominant cultures in scholarly discourse. Western academia has placed value on empirical data, the written word, and concrete facts while ignoring or disregarding traditional modes of acquiring knowledge by indigenous peoples.[4] In North America, the issue of education has been historically steeped in colonialism and goals of assimilation. This is perhaps most obvious in the previous creation and existence of residential and industrial schools across the continent in the nineteenth and twentieth centuries.

These institutions were run in collaboration with church and Crown and worked toward the goal of assimilating the indigenous population. This involved the dismantling of traditional culture by removing children from their communities and "subjecting them to cultural reprogramming" (Stonechild 2006:8) by enforced mandatory attendance. Though residential schools have now been recognized as unethical, these schools, just like the File Hills Farm Colony, were extreme tools designed "to quickly absorb Indians into the allegedly superior and more desirable British language and culture" (2006:19). Polynesian scholar Vilsoni Hereniko (from Rotuma Island) acknowledges this as a commonality in colonized peoples: "The school and church are institutions that work hand in hand to colonize the mind. As native people were taught to read and write, they paid less attention to oratory" (2000:83).

The value of the written word over and above oratory in schools, colleges, and universities is a cause for concern, as indigenous ways of being are marginalized when testing or teaching is primarily in written form (Hereniko 2000:84). Elaborating on this, Hereniko states that the written word undermines oratory and implies that there is one sole truth, which can only be discovered through rigorous research. To rectify or work against this, we should consider alternate ways of finding and publishing the "truth." When conducting research and seeking answers, we should consider and address the following questions: What kind of truth is being told? Whose truth is it? Will the truth favor the colonizer or the colonized? (2000:86). Reinforcing these ideas put forth by Hereniko, Comanche writer Paul Chaat Smith reminds his readers to consider that history "is always about who is telling the stories and to whom the story teller is speaking, and how both understand their present circumstances" (2009:53). In other words, when we seek knowledge about the past, it is important that we hear many voices and contextualize them in their individual perspectives, as well as within cultural principles.

The importance of oral traditions and indigenous ways of gathering knowledge has commonly been placed on the back burner by Western academia. Native American scholar Vine Deloria Jr. has spoken out about the utilization of and attention to indigenous knowledge in the academy. He states that in the past it did not matter what tribal leaders and elders might have wanted to say, as "nothing was understood as authoritative unless a non-Indian had written it" (Deloria 2004:16). Deloria admits that although this attitude may now be in decline, it may still linger in "the minds of academics and the public at large" (2004:16).

Historically, the researching of indigenous peoples was carried out and analyzed solely for Western purposes. The outcome of such studies has usually been for the benefit of the researcher and not those being researched, as published results are typically steeped in theoretical discourse to serve a community of academic peers and to gain prestige for presenting original data. Readers lacking initiation into the language of academia are excluded from the audience. As pointed out by Hereniko, the employment of Western theories to understand the unfamiliar results in "academics ... talking to each other rather than to the people about whom they are writing" (2000:88). Other scholars agree with this sentiment, such as Thomas McLaughlin, who states that theory is a tribute to the power of ideology, and its use of dense language has "opened it to criticism as an elitist, merely academic exercise" (1996:5). These are not isolated opinions, as demonstrated by Holly Devor, who has also discussed her frustration when initially entering into the academic world: "Theory was written in arcane, difficult-to-read language. In its highest form it was highly intellectual commentary on the commentaries produced by other theorists, none of which was easy to track back to the real lives of real people" (2000:41).

Other problems that occur in academic publishing involve the "ownership" of gathered information. The first researchers to publish their findings or facts about a culture have the ability to claim ownership of that information. This ensures that "knowledge that belonged to indigenous people, like their land in many cases, is slowly appropriated by the colonizers" (Hereniko 2000:88). However, through recognizing the act of academic imperialism, it is possible to work on correcting this situation. Plains Cree and Saulteaux scholar Margaret Kovach advocates the use of "indigenous methodologies." Kovach uses the term "indigenous methodologies" in plural to "describe the theory and method of conducting research that flows from an indigenous epistemology" (2009:20). Described as being in line with indigenous values, the methodology seeks to gain and process knowledge in a manner that not only holds some form of community accountability but also allows researchers to present themselves as allies with the intent to use the acquired knowledge in a manner that "gives back to and benefits the community in some way" (2009:48). It is only when researchers choose to acknowledge the importance of memory and oral traditions in indigenous knowledges and also provide appropriate credit to those who have shared such knowledge that an accurate representation of indigenous people can be achieved in scholarly discourse.

ANTHROPOLOGY AND THE ETHNOGRAPHIC PRESENT

In the field of anthropology, many of the early ethnographers who focused on First Nations or Native American societies were concerned with the idea of salvage anthropology. That is, these ethnographers were intent on documenting a way of life that was feared to be in danger of disappearing through colonial contact and imperial expansion. Their methods involved the use of the ethnographic present, a literary device in writing that can be seen as situating cultural groups in the past. This style of writing generally does not allow for the recognition of contemporary issues. Other problems that have occurred in such research involve the acknowledgment of indigenous methods of transmitting and gaining knowledge. Society and culture are not static, and just as people change, so too must the academic discourses employed when studying indigenous cultural groups.

Native North America has historically held fascination for academics and nonacademics alike. One could even say that the practice of anthropology in North America was built on the study of American Indians and Canadian First Nations. Orin Starn (2011) explores the various aspects of this relationship and the representation of Native Americans in both academia and the general public. Starting with the father of American anthropology, Franz Boas, Starn states that Boas and his students highlighted the centrality of aboriginal peoples in American anthropology. Boas was known for building his career on the work he produced through research on the Kwakuitl (or Kwakwaka'wakw, as they are now known) in British Columbia. He also encouraged his students to follow in his footsteps and work with the indigenous people of North America. Alfred Kroeber, his star pupil, is famous for his work with Ishi, "The Last Wild Indian in North America" (Kroeber 1961). Margaret Mead, most recognized for her work in the South Pacific, also studied the Omaha at Boas's encouragement.

The pioneers of American anthropology sought to record and document an indigenous way of life that was perceived to be in danger of disappearing due to colonial conquest. Early ethnographic films also attempted to capture dying lifestyles, as can be seen in Robert J. Flaherty's *Nanook of the North* (1922). Described as "ethnographic taxidermy" by Fatimah Tobin Rony (1996:100), *Nanook of the North* sought to show the daily activities of the "unspoiled savage" (Jarvie 1978:197) in the Quebec Arctic Circle. This film has been praised for being one of the first documentary films, as well as one of the first ethnographic films to be made. Unfortunately, when it comes to anthropological contributions, the film is somewhat stunted. Yes, Flaherty follows an

Inuit family for a year and visually documents their day-to-day activities; however, he fails to explain why certain actions are performed or what social organizations existed beyond this one family. Rony elaborates on these points and explains that Flaherty himself stated that "he did not want to show the Inuit as they were at the time of the making of the film, but as (he thought) they had been" (1996:101).

It is not just early ethnography that practiced salvage anthropology. Many of the existing ethnographic resources written by scholars on the Plains Cree in Canada are situated in the past and only provide a glimpse into precolonized life. David G. Mandelbaum's oft-cited work, originally published in 1940, on the Plains Cree can provide an example. Mandelbaum states in the preface of the reprinted edition that his ethnographic focus was mainly on "the buffalo-hunting way of life, and not on the experiences of the Plains Cree on reservations as I witnessed them in the summers of 1934 and 1935" (1979:xiii).

The use of the ethnographic present has been stated as perpetuating a failure to recognize indigenous people as contemporary beings. Johannes Fabian explains that "in simple terms, the ethnographic present is the practice of giving accounts of other cultures and societies in the present tense" (1983:80). Critics of the ethnographic present state that it "'freezes' a society at the time of observation; at worst, it contains assumptions about the repetitiveness, predictability, and conservatism of primitives" (1983:81). At face value, this can be seen as problematic; however, Fabian stresses the importance of differentiating between the use of present tense as a linguistic device and "Time in the 'real world' outside of communicative situation of the text" (1983:83). With this in mind, writing in the ethnographic present, "despite the fact that it is descriptive of experiences and observations that lie in the author's past, would be indifferent because tense does not locate the content of the account in Time" (1983:83). In other words, describing an event in the present tense does not necessarily mean that the circumstances of that event are located in a fixed point in time.

It would be implausible to state or request that the use of the present tense be discontinued in ethnographic writing. Though it is important to understand the history of people, continual dwelling in the past can result in anthropologists refraining from and neglecting to discuss and address the trauma, poverty, displacement, and other hardships experienced as a result of colonial influence. However, as a solution, I submit to Fabian's approach that the use of the present tense in anthropological writing should be used alongside the recognition that culture and society are not stagnant, nor are the issues and problems faced by such people. Failure to recognize this will result in a failure to realize that what may have been true yesterday or even today may not necessarily be true tomorrow or at another point in the future. It is with these theoretical tools in hand that I will approach the case of the File Hills Farm Colony on the Peepeekisis reserve, shifting from a "frozen" history to accounts from living people whom I had the privilege to work with during the summer and autumn of 2013.

PREVIOUS REPRESENTATIONS OF THE FILE HILLS FARM COLONY

The acknowledgment and validation of memories and attitudes toward both the past and the present play a vital role in understanding a people's history. The subject of the File Hills Farm Colony is no exception, as reflected in several substantial pieces of writing that discuss its implementation and existence from the perspective of government agents, scholars, and descendants of colony placements. In the research I have conducted, it has become apparent that there is a lack of representation of the Peepeekisis reserve and the File Hills Farm Colony from the perspective of the original members and the descendants of original members of the band.

William Morris Graham discussed the development of the colony on Peepeekisis and the relationships that he maintained with those selected to participate. Additionally, his interactions with other leaders and members of First Nations reserves in Alberta, Saskatchewan, and Manitoba are also documented in his book, *Treaty Days: Reflections of an Indian Commissioner* (1991). While Graham is able to provide first-hand accounts of events that occurred during the time of the colony's existence, his disdain for First Nations that were not seen as progressive is apparent. Readers of his work must take into account that the version of events he tells is focused on Western ideas of civilization, Canadian public policy, and his own government ambitions.

The location of the File Hills Farm Colony on Peepeekisis Cree Nation reserve was the focus of C. Drew Bednasek's PhD dissertation, "Aboriginal and Colonial Geographies of the File Hills Farm Colony" (2009a), and journal article "The Influence of Betterment Discourses on Canadian Aboriginal Peoples in the Late Nineteenth and Early Twentieth Centuries" (2009b), which explored the history surrounding the colony and the "betterment" policies of the Canadian government in regard to the civilizing of the First Nations population. I discussed his work on the colony with members of Peepeekisis, and his writings were criticized as being a "glossed-over" history of Peepeekisis, in addition to being described as "riding the fence" between original and colony placements (personal communication, October 25, 2013). While he does produce information from oral histories, the fruit of his research is mainly composed of a reconstructed history dependent on archival documents and theoretical discussion. Conversely, "Remembering the File Hills Farm Colony" (2009c) is a much smaller journal article of his that directly addresses the benefits that oral knowledge and social memories can contribute to formal studies. Despite this, his work refrains from an in-depth exploration of the history and lives of colony placements or original band members.

Sarah Carter, a historian and professor at the University of Alberta, has written about the File Hills Farm Colony in her book *Lost Harvests: Prairie Indian Reserve Farmers and Government Policy* (1990) and in a later article, "Demonstrating Success: The File Hills Farm Colony" (1991). Both of these works are substantial pieces of writing; however, the main focus is on the establishment of the colony and the participants who were chosen to reside on and work the land. As an outsider to the community, she provides thorough discussions about the government policies that structured the agricultural experiment. Very little attention, if any, is given to the original members of the Peepeekisis band. Furthermore, there is a distinct lack of acknowledgment or personal engagement with the oral histories of either colony placements or original band members as they relate to the government experiment.

Eleanor Brass is perhaps one of the most recognized names when it comes to published works on the File Hills Farm Colony. Daughter of Fred Dieter, one of the first and reportedly most successful participants in the agricultural scheme, Brass has written extensively about her childhood and life growing up as a colony member of File Hills. There is not much mention of the original members of the Peepeekisis band, though in her recollection of attending the residential boarding school, which mixed colony and noncolony children, she states that the "full-blooded Indian children were more passive and were far easier to handle than we were. This showed a natural inherited trait from their native background. Politeness was one of the main virtues of their forefathers" (Brass 1987:26). While Brass's work is representative of colony members, it is an idealized account of the past that is prone to romanticism and does not fully discuss the impact the colony had on both placements and original members of Peepeekisis Cree Nation.

"The History of the File Hills Farming Colony" (1974) is a journal article that was written by Donna Pinay, also a member of the Peepeekisis Cree Nation. Pinay is a descendant of colony placements, and her work praises the innovation and hard work put forth by those who participated in and lived the colony life. Like Brass's account, her article romanticizes the past and refrains from critically examining the government policies that enabled the colony's existence.

Pinay refers to the original members of the Peepeekisis reserve as "protesters" whose request for band membership inquiries in 1955 would have "reduced [the population of the band] greatly and all of the Colony members would have been homeless with years of work for nothing" (1974:18). Pinay presents an idealized perspective on colony life, a one-sided history. When I read her work, I found that there was a distinct lack of representation of those who were the original members of Peepeekisis Cree Nation.

When I reviewed the literature on the File Hills Farm Colony, I discovered that most, if not all, of the documents were presented from a European Canadian standpoint. These early works do not include a clear depiction of the lives that were directly influenced and displaced by the government's attempt to assimilate the aboriginal population. Recalling the words of Hereniko, Smith, and Kovach, we must critically examine the sources of written history when researching indigenous topics. In my own research on the File Hills Farm Colony, I have taken their scholarly advice to heart and have considered the way these early writers have represented the colony. Rather than completely focus on the written record, which has been proven to be flawed and one-sided, I have chosen to explore and represent the voices of the overlooked and unrecognized: the original band members and their descendants of Peepeekisis Cree Nation.

THE FILE HILLS FARM COLONY: A SITUATION DIVIDED

The first time I learned about the File Hills Farm Colony was as an adolescent. I am not only of Plains Cree and Lakota descent but also a registered member of the Peepeekisis Cree Nation. My family has not lived on the reserve since I was an infant; however, my father was an elected headperson and commuted daily to the Peepeekisis reserve to serve on the band council. As a council member, it was his duty to look after several portfolios related to the band's governance. One such portfolio regarded the File Hills Farm Colony and the band's ongoing claim with the Canadian government. During his time in office, my father spent several years researching the history of Peepeekisis, working with archival documents, meeting with lawyers, and engaging with the community and the (now-defunct) Indian Claims Commission. However, at that time I was merely a teenager and paid more attention to my part-time job and hanging out with friends than I did to studying colonial history.

It was not until much later, while I was in my third year as an undergraduate studying anthropology, that my mind found its way back home. Like most other anthropology students, I entertained dreams of someday traveling to an "exotic" location where I would study the workings of society and gain knowledge about the various ways people lived their lives. Every time I thought about this, one question kept forming in the back of my mind: How could I go elsewhere to learn about people when there is still so much about my own people and history that I have not explored? A chance assignment in a political anthropology class allowed me to dip my toes in and begin to reconnect with my roots. Little did I know that the six-page essay I produced would be the beginning of a larger project and a stronger desire to understand the contemporary social issues faced by members and residents of Peepeekisis Cree Nation.

During the task of establishing this undergraduate honors thesis, I obtained a large number of documents released by the (former) Department of Indian Affairs and Northern Development, as well as by the Indian Claims Commission. I also gathered published material pertaining to the formation of the File Hills Farm Colony and William Morris Graham (see Bednasek 2009; Brass 1987; Carter 1990, 1991; Titley 1983, 1986; Pinay 1974). This collection of written information contains both government archival documents and contemporary primary and secondary sources. These physical literary remnants of the colony not only describe the history of the band prior to colonization but also reveal much about the government's experiment in civilization and assimilation policies.

In order to explore the social consequences that were a result of the colony's impact, I actively pursued the involvement of various community members of Peepeekisis Cree Nation. When I conducted interviews and created spoken records with members of the community, their memories of the past and ideas about the present revealed painful feelings, questions of identity, and a desire for unity. Participants I have spoken with are "original" registered members of the band who not only have lived the band history but also have a research interest in it. My approach to interviews utilized Kovach's recommendation of conversational and indigenous methodology (2009, 2010) in order to appreciate and visit the personal histories of Peepeekisis members. Rather than sit down with my interview subjects in a formal setting where I asked specific questions in a specific order, I adopted a more casual approach. Meetings generally took place in the comfortable living room of Freda and Don Koochicum's house, with a pot of coffee brewing in the kitchen. We had conversations about the colony, but speakers presented and shared their own specific stories. By aligning myself with these methods, it was my desire to contribute, share, and enrich the cultural, social, and historical knowledge and interpretation of the band's past.

While I may have grown up in a primarily urban environment, I was still raised in a manner that enabled me to be familiar with the transmission of knowledge through oral means. This same urban upbringing also had the unintended consequence of not allowing me to establish many relationships with Peepeekisis band members aside from my family prior to the undertaking of this project. Despite my initial lack of personal relationships, band members were willing to grant me a unique position as both a researcher and a young member of the community who wishes to learn and acknowledge the band's unique history. Many people on Peepeekisis are familiar with my father, and it was through this affiliation that participants agreed to meet and discuss the colony with me. My interest and desire not only to learn but also to share the collective history of the community facilitated an environment of cooperation and encouragement by my fellow band members as I conducted this project.

Despite my intimate relationship with the community and my commitment to my thesis topic, I have maintained a strict observation of ethical requirements. Before I was able to meet and speak with members of the community for research, I was required to undergo an application process with the University of Regina Research Ethics Board (REB). Furthermore, the government of Canada's *Tri-Council Policy Statement: Ethical Conduct for Research Involving Humans* (Canada 2010) contains numerous regulations and standards that have to be considered and complied with preceding the engagement of a research project that directly involves aboriginal communities and participants. It was only after I filled out the REB application form, a necessary document that outlines research procedures and goals more suited to fields other than anthropology, and after I familiarized myself with the Tri-Council policy guidelines that I was able to proceed with the execution of this research project.

DISCUSSING THE DIVISION

It was not easy when I initially decided to return to the Peepeekisis reserve. As I stated, I have not lived on the reserve since infancy, although I have many family members who do. My eldest sister resided on Peepeekisis for a number of years until she passed away under tragic circumstances. Following that, I stayed away for a long time and refrained from visiting the area out of grief. Although I was initially slightly apprehensive about visiting the reserve, these feelings soon melted away as I was introduced to relatives I had never met, as well as friends of my parents and grandparents. Chief Mike Koochicum took the time to listen intently to me as I explained my project to him, and he wished me well in my research. In a way, the project was both a homecoming and an education in the history of my band.

I met many people as I attended meetings and went to summer pow-wows, but it would not be until the beginning of autumn that I would meet Donald and Freda Koochicum. Married in 1963, Don and Freda have lived and worked both off and on the reserve. Currently residing on Peepeekisis and in their seventies, the couple are still engaged with agricultural practices. In the mornings, Freda tends to her chickens, while during the day, Don works in their fields and pasture. Born in 1941 to John and Dorothy Koochicum, Donald is descended from a line of members who were "original" to the Peepeekisis band prior to the colony transfers. Although Freda is originally from Star Blanket reserve, she gained her Peepeekisis membership through marriage to Don and has been actively involved with studying and researching the Peepeekisis band history. In addition to this, she has also been employed as band administrator and served on multiple committees that sought to further the progress on the dispute between Peepeekisis Cree Nation and the government of Canada in regard to the colony's existence.

Driving the dusty grid roads of Peepeekisis Cree Nation, one would never know that it is home to a questionable colonization scheme put forth by the Canadian government. The reserve is home to roughly 600 band members and has approximately 1,800 registered members who live off-reserve (Aboriginal Affairs 2013). As mentioned earlier, any buildings that were once present during the existence of the File Hills Farm Colony are no more—they have been either torn down by band members or burned. This also applies to William Morris Graham's house, located just outside of Peepeekisis's boundaries. According to Donald, all that remains of Graham's former residence are a few trees. To my knowledge, this location is not something known to the general public but is something that marked the hearts and memories of those who are familiar with Peepeekisis history.

It was a warm autumn morning when I pulled my car into Donald and

Freda's yard on the Peepeekisis reserve. The gravel crunched beneath my feet as I made my way to their house. A friendly black dog greeted me with a sniff and lick to the hand. I let myself into their home and called out to announce my arrival. This was not my first visit to their house, and just as she had during our initial meeting, Freda welcomed me with a grandmotherly hug.

Settled in on one of the sofas in their living room, Donald spoke to me about growing up on the reserve with his grandparents. He recalled seeing the houses that colony placements lived in, and as a youth he asked his grandmother about the people who were living there. "I didn't realize that Indians lived there," he told me. "*We* were Indians, but we were poor. Our house didn't look like theirs" (personal communication, October 30, 2013). Elaborating on this, he explained to me that he lived on the west side of the reserve with his grandparents in a house that had a sod roof and dirt floors. "My grandmother," he recalled, "used to peel potatoes and then go outside and throw the peelings on the roof of our house. They would start to sprout! You could be sitting inside and see dirt falling from the ceiling, and all of a sudden there would be a big potato!" He related this story to me with a hint of amusement but explained that in the continual struggle to make ends meet, the ceiling potatoes were harvested and used as a supplementary source of food for the family.

The thoughts he expressed to me echoed the ones he shared with the Indian Claims Commission during a community session in support of an inquiry on the File Hills Farm Colony: "We had nothing, and we lived in a sod hut until 1951. It was dirt floor, and we used to wake up in the morning and have frost on our heads and . . . we had no winter clothes. . . . That's a hardship that we faced over there, and I lived through that" (Indian Claims Commission 2002:252). Growing up under these circumstances, Donald witnessed a burgeoning social divide between the colony placements and the original band members. The colony may have disintegrated in the 1950s, but the split in the community remains in place. He states that "it created a lot of hard feelings between colonized people and the original members, and . . . it's still that way. We're still divided, not united, and it shouldn't be that way, . . . it should be together we stand and together we fall" (2002:275).

Don's words reveal an unhealed wound left on the community as a result of Graham's social manipulation. Speaking of the community as a whole, he further impressed the need for the community to act as one when dealing with the history of Peepeekisis: "The people should understand that they too went through this turmoil, this whole hardship that we are having here. They should get to understand and . . . live together in peace. The fight has been so long now. When are the people going to stop—start to think 'let's stand together' and 'let's do this together,' and 'let's be a nation, not divided,' but I guess it's up to the people, not me" (2002:294–295). By purposely creating an environment that did not allow for freedom of communication or interaction between placements and originals, the File Hills Farm Colony fostered both a chasm of distrust and a desire for unity by placements and original members.

Voicing this observation to Freda, I wondered how this state of being could still be felt between the two "factions" of the reserve. A common theme in many of our conversations was the loss of identity and displacement of land experienced by both the placements and the originals. Since the 1950s, the Peepeekisis band has been fighting with the government of Canada for recognition of Graham's agricultural scheme. The towns of Lorlie and Melville, located southeast of the reserve, were host to two important court cases that determined the fate of the colony placement's band memberships. The first inquiry confirmed that the originals had a legitimate cause for complaint. However, a follow-up decision ruled that the placements were to be considered full members of the Peepeekisis band due to the amount of time that they and their families had resided there (Indian Claims Commission 2004a:3).

Instead of unifying the band, these decisions created a divided community: the placements felt as though they were being threatened with removal, and the originals felt as though their concerns had been disregarded. Band members who are aware of Peepeekisis's complicated history are still struggling with the need for unification of both sides. On behalf of their members, the band council has submitted a claim to Aboriginal Affairs that implores Canada to recognize the role it has played in creating this divisive environment.

In the early 2000s, the Indian Claims Commission paid several visits to the reserve and conducted a third-party investigation surrounding the creation and operation of the File Hills Farm Colony (Indian Claims Commission 2002, 2004c). Questions posed to band members focused on the band's historical past and the role that Graham played in creating it. According to Freda, there were still many concerns that had not been addressed. Speaking of the interviewed colony members, she explains, "They [the colony descendants] could have talked about the lands that they lost. They could have been chiefs or councillors. They could have been so much more, had they gone to their own reserves [after graduating from industrial and residential school]. They could have been examples to their members. When they came here, their hands were tied" (personal communication, September 30, 2013).

The commission did find that the government of Canada had breached its lawful obligations to the band and recommended that the Crown acknowledge this (Indian Claims Commission 2002); however, the present community divide also demands recognition. To explain the fissure felt between colony placements and original members, Freda explained that it has arisen from a loss of identity rather than just from a sense of displacement: "They didn't lose the land so much as they lost themselves. It's the essence of who they were that they have lost. When you lose that, you're like a coyote that is backed up against a wall. There is nothing left anymore. All you have to do is fight, and you [begin to fight] for your own self. You don't care about these other people, because they are the ones who are causing this hurt [and anxiety]" (personal communication, October 25, 2013).

Freda and Don are not the only ones to acknowledge this division; others have also spoken of the fractured situation the community now finds itself in. Alice Sangwais, the granddaughter of hereditary chief Peepeekisis, discussed the divide with the Indian Claims Commission: "It was two reserves. It still is. It still is a colony and Peepeekisis. It's two reserves [existing] on one reserve" (2002:35). Rather than pit the two sides of the reserve against one another, Freda suggests that both sides need to work in unison if an agreement is to be reached with the Canadian government: "It has to be an understanding that this is Graham— the government—that did this to us. We have to fight from both sides" (personal communication, October 25, 2013).

For this conversation we were joined by former band council member Claude Desnomie, now in his midfifties.[5] He explained that during his first term in office he concentrated on the originals' side with regard to furthering the claim with Canada. Unfortunately, in doing so he was perceived to be one-sided in his work. He explained to me that he had intended to devote his next term to the perspective of the colony descendants so that a comprehensive view of Peepeekisis could be presented in the claim against the government. Unfortunately, he was not able to achieve this goal, as he did not win the election for a second term in office: "My position [on council] was open, and that is when [certain band members] went and made a massive campaign to not vote for me. None of their kids or any of their relatives voted for me. But what they did was they lost their land claim by doing that, because I had them on the doorstep of going into the negotiation stage [with Canada]" (personal communication, August 15, 2013).

Despite this, Claude holds firm to his belief that the first step to achieving a unified membership is the need to acknowledge and identify with the band's past. This applies to both descendants of colony placements and original members. He expressed the opinion that unification has not happened in the band because "a lot of people are scared to know what is inside of them" (personal communication, October 25, 2013).

Sharing his own personal history, Claude speaks of identifying with both colony and original membership: "To throw it out there, I know who I am. My dad is who he is, and my mother is who she is. Together, they created me: the perfect half-breed on Peepeekisis. Literally. My mother was a full blood original member, and my dad's family transferred in 1882 from strong Métis roots. For some reason, there are very few [band members] who want to know who they are. In my family, we know who we are. We're quite proud that we're one-sixteenth French, while others continue to deny their heritage" (personal communication, September 30, 2013).

Though there may be a social divide between colony placements and original members, Claude's words carry a message. While original Peepeekisis members may be related by blood and through marriage, colony placements have also created strong kinship ties through their shared history of membership transfers. Regardless of what lineage a Peepeekisis member is descended from, they are now members of the same reserve and hail from the same band. To forget one's past and present is to forget that there is a common cause for grievance and need for reconciliation. Claude also voiced these thoughts to me during an earlier meeting: "Peepeekisis will not go anywhere until the past is dealt with. You have to deal with the past before you can walk forward. Any person in [the] mental health [profession] will tell you that. Peepeekisis has to deal with the past and the federal government has to deal with the past, otherwise you're going to keep having problems" (personal communication, August 15, 2013).

When dealing with the band history, it has to be recognized that both sides of the colony scheme were affected by its existence, just as both sides were equally displaced—original band members were forced to live in poverty on one side of the reserve while carrying a lower social status, whereas colony placements were manipulated and removed from their home bands and lost any opportunity to contribute to their former communities.

The Peepeekisis band has been attempting to reconcile with the government of Canada over the implementation of the File Hills Farm Colony for decades. Recently the band was told that their claim against the government has been rejected, leaving the community with two options: file an appeal with the Supreme Court of Canada or submit their claims through the Specific Claims Tribunal, "an independent adjudicative body comprised of up to 6 full time Federal judges appointed from Provincial Superior Courts across the country" (Specific Claims Tribunal 2013). This bid for reconciliation and recognition is not solely for the benefit of the current Peepeekisis membership but also for its future.

Freda believes that in order to win the claim against Canada, the band should present it as a group. "I have never only talked about the original members," she had declared in a passionate tone. "I went into [the claims process] as the band as a whole, and that's the way I treated it" (personal communication, September 30, 2013). Simply winning the claim against Canada is not enough to secure a stable community for Peepeekisis. Though the matter of the colony has yet to be settled,

Freda knows that the current situation is one that will affect future generations of Peepeekisis members. "When push comes to shove and [we win our claim], what do we want out of it? Those are things we need to know. [Future generations] are going to know the true story of what really happened, and did we do anything? . . . What did we do to improve our situation? *That* is what the next generation is going to judge us by. We have to think about them."

Listening to Freda, Donald, and Claude speak, I realized that there is a sense of bitterness, anger, and hurt when it comes to the history of Peepeekisis. Freda told Bednasek during his research that "many people are angry about what happened here" (2009b:179). Despite this sense of loss, displacement, and divide that now exists, what remains is a feeling of hope. Freda tells me that despite the current lack of resolution, what matters is the truth of the people when it comes to the colony's impact on the community. "To me, that is more important than anything else."

DISCUSSION

Although Peepeekisis looks like any other reserve, the lack of physical evidence left behind by the colony does not mean that the colony no longer exists. The File Hills Farm Colony is still present and very much alive today. When Bednasek conducted his research on the colony, he was initially discouraged by the lack of physical remnants left behind by the colonial experiment. Asking band member Martine Desnomie about what still existed from the colony, she looked at him and said that what remained was "the people" (2009b:137).[6] In my experience with researching and talking with members of Peepeekisis, this statement condenses the profound impact of the former colony.

As a Peepeekisis band member who did not grow up on the reserve, I have been granted a privileged position. Not only have I had the opportunity to learn about and discuss the history of the File Hills Farm Colony from a distanced perspective, my ancestral ties have also allowed me to connect with, feel close to, and represent the voices of the present in a way that has not been previously achieved by my scholarly predecessors. I have learned that when studying the history of Peepeekisis and the File Hills Farm Colony, it is not enough to solely focus on the past. Doing so results in losing sight of the people who lived through the history and continue to live with it. The past is what dictates the present, and by recognizing this we can see that the social stratification currently experienced by the Peepeekisis community is a direct result of the colony's legacy. Had I relied solely on the existing literature for this chapter, I would have assumed that it was all over, a past mistake that has long been rectified (and "gotten over").

The current social divide can be attributed to the File Hills Farm Colony, which not only contributed to a fractured, disempowered community but also perpetuated a loss of identity experienced by both sides of Peepeekisis Cree Nation. Placements who were chosen to participate had marriages arranged for them by Crown and church, and they lost band membership on their home reserves. Original Peepeekisis members were displaced and prohibited from using the entirety of the land initially assigned to them by the Canadian government. Both sections of the reserve were prohibited from engaging in cultural practices, dances, and ceremonies with the threat of punishment by Graham.

Through my discussions of the past and its effect on the present community, it became apparent that for my informants it is not a question of when the colony ended. Nor is it a question of which side of the reserve had it worse or better. Although I spoke mainly with descendants of the original members of the Peepeekisis band, the focus of our conversations were never one-sided. Equal concern and attention was paid to both the injustices suffered by the colony placements and the hardships endured by the original members.

When discussing the past and learning about the colony, I noted that there remained an underlying bitterness and hurt in people's voices. That said, there is another thing that became apparent to me: the presence of hope. There is hope that the band can settle their claim, hope that the community will come together, and hope that the story of the band's past and present will be told. Summing up what I heard many times, it is the future generations of Peepeekisis members who will question the actions and conduct of their predecessors. This belief has fostered a determination to achieve both political and social unity, despite the difficulties both sides have endured. If the present determines the future, then I would say that the future is hopeful.

After engaging in some preliminary archival and ethnographic research, I have found that many questions remain open. To me and to the people I spoke with, one key question is: How can a satisfactory conclusion between Peepeekisis's and Canada's colonial history be reached? Claude suggested that it requires Peepeekisis members to embrace the past and know personal histories as they apply to the colony. Don stated that the band needed to work together to become a unified front to achieve their goals. Freda stressed the importance of knowing the story behind the government documents as it is told and known by the people. Perhaps a combination of all three methods will prove to be successful. Knowing and acknowledging a shared history of the band and telling the stories of the people who lived that history can not only serve to further and help settle the land claim with Canada but also educate current and future generations of both band members and nonband members alike.

CONCLUSION

The use of oral history and social memory is not a unique concept when writing about First Nations and other indigenous peoples. Histories and stories are shared that tell of the injustices that have been experienced as a result of imperial expansion and colonial ambitions. This is true for members of Peepeekisis Cree Nation; however, their situation is one of a unique and particular history in North America. The File Hills Farm Colony was implemented at the hands of government agent William Morris Graham and has resulted in a social divide between band members. The colony may no longer have a recognized standing with the government, but through the conversations I have participated in, it appears to still be very much alive. Emotions of anger, bitterness, and hurt were expressed when the subject of the colony and Graham came up in conversation. Despite these feelings, there remained expressions of hope and determination to unite as a community and heal the lingering wound.

Canadian First Nations and American Indians have often been told to "get over it" by insensitive souls when the consequences of colonialism have been raised. Those who express such sentiments fail to recognize that the event a person is usually told to get over is not necessarily a thing of the past. Rather than advocate that a person get over whatever hardship or traumatic incident has occurred, we need to understand how that event has shaped the people or situations in the present. To undertake a study of the File Hills Farm Colony that solely focuses on the history of the project would not accurately portray the community as it is today. Focusing on the historical past of the Peepeekisis band places the current membership and residents ahistorically in time and fails to acknowledge the current situation of the band.

I have discussed the methods one should adopt when writing about indigenous topics and utilizing the knowledges of indigenous people. To reiterate, it is important that the information be used to benefit the community in some way. With this in mind, I have purposely refrained from writing in a manner that can alienate those who are not well versed in academic language. Additionally, I have also sought to record and tell the stories and thoughts as they were told to me. Rather than write this chapter as an academic for other academics, I have attempted to portray this particular case study as being written by a member of the people for the people. In this case, I refer to "the people" as all people: scholars, students, indigenous people, nonindigenous people, and any other interested parties.

NOTES

The chapter was originally presented as an honors thesis in anthropology at the University of Regina.

1. I have decided to use the word "knowledges" in plural when referring to indigenous ways of knowing and learning. By using the word "knowledges," I am recognizing that there are many types of indigenous peoples and, subsequently, many types of indigenous knowledge that can be passed on.
2. In several conversations with Peepeekisis band members, the File Hills Farm Colony was referred to not only as a social experiment but also as a "scheme" put forth by Indian Agent William Morris Graham in order to further his own career and manipulate the lives of First Nation peoples.
3. Desnomie is a common last name on the Peepeekisis Cree Nation and includes several family lines. In this case, Florence was married to my paternal great-grandfather's second cousin.

4. I am using the term "Western" as a method of describing nonindigenous peoples and ideologies; however, it is important to acknowledge that this is a problematic term. Just as there is no singular panindigenous identity, there is also no singular Western identity or persona. However, for the purposes of this chapter I will use the term "Western" to indicate a way of being that originates from a European-based society or culture.

5. Claude Desnomie is my father.

6. Martine Desnomie is married to my father's second cousin.

REFERENCES

Aboriginal Affairs and Northern Development Canada. 2013. Peepeekisis—Connectivity Profile. https://www.aadnc-aandc.gc.ca /eng/1357840942266/1360166524706.

Bednasek, C. Drew. 2009a. Aboriginal and Colonial Geographies of the File Hills Farm Colony. PhD dissertation, Department of Geography, Queen's University.

———. 2009b. The Influence of Betterment Discourses on Canadian Aboriginal Peoples in the Late Nineteenth and Early Twentieth Centuries. Canadian Geographer 53(4):444–461.

———. 2009c. Remembering the File Hills Farm Colony. Historical Geography 37:53–70.

Brass, Eleanor. 1987. I Walk in Two Worlds. Calgary: Glenbow-Alberta Institute.

Canada. 1874. Treaty No. 4 between Her Majesty the Queen and the Cree and Saulteaux Tribes of Indians at the Qu'appelle and Fort Ellice. http://www.aadnc-aandc.gc.ca/eng/1100100028689/1100100028690.

———. 2010. Panel on Research Ethics. Tri-Council Policy Statement: Ethical Conduct of Research Involving Humans. 2nd ed. http://pre .ethics.gc.ca/eng/policy-politique/initiatives/tcps2-eptc2/Default/.

Carter, Sarah. 1990. Lost Harvests: Prairie Indian Reserve Farmers and Government Policy. Montreal: McGill-Queen's University Press.

———. 1991. Demonstrating Success: The File Hills Farm Colony. Prairie Forum 16(2):157–183.

Clifford, James, and George E. Marcus, eds. 1986. Writing Culture: The Poetics and Politics of Ethnography. Berkeley: University of California Press.

Deloria, Vine, Jr. 2004. Marginal and Submarginal. In Indigenizing the Academy: Transforming Scholarship and Empowering Communities.

Devon Abbott Mihesuah and Angela Cavender Wilson, eds. Lincoln: University of Nebraska Press.

Devor, Holly. 2000. Speaking Subjects: Theory in the Vernacular. Feminism & Psychology 10(1):41–45.

Fabian, Johannes. 1983. Time and the Other: How Anthropology Makes Its Object. New York: Columbia University Press.

Flaherty, Robert J., dir. 1922. Nanook of the North. 78 mins. Quebec: Pathépicture.

Graham, William Morris. 1991. Treaty Days: Reflections of an Indian Commissioner. Calgary: Glenbow-Alberta Institute.

Hereniko, Vilsoni. 2000. Indigenous Knowledge and Academic Imperialism. *In* Remembrances of the Past: An Invitation to Remake History. Robert Borofsky, ed. Pp. 78–91. Honolulu: University of Hawai'i Press.

Indian Claims Commission. 2002. Peepeekisis First Nation Community Session. http://iportal.usask.ca/docs/ICC_CD/Peepeekisis%20first%20nation/05/t.pdf.

———. 2004a. File Hills Colony: A Breach of Treaty, Indian Act, and Canada's Fiduciary Responsibility. Landmark 10(1):1–4.

———. 2004b. Peepeekisis First Nation, File Hills Colony Claim. http://iportal.usask.ca/docs/ICC_CD/Peepeekisis%20First%20Nation/open.pdf.

———. 2004c. Peepeekisis First Nation Inquiry, File Hills Colony Claim. http://publications.gc.ca/collections/Collection/RC31-21-2004E.pdf.

Jarvie, Ian. 1978. Review of *Nanook of the North*. American Anthropologist 80(1):196–197.

Kovach, Margaret. 2009. Indigenous Methodologies: Characteristics, Conversations and Contexts. Toronto: University of Toronto Press.

———. 2010. Conversational Method in Indigenous Research. First Peoples Child & Family Review 5(1):40–48.

Kroeber, Theodora. 2002 [1961]. Ishi in Two Worlds: A Biography of the Last Wild Indian in North America. Berkeley: University of California Press.

Mandelbaum, David G. 1979. The Plains Cree: An Ethnographic, Historical, and Comparative Study. Regina: Canadian Plains Research Centre.

McLaughlin, Thomas. 1996. Street Smarts and Critical Theory: Listening to the Vernacular. Madison: University of Wisconsin Press.

Morris, Alexander. 1991 [1880]. The Treaties of Canada with the Indians of Manitoba and the North-West Territories Including the Negotiations on Which They Were Based. Toronto: Belfords, Clarke & Co.

Pinay, Donna. 1974. The History of the File Hills Farming Colony. Saskatchewan Indian 4(6):16–19.

Ray, Arthur J., Jim Miller, and Frank J. Tough. 2000. Bounty and Benevolence: A History of Saskatchewan Treaties. Montreal: McGill-Queen's University Press.

Rony, Fatimah Tobin. 1996. The Third Eye: Race, Cinema, and Ethnographic Spectacle. Durham: Duke University Press.

Sanjek, Roger. 1991. The Ethnographic Present. Man, new series, 26(4):609–628.

Smith, Paul Chaat. 2009. Everything You Know about Indians Is Wrong. Minneapolis: University of Minnesota Press.

Specific Claims Tribunal. 2013. Welcome to the Specific Claims Tribunal Canada. http://www.sct-trp.ca/hom/index_e.htm.

Starn, Orin. 2011. Here Come the Anthros (AGAIN): The Strange Marriage of Anthropology and Native America. Cultural Anthropology 26(2):179–204.

Stonechild, Blair. 2006. The New Buffalo: The Struggle for Aboriginal Post-secondary Education in Canada. Winnipeg: University of Manitoba Press.

Titley, E. Brian. 1983. W. M. Graham: Indian Agent Extraordinaire. Prairie Forum 8(1):25–41.

———. 1986. A Narrow Vision: Duncan Campbell Scott and the Administration of Indian Affairs in Canada. Vancouver: University of British Columbia Press.

CONTRIBUTORS

DMITRY V. ARZYUTOV, Department of Anthropology, University of Aberdeen (UK) and Department of Siberian Ethnography, Peter the Great Museum of Anthropology and Ethnography (Kunstkamera) (Russia); email: darzyutov@gmail.com

REGNA DARNELL, Department of Anthropology, University of Western Ontario; email: rdarnell@uwo.ca

CHEYANNE DESNOMIE, Department of Anthropology, University of Regina, Canada; email: cheyanne.desnomie@uregina.ca

PRISCILA FAULHABER, History of Science Department, Museum of Astronomy and Related Sciences, Brazil; email: pfaulhaber@globo.com

PATRÍCIA FERRAZ DE MATOS, Instituto de Ciências Sociais, Universidade de Lisboa, Portugal; email: patricia_matos@ics.ul.pt

FREDERIC W. GLEACH, Department of Anthropology, Cornell University; email: f.gleach@cornell.edu

GEOFFREY GRAY, The School of Historical and Philosophical Inquiry, University of Queensland; email: g.gray1@uq.edu.au

DENISE NICOLE GREEN, Department of Fiber Science and Apparel Design, Cornell University; email: dng22@cornell.edu

RAINER HATOUM, Goethe University, Frankfurt am Main, Germany.

SERGEI A. KAN, Department of Anthropology, Dartmouth College; email: Sergei.A.Kan@dartmouth.edu

ADAM KUPER, Department of Anthropology, London School of Economics; email: adam.kuper@gmail.com

FREDERICO D. ROSA, Department of Anthropology, CRIA-FCSH / NOVA University, Lisbon, Portugal; email: fdelgadorosa@fcsh.unl.pt

www.ingramcontent.com/pod-product-compliance
Lightning Source LLC
Chambersburg PA
CBHW032342280326
41935CB00008B/425